92
Pater

$ 27.50
6-16-99

This book was donated by:

The Book Warehouse
St George
Utah

WALTER PATER

WALTER PATER

Lover of Strange Souls

Denis Donoghue

ALFRED A. KNOPF
New York 1995

THIS IS A BORZOI BOOK
PUBLISHED BY ALFRED A. KNOPF, INC.

Copyright © 1995 by Denis Donoghue

All rights reserved under International and Pan-American
Copyright Conventions. Published in the United States by
Alfred A. Knopf, Inc., New York, and simultaneously in Canada by
Random House of Canada Limited, Toronto. Distributed by
Random House, Inc., New York.

Owing to limitations of space, all permissions to quote
from previously published material can be found immediately
following the index.

Library of Congress Cataloging-in-Publication Data
Donoghue, Denis.
Walter Pater : lover of strange souls / Denis Donoghue.—1st ed.
        p.   cm.
ISBN 0-679-43753-3
1. Pater, Walter, 1839-1894. 2. Authors, English—19th century—
Biography.   I. Title.
PR5136.D66   1995
824'.8—dc20
[B] 94-12843
CIP

Manufactured in the United States of America
First Edition

For Frances and the Children

Contents

PART IV

Part I

1

Preliminaries

I

MY EARLY READING did not include much of Walter Pater's work. I recall from some anthology of English prose a passage about the Mona Lisa that I thought gorgeously purple, another about a hawthorn tree, and one about a man seeking something in the world that is there in no satisfying measure or not at all. At University College, Dublin, I read anything that came my way, subject to two considerations. I was much taken with the work of the American New Critics, especially those who seemed to have issued from T. S. Eliot's overcoat: Cleanth Brooks, John Crowe Ransom, R. P. Blackmur, and Kenneth Burke. Closer to home, I kept up with the work of F. R. Leavis and the critics he published in *Scrutiny*. But I read those critics unequally. I took my general sense of modern literature mainly from Eliot's *The Sacred Wood* and Leavis's *New Bearings in English Poetry*. According to that view, literature is the supreme means by which, as Leavis wrote in an early essay on D. H. Lawrence, we "undergo a renewal of sensuous and emotional life, and learn a new awareness."[1] It is in this consideration a signal achievement of language, a focus of discovery within a language, hence the necessity of paying attention to linguistic acts. Language is the form in which values—personal, social, moral, religious, political—are most compellingly found in action. Eliot took it for granted that he could indicate the superiority of one culture over another, one phase of civilization over another, by quoting a few lines of verse. Leavis made his readers feel that by concentrating his mind on *The Waste Land*, *The Rainbow*, *Women in Love*, and "St. Mawr" he could diagnose the spiritual condition of nations. The crucial issues in modern literature were those which Matthew Arnold produced in *Culture and Anarchy* and *Essays in Criticism*. Their bearing upon culture and society was most powerfully met in Eliot's early poems, culminating in *The Waste Land*. Leavis's attention to these issues was to be found not only in *New Bearings* but later in *The Great Tradition* and the essays he selected for *The Common Pursuit*. Pater did not come into that reckoning except in passing, as a symptom of the decadence the great modern writers, especially Eliot and Lawrence, had to challenge. Typical in this respect was Leavis's aside, in an essay on Hopkins, that in D. G. Rossetti's verse "we find nothing more of the 'hard gem-like flame' than in Pater's prose."[2] Pater was not thought to be as dangerous, because he was not as sinister, as the BBC and the journalists of Fleet Street. If mentioned at all, he was taken to exemplify the genteel tradition in English life, a body of sentiment already discredited. Reviewing Santayana's *The Last Puritan* in *Scrutiny* under the title "The Last Epicurean," Q. D. Leavis thought it sufficient to make the point by associating Santayana and Pater with gentility:

> Professor Santayana is probably the last very distinguished mind to cherish that tradition, which is the reason that this review is headed "The Last Epicurean." Not "Epicurean" with reference to the original Epicurus of course; the adjective is intended delicately to suggest a relationship with the Oxford branch of the family. Pater, though his literary art was at the opposite extreme from Professor Santayana's, was also a victim of the feminine charm of Oxford.[3]

In the same review, Q. D. Leavis compared *The Last Puritan*, to its disadvantage, with *The Education of Henry Adams* and L. H. Myers's *The Root and the Flower*.

F. R. Leavis was a major critic, a great rhetorician on the social ramification of literature, comparable to Johnson, Coleridge, and Eliot, but he rarely wrote a sustained analysis of a poem, a play, or a novel. He quoted long passages and pointed to their demonstrable qualities, but his force in critical practice was a matter of intervening on literary issues, challenging received opinions on the value of one writer or another. I read the American critics mainly to see what close reading meant and to find the modern literature of England, Ireland, and America considered in relation to the European novel. Burke and Blackmur were masters of close reading, especially in early essays on Eliot, Pound, Yeats, Williams, and Marianne Moore. Philip Rahv and William Phillips edited *Partisan Review* and printed there some of the most formidable essays on social and literary issues. But I felt special admiration for Ransom. Like Wallace Stevens and Paul Valéry, Ransom had nearly as much interest in aesthetics as in poetry. The essays he printed in *The Kenyon Review* attended mostly to the theory of poetry and assumed that a steady reading of Aristotle, Kant, and Hegel would help anyone in reading Shakespeare, Donne, and Milton. Pater's name appeared occasionally, but Kenneth Burke's commentary on *Gaston de Latour* in his *Counter-Statement* is the only essay on Pater I recall reading in the context of the New Criticism. Burke's chapter is called "Adepts of Pure Poetry," and his adepts are Flaubert, Pater, and Remy de Gourmont.

So I didn't come to Pater on the clear recommendation of the masters in criticism. The writers most frequently recommended were Leavis's major novelists, Jane Austen, George Eliot, Henry James, Conrad, and Lawrence. The poets to be reckoned with were Eliot, Pound, and (with reservation) Yeats. The writers most admired in *The Kenyon Review* and *Partisan Review* were James, Kafka, Joyce, Hopkins, Mann, Dostoevsky, and Tolstoi.

But there was another map of modern literature available to me. I read Yeats's autobiographical volumes and his *Oxford Book of Modern Verse*. It is customary to regard the *Oxford Book* as eccentric, Yeats's silly tribute to his friends. His introduction to the book is thought to be bizarre. And what did he think he was doing, choosing as the first poem in the anthology Pater's sentence about the Mona Lisa and turning it into mediocre free verse? In "The Phases of the Moon" Yeats's Robartes says: "He wrote of me in that extravagant style / He had learned from Pater. . . ." In his autobiographical books Yeats presents Pater as the sage of Oxford, a remote figure to be approached occasionally by Lionel Johnson and Arthur Symons and yet in his reserved way the man chiefly responsible for the poetry of the nineties and its consequence in modern literature. Yeats was suggestive rather than specific. He didn't make it clear to me how the poetry of Pater's day had turned into the poems written by Yeats himself in his later years and by Eliot,

Pound, and Auden. Nor did he explain his remark, in the *Autobiographies*, that Pater's ideal of culture could only create feminine souls: "The soul becomes a mirror not a brazier."[4] I think, but can't prove, that Yeats associated homosexuality with feminine souls in men, the passive role in experience.

Yeats wasn't much help, either, when I started wondering how Pater chose the major interests of his work: Italian Renaissance painting and sculpture, Greek mythology and sculpture, nineteenth-century German criticism and aesthetics. Why those? They would not now be regarded as self-evidently the cultural artifacts most worth thinking about. A young critic today interested in art, literature, and aesthetics would probably choose to pay attention to nineteenth-century French art, the art of Africa or Mexico, and contemporary American painting and photography as the interests worth having. The reason for those choices may be politically opportunist: Greece and Rome are no longer the imperative virtualities they were to Pater's generation. This, too, may pass. But one way of describing Pater's work is that he set out to create a personal style by paying a special kind of attention to ancient Greece and Rome, Renaissance Italy, and modern German aesthetics. He sensed that these were the materials he could convert to his own spirit. Yeats was Pater's disciple in this respect, except that he thought of style in public terms, embodied however inadequately in the Abbey Theatre, and he added the Japanese Noh plays and the lore of pagan Ireland to Greek tragedy and Italian Renaissance art, the culture of Urbino and Ravenna.

The Introduction to *The Oxford Book of Modern Verse* is a wild fling at a subject Yeats in 1936 was nearly done with. Eliot was then in command, authoritative in poetry and criticism despite the abrasiveness of his social commentary. But the situation has changed. It is hard to believe that modern literature, or even modern poetry, has issued from anyone's overcoat, despite the case that Hugh Kenner has argued so insistently in *The Pound Era*. There are many masters: in English, Irish, and American poetry Whitman, Hardy, Hopkins, Pound, Yeats, Eliot, Frost, Stevens, Auden, and Olson have had their following in writers and readers. In such a plural context, Yeats's account of modern literature doesn't seem bizarre to me. It starts with Pater.

The main justification for writing a book on Pater at this point is to clarify the recognition one is claiming for him. It is not a question of influence but of presence. Pater is a shade or trace in virtually every writer of any significance from Hopkins and Wilde to Ashbery. Some writers have resented his presence and tried to remove it, as Eliot tried and failed in his essay "Arnold and Pater." Pater is as evident in Eliot's poems as in Joyce's fictions. It was Pater, more than Arnold, Tennyson, or Ruskin, who set modern literature upon its antithetical—he would say its antinomian—course. In practice this means he made modern English literature European, just as he opened modern English criticism to German motifs and set readers thinking differently about Greek art and myth. He is the enabling force, however frail Henry James thought him to be, in gathering into English literature the concerns otherwise found only in Baudelaire, Stendhal, Rimbaud, Flaubert, Verlaine, and Mallarmé. Pater had to write *Studies in the History of the Renaissance* before Arthur Symons could write *The Symbolist Movement in Literature* or, more than thirty years later, Edmund Wilson could write *Axel's Castle*, the books that elucidated the origins of modern poetry and fiction in French Symbolism. It was Pater who first expressed in English the feelings and the misgiving about them which we hear again, with a different tone, in "The Love Song of J. Alfred Prufrock" and, allowing for further difference, in *A Portrait of the Artist as a Young Man*. Pater is audible in virtually every attentive modern writer—in Hopkins, Wilde, James, Yeats, Pound, Ford, Woolf, Joyce, Eliot, Aiken, Hart Crane, Fitzgerald, Forster, Borges, Stevens, Ammons, Tomlinson, and Ashbery. The nature of his presence is elusive. It is harder to say that he is there than that he has been there. Literary historians find him in familiar chapters: "Art for Art's Sake," Aestheticism, Pre-Raphaelitism, Decadence. I have no quarrel with these ascriptions. But "the Pateresque" is more pervasive than they imply. Pater was not an original thinker. Every idea he expressed may be found elsewhere, mainly in French and German criticism. But it is misleading to refer to ideas. Pater's significance is that he invented the Pateresque: he added to literature a certain tone, a style. The invention of a style is a far more considerable act in literature than the invention of an idea. In literature, ideas are merely raw matter, congealed feelings. Pater devised a style, using the ideas of other writers as means and incentive. This has often been misunderstood. It is common to offer to dispose of Pater as a "representative man" lost in the meandering expression he is deemed to present. That is James's method of patronizing him. But Pater floats free of the movements and schools for which he is held accountable. He never gave himself over to any of them. But whatever we mean by modernity, he is an irrefutable part of it, if not as I sometimes fancy its "onlie begetter."

But I should emphasize that this book is not much concerned with Pater's influence. It is a critical biography, a Brief Life. I am interested in diverse literary relations, not merely in the particular relation designated as the influence of one writer on another. Influence is a quaint consideration in literary history and criticism. In *La Terre et l'évolution humaine* Lucien Febvre noted that the word "influence" is not to be found in science: "*Et 'influence,' ce n'est pas un mot de la langue scientifique mais la langue astrologique.*"[5] Influence is merely one motif, often recited with undue decisiveness: it does not exhaust the affiliations between the two writers brought together. "Relation," as Febvre maintained, is a sane word; its history is free of fog and obscurity. To be specific: I do not claim that Pater influenced Ashbery, but I note that on one occasion Ashbery's reading of a passage in Pater's *Plato and Platonism* led to his writing a poem. For that occasion, Pater was a presence to Ashbery; the two writers came into one field of force. I feel shy using the word "intertextuality," but it is a better word than "influence" because it establishes a field of action and leaves readers free to consider many lines of force, affiliations, trajectories.

The writer I emphasize in this book is the antinomian Pater. The first meaning of "antinomian" is "against the law," a meaning invoked in A. L. Morton's *The Everlasting Gospel* and E. P. Thompson's *Witness Against the Beast: William Blake and the Moral Law*. These books find Blake in a tradition of antinomianism dating from the seventeenth century in England: a tradition of dissent, the work of artisans, pamphleteers, radicals, men with ink and grit on their hands. Antinomianism in that sense makes a counterculture, and rejects the complacent law of reason and enlightenment. Pater had not the temper for such dissent; there is nothing of the artisan in him. He was fairly comfortable in the professional middle class of Oxford and London: the Empire had nothing to fear from him. But by interpreting the antinomian impulse as independent of the law rather than against it, Pater took to himself the tone of dissent and inscribed it in an otherwise polite culture. He represents, however mildly, the perfection of standing aside. So he made the law of culture, for those who read him, a little less sure of itself. If he anticipates the early work of Yeats, Eliot, and Joyce, rather than of Shaw, Chesterton, and Belloc, it is because he judged that he could best live by minding, for the most part, his own business.

II

From Gosse's "Walter Pater: A Portrait" (1894) to Gerald Mons-man's *Pater's Portraits* (1967), Michael Levey's *The Case of Walter Pater* (1978), and more recent work, those who have taken an interest in Pater have acted upon two assumptions: that he must have had more life than appears, since otherwise he would have to be deemed a freak of nature and culture, obstinate in the penury of his appearances; and that if he put whatever life he had into his work, it should be possible even now to thwart him and to remove the concealed life from the work by biographical deduction. As a result, it has become standard practice to regard Pater as an autobiographical writer and to assume that the main motifs of his writing are there because they happened to him, not because he imagined them. He is rarely allowed to have imagined anything, but only to have transcribed it, the writing being its trace. He wrote "The Child in the House," so he must have been the child in that house.

These assumptions are strange. I can't see why we claim to take the creative imagination seriously while slighting it in every practice. In the literature of Romanticism—in which Pater evidently though not squarely takes his place—the concept of imagination is supposed to be a fundamental capacity. Artists imagine experiences they have not had, lives they have not lived. Other voices, other rooms. We regularly distinguish between the biographic self and the poetic self, as between the *pneuma* and the *psyche*. But we appear to derive grim satisfaction from the assumption that a writer merely recites what happened. It is hard to say why we find this notion congenial, unless it is that we resent the claim, explicit in the word "genius," that there is a difference of kind between a great writer—Shakespeare, Milton, Wordsworth, Blake—and other people. I assume that genius denotes the availability, in a particular person, of energy to an extraordinary degree beyond local need. The signs of it are *copia*, excess, waste. The energy is not exhausted in merely remembering or reporting an experience. The reason why there is little to be said about genius is that a difference in degree at some point becomes a difference in kind. Leonardo was a genius: he had more energy than anyone else. Pater was not a genius: his energy was not enough. Nor had he a great dramatic imagination. But he was capable of imagining forms of life other than his own, even though in the end these may seem to evanesce into yet another semblance of his own.

As a theoretical issue, this might have been resolved by T. S. Eliot's assertion, in "Tradition and the Individual Talent," that the more complete the artist, the more separate in him will be the man who suffered and the mind that created. But few artists are as complete as that. Eliot might have asked: When you have deduced a suffering man or woman from the evidence of a mind that created, what do you suppose you have achieved? What status do you ascribe to the figure you have divined? The work of art and the man or woman who created it are still separate. There is a relation between them. Blake's works did not issue from Wordsworth's life. But the relation is occult; it can't be specified. The best reason for invoking the creative imagination is that the phrase indicates our sense of this opacity. Using the phrase, we are not engaged in obscurantism, bewildering ourselves, or driving our minds beyond the reach of syntax. We are acknowledging the mysterious character of such a mind, and confessing that it can't finally be explained or explained away by reciting the personal, domestic, social, economic, and political conditions of its production.

In this book I assume, unless contrary evidence is irresistible, that the constituents of Pater's work are there because he invented them. If a detail in the work is also known to correspond to something in the life—Marius the Epicurean dreaded the sight of copulating snakes, and so did Pater—I don't regard the correlation as embarrassing.

2

The Funeral and Henry James

WALTER PATER DIED on July 30, 1894, from a heart attack after a bout of pleurisy. He was buried in the cemetery of St. Giles's at Oxford on August 2. Attendance at the funeral was small because dons and students were on their Long Vacation, but a few officers of the university turned up. The chief mourners were Charles Shadwell, Charlotte Green, Frederick Bussell, Edmund Gosse, and Pater's sisters Clara and Hester. Henry James, who might have been expected to attend, did not, for reasons he gave in a letter to Gosse on August 10:

> You were very happily inspired in writing me about Pater's interment—&, in particular, in writing so charmingly. Your letter makes me much regret that, having, as I had, fifty minds to go to his funeral, I didn't have the fifty first which might have carried me there. If I had known you would go I would have joined you—very possibly. But I was deterred by considerations—that of my very limited acquaintance with Pater, my non-communication with him for so long, & above all by (what I supposed would be) the compact Oxfordism of it all; in which I seem to feel myself to have no place.[1]

These reasons were enough not only to keep James away but to let him present his absence as an esoteric tribute to the deceased. The revision of "I would have joined you" to "very possibly" propels a typical sequence in his references to Pater: first an acknowledgment of his distinction, then with notable speed a recital of several reasons for slighting it, and finally an interpretation of those reasons as amounting somehow to a tribute:

> It was not to be dreamed of, however, I think, that the event should have been more "noticed." What is more delicate than the extinction of delicacy—& what note more in place than that of "discretion"—in respect to the treatment of anything that might have happened to Pater—even the last thing that *could* happen? It presents itself to me—so far as I know it—as one of the successful, felicitous lives and the time & manner of the death a part of the success.[2]

In that last phrase, according to Leon Edel, James is probably alluding to the success of Pater's books, "his *Plato and Platonism* of the previous year having confirmed the already large reputation of the author of *Marius the Epicurean*."[3] It may be true. But James's reference to delicacy, to the supreme delicacy of its extinction, and to "discretion," such that the word requires the attention of inverted commas, suggests that he has more in view than two successful books. He appears to say that the suddenness of Pater's death, by ruling out the vulgar possibility of its having long been anticipated, was yet another mark of his delicacy. He died in such a manner as to draw few to the cemetery. Even in that respect, he had the distinction of keeping "the last curiosity" to himself.

Pater also enabled James to express, in the same letter, one of his favorite emotions, unassertive regret:

> I don't cease to regret that being last February (I think,) at Oxford, and Herbert Warren taking me on the Sunday afternoon to see him, took me to the spare little house where Miss P. only was drearily visible, instead of to Brasen nose [*sic*], where I learned with a pang, that evening, from the curious Bussell, W.H.P. had been "disappointed" at my non-arrival.[4]

The pang was not intense. James and Pater met for the first time probably in January 1879, introduced by a mutual friend, the American novelist Julia Constance Fletcher. James's letter of January 18, 1879, to his mother implies that the occasion he describes was the first:

> . . . a Sunday evening *conversazione*, at the Herz's—German Jews, living in a very pleasant old house in Harley Street, who are insatiate lion-hunters, and most naifs in their pursuit of notabilities. They go in for having a literary *salon* and also have, I believe, every Sunday, when they first gave a very good dinner, a very well-frequented one. The evening I was there, there were a lot of people, and I talked with Frederic Harrison, Lyulph Stanley, C. G. Leland, W. Pater (who is far from being as beautiful as his own prose), etc. Such, dearest mother, is the history of my small outgoings. . . .[5]

When Pater moved to London in August 1885 and started living at 12 Earl's Terrace, Kensington, he met James fairly often at literary parties, especially those given by his neighbors the Robinsons. They did not become close friends. In temper, they were far apart: James, socially voluble; Pater, withdrawn as if it were a matter of principle from anything that presented itself for attention. Thomas Hardy noted, after meeting Pater in London in 1886, that his manner was "that of one carrying weighty ideas without spilling them."[6] But I don't think Pater's manner proclaimed that he wouldn't spill them. Or proclaimed anything, except that the heroic mode of living was not his. "His nature shyly asserted itself," Edward Thomas wrote of him.[7] I think that James regarded Pater as one of those who take undue pride in their reserve. In "*Daniel Deronda*: A Conversation" (1876) he has one of the speakers refer to George Eliot's Grandcourt as "the most detestable kind of Englishman—the Englishman who thinks it low to articulate." James couldn't have had Pater in mind—he hadn't at that point met him—but I speculate that, upon meeting him, he found his prejudice confirmed, though not to the degree of disliking Pater as manifestation of the type in question. What Pater regarded as low is a necessary consideration in one's sense of him.

On December 13, 1894, James took another opportunity to convey his sense of Pater's life. Gosse sent him a copy of his obituary essay, "Walter Pater: A Portrait," and James thanked him for its "vivid pages":

Much as they tell, however, how curiously negative & faintly-grey he, after all telling, remains! I think he has had—will have had—the most exquisite literary fortune: i.e. to have taken it out all, wholly, exclusively, with the pen (the style, the genius,) & absolutely not at all with the person. He is the mask without the face, & there isn't in his total superficies a tiny point of vantage for the newspaper to flap its wings on. . . . Well, faint, pale, embarrassed, exquisite Pater! He reminds me, in the disturbed midnight of our actual literature, of one of those lucent matchboxes which you place, on going to bed, near the candle, to show you, in the darkness, where you can strike a light: he shines in the uneasy gloom—vaguely, and has a phosphorescence, not a flame. But I quite agree with you that he is not of the little day—but of the longer time.[8]

James knew that Gosse would recognize, in that last sentence, an allusion to one of Pater's most noticed passages from the Conclusion to *Studies in the History of the Renaissance*—"to burn always with this hard gem-like flame, to maintain this ecstasy, is success in life."[9] Gosse could be relied on to take the point, that Pater was a genuine artist, distinctive in his way, but not one of the masters. The repetition of "exquisite" in James's letter, like the reference to phosphorescence in default of flame, conveyed a firm assessment, that Pater's merits, fine as they were, added up to minor artistry.

On November 8, 1896, James wrote to Gosse again, thanking him for the volume of Pater—it was probably the unfinished *Gaston de Latour*—he had sent him:

All thanks for the little grey, pretty Pater, of which I have tasted fully the faint, feeble sweetness. Of course it's casual work, but it gives one that odd, peculiar sense that reading him always gives—that kind of little illusion that some refined, pathetic object or presence is *in the room* with you—materially—& stays there while you read. He has too little point, & a kind of wilful weakness; but he's divinely uncommon. I went, by the way, yesterday to see his sisters, my neighbors; & found them in a state of subdued flourish & chaste symmetry which I hope means all manner of solid comfort.[10]

James's way of making "refined"—one of Pater's favorite words—yield to "pathetic" enacts the same rhythm; he pays tribute, then reduces the amount he appears to have paid, and in the end restores some of the good of it by improving "object" to "presence," even though it is a presence soon to be put by.

James acknowledged that Pater was a person to whom it was difficult to pay appropriate tribute. He thought him a distinctive writer, a rare individual, but he didn't regard him as a presence large enough to constitute a type. In 1902 James gave some thought to the aesthetic type, but mainly to assert that it hadn't established itself in English society:

> Many of us will doubtless not have forgotten how we were witnesses a certain number of years since to a season and a society that had found themselves of a sudden roused, as from some deep drugged sleep, to the conception of the "esthetic" law of life; in consequence of which this happy thought had begun to receive the honours of a lively appetite and an eager curiosity, but was at the same time surrounded and manipulated by as many different kinds of inexpertness as probably ever huddled together on a single pretext.[11]

He means, I think, the inexpertness evident in *The Yellow Book*, Beardsley, Lionel Johnson, and Arthur Symons, thickened into the appalling muddle of Wilde:

> The spectacle was strange and finally was wearisome, for the simple reason that the principle in question, once it was proclaimed—a principle not easily formulated, but which we may conveniently speak of as that of beauty at any price, beauty appealing alike to the senses and to the mind—was never felt to fall into its place as really adopted and efficient.[12]

It remained, this Aestheticism, an exotic import from France; it did not settle down to enrich the society that briefly considered it:

> It brought with it no repose, brought with it only agitation. We were not really, not fully convinced, for the state of conviction is quiet. This was to have been the state itself—that is the state of mind achieved and established—in which we were to know

ugliness no more, to make the esthetic consciousness feel at home with us, or learn ourselves at any rate to feel at home with *it*. That would have been the reign of peace, the supreme beatitude; but stability continued to elude us. We had mustered a hundred good reasons for it, yet the reasons but lighted up our desert. They failed to flower into a single concrete esthetic "type." One authentic, one masterful specimen would have done wonders for us, would at least have assuaged our curiosity.[13]

I take this to mean that Wilde's trials and imprisonment ruled out the entire possibility, and that Pater, who seemed to proclaim the aesthetic law of life, was not masterful enough to embody it. Pater's being an individual was excellent, but he never made himself a type; as James's artists, in several stories, embodied a type. D'Annunzio embodied it, too, but had the disability of being a foreigner, too far from Rye to impinge upon "us."

In 1906 James made his final attempt to "place" Pater. When A. C. Benson's *Walter Pater* came out, James wrote him a letter of congratulation:

> You have done in especial *this* delightful and interesting thing —that you have ministered to that strange, touching, edifying (to me quite thrilling) operation of the whirligig of time, through which Pater has already, in these few years, and little as he seemed marked out for it, become in our literature that very rare sovereign thing, a Figure: a figure in the sense in which there are so few! It is a matter altogether independent of the mere possession of genius, or achievement even of "success." I think—it's a matter almost of tragic or ironic (or even comic) felicity; but it comes here and there to the individual— unawares—and it leaves hundreds of the eminent alone. Well, I feel that it has come to dear, queer, deeply individual and homogenous W.H.P., crowning his strong and painful identity—and that your study of him, in which many of your observations do go deep, will really quite have settled the thing.[14]

We can only guess, despite James's effort to explain the word, what it meant for Pater to have become a figure rather than a type. I think it meant his having become a character, as in a novel, a personage with enough space around him to appear to stand free of his social and other conditions. Arnold, perhaps, was not in that sense a figure, because he was immersed in those conditions to the extent of hardly being separable from them. But I am guessing. A figure, in any case, is not a type.

James's note, in the end, is one of patronage. He does not dismiss Pater, but he puts him in a category of secondary writers. If Pater were a character in one of James's novels, he would be a *ficelle*, ministering to heroine and hero without drawing light away from them. "Curiously negative & faintly-grey" is not James's last word on Pater, but as a first indication of his judgment it sets a limit beyond which subsequent praise can't go. Perhaps there is a trace of homophobia here. James knew that he and Pater were of similar sexual disposition, but he does not imply any sympathy or fellowship, unless the word "painful" in the letter to Benson, himself homoerotic, is code between them. But even if it is, James's impatience with Pater seems to say that whatever Pater was, he wasn't masterful in that being.

But there is a complicating factor. In James's fictions of the aesthetic and artistic life—*Roderick Hudson*, *The Tragic Muse*, and "The Lesson of the Master" sufficiently mark this emphasis—we find two forms of it. In one, the artist hands himself over to his work, to the degree of giving up any personal or biographical claim. He does not reward the attentions of a newspaper: he has lost himself in his work and wishes to be found only there. James's reference—which admits a phallic interpretation without demanding one—to Pater as having "taken it out all, wholly, exclusively, with the pen (the style, the genius,) & absolutely not at all with the person" establishes him as an artist of that ascetic character. In the Preface to *The Tragic Muse* James describes this form of the artistic life:

> Any presentation of the artist *in triumph* must be flat in proportion as it really sticks to its subject—it can only smuggle in relief and variety. For, to put the matter in an image, all we then—in his triumph—see of the charm-compeller is the back he turns to us as he bends over his work.[15]

James admired such artists, and thought them especially well advised in the years of the yellow press to conduct their visible lives with reserve. But he recognized a second and in the end a greater form of the artistic life. When he thought of the major writers—Balzac, Stendhal, Flaubert preeminently among those he cared about—he found them exhibiting such abundance that it suffused their lives and works. It was possible to distinguish, even in these cases, between life and work, but only for a local descriptive reason: it made for a distinction between the two forms abundance took. James's tribute to those writers did not include the limiting word "exquisite" or propose a demarcation between the pen and the person. Pater, rich in other merits, lacked abundance; his energy went wholly into his books, leaving little or no remainder. That is what James's tribute comes to. He hoped that in his own case there was abundance enough, and he made his career in that confidence. His appreciation of social life was a sign of his choice. Gregarious by nature as well as on principle, he knew that he would hear at the dinner-table much lore and gossip that he could turn to account in his fiction. From that post of vantage and armed with a corresponding prejudice, he saw Pater as necessarily constricted: there was not enough energy available to animate a large life and major creative work. Or so James thought.

The difference between James and Gosse, when Pater was in question, was simple. James assumed that Pater had virtually no life apart from his work, and he read the work as creation nearly independent of its author. Gosse knew Pater far more familiarly than James did and saw him in more various circumstances. He received from him the gift of a cat called Atossa, her sister Pansie remaining with the Paters at Oxford: a trivial matter to those who don't care for cats. No cat passed from Pater to James. Nor did James ever see Pater, as Gosse did, emerging with Swinburne from a hansom cab at William Bell Scott's house in Cheyne Walk, Pater not only sober but dainty, sporting lemon-yellow kid gloves, Swinburne falling drunk on the pavement. Presently, according to Gosse, Pater appeared in Scott's upper room, "talking with dreamy detachment on indifferent subjects" while the servants removed Swinburne to the kitchen to be cleaned and sobered.[16] Such an episode may not amount to much, but Gosse wanted to bring Pater's life forward, subject to considerations of decorum and privacy. He hoped to make the mere life, such as it palely was, count for something when in James's ironic sense of it, it counted for little or nothing. Pater's books might be left to come into their own; two or three of them had a chance of surviving. But the chance would be improved if they could be seen as having issued from a life more substantial than the common image of it.

But James's patronizing tone, when Pater's name and work came up, was misleading. Several of Pater's sentences from *Studies in the*

History of the Renaissance, especially from the "Mona Lisa" passage, stayed in James's mind, as Adeline R. Tintner has shown,[17] for the rest of his life. He had also to curb a Pateresque or aestheticist force in himself by inventing Gilbert Osmond in *The Portrait of a Lady* and Adam Verver in *The Golden Bowl* to show it subdued. These characters, and the fate James imposed upon them, are his answer to the temptation of living one's life in the spirit of a connoisseur. But the case was difficult. In "The Author of 'Beltraffio' " James allows Mark Ambient to go his own aesthetic way. Of "Beltraffio" he says that nothing had been done in that line "from the point of view of art for art." If Mrs. Ambient finds her husband's mind so repellent that she is willing to see her son die rather than grow up in the scene of such corruption, the story does not endorse her logic. There is something of Pater in Ambient, if to the Pater we know we add, however implausibly, a Philistine wife. A child who dies without palpable cause is entirely Paterian. In *The Princess Casamassima* James had to send Hyacinth to Paris and Venice and let him see "the splendid accumulations of the happier few, to which doubtless the miserable many have also in their degree contributed." Hyacinth reaches a conclusion, alien to his political faith, that he loved the monuments and treasures of art, the palaces, conquests of learning and taste, indeed "the general fabric of civilisation as we know it," despite the fact that these treasures were raised upon "the despotisms, the cruelties, the exclusions, the monopolies and the rapacities of the past." Because of those great works, as he tells the Princess, "the world is less of a 'bloody sell' and life more of a lark."[18] The Princess, like Paul Muniment, is determined to effect restitution. Hyacinth comes to regard "the intolerance of positions and fortunes that are higher and brighter than one's own" as merely a grudge that leaves an odious stain upon one's soul. He kills himself rather than settle for the simplification by which one value is allowed without misgiving to displace another.

In these and other stories of artistic life, James imagines several nuances of a life contiguous to his own but separable from it, too. The stories acknowledge aspects of the aesthetic life that James didn't otherwise wish to talk about. He argued patiently enough with his brother William and with H. G. Wells, R. L. Stevenson, Henry Adams, Gosse, and other writers about fiction, form, language, style, and the merit of the imaginative act. But not about the sinister aspects of art: these he consigned to his stories. Even in private letters he commented on Wilde's life only to the extent of declaring him a fatuous boor. James couldn't entirely ignore Pater, Beardsley, or even a man as bizarre in a minor way as Howard Sturgis, but he condescended to them, and observed their lives from a distance. He mainly wondered why Pater, so interesting up to a point, hovered there as if he feared to exceed himself.

Part II

Brief Life

3

From Stepney to Oxford

Now, once more, it is not altogether easy to interpret Pater.
—George Saintsbury in *The Bookman*, August 1906

IN HIS ESSAY ON Leonardo da Vinci, Pater remarks that during his years at Florence "Leonardo's history is the history of his art; for himself, he is lost in the bright cloud of it."[1] Reciting Pater's life, we have to look for him in the cloud of his occasional writings. He is rarely visible anywhere else. There are weeks or even months in which he seems to have taken literally his favorite motif of evanescence and drifted away. We assume that he is still alive, but the evidence for his breathing is meager. We take it for granted that he is lost in the cloud of his interests, bright or not. Normally, an essay, a lecture, or a book at last sets the life astir, resumes the narrative, and we conclude that during the vacant weeks he has been living what he regarded as his true life: reading classical or modern philosophy, German metaphysics, the German scholarship on mythology, looking at Italian Renaissance pictures in the National Gallery in London, Greek sculptures in the British Museum. In retrospect, we find his silences not wasteful but enabling; he has been teaching, tutoring a few students, or spending the Long Vacation in France or Italy. The weeks have an air of meaning, short of meaning anything in particular. We are used to finding the lives of nineteenth-century writers rampant with incident, and the biographical problem is to discover the dominant motive or pressure the events inscribe. It is the problem of making particular sense of a life, given so much evidence upon which to work. Goethe, Balzac, Stendhal, Ruskin, Flaubert, Carlyle, Arnold, Newman, Dickens, George Eliot: they are never lost in the cloud of their art. If there is opacity, it is not for lack of significant incident. But Pater had little producible life, or only such life as declared itself in his prose: certain tones, cadences, gestures. By comparison with his grand contemporaries, he seems hardly to have lived. But when we reach that conclusion, we know we have asked the wrong question.

Pater was born on August 4, 1839, at 1 Honduras Terrace, Commercial Road, a grubby district on the north shore of the Thames between Wapping and Stepney. He was christened Walter Horatio Pater in honor of his cousin and godmother, Mrs. Walter Horatio May. His father, Richard Glode Pater, was a surgeon: not a surgeon or a physician in the exalted modern sense but a medical man in useful general practice among the poor of the East End. Walter was the third child of Richard and Maria Pater; preceded by a brother, William Thompson Pater, born in 1835, and a sister, Hester Maria, born in 1837. A fourth child, Clara Ann, was born in 1841. On January 28, 1842, Richard Pater died at the age of forty-five: the cause of death was given as "an affection of the brain." Soon after, the widow and children moved to Enfield, a far more salubrious place than Stepney. On September 19, 1845, Pater's uncle William died, also at the age of forty-five.

A child two and a half years old can hardly be supposed to remember his dead father with much clarity. Pater retained, as a consequence of his father's death, mainly a sense of lack as an incorrigible factor in human life. He grew up with the conviction not only that life was brief but that, in a particular case, its tenure was arbitrary; it might end at any time and without apparent cause. In Pater's fiction, heroes die young, as if early death were in the nature of life and life itself a gratuitous concession. I am urged to live intensely, if only because my life is likely to be short, my death abrupt. In Pater, as in Wallace Stevens, death is the mother of beauty and the cause of our seeing beautiful things with a correspondingly acute sense of their transience. So at the end of *The Renaissance* Pater speaks of Rousseau when he might well have spoken for himself:

An undefinable taint of death had clung always about him, and now in early manhood he believed himself smitten by mortal disease. He asked himself how he might make as much as possible of the interval that remained; and he was not biassed by anything in his previous life when he decided that it must be by intellectual excitement, which he found just then in the clear, fresh writings of Voltaire. Well! we are all *condamnés*, as Victor Hugo says: we are all under sentence of death but with a sort of indefinite reprieve—*les hommes sont tous condamnés à mort avec des sursis indéfinis*: we have an interval, and then our place knows us no more.[2]

Pater adds to this passage from Hugo's *Le Dernier Jour d'un condamné* "a sort of"—a favorite phrase of his own misgiving, as if he thought Hugo too resolute even in affirming the common fate. The sentiment required an uncertain hovering before its expression. It is typical of Pater in his reflective moments to inscribe hesitation into conclusions which, in the event, are sufficiently bold to satisfy one's gloomiest anticipation. Hugo's sentence marches to its comprehensive end; Pater's suspends the cadence, postponing the certitude he doesn't offer to avoid. The sentence is written under the shadow not of Pater's death but of the arbitrary duration of life as the condition under which we are permitted to live at all.

The years at Enfield were a period of contentment, if not of vivacity. Pater's mind, gratified by rural life, transcribed a new circle of images: trees, flowers, heat, light, walled gardens, an old house. Later, in an essay on Charles Lamb, he recalled his own Enfield:

He felt the genius of places; and I sometimes think he resembles the places he knew and liked best, and where his lot fell— London, sixty-five years ago, with Covent Garden and the old theatres, and the Temple gardens still unspoiled, Thames gliding down, and beyond to north and south the fields at Enfield or Hampton, to which, "with their living trees," the thoughts wander "from the hard wood of the desk"—fields fresher, and coming nearer to town then, but in one of which the present writer remembers, on a brooding early summer's day, to have heard the cuckoo for the first time.[3]

It is a sentence as if set to Delius's music, the phrases issuing one from another by association or mild contrast and coming to rest upon an evocation. Pater's claim to have had a sensuous childhood could not be more quietly made. We know that it is a claim only because he so rarely speaks of himself.

In February 1853 the family moved to 12 Harbledown Place, Harbledown, near Canterbury. The main reason for the move was that Pater could attend the King's School in Canterbury as a day boy. In "Emerald Uthwart," written after a visit to his old school in the summer of 1891, he transferred Kent to Sussex and enhanced a setting in some respects like the Canterbury he remembered:

> . . . little velvety fields, little with the true sweet English little-
> ness of our little island, our land of vignettes. Here all was little;
> the very church where they went to pray, to sit, the ancient
> Uthwarts sleeping all around outside under the windows, de-
> posited there as quietly as fallen trees on their native soil, and
> almost unrecorded, as there had been almost nothing to record.[4]

On February 25, 1854, Pater's mother died. One of Pater's early biographers, Thomas Wright—not a reliable source and on this matter the only one—reports that Pater had quarreled with his mother and that a "peculiar bitterness" persisted beyond her death. The only evidence for this is that there is a similar breach in *Marius the Epicurean* between Marius and his mother. Pater's aunt Elizabeth took charge of the children. Meanwhile he continued to be reasonably happy at the King's School, though on one occasion he was set upon by some of the boys. Pater formed with his schoolmate Henry Dombrain the first of his intense friendships. Another schoolboy, J. R. McQueen, joined them to make "the inseparables." Their favorite pastime was to walk in Blean Woods, reading to one another poems by Wordsworth and Keats. Many years later McQueen gave Wright a description of Pater's appearance in 1855:

> . . . thin, rather hump-backed, pale, with a most singular face,
> and prematurely whiskered. He had an overhanging forehead,
> deep set mild eyes: a nose very low at the bridge and neither
> Grecian nor Roman; a curious misformation of the mouth,
> resembling slightly some species of ape; and those strange
> whiskers.[5]

In 1855 Pater, already high church, met Rev. John Keble, author of *The Christian Year*, who encouraged him to enter the ministry and devote his life to Christianity. He was a somewhat grave boy, kind enough but reserved in temper. He was also an aspiring but not a budding religious poet. One poem is "St. Elizabeth of Hungary," another "The Chant of the Celestial Sailors": he used poetry mainly to tempt himself to sublimities he was otherwise unable to practice. One of his poems, "Watchman, What of the Night?," questions the immortality of the soul.

On Speech Day, 1858, Pater made the unusual choice of a modern poem for recitation, a selection from Tennyson's "Morte d'Arthur." Leaving King's, he brought with him a small garland of prizes in Latin scholarship and church history: more to the point, an exhibition of £60 a year for three years at Oxford. The school added £30 for books, and McQueen's family may have given him some money. In October 1858 he went up to Queen's College, Oxford. He soon made friends with two of the most formidable undergraduates, Ingram Bywater and Matthew Moorhouse. Within a year or so, much influenced by the writings of Kingsley, F. D. Maurice, and in due course Darwin, Pater discarded his religious faith. He was now a skeptic in the tradition of Hume. But he retained the bizarre plan of taking orders in the Church of England.

In 1860 and 1861 Pater and Bywater received private tuition in Greek from Benjamin Jowett. But Pater's most influential teacher was William Wolfe Capes, Reader in Ancient History. Pater soon became an Arnoldian; he attended Arnold's lectures "On the Modern Element in Literature," enjoyed their mischievousness, and committed to memory several stanzas of "The Scholar Gypsy." Never an idler, he learned enough German to read Hegel and recent philosophy. He kept himself up to the minute with English and French fiction. An early reader of *Modern Painters*, he recognized Ruskin and Arnold as his masters in criticism. The one thing he neglected to do was to prepare for his examinations. On December 11, 1862, he graduated with a disappointing second-class degree in Literae Humaniores.

Meanwhile his aunt took Clara and Hester to Heidelberg to complete an education that had hardly begun. Pater visited them there in the Christmas vacation 1858, again in October 1859, and in the Long Vacation 1860. Returning from one of these visits, he perused the cathedral at Mainz, attended service in the cathedral at Cologne, and committed the indelicacy of attending High Mass at Antwerp. His letters to McQueen showed that his relation to Christianity was now frivolous. He still intended to seek ordination and was heard to say that it would be fun to become a minister without believing a word of Christian doctrine. McQueen was appalled by Pater's bravado. On February 21, 1859, he told Pater that he would do anything he could to prevent his ordination. He asked him to desist, and when Pater ignored the request he consulted Henry Parry Liddon, a high church-man at Christ Church. Liddon advised him to write to the Bishop of London, Archibald Tait, objecting to Pater's proposed ordination and referring the Bishop, if he needed further evidence, to Rev. John B. Kearney, one of Pater's teachers at King's. In the event, Pater didn't persist in his impudence.

His loss of faith didn't constitute a crisis. He assumed that he could fulfill his spiritual nature just as well in secular as in religious terms. Arnold and Renan made that assumption respectable, with little dif-ficulty since they released their readers from the obligation of believing anything. By translating soul into spirit, Pater acquired a sense of spirituality on easy terms. He was free to merge it with any current notion of mind, consciousness, or sensibility. Like Georg Simmel, he found it congenial to believe that life, in its flow, is not determined by a soul but driven by a force. Pater dissolved theology in states of feeling, for which the terms of individual psychology were fully adequate. He had, it appears, no sense of guilt or sin. Or if he had, he soon consigned it to a more comprehensive sense of the lack, the empty necessity in life, for which he was not responsible. If he had been allowed to take orders and to become a minister, he would have taken his duties lightly by taking them aesthetically. His interest in religious ritual and cere-mony was keen but entirely picturesque, it fulfilled itself in the charm of hieratic appearances, elegant forms. But when McQueen intervened and took the matter of ordination to the Bishop of London, Pater felt a certain disturbance, the first in his not yet public life. As in later episodes, he could not understand what the fuss was about, though any undergraduate could have explained it in every particular. Pater was a sensitive young man, but not in any respect that dissuaded him from being pert.

A matter that distressed Pater far more than his loss of Christian faith was his appearance. He was ugly. None of his features was dis-tinguished. He was regarded as the Caliban of letters. "I would give ten years of my life to be handsome," he said.[6] He was already thinking of beauty as not only a value but perhaps the supreme one. That he should so lack it while admiring it in the choice young men of Oxford was painful to him. There was little he could do. A few of his friends took up the problem to the extent of suggesting that he grow a mustache. Pater accepted the suggestion and, as William Gaunt has remarked, "shortly there burgeoned on his upper lip that formidable luxuriance which provided him with a distinct character not his own."[7]

On December 28, 1862, Pater's aunt Elizabeth died in Dresden. He attended the funeral there and returned with Hester and Clara to settle for the time being in London.

Late in 1862 Pater joined the Old Mortality, a discussion-group of undergraduates and junior fellows most of whom were agnostic. In January 1863 he had the audacity to seek a clerical fellowship at Brasenose. In the summer, another clerical fellowship turned up at Trinity College. Pater won neither of them. But on February 5, 1864, he was elected to a probationary fellowship in classics at Brasenose, a non-clerical one, fortunately. His academic qualifications were poor, but he was known to be widely read, to be familiar with German philosophy and scholarship, and to have an air of distinction. These qualities were enough for Brasenose, intellectually a nondescript college, its students distinguished only on the playing fields. They toiled at games and played at books, as Humphry Ward said. Pater's main duty was to coach them for their examinations in Greek and Latin, a task he performed well enough. He was now known to be an agnostic. On February 20, 1864, he read to the Old Mortals a paper on "Fichte's Ideal Student" in which he advocated "self-culture" and declared that he did not believe in the immortality of the soul. S. R. Brooke, a devout Anglican, wrote in his diary that Pater's talk was "one of the most thoroughly infidel productions" it had ever been his pain to hear.[8] Brooke conveyed his sense of outrage to Gerard Manley Hopkins, an undergraduate at Balliol. Hopkins then suggested to Liddon that they should start a rival essay-club to oppose the agnosticism of the Old Mortality. The result was the Hexameron Essay Society, established "to promote discussion upon subjects of interest so far as may be consistent with adherence to the doctrines of the Catholic Faith."[9] Edward Caird's note on Pater for the *Dictionary of National Biography* describes his first essay as "a hymn of praise to the Absolute." This probably refers to Pater's first performance at the Old Mortality, or to an extended version of it called "Diaphaneitè" that he wrote a few months later. These performances shocked a few of the members and caused local scandal. Pater liked to show off his irreligious character as a token of his modernity and to exemplify an *avant-garde* by uttering this version of it. He enjoyed breathing the thin air of speculation.

On February 5, 1865, Pater's fellowship was confirmed. The fact that he hadn't earned it wasn't allowed to count. He was evidently the sort of Fellow his college wanted. Little in the way of scholarship was required. Many years later Bernard Berenson committed to his diary a note of envy, that Wolfflin's doctoral thesis in 1886, "*Prologomena zu einer Psychologie der Architektur*," had anticipated Berenson's entire philosophy of art. "He, however, had Burckhardt and Volkelt as teachers and generations of German thinkers, while I had what? Only Pater."[10] Not that Berenson was ever one of Pater's pupils. They met once. "I did meet Pater, although against my will, and it was very disappointing."[11] But in 1865 Pater got the fellowship, so the problem of a career was solved. Under the Commissioners' Statutes of 1854 a fellowship was a benefice for life, provided the holder accepted the conditions attached to it. These were not arduous. Pater was now secure, a bachelor don, a middle-class Fellow of moderate but never endangered means, as Edward Thomas described him. For the rest of his life he moved between Oxford and London: Oxford for teaching, reading, writing, and the company of good-looking young men; London for the flourish of being, if only for a few years, a man of the world as well as a man of letters. At Oxford he was that comfortable being, a bachelor don of homosexual disposition. Cared for by his sisters, he lived a life mostly of reserve, but occasionally among friends he darted forth with an intrepid opinion.

To one matter he paid particular attention: the adornment of his rooms at Brasenose. He had two rooms on the first floor, with a direct view of the Radcliffe Camera and a slant view of St. Mary's Church. The rooms were paneled in pale green, with matting on the floors. The furniture was oak. He hung a few choice prints, *Three Fates*, attributed to Michelangelo, a head after Correggio, something by Ingres. His books were mainly Greek philosophy, modern French fiction, German aesthetics, and a few inscribed volumes of poetry. There were also, if Lionel Johnson is to be believed, some books on political economy. Johnson reported the matter to Yeats with Pater's explanation, that "everything that has occupied man, for any length of time, is worthy of our study." Yeats thought the point worth recalling in "The Tragic Generation," along with the remark that Johnson's reports "were not always to be trusted."[12] There is better authority for noting that a table in Pater's living room sustained a dwarf orange-tree with real oranges on it.

In the summer of 1865 Pater made his first visit to Italy. Accompanied by Shadwell he went to Ravenna, Pisa, and Florence. The experience was a revelation, a glimpse of more liberal intuitions than Pater had ever known. He divined from Renaissance paintings the imagery of a richer, more daring sense of life than any to be seen in Oxford. He began to associate the Italian Renaissance with freedom, sensuous experience, "the exercise of sight and touch" which he attributed to his master in these fulfillments, Winckelmann. Mostly he saw in those paintings an ideal human image, the love of a man for a beautiful boy. After the Long Vacation he returned to Brasenose.

4

Hopkins, Oscar Browning, Simeon Solomon, Symonds

IN THE TRINITY TERM of 1866 Jowett sent Hopkins to Pater for tutoring. Hopkins had come up to Balliol on a scholarship in April 1863. He was now fairly well established as an undergraduate, and he was respected by colleagues who shared his concern for ritual and Anglican doctrine. His personal life in other respects was often a torment. Mainly but not exclusively attracted to young men, he worried over his susceptibility to beauty in any form; it distracted his spiritual life. In a period of ten months, according to one of his diaries, he found himself guilty of 1,564 sins, an average of five a day; 238 of these were sexual. He was much troubled by nocturnal emissions, and given to masturbation. Fasting and other forms of penance were his response to these sins of the flesh.

On May 2, 1866, Hopkins made a note in his journal:

Coaching with W. H. Pater this term. Walked with him on Monday evening last, April 30. Fine evening bitterly cold. "Bleak-faced Neology in cap and gown." No cap and gown but very bleak.[1]

"Bleak-faced Neology in cap and gown" is a line from Rev. Charles Turner's sonnet "A Dream." Neologists were theologians who tried to subdue the doctrines of Christianity to a rationalist interpretation. Turner thought he could thwart such men by firing twenty sonnets across their bows. For May 31 Hopkins's journal reads:

> A little rain and at evening and night hard rain.—Pater talking two hours against Xianity.[2]

Presumably the sentiments Hopkins had to listen to were the ones Pater delivered to the Old Mortality. The text, like the soul in Pater's account of it, has not survived, but "Diaphaneitè" probably gives the gist of it. A barely disguised love-letter to Shadwell, it dreams of a beautiful form of life that only a few figures from literature and history adumbrated.

But Hopkins was immune to Pater's two hours of agnosticism. No church was high enough for him. The particular issue that impelled him to become a Roman Catholic was his doubt about the historical legitimacy of the Church of England in administering the Sacrament of the Eucharist. Belief in the Real Presence required a ground in Infallibility, and the only such ground was papal infallibility. On July 17, 1866, Hopkins decided that he could no longer receive Communion in the Church of England. Three months later, on October 21, Newman received him into the Roman Catholic church. On November 7, 1866, he wrote to Liddon, denying that he had let himself be dazzled into Catholicism. On the contrary, he told him, he became a Catholic because two and two make four.

Meanwhile he wrote essays for Pater, including "The Origin of Our Moral Ideas," an attack on Utilitarianism. Pater underlined a few notable phrases in it but otherwise did not annotate it. Hopkins's papers during that term were mostly on Plato, morality and aesthetics, and the discrimination of pagan and Christian virtues. Hopkins's conversion suspended for a few months the relation between him and Pater. An invitation to join Pater on a reading party, much appreciated in advance, did not arrive. But the relation was soon mended. Pater was capable of resentments but not inclined to maintain them for long. Hopkins was moving resolutely toward the priesthood and eventually committed himself to the Society of Jesus. He entered the Jesuit novitiate at Roehampton on September 7, 1868, and was ordained priest on September 23, 1877. Pater couldn't divert him from the path to Rome.

But Hopkins still kept doubtful company. On May 29, 1868, he saw Swinburne and was introduced to Simeon Solomon. On June 17 he lunched with Pater and they went to Solomon's studio and the Royal Academy. Hopkins and Pater were divided on religious belief, but their interest in art, aesthetics, and homoerotic sentiment kept a mild friendship going. Even when Hopkins became a priest, he continued to visit Pater. In February 1879, assigned to St. Aloysius's Church at Oxford, he dined with him and his sisters.

As a writer, Hopkins was closer to Ruskin's spirit than to Pater's. Like Ruskin, he paid attention to the glowing sundry of the world. He looked at things. "What you look hard at seems to look hard at you," he noted, and enjoyed the double hardness. Pater was already a relativist, a modernist of drift; he looked at objects only in the hope of provoking himself to a tone or a sensation somewhat aside from them. Phenomena did not interest him for any other reason. As his pupil for a term, Hopkins learned from Pater how to conduct an argument in philosophic terms which would at least be understood if not accepted by an opponent. On the question of belief, Pater should have minded his own business. But Hopkins's faith was not at risk on that cold evening.

So they were at Oxford, but each had his own sense of the place. It was fashionable during those years to display one's sensibility in an expressed sense of Oxford. Cambridge was already moving toward science and worldly versions of philosophy, but Oxford was still to be found between Plato, Aristotle, and Hegel, its terms of allusion linguistic, ethical, and aesthetic. Its typical achievement, and one of its supreme accomplishments, was the *Oxford English Dictionary*, begun in 1884 and, till supplements became necessary, completed in 1928. Pater liked Oxford, but he did not share the sense of historical radiance which it incited in Newman, Arnold, and Hopkins. In Easter 1865 Hopkins wrote a poem "To Oxford":

> . . . *for nothing here*
> *Nor elsewhere can thy sweetness unendear.*
> *This is my park, my pleasaunce.*[3]

In "Duns Scotus's Oxford" he writes of "Towery city and branchy between towers." Duns Scotus, who is thought to have lectured at Oxford about 1301, gave Hopkins cause to imagine that the true spirit of the university proceeded from medieval Christianity through the honorable error of the Oxford Movement to Dr. Newman. Hopkins's

Oxford was not, therefore, the sum of Newman, Jowett, Max Muller, Ruskin, Arnold, Pater, and the Oxford Hegelians; it was Catholic Oxford, baptized by Father Hopkins's desire.

Pater did not think of Oxford in this numinous style. The choice between Oxford and London was always available, but nothing much depended upon making it or sticking by it. Domestic convenience, rather than his spirituality, was the issue. Sometimes, he thought that the chief merit of Oxford was that it was not London; at other times, that the merit was not especially felicitous. But he did not doubt that the Oxford of Newman, Arnold, and Jowett was a significant force in cultural life. In the poem "Oxford" Edward Dorn expresses feelings about the place that Pater would not have understood:

> *Oxford was never intended for defeat*
> *as I understand it it was born*
> *as a dirty necked attempt*
> *to keep clear of the establishment.* . . .

and later in the same poem:

> *Can't*
> *you tell yourselves it is time*
> *Oxford stopped having a place*
> *in English life as sanctuary.* . . .[4]

It was as sanctuary that Pater and Hopkins, in their different tones, valued Oxford even when it became the scene of distress for each of them.

In late 1866 or early 1867 Pater branched out and gave a series of lectures on the history of philosophy. They were memorable, short of being useful to the students to whom they were addressed. They were unusual in at least one respect, according to Humphry Ward, who attended them—they rarely mentioned any philosopher's name:

They presupposed, I fear, much more knowledge than any of the class possessed; and I remember that, after the first, one man who had easily gained his First in Moderations resigned Greats work on the spot. Not that they were difficult, still less dry; but the easy way the teacher moved amid his material was a little confusing to slow-moving minds.[5]

But Pater was a fairly good teacher, far better than most of his colleagues. Mark Pattison was not thinking of him when he said that Oxford colleges decently shrouded the incompetence of their tutors in the seclusion of a private apartment.

In May 1869, as if to divert attention from his plain features, Pater started dressing as a dandy: top hat, black tailcoat, silk tie of apple-green, dark striped trousers, yellow gloves, patent leather boots. On vacation, he traveled mainly in France, Germany, and Italy, either with his sisters or, as in the summer of 1865, with Shadwell. Sometimes, as in the Long Vacation of 1867, he contented himself with the pleasures of a reading party at Sidmouth.

The circle of Pater's friendships in Oxford and later in London was not large. Shadwell, Gosse, Bussell, Mark Pattison and his wife, Mr. and Mrs. Humphry Ward, Bywater, and Mandell Creighton occupied most of it, and there were additions from time to time, such as Vernon Lee and William Sharp. There were also a few with whom Pater formed literary affiliations, notably Swinburne, George Moore, Lionel Johnson, and Arthur Symons. These relations were pleasant, but Pater also required them to be serviceable. Ethereal as he generally appeared, he was not above nudging his friends to review his books or otherwise to write in his favor. He found adverse criticism painful, even when it came from insignificant people, so he went out of the way of decorum to arrange for cordial reviews. Oscar Wilde and D. S. MacColl responded congenially to his requests that they might review his books. He was not a relentless impresario in such matters, but he was worldly enough, if it could be quietly managed, to do himself a good turn. It is surprising, then, that he was not more careful in his choice of associates. He became prudent, but only when a scandal obtruded.

Pater's friendship with Oscar Browning was a case in point. Browning was greatly taken with Pater's essay on Winckelmann, published anonymously in January 1867, and he contrived to meet its author in Oxford through a mutual friend, the journalist John Burnell Payne. Browning and Pater became friends, and remained on visiting terms for several years. Browning was a housemaster at Eton, and Pater accepted occasional invitations from him to come to the school and perhaps speak to the boys. On one such visit early in 1875 there was a water-party. In the boat, one of Browning's pupils, William Graham, showed remarkable familiarity with French fiction, discussing Mérimée, Gautier, and other writers with Browning, Pater, and some women of the party. The next day, Pater praised the boy for his literary knowledge and remarked to one of the women that when a boy of his tender years showed any kind of literary taste it was generally for poetry of a commonplace nature, such as Alfred Tennyson's. The woman repeated the remark, it appears, to Anne Thackeray, who passed it on to Leslie Stephen, who in turn delivered it to his brother James Fitzjames Stephen. Enhanced in the telling, the remark was conflated with a report that Browning had lent one of his pupils a copy of Gautier's *Mademoiselle de Maupin*. J. F. Stephen had a son at Eton, and he wrote to Browning about the book, adding that "a man called Pater" was named as "approving the supposed proceeding." Browning, much amused, sent the correspondence to Pater, who replied—the date of the reply is not known:

> My dear Browning,
>   I was not at all amused but much pained at the letters you enclose. You heard all I said to Graham. I think it is not possible that I mentioned the book in question. I should greatly disapprove its being lent to any boy or young man, or even allowed in his way, and it would be quite impossible for me to recommend it to anybody. I read it years ago but do not possess it. Please give an unqualified denial to the statement that I approved anything of the kind. Such statements misrepresent and pain me profoundly. . . . I remember that, the subject arising in the natural course of conversation, I mentioned an innocent sort of ghost story by Gautier as a very good specimen of its kind. I am sorry now that I did so, as I can only suppose that the report in question arose in this way.[6]

On September 16, 1875, Browning was sacked, for reasons quite unconnected with Pater or the boating-party. He was a generous man, but some of his colleagues at Eton thought him meddlesome. Besides, there was a suspicion of pederasty. His interest in one of the boys, George Curzon, was thought to be sinister. None of these considerations made him unacceptable to Pater or to the Fellows of King's College, Cambridge. He went back to King's at Christmas and had a career in the college that lasted till 1908. His friendship with Pater survived the tiff over *Mademoiselle de Maupin* and the dismissal. An entry in Mark Pattison's diary for May 5, 1878, reads:

To Pater's to tea, where Oscar Browning, who was more like Socrates than ever. He conversed in one corner with 4 feminine looking youths, "paw dandling" there in our presence, while the Miss Paters and I sate looking on in another corner—Presently Walter Pater, who, I had been told, was "upstairs" appeared, attended by 2 more youths of similar appearance.[7]

The friendship lasted till the summer of 1880 and ended for no known reason.

For a few years, the artist Simeon Solomon was another of Pater's dangerous friends. They met, probably through Oscar Browning, in 1868. Solomon was much influenced in his art and poetry by D. G. Rossetti and Swinburne, but he also had time for the crazy Count Eric Stenbock. Solomon's prose poem *A Vision of Love Revealed in Sleep* (1871) owes a good deal to Pater and to theories of symbolism in Pater's vicinity. Solomon's *Bacchus*, exhibited at the Royal Academy in 1867, caught Pater's attention as did another painting on the same congenial theme that Solomon exhibited, also in 1867, at the Dudley Gallery. Solomon's drawing of Pater, done at Brasenose in 1872, is a work of unasserted charm and probably a decent likeness, improved a little by the artist's admiration of his subject. One of his drawings, on the *Song of Solomon*, was a gift to Pater. In May 1873 Solomon was arrested for importuning a man in a public urinal in London. Swinburne, Pater, and Bywater met by arrangement in Oxford on May 23 to consider how they might deal with the situation of their "wandering Jew." There was nothing to be done. Solomon was sentenced to eighteen months in Clerkenwell House of Correction, a sentence later commuted to police supervision. Swinburne was characteristically quick to be rid of the nuisance. He didn't even allow to be reprinted the article on Solomon's *Vision of Love* that he had published in *The Dark Blue* in July 1871. Pater at least went to the trouble of discussing the arrest with Solomon's sister Rebecca and drawing the conclusion, naive as it turned out, that Solomon might yet be recovered. Pater's affection for him was not diminished by the episode.

In "A Study of Dionysus," published in December 1876, Pater referred to Solomon, without naming him but in terms clear enough to be understood by anyone who kept up with artistic events. Discussing various representations of Dionysus, Pater noted that the god was usually shown "in his joy, as an embodiment of that glory of nature to which the Renaissance was a return." But in an early engraving by

Mocetto, Pater remarked, Dionysus appears in "a posture of statuesque weariness," with an expression of "painful brooding":

> One knows not how far one may really be from the mind of the old Italian engraver, in gathering from his design this impression of a melancholy and sorrowing Dionysus. But modern motives are clearer; and in a *Bacchus* by a young Hebrew painter, in the exhibition of the Royal Academy of 1868 [*sic*], there was a complete and very fascinating realisation of such a motive; the god of the bitterness of wine, "of things too sweet"; the sea-water of the Lesbian grape become somewhat brackish in the cup.[8]

The reference is typical of Pater; three years after Solomon's disgrace, his name can't be mentioned in print, but superior readers who know such things—"Lesbian grape" is homosexual code—are reminded that the artist was (and still is) to be admired. To call him a Hebrew painter was not thought rude.

A few days after his fiftieth birthday, August 4, 1889, Pater received a gift from his friend Herbert Horne, of a drawing by Solomon. Horne acted informally as Solomon's agent during the years of his disgrace. Pater was pleased with the gift:

> My dear Horne,
>   I think it very kind of you to send me this beautiful and characteristic drawing by S. Solomon.—Accept my sincere thanks for so choice a gift.[9]

I take "choice" to mean not merely superior in itself but delicately chosen in all the aspects of the occasion: the drawing was beautiful, presumably—it has not been traced—and its being the work of poor Solomon, a friend of both Horne and Pater, made it a welcome communication among the three of them.

The extent of Solomon's deterioration, Pater did not live to see. Solomon was often an inmate of St. Giles's Workhouse during the last five years of his life.

Pater conducted some of his relations with a more judicious mixture of public and private acknowledgments. His friendship with John Addington Symonds was typical of this precision. They met in March 1860. In November 1862 one of Symonds's resentful friends, G. H. Shorting, circulated to six Fellows of Magdalen certain love-poems and passages of love-letters from Symonds. The implication was that Symonds intended corrupting the choristers of Magdalen. An inquiry was held in the college. On December 28 Symonds was acquitted, but the episode put him under such strain that his health deteriorated. He resigned his fellowship at Magdalen and moved to London. The friendship between Pater and Symonds may already have waned. Nothing is known of it for several years. But they evidently met, however infrequently. On a visit to Oxford in May 1872 Symonds found Pater "well dressed & ghastly." When *Studies in the History of the Renaissance* appeared on March 1, 1873, careful readers noted an insult. Pater quoted three of Michelangelo's sonnets, in Symonds's translation, praised the translations as "executed with great taste and skill," but neglected to name the translator. The offense is strange, because Symonds had already praised Pater's essay on Michelangelo as a work exhibiting "the purest and most delicate sympathy with the poet's mind."[10] Naturally, Symonds resented Pater's snub: the translator's name did not appear till the third edition of *The Renaissance* in 1888.

By 1873 Pater and Symonds were rivals, divided by a common interest in Renaissance art and culture. Symonds got *Studies in the History of the Renaissance* for review, and on February 20, 1873, wrote to Henry Dakyns:

> You shall have Pater reviewed by me when *The Academy* comes. There is a kind of Death clinging to the man, wh[ich] makes his Music (but heavens! how sweet that is!) a little faint & sickly. His view of life gives me the creeps, as old women say. I am sure it is a ghastly sham; & that live by it or no as he may do, his utterance of the theory of the world has in it a wormy-hollow-voiced seductiveness of a fiend.[11]

This says: if Pater is indeed a lover of young men, I wish he would act boldly upon his desires and stop etherealizing them in that sickly way.

In the event, Symonds's review of Pater's book showed no sign of resentment. Symonds welcomed Pater as an aesthetic critic and thought his book a masterpiece in that kind:

> Each paragraph, each sentence is saturated with thought; not with that kind of thought which Novalis described as a "dead feeling, a wan, weak life," but with the very substance of the

feeling which only becomes thought in order that it may receive expression in words.[12]

Only the chapter on Botticelli was seriously questioned. Symonds thought Pater had ascribed to him "a far greater amount of sceptical self-consciousness than he was at all likely to have possessed." The melancholy of Botticelli's Madonnas was better explained, Symonds affirmed, by his having "tried to delineate her premonition of the coming sword, and not her weariness in being the mother of the sinless Saviour."[13] Pater was pleased with the review.

In 1873 Symonds wrote but didn't publish *A Problem in Greek Ethics*; he published it in a private edition in 1883. The main effort of the book was to distinguish two forms of masculine passion in Greek literature and myth. The first is spiritual and is under the protection of Ouranios; the second is base and sensual and is enforced by Pandemos. Greek love was in its origin and essence a military sentiment. "Fire and valour, rather than tenderness or tears, were the external outcome of this passion," Symonds argued, "nor had *Malachia*, effeminacy, a place in its vocabulary." He then quoted from Pater's essay on Winckelmann the letter in which Winckelmann told Friedrich von Berg that the supreme beauty of Greek art "is rather male than female." Symonds accepted this and said that it was due "not so much to any passion of the Greeks for male beauty as to the fact that the male body exhibits a higher organization of the human form than the female." Symonds had an interest in emphasizing the military and noble character of Greek boy-love:

An expressive Greek phrase, "youths in their prime of adolescence, but not distinguished by a special beauty," recognises the persuasive influence, separate from that of true beauty, which belongs to a certain period of masculine growth. The very evanescence of this "bloom of youth" made it in Greek eyes desirable, since nothing more clearly characterises the poetic myths which adumbrate their special sensibility than the pathos of a blossom that must fade. When distinction of feature and symmetry of form were added to this charm of youthfulness, the Greeks admitted, as true artists are obliged to do, that the male body displays harmonies of proportion and melodies of outline more comprehensive, more indicative of strength expressed in terms of grace, than that of women.[14]

Like many Victorian homosexuals, Symonds derived immense satisfaction from talking and writing about boy-love, pederasty, and "the early Greek enthusiasm." In *A Problem in Modern Ethics* he fusses over Whitman's "Calamus" poems in the hope of evoking "a new chivalrous enthusiasm, analogous to that of primitive Hellenic society, from emotions which are at present classified among the turpitudes of human nature."[15] Symonds thought that the question of sexual inversion should be examined as a fact of embryology rather than of psychical pathology. Noting, as everyone did, that higher education in England still rested on the study of Greek and Latin philosophy, literature, and drama, and that these were "impregnated with paederastia," he argued that the whole question could safely be ignored. The few men who exercised "sterile and abnormal sexual inclinations" were not a nuisance to anyone. The laws prohibiting sodomy, even between consenting adults, should be repealed.

Pater approached these themes far more obliquely than Symonds did; he chose to write about Winckelmann rather than about himself, while enjoying the warmth of homosexual motifs. He stayed silent on the question of legislation. Symonds associated himself with Winckelmann and Pater while claiming to be a more robust scholar of the subject than either of them.

In 1873 Symonds published the first volume of *Studies of the Greek Poets*. In the second volume (1876) he took the occasion to say a good word for pederasty. Pater referred to the first volume in a single phrase—"his former eloquent volume"—in his review of Symonds's *Renaissance in Italy: The Age of the Despots* (1875). The review appeared in *The Academy* on July 1; it is highly laudatory. Pater points out that in many respects Symonds has been anticipated by Taine and Stendhal, so that the distinction of the book under review lies not in its originality but in Symonds's dramatic imagination, powerful indeed. Pater was disturbed by Symonds's representation of the violence of the Italian Renaissance: his own sense of the Renaissance as a humanistic movement was hard to maintain in the lurid company of Symonds's murderous popes and princes. That it survived his reading of Taine and Stendhal is curious enough. Pater was capable of ignoring Renaissance mayhem which he could not accommodate in his sense of the art of sixteenth-century Italy, but Symonds's book was embarrassingly explicit. Pater tried to mitigate this element by stressing, in the Italian princes, the need of civic order. Even the activities of Machiavelli could be justified on conservative grounds:

The chapter on "The Prince" corrects some common mistakes concerning Machiavelli, who is perhaps less of a puzzle than has sometimes been supposed, a patriot devising a desperate means of establishing permanent rule in Florence, designing, in the spirit of a political idealism not more ruthless than that of Plato's Republic, to cure a real evil, a fault not unlike that of ancient Athens itself, the constant exaggerated appetite for change in public institutions, bringing with it an incorrigible tendency of all the parts of human life to fly from the centre, a fault, as it happened in both cases, at last become incurable.[16]

Special pleading, indeed; but Pater's own book on the Renaissance was then a mere two years before the public. That he had given a memorable account of the Renaissance while subliming its murders away was a point any reader of Symonds's book could now make. Reluctant to wait for such a comparison, Pater rebuked Symonds, at the end of an otherwise appreciative review, for his lack of reserve. Pater's reserve is such a matter of principle that he can't let himself quote examples of Symonds's lack of it:

Notwithstanding Mr. Symonds's many good gifts, there is one quality which I think in this book is singularly absent, the quality of reserve, a quality by no means merely negative, and so indispensable to the full effect of all artistic means, whether in art itself, or poetry, or the finer sorts of literature, that in one who possesses gifts for those things its cultivation or acquisition is neither more nor less than loyalty to his subject and his work.[17]

Symonds found the review "extremely gratifying." He did not regard lack of reserve as a defect but as a merit Pater lacked the courage to practice.

When *Marius the Epicurean* was published, on March 4, 1885, Symonds put off reading it for several weeks. On March 30 he wrote to Mary Robinson:

I cannot sympathise with Pater's theory of life; & as this book seems to give it elaborate utterance, I do not want to study it in discordant circumstances—for I want at least to respect it. But I have always thought it the theory of one who has not lived & loved.[18]

More pungently, he wrote to Henry Sidgwick on April 5:

> "Marius," I have not read. I suppose I must. But I shrink from approaching Pater's style, which has a peculiarly disagreeable effect upon my nerves—like the presence of a civet cat. Still, I believe I must read it.[19]

In later years, Pater and Symonds were thought of chiefly as opponents in the interpretation of the Renaissance. But in June 1876, when each had been reviewing the other's work, they were regarded as associates in a highly suspect movement, Aestheticism. Sidney Colvin warned André Raffalovich to have nothing to do with Symonds or Pater, a warning the recipient ostentatiously ignored. In 1876 Symonds and Pater were rival candidates for the Chair of Poetry at Oxford. Both were rumored to be homosexual, decadent, and pagan. By March 15, 1877, Pater had withdrawn from the contest. In that month, R. St. John Tyrwhitt, rector of St. Mary Magdalen, Oxford, attacked Symonds in an article, "The Greek Spirit in Modern Literature," in the *Contemporary Review.* "There are vices," he said, "which are not ever named among us," and he denounced Symonds not only for naming them but for presenting them as natural. Tyrwhitt's point was that the concept of Hellenism in Arnold was "an accurate study of truth by pure reason" but that in Symonds it was "a standard of the artistic wing of the great army of atheism." In *The Oxford and Cambridge Journal*, May 21, 1877, Edward C. Lefroy attacked Symonds and Pater for urging people to live by the promptings of their nature. By the time the *Journal* appeared, Symonds, too, had withdrawn his name from the list of candidates for the chair. John Campbell Shairp, Arnold's candidate, was elected.

Long after Pater's death, his name continued to be associated with Symonds's even by those who, in the end, emphasized the differences between them rather than the aestheticism they shared. Symonds was a married man and a father, uncomfortable in both capacities. He made no serious effort to conceal his desire for men. *A Problem in Modern Ethics* was privately printed, but it went the rounds quickly enough. Gosse sent James a copy of it. James thought it a gallant performance on Symonds's part and admirable in every respect except for its lack of humor, "*the* saving salt," as he told Gosse. Pater wrote no such pamphlet. But Symonds and Pater continued to be associated with irregular sentiments. When A. C. Benson was preparing his biography of Pater, he interviewed Herbert Warren of Magdalen College, Oxford, a friend of Pater and of James. Warren, according to Benson's diary, talked of "the aesthetic movement, Symonds, Pater, Jowett, + others." Benson comments:

> Rather a dark place, I am afraid. But if we give boys Greek books to read + hold up the Greek spirit + the Greek life as a marvel, it is very difficult to slice out one portion, which was a perfectly normal part of Greek life, and to say that it is abominable etc. etc. A strongly sensuous nature—such as Pater or Symonds—with a strong instinct for beauty, + brought up at an English public school, will almost certainly go wrong, in thought if not in act. But Warren revealed to me a depth of corruption in Symonds of which I had not dreamed. When he was well + strong he remained free from the shadow.[20]

5

Scandal

IN HIS ESSAY on Botticelli, published in August 1870, Pater remarked of him that "in an age when the lives of artists were full of adventure, his life is almost colourless." There was not even a legend to dissipate. "Only two things happened to him," Pater said, "two things which he shared with other artists:—he was invited to Rome to paint in the Sistine Chapel, and he fell in later life under the influence of Savonarola, passing apparently almost out of men's sight in a sort of religious melancholy, which lasted till his death in 1515, according to the received date."[1] It is typical of Pater to speak of colorlessness and then to add without comment the color of a name luridly ascetic. Savonarola was not as vivid to Pater as he was to Hopkins, who took Origen and Savonarola as his masters in discipline and burned his poems, it may be, in imitation of Savonarola's more famous bonfire of vanities. Pater was drawn to people to whom nothing had happened. But he often qualified his appreciation of them by mentioning in their vicinity someone to whom much had happened.

Pater's own life was colorless; whatever color it had, he added from the impulsions of his desire to an almost blank canvas. Two things happened to him. He conceived the frivolity of becoming a minister of the Anglican church, and was thwarted in the conceit. Then in the years between 1873 and 1877 he became something of a scandal. Specifically, between the publication of *Studies in the History of the Renaissance* (1873) and that of W. H. Mallock's *The New Republic*, which appeared in *Belgravia* from June to December 1876 and as a book in 1877, he got himself into endless trouble.

The scandal might have started in January 1867 when Pater published in the *Westminster Review* a review-essay on Winckelmann's *History of Ancient Arts among the Greeks*. The essay is in all essentials an account of Winckelmann's life and work, relying mainly on Joseph Eiselein and Otto Jahn for the biography, and on Hegel for the theory of Greek sculpture. It is also a revision, indeed a correction, as David J. DeLaura has shown in *Hebrew and Hellene in Victorian England* (1969), of Arnold's essay "Pagan and Medieval Religious Sentiment." If Pater had not published it anonymously, he would have caused offense by several paragraphs on Winckelmann, including this one:

> That his affinity with Hellenism was not merely intellectual, that the subtler threads of temperament were interwoven in it, is proved by his romantic, fervid friendships with young men. He has known, he says, many young men more beautiful than Guido's archangel. These friendships, bringing him in contact with the pride of human form, and staining his thoughts with its bloom, perfected his reconciliation with the spirit of Greek sculpture.[2]

"Perfected" is a bold claim. Long after Pater's death, Ingram Bywater said of the essay, in a letter to Hermann Diels:

> You will notice, I think, a certain sympathy with a certain aspect of Greek life; I must tell you that that was not confined to him.[3]

Pater's essay on Winckelmann, if it had been widely recognized as his, would have shocked his clerical colleagues at Brasenose by its claim that "the broad characteristic of all religions as they exist for the greatest number, is a universal pagan sentiment, a paganism which existed before the Greek religion, and has lingered far onward into the Christian world, ineradicable, like some persistent vegetable growth, because its seed is an element of the very soil out of which it springs."[4]

Not content with that affront, Pater published in October 1868 a review-essay—anonymous, again—on William Morris's poems, in which he warmed to a pagan sense of life:

> One characteristic of the pagan spirit these new poems have which is on their surface—the continual suggestion, pensive or passionate, of the shortness of life; this is contrasted with the bloom of the world and gives new seduction to it; the sense of death and the desire of beauty; the desire of beauty quickened by the sense of death.[5]

Up to that point, Pater's article was just a review, though an exotic one, especially when he permitted himself to say of "that whole religion of the middle age" that it was "but a beautiful disease or disorder of the senses," and that such a religion "must always be subject to illusions."[6] But he would not let well—or reasonably well—alone. He ended the review with seven paragraphs for which Morris's poems provided little warrant. These paragraphs, when they appeared in somewhat changed form as the Conclusion to *Studies in the History of the Renaissance*, impelled readers to associate Pater with high-toned corruption.

"To regard all things and principles of things as inconstant modes or fashions," Pater says, "has more and more become the tendency of modern thought." In the first paragraph he supposes himself a materialist or an objectivist and lets modern science have its destructive way—one's conviction of stability in an apparently objective world is a delusion:

> Let us begin with that which is without,—our physical life. Fix upon it in one of its more exquisite intervals—the moment, for instance, of delicious recoil from the flood of water in summer heat. What is the whole physical life in that moment but a combination of natural elements to which science gives their names? But those elements, phosphorus and lime, and delicate fibres, are present not in the human body alone; we detect them in places most remote from it. Our physical life is a perpetual motion of them—the passage of the blood, the wasting and repairing of the lenses of the eye, the modification of the tissues of the brain by every ray of light and sound—processes which science reduces to simpler and more elementary forces. Like the elements of which we are composed, the action of these forces

extends beyond us; it rusts iron and ripens corn. Far out on every side of us these elements are broadcast, driven by many forces; and birth and gesture and death and the springing of violets from the grave are but a few out of ten thousand resulting combinations. That clear, perpetual outline of face and limb is but an image of ours under which we group them—a design in a web the actual threads of which pass out beyond it. This at least of flame-like our life has, that it is but the concurrence renewed from moment to moment of forces parting sooner or later on their ways.[7]

In that long paragraph Pater is not endorsing the scientist's account of what we call life. But in speaking for modern science he tempts himself with the vertigo of an alien vocabulary. He dares himself to think these thoughts. Not that the thinking is decisive. He doesn't explain, for instance, how we come to group certain sensory events under one image rather than another; why we deem one group to be a face, another a limb. He is inciting himself—and exciting himself—to think like this.

In the next paragraph, more plausibly, he supposes himself an idealist, beginning with "the inward world of thought and feeling" and directing his mind upon the apparently external world:

At first sight experience seems to bury us under a flood of external objects, pressing upon us with a sharp, importunate reality, calling us out of ourselves in a thousand forms of action. But when reflection begins to act upon those objects they are dissipated under its influence, the cohesive force is suspended like a trick of magic, each object is loosed into a group of impressions, colour, odour, texture, in the mind of the observer. And if we continue to dwell on this world, not of objects in the solidity with which language invests them, but of impressions unstable, flickering, inconsistent, which burn, and are extinguished with our consciousness of them, it contracts still further, the whole scope of observation is dwarfed to the narrow chamber of the individual mind.[8]

The sliding from "world" and "objects" to "impressions" makes it inevitable that even these impressions are voided by one's consciousness of them. "Impression" is Pater's word for that event which is neither objective nor subjective but compounded of both considerations. An impression is an impression of something, but it is well on the way to becoming independent of its source, a trace without memory. In this paragraph Pater is tempting himself with the frisson of solipsism:

> Experience, already reduced to a swarm of impressions, is ringed round for each one of us by that thick wall of personality through which no real voice has ever pierced on its way to us, or from us to that, which we can only conjecture to be without. Every one of those impressions is the impression of an individual in his isolation, each mind keeping as a solitary prisoner its own dream of a world.[9]

The damage here is done by "of"—the impression of an individual—because it removes the impression from the object that occasioned it and makes it the individual's desperate possession. At that point, by a remarkable turn of phrase, the impression becomes a solitary prisoner, as if it were locked in a mind conceiving "its own dream of a world." It is like a story by Kafka. But Pater is not done yet; mention of prison and a prisoner incites him to subject these, too, to the Heraclitean fire:

> Analysis goes a step further still, and tells us that those impressions of the individual to which, for each one of us, experience dwindles down, are in perpetual flight; that each of them is limited by time, and that as time is infinitely divisible, each of them is infinitely divisible also, all that is actual in it being a single moment, gone while we try to apprehend it, of which it may ever be more truly said that it has ceased to be than that it is. To such a tremulous wisp constantly reforming itself on the stream, to a single sharp impression, with a sense in it, a relic more or less fleeting, of such moments gone by, what is real in our life fines itself down. It is with the movement, the passage and dissolution of impressions, images, sensations, that analysis leaves off, that continual vanishing away, that strange perpetual weaving and unweaving of ourselves.[10]

Wisp: as a wisp of cloud, or of haze on the surface of a stream. It is not clear how "a single sharp impression" could be arrived at and maintained from an object so tenuous, unless by a mind struggling to keep itself going on such penury. The effort makes the impression, provoked by traces of the images that have already lapsed or been dissolved. Pater has started by personifying "analysis" as a messenger of loss; now he personifies "what is real in our life" as a minimalist, a Giacometti paring away what he regards as surplusage—"fines itself down"—presumably to the point at which, with one more stroke, there is nothing left but the sense that something has been. Such thoughts "seem desolate at first," Pater concedes, as if upon further reflection in the same spirit they might come to seem exhilarating:

> . . . at times all the bitterness of life seems concentrated in them. They bring the image of one washed out beyond the bar in a sea at ebb, losing even his personality, as the elements of which he is composed pass into new combinations. Struggling, as he must, to save himself, it is himself that he loses at every moment.[11]

The diverse glooms of Tennyson and Arnold are here combined, with a further cadence of dissolution entirely Pater's.

A ponderous sentence in Novalis's German at this point allows Pater to draw a breath and speak in his own voice. Ignoring the proof he has just given of Heraclitean instability and loss, he makes the first assertion without saying whether it is true or merely appears to be true:

> Every moment some form grows perfect in hand or face; some tone on the hills or sea is choicer than the rest; some mood of passion or insight or intellectual excitement is irresistibly real and attractive for us for that moment only. Not the fruit of experience but experience itself is the end.[12]

"For that moment only" hardly counts as a disability, the gratifications that gather into the moment being so rich. Still, it is painful that one's life consists only of moments, and those perhaps few:

> A counted number of pulses only is given to us of a variegated, dramatic life. How may we see in them all that is to be seen in them by the finest senses? How can we pass most swiftly from point to point, and be present always at the focus where the greatest number of vital forces unite in their purest energy?[13]

It is not clear who is counting those pulses. Presumably some lives have them in great abundance because the mind in those cases makes the most of its occasions. The answer to the next question—How may we see in them all that is to be seen?—is, by taking care to have the finest senses and to set them astir. "From point to point": point is, I suppose, the moment of supreme focus or concentration. The vocabulary glances back at Blake, supreme adept of pulsations, but it means, too, what James meant by the admonition—be someone upon whom nothing is ever lost:

> To burn always with this hard gem-like flame, to maintain this ecstasy, is success in life. Failure is to form habits; for habit is relative to a stereotyped world; meantime it is only the roughness of the eye that makes any two things, persons, situations—seem alike. While all melts under our feet, we may well catch at any exquisite passion, or any contribution to knowledge that seems by a lifted horizon to set the spirit free for a moment, or any stirring of the senses, strange dyes, strange flowers and curious odours, or work of the artist's hands, or the face of one's friend. Not to discriminate every moment some passionate attitude in those about us and in the brilliance of their gifts some tragic dividing of forces on their ways, is on this short day of frost and sun to sleep before evening.[14]

The main emphasis is on the motive: "to set the spirit free for a moment." People want to feel alive, but they want their own forms of life, not those accredited by society as habits and conventions. To get as many pulsations as possible into the given time, we should discriminate between sensory occasions, deeming one more intense than another:

> High passions give one this quickened sense of life, ecstasy and sorrow of love, political or religious enthusiasm, or the "enthusiasm of humanity." Only, be sure it is passion, that it does yield you this fruit of a quickened, multiplied consciousness. Of this wisdom, the poetic passion, the desire of beauty, the love of art for art's sake, has most; for art comes to us professing frankly to give nothing but the highest quality to your moments as they pass, and simply for those moments' sake.[15]

There is nothing here that was not already in Hume, Pater's precursor in skepticism. Pater accepts the philosophic terms of his day: subject and object. He is sufficiently an idealist to think subject the superior term, in any practice that counts. Object is whatever the mind can't help adverting to, but it has few further rights. Science shows that every object dissolves into its particles: an object seems palpable but only because we have acquired the habit of not analyzing it. The mind, too, loses its appearance of stability as soon as one examines it. Pater is compelled, therefore, to see mobility as the condition of both terms. He knows that he risks solipsism, but meanwhile he makes up for the loss of stability by finding the experience of change, transience, ebb-and-flow at least interesting. He then introduces the criterion of intensity and distinguishes between experiences more or less intense. He is modern because he accepts this criterion: it constitutes his entire thought. It explains why he is not a formalist; his supreme value is not form but force, energy, the flow of mind among phenomena. He settles for mobility as the condition under which he has access to either subject or object, and makes the best of every moment by making the most of it. "Paterian" is the adjective for this way of being alive. That the experience continues to be interesting is the only blessing at hand, but it is enough. Pater doesn't demand anything more, though he is sometimes rueful about the predicament it entails. The trajectory of this interest eventually reaches Valéry's Teste, Eliot's J. Alfred Prufrock, and Joyce's Stephen Dedalus.

Pater concedes that you could enjoy this quickened sense of life through any passionate commitment: a great love or a political cause. Only be sure it is passion. What else could it be? He is relying on us to remember the criterion from the earlier passage and to put it beside this one. It is passion if it sets your spirit free, if only for a moment. This might exclude a political cause, since it would bind you to worldly obligations beyond the moment. The wisest recourse, after all, is to beauty and to art for its own sake because these don't throw you into stereotypes and general considerations.

When Pater transposed these paragraphs, or much of them, into the Conclusion to *Studies in the History of the Renaissance*, he excised the passage about the pagan spirit, presumably because it was too closely attached to his brooding on Morris's poems. He also deleted the sentence about the loss of self, "washed out beyond the bar in a sea at ebb." The sentence about having an interval "and then we cease to be" was toned down to read "and then our place knows us no more." He may have thought these changes secured him against rebuke. If he did, he erred. They gave offense, not only in 1873 but as late as 1930 when

T. S. Eliot quoted them as evidence that Pater was not a harmless aesthete but a moralist, and a damnable one.

By 1873, Pater was settled in his disposition, manner, and tone, if not in his opinions and beliefs. It was his social style not to be entirely at ease. Henry James said of Mr. Longdon, in *The Awkward Age*, that he was master of two distinct kinds of urbanity, the kind that added to distance and the kind that diminished it. Pater had none of the latter kind, and only enough of the former to make him distinguishable. His desire for young men was strong, otherwise he would not have taken such risks in consorting with them, but between himself and people of his own generation he generally kept his distance or added to it. His speech embodied the choice: in company he was often silent, withdrawn, and when he consented to speak he spoke hesitantly, with long pauses between the words, as if he found conversation at regular speed and vivacity an effort. Expansive tones he reserved for written work.

6

John Wordsworth,
W. M. Hardinge, W. H. Mallock

B EFORE THE REVIEWS of *Studies in the History of the Renaissance*
started appearing, Pater knew that he had given offense. Rev. John
Wordsworth was not only a Fellow of Brasenose but chaplain and tutor
of the college. He was a friend of Pater's, a former private pupil of his,
and on one occasion joined a reading-party with Pater on a trip to
Wales. On March 17, 1873, he wrote to Pater to explain the distress
the book had caused him and other readers:

> No one can admire more than I do the beauty of style and the
> felicity of thought by which it is distinguished, but I must add
> that no one can be more grieved than I am at the conclusions
> at which you represent yourself as having arrived. I owe so
> much to you in time past, and have so much to thank you for
> as a colleague more recently, that I am very much pained in
> making this avowal. But after a perusal of the book I cannot
> disguise from myself that the concluding pages adequately sum
> up the philosophy of the whole; and that that philosophy is an
> assertion, that no fixed principles either of religion or morality
> can be regarded as certain, that the only thing worth living for

is momentary enjoyment and that probably or certainly the soul dissolves at death into elements which are destined never to reunite.

Wordsworth knew that the Conclusion came, with minor changes, from the review of Morris's poems in the *Westminster Review*:

> But that article was anonymous, whereas this appears under your own name as a Fellow of Brasenose and as the mature result of your studies in an important period of history. If you had not reprinted it with your name no one would, I presume, have had a right to remonstrate with you on the subject, but now the case appears to be different; and I should be faithless to myself and to the beliefs which I hold, if in the position in which I find myself as tutor next in standing to yourself I were to let your book pass without a word.

Wordsworth's next sentences brought the issue more particularly home:

> My object in writing is not to attempt argument on the conclusions, nor simply to let you know the pain they have caused me and I know also many others. Could you indeed have known the dangers into which you were likely to lead minds weaker than your own, you would, I believe, have paused. Could you have known the grief your words would be to many of your Oxford contemporaries you might even have found no ignoble pleasure in refraining from uttering them.

That Pater took ignoble pleasure in uttering his conclusions is Wordsworth's clear implication: "ignoble" was meant to punish him. Wordsworth's later reference to the Tests Act of 1871 implied that Pater was lucky to be able to take advantage of legislation which removed the obligation of subscribing to the Thirty-nine Articles:

> But you may have already weighted these considerations and have set them aside, and when they are pressed upon you you may take your stand on your right under the University Tests Act to teach and publish whatever you please.

Wordsworth finished by warning Pater that the dispute between them must become "public and avowed," that "it may be my duty to oppose you," and that Pater meanwhile should give up his share in the divinity examinations of the college.[1] Pater's reply—assuming that as a gentleman and a colleague he made one—has not survived.

When the reviews started coming, he stayed quiet. A few of them were laudatory, notably those by John Morley, Sidney Colvin, Symonds, and Frederick G. Stephens. Emilia Pattison's was severe, but on grounds which Pater could not have resented. She took issue with the title of the book and claimed that "the historical element is precisely that which is wanting":

> Mr. Pater writes of the Renaissance as if it were a kind of sentimental revolution having no relation to the conditions of the actual world. . . . Whilst he discriminates or characterizes with great delicacy of touch the sentiment of the Renaissance, he does not let us know that it was precisely as the expression of vital changes in human society that this sentiment is so pregnant for us with weighty meaning.[2]

Pater accepted the rebuke silently and removed the word "history" from the title in subsequent editions. *The Renaissance: Studies in Art and Poetry* has been its title since 1877.

Pater was not distressed by Mrs. Pattison's review, or even by Symonds's charge that he had inflicted his own self-consciousness on Botticelli. But he was not indifferent to a note that emerged in several reviews a few weeks after Wordsworth's protesting letter: that the book was irreligious, blatantly hostile to Christianity, and designed to subvert the morals of impressionable young men. An anonymous essay in the *Examiner* on April 12 made much of Pater's Cyrenaicism, the assertion that the best way to live is to crowd as many pulsations as possible into one's inevitably brief life, and that the best way to do this is by cultivating art for art's sake:

> Get your self-contained pleasure, cried Aristippus; get your "pulsation," cries Mr. Pater. Yes, but we surely need a criterion of "pulsations." The housemaid who revels in the sensation novels of the "London Journal" holds with Mr. Pater—only less consciously—that it is its pulsations that make life worth the living.[3]

On May 11, 1873, F. W. Farrar, Dean of Canterbury, preached a sermon before the University of Cambridge in which he denounced as base the suggestion that people should fill their lives with pleasurable sensations.

This flurry culminated in an unsigned review, now known to be the work of Margaret Oliphant, in *Blackwood's*, November 1873, mocking Pater for his "grand pursuit of self-culture." Coming to the Conclusion of the book, Mrs. Oliphant remarked its "elegant materialism":

> The book is rococo from beginning to end,—in its new version of that coarse old refrain of the Epicureans' gay despair, "Let us eat and drink, for to-morrow we die"—as well as in its prettiness of phrase and graceful but far-fetched fancies.[4]

When George Eliot read Mrs. Oliphant's review, she wrote to the editor, John Blackwood, on November 5:

> I agreed very warmly with the remarks made by your contributor this month on Mr. Pater's book, which seems to me quite poisonous in its false principles of criticism and false conceptions of life.[5]

On November 23 W. Wolfe Capes preached a sermon implicitly rebuking Pater and denouncing the "humanitarian culture" he advocated:

> That is a poor philosophy of life which would concentrate all efforts upon self, and bid us to console ourselves amid our short-lived pleasures, so they be only intense and multitudinous enough. It needs a loftier spirit to give its true dignity to manhood, and happiness itself so hotly wooed, will surely slip like an unsubstantial phantom from the grass.[6]

Pater did not reply to this, or to any other attack on the book. Within a few weeks it was widely murmured against, and taken as proof that the suspicions buzzing around his name were justified. Those readers who knew or guessed that the essay on Winckelmann was Pater's work were now assured that he was corrupt, however mild his social bearing.

One embarrassment was followed by several. In February 1874 an Oxford undergraduate, William Money Hardinge, got into trouble. Colloquially known as "the Balliol Bugger," he had made himself notorious. A gifted poet, winner of the Newdigate Prize in 1876, he was mainly known for his sexual activities. Two of his colleagues, one still not known, the other Leonard Montefiore, complained to Richard Lewis Nettleship, a Fellow of Balliol, that Hardinge's "unnatural" behavior was giving the college a deplorable name. Hardinge was also known to have written several indecent sonnets and circulated them. Nettleship conveyed these reports to Jowett, Master of the College. Jowett was always sympathetic to young men in trouble, so he merely asked Hardinge's father to remove the boy and keep him at home for some months. Pater was involved with Hardinge, according to Benson's diary and to a batch of letters that passed between Hardinge's friends. The main documents are Arnold Toynbee's letter of February 25, 1874, to Philip Gell, and another to Gell from Alfred Milner, dated March 1, 1874.

Toynbee's letter reads in part:

> Hardinge has gone down till November, and as Jowett now (?) knows all about Pater—at any rate quite enough—and his parents' eyes before strangely closed are now wide open to the inferences that are & may be drawn from his manner & conversation, and as Hardinge himself for the first time seems distinctly to realize the peril in which his conduct has placed him, there is some hope of his working sufficient change in character & circumstances to prevent the catastrophe which otherwise must only have been a question of time.

Milner's letter of March 1 to Gell claimed that Montefiore acted correctly in telling Nettleship about Hardinge. Milner had had a visit from Hardinge, who asked him to tell Jowett, should the occasion arise, that he had never heard from Hardinge's lips "any indecent poetry or words wh. could be construed into an allusion to *unnatural* profligacy." Milner told Hardinge he couldn't tell such a lie. He then wrote to Gell:

> For my own part, I do not see, that Montefiore was to blame even in the time of the step. ~~You~~ The very fact, that Hardinge had not yet irretrievably committed himself with Pater was all the more reason why the evil should be prevented. It seems more strongly absurd to say, that one should not interfere till the mischief was done. And it is vain to pretend that there was not evidence of the strongest character against Hardinge. When

a man confesses to lying in another man's arms kissing him &
having been found doing it, as there is the strongest evidence to
prove, ~~in Hardinge's case~~, or when letters pass between them
in wh. they address one another as "darling" & sign themselves
"yours lovingly," & such a letter *I* have seen, when verses are
written from one man to another too vile to blot this paper,
what hope can you have, that a criminal act, if not committed
already, will may not be committed any day? Why, if it does
not occur, it is pure "good luck," & not "good management."

In a further letter of March 13, 1874, to Gell, Milner writes:

Hardinge with his usual delicacy has written an abusive letter
to Rawnsley, in wh. he says, that he has just heard from you,
telling him that the three chief agents in his removal were Miss
Pater, Montefiore & Rawnsley. . . .[7]

It is not known how Miss Pater—Clara, probably—comes into the
story. According to Benson's diary for September 1, 1905, a week after
he had completed his biography of Pater, he had a conversation with
Gosse. Gosse told him that there were indeed incriminating letters;
that they were brought to Jowett by W. H. Mallock, author of *The
New Republic*; and that Jowett summoned Pater to his presence. The
diary continues:

What a donkey P. must have been to write them—it is a mistake
one makes to feel that writing is somehow more impersonal than
speech—It is: but it is also imperishable!
    Pater's whole nature changed under the strain, after the
dreadful interview with Jowett. He became old, crushed,
despairing— + this dreadful weight lasted for years; it was
years before he realised that J. would not use them.

Most of this passage is probably Gosse's report, transcribed by Benson.
Gosse and Benson had been friends since 1893, but Benson didn't know
Pater. It is evident that Gosse told Benson many things he himself
hadn't chosen to include in his obituary essay on Pater in December
1894. I interpret Benson's diary as evidence that Gosse told him about
Jowett, Mallock, and some compromising letters, but prompted him
to the urbane conclusion contained in the diary for November 12, 1904:

Probably some indiscreet devotion, Pateresquely expressed—
for that Pater was ever anything but frigidly Platonic in his
affections I decline to believe.

It is possible that Clara Pater came upon some letters in her brother's
study and that she sought Gosse's aid in having Jowett remove Hardinge
from Oxford. Possible, too, that Gosse used Mallock as his messenger
to Jowett. Mallock didn't like Jowett, but he was on good enough terms
with him to accept invitations to dine and to meet in Jowett's rooms
some of the most celebrated writers of the day. But the letters present
a difficulty. It is unlikely that Clara snatched them from Walter's desk
and conveyed them to Gosse or to anyone else. Unlikely, too, that
Hardinge gave Mallock any letters from Pater or copies of his own to
Pater: Why would he do such a foolish thing? Report of the nature of
the letters would have been enough for Jowett; he would have felt
justified, even without seeing them, in sending Hardinge down for a
few months till the dust settled, and in having a sharp interview with
Pater.

Pater and Hardinge met socially, at least once, several years after
this affair. André Raffalovich's memoirs include this passage:

> What I ventured to call bumping into Pater's legend happened
> one evening when I brought him together again with W.M.H.
> (shall we call him Leslie as, in one of the keys to The New
> Republic, Leslie is asserted to be W.M.H.?), to whom he had
> been attached when Leslie was a slender and willowy under-
> graduate. A dozen years had made him bald and stout. Pater's
> astonished lips uttered the astonished and astonishing words:
> "Why! he looks like the Duke of Cambridge." On this occasion
> another great friend of mine of quite another tradition exclaimed:
> "Pater looks like a man pursued by the Furies."[8]

Raffalovich's knowledge of Pater's attachment to Hardinge was only
hearsay: in 1874 he was ten years old. But it is significant that the
rumor had lasted more than fifty years by the time Raffalovich referred
to it in print.

There is no evidence that Jowett used the letters—or even talk of
them—to warn Pater against putting himself forward for any university
appointments. On the other hand, a word from Jowett would have
been enough to set Oxford against Pater, whose reputation was already

dubious. Within a few months, a junior proctorship fell vacant, and Brasenose had the right to nominate a candidate. Pater was next in line for the job, but his name was not sent forward. On September 25, Brasenose nominated Rev. John Wordsworth.

On April 20, 1875, the Bishop of Oxford, John Fielder Mackarness, delivered an address at his second visitation in the Cathedral Church at Christ Church. He quoted a passage from the Conclusion to *Studies in the History of the Renaissance* to illustrate the "school of unbelief" and its rampancy in Oxford. The Bishop then asked:

Can you wonder that some who played an honourable part in Oxford life a generation since, refuse to let their sons imbibe lessons so alien from the lore they learned? Can you wonder that to young men who have imbibed this teaching the Cross is an offence, and the notion of a vocation to preach it an unintelligible craze?[9]

A further exacerbation followed in the summer of 1876. Mallock started serial publication of *The New Republic*, a sequence of imaginary conversations making fun of Arnold, Ruskin, Jowett, and Pater. Not under their names, but they were instantly recognized. It is hard to estimate whether Pater was more dismayed to find himself mocked, or gratified to know that he was taken as seriously, for that purpose, as Arnold, Ruskin, and Jowett. According to Gosse's obituary essay, Pater took the skit lightly: "he thought the portrait a little unscrupulous, and he was discomposed by the freedom of some of its details."[10] But not distressed, apparently. According to Gosse, Pater was far more ruffled by newspaper references to him and his aestheticism. "I wish they wouldn't call me a 'hedonist,' " he said to Gosse in 1876: "it produces such a bad effect on the minds of people who don't know Greek."[11]

Mallock's book is an ironic version of Plato's *Republic*. A party is gathered at an English country-house to discuss major issues of the day and certain issues of a longer day such as the Aim of Life. Pater appears as Mr. Rose the Pre-Raphaelite, "the pale creature, with large moustache, looking out of the window at the sunset." If Hardinge appears as Lesley, it is of no account: he is not brought into any embarrassing relation to Mr. Rose. Before Mr. Rose is given anything to say, we hear that "he always speaks in an undertone, and his two topics are self-indulgence and art." Some of the irony directed upon him is harmless:

I rather look upon life as a chamber which we decorate as we would decorate the chamber of the woman or the youth that we love, tinting the walls of it with symphonies of subdued colour, and filling it with works of fair form, and with flowers, and with strange scents, and with instruments of music. And this can be done now as well—better, rather—than at any former time: since we know that so many of the old aims were false, and so cease to be distracted by them. We have learned the weariness of creeds; and know that for us the grave has no secrets. We have learned that the aim of life is life; and what does successful life consist in? Simply . . . in the consciousness of exquisite living—in the making our own each highest thrill of joy that the moment offers us—be it some touch of colour on the sea or on the mountains, the early dew in the crimson shadows of a rose, the shining of a woman's limbs in clear water, or—

Mr. Rose is interrupted at that point, not a moment too soon. The parody of Pater is fairly well done, especially when he is indulging his infatuation with belatedness, a familiar mark of Decadence:

I look upon social dissolution as the true condition of the most perfect life. For the centre of life is the individual, and it is only through dissolution that the individual can re-emerge. All the warrings of endless doubts, all the questionings of matter and of spirit, which I have myself known, I value only because, remembering the weariness of them, I take a profounder and more exquisite pleasure in the colour of a crocus, the pulsations of a chord of music, or a picture of Sandro Botticelli's.

One of the guests, Lady Ambrose, wonders in a loud whisper why Mr. Rose talks of everybody "as if they had no clothes on." But this is badinage. It unbecomingly becomes more only in one passage, where Mallock's malevolence is the chief exhibit. Mr. Rose has been murmuring to himself at intervals for some time:

I was merely thinking of a delicious walk I took last week, by the river side, between Charing Cross and Westminster. The great clock struck the chimes of midnight; a cool wind blew; and there went streaming on the wide wild waters with long vistas of reflected lights wavering and quivering in them; and I roamed about for hours, hoping I might see some unfortunate cast herself from the Bridge of Sighs. It was a night I thought well in harmony with despair. Fancy . . . the infinity of emotions which the sad sudden splash in the dark river would awaken in one's mind—and all due to that one poem of Hood's.[12]

The poem of Hood's is "The Bridge of Sighs," about a young woman who drowns herself:

> *Take her up tenderly,*
> *Lift her with care;*
> *Fashion'd so slenderly,*
> *Young, and so fair!*

It is hard to believe that that episode in *The New Republic* left Pater unmoved, unwounded. He probably maintained a show of indifference when Gosse mentioned it, a device Pater often practiced. There is no reason to think he was overwhelmed by Mallock's parody of him, but he must have winced.

7

Arthur Symons, George Moore, Lionel Johnson, Wilde

Everything in Pater was in harmony, when you got used to its particular forms of expression: the heavy form, so slow and deliberate in movement, so settled in repose; the timid yet scrutinising eyes; the mannered, yet so personal voice; the exact, pausing speech, with its urbanity, its almost painful conscientiousness of utterance; the whole outer mask, worn for protection and out of courtesy. . . .
— Arthur Symons, *A Study of Walter Pater* (1932)

MOST OF THE CONSEQUENTIAL EVENTS in Pater's life happened between 1873 and 1877 and left him mainly bewildered or dismayed. He did not anticipate the fuss caused by the Conclusion to *Studies in the History of the Renaissance*, even though he prepared the book with care and knew that several of his colleagues in Oxford were alert to his paganism. Assembling for inclusion in the book the essays already published, he toned down a few of the insults they contained. In a reference to Leonardo's religion, he had dismissed "such hurried candle-burning"; he changed this to "these hurried offices." An offensive sentence about the Protestant response to the *Last Supper* was deleted:

> Protestants, who always found themselves much edified by a certain biblical turn in it, have multiplied all sorts of bad copies and engravings of it.[1]

But these gestures were not enough. Pater saw small offenses but was strangely blind to large ones.

After the fuss, he set a new course for his professional life. He kept his head down. For a time, he confined his attention to safe subjects: Wordsworth, *Measure for Measure*. He resented the charge of hedonism, but he expressed his resentment obliquely. In his literary essays he kept up an impeccable demeanor, but in his commentaries on certain Greek myths—Dionysus, Demeter, Persephone—he consorted with violent feelings which arose naturally in their vicinity. Through these, he distanced himself from the received version of Greek culture as the supreme achievement of patience—Winckelmann, Goethe, and Arnold made this a commonplace, and till now Pater accepted it. In the Greek essays of 1875 and 1876 he moved among images of dismemberment and vengeance. He continued to read morally questionable writers, especially Gautier, Baudelaire, and Swinburne, but he avoided naming them in print. Not that he was scrupulous in acknowledging his sources, even when they were respectable. He appropriated ideas from Hegel, Schiller, Arnold, Grote, Ruskin, Alexander Grant, and many other writers, but he rarely bothered to pay his debts. He took particular care to conceal his indebtedness to French writers who were thought to be immoral. German writers were assumed to be acceptable, and Pater freely quoted them. But the French were suspect, except for the few who were known to be wholesome. In the 1888 edition of *The Renaissance* Pater changed "strange flowers" to "strange colours" to avoid any whiff of *Les Fleurs du mal*. In "The School of Giorgione" (1877) he took without acknowledgment a phrase from Baudelaire's essay on Delacroix, discretion being for the moment the better part of scholarship. Revising the essay on *Measure for Measure*, first published in November 1874, he changed "manly" to "many"—unless this is merely a printer's error, corrected—in a sentence that began, "They are capable of manly friendships . . ." and he removed "naked" from a sentence about Isabella: ". . . stripped naked in a moment of all convention, she stands before us clear, detached, columnar, among the tender frailties of the piece." In the unpublished tenth chapter of *Gaston de Latour*, Pater refers to "sinful Abelard," whom he presented in the book on the Renaissance as sinless victim of an unnecessarily harsh orthodoxy.

In these and other changes, Pater gradually recognized and accepted the case which W. W. Capes, Sarah B. Wister, W. J. Courthope, John Wordsworth, and other readers made against the Conclusion to *Studies in the History of the Renaissance*. In the 1877 edition he silently removed the offending pages. When he restored them in the 1888 edition, he added a footnote to justify both the removal and the restoration:

This brief "Conclusion" was omitted in the second edition of this book, as I conceived it might possibly mislead some of those young men into whose hands it might fall. On the whole, I have thought it best to reprint it here, with some slight changes which bring it closer to my original meaning. I have dealt more fully in *Marius the Epicurean* with the thoughts suggested by it.[2]

In the "slight changes" he deleted every reference to religion and replaced every highly charged phrase by an innocuous version of it; so "abstract morality" became "abstract theory." In the 1893 edition, the last published in Pater's life, "the love of art for art's sake" became "the love of art for its own sake," a change mainly acoustic but enough to reduce the echo of Pater's association with decadence.

But it took him several years to reach this degree of abjection. Between 1873 and 1877 he recognized the necessity of being prudent, but his concessions had a certain pattern. He removed the cause of offense while making it clear that he had removed it, and he added some token, timidly indeed, of the feelings he had been forced to proscribe. He was not willing wholly to be penitent. While he omitted the Conclusion from the 1877 edition, he gratuitously added to the passage about "Aucassin and Nicolette" a long account of the thirteenth-century story, "Li Amitiez de Ami et Amile," of passionate friendship between two men. In his commentary on "Aucassin and Nicolette," he omitted from the 1877 text one of Aucassin's most spirited outbursts, "a passage," Pater explained, "in which that note of rebellion is too strident for me to translate it here, though it has its more subdued echoes in our English Chaucer."[3] In later editions he continued to withhold Aucassin's speech, even though it had by then been translated into English by F. W. Bourdillon and by Andrew Lang.

The changes Pater made in the 1877 edition reduced the temperature of its phrases. In the early essay on Winckelmann (1867) and in the 1873 edition, Winckelmann had "romantic, fervid friendships with young men"; now he had only "romantic, fervent friendships" with them, his fever having been cooled by the damp cloth of religion. Sometimes the change removed excess, especially when a repeated phrase seemed too much of a thing otherwise good. In 1873 Pater transcribed from his then unpublished "Diaphaneitè" two sentences on Greek statuary:

The beauty of the Greek statues was a sexless beauty; the statues of the gods had the least traces of sex. Here, there is a moral sexlessness, a kind of impotence, an ineffectual wholeness of nature, yet with a divine beauty and significance of its own.[4]

In 1877 the first sentence was retained, but "a kind of impotence" was deleted from the second, and "a kind of"—regrettably one of Pater's favorite phrases—was transferred to the already ineffectual wholeness. He allowed the internal rhyming of *sex* to persist. In the chapter on Botticelli a reference to God, which might have offended Christians, was changed to refer to Jehovah, which would not have offended anyone.

So much in the cause of discretion. Yet in November 1876 and for several months thereafter, Pater pressed Macmillan to add to the title page of the new *Renaissance* a small vignette of doubtful provenance and considerable suggestiveness. "The subject of the vignette," he wrote to Macmillan on March 13, 1877, "has no recognised name, being only a small drawing;—the words of the advertisement might run,—'with a vignette after Leonardo da Vinci, engraved by Jeens'; and in any gossip on the subject it might be described as being from a favourite drawing by L. da V. in the Louvre."[5] I am not aware of any gossip, but a vigilant reader might have wondered why, in the second but not in the first edition, Pater chose from many available drawings that one. It was thought to be a portrait of Francesco Melzi, a beautiful boy whose head Leonardo often drew to make an angel's head.[6] Pater described it in the essay on Leonardo:

> . . . a little drawing in red chalk which every one will remember who has examined at all carefully the drawings by old masters at the Louvre. It is a face of doubtful sex, set in the shadow of its own hair, the cheek-line in high light against it, with something voluptuous and full in the eyelids and the lips.[7]

The drawing is now thought not to be by Leonardo but by one of his school. On the title-page of the 1877 edition the face looks erotically androgynous, like beautiful Tadzio in the film of *Death in Venice*, and it seems an emblem of the heterodox recognitions which Pater felt obliged to suppress. But he suppressed them while adding new traces of the banned sentiments, words to the wise.

The most far-reaching change between the editions of 1873 and

1877 was Pater's movement from a vocabulary of conflict to one of difference and independence. Temperamentally he was averse to conflict, even to the mildest disputes: his most typical conversational gesture was a murmured "no doubt, no doubt." Recognizing that his book had given offense, he bowed his head and quietly decided not to repeat the fault. There was no question of a public quarrel, or of pursuing the matter in essays or letters: the damage was done. Instead of defending himself, Pater internalized his subversive values and retained them in the form of difference. Provided he did not express them in a public or tendentious form, he was reasonably safe, even though he continued to be associated with irregularity of sentiment and desire. So he retained, as private property, feelings that could not be avowed. Precedents for this device included Byron's recourse to Cain and Blake's appropriation of the truculence embodied in Milton's Satan.

In his private life Pater was not entirely circumspect. Even after the episode with Hardinge, he continued to cultivate good-looking young men, especially undergraduates of an athletic disposition. When he went to have his hair cut at Spier's, he observed the barbers. One of them, Ed Dugdale, recalled many years later that he had been a person of interest to Pater:

> Mr. Pater was a frequent visitor to the hair-cutting salon of Spier's and Son, his hair being very scanty and fine. I was the lucky individual whom he selected to wait upon him; and being a mere youth of two-and-twenty, I was almost alarmed when one day, as I stood in front of him arranging his hair, he suddenly stooped down and gazed intently at my slippered feet; without saying a word, he took up one of my feet and placed it upon his knee, stroked it and observed it from every angle possible. Evidently he admired some curves or lines which the foot exhibited. He invited me to come to his rooms at Brasenose College, but being then unacquainted with the reputation of this great man (this was in the late 1870's) I did not avail myself of what would now appeal to me as a high privilege.[8]

Raffalovich, ever implicative, adds a suggestive footnote to Gosse's account of going with Pater to see a performance of Pinero's farce *The Magistrate* in London in 1885. "I am pleased to remember," Raffalovich says, "that [Pater] several times met Harry Eversfield, so successful as the boy in Pinero's play."[9]

Most of Pater's friendships during his later years, if friendship is not too strong a word for them, were with writers: he made himself available to several, including Gosse, Arthur Symons, George Moore, Lionel Johnson, William Sharp, Vernon Lee, and Oscar Wilde, and he retained them in his circle unless prudence indicated that he should be rid of them. His relation to Symons is typical of his enthusiasm, and of the ease with which he curbed it when Symons became a nuisance.

Symons admired Pater long before he had a chance to meet him. At the age of seventeen or eighteen he read *Studies in the History of the Renaissance*,

> which opened a new world to me, or, rather, gave me the key or the secret of the world in which I was living. . . . It taught me that there was a beauty besides the beauty of what one calls inspiration, and comes and goes, and cannot be caught or followed; that life (which had seemed to me of so little moment) could be itself a work of art; from that book I realised for the first time that there was anything interesting or vital in the world besides poetry and music. I caught from it an unlimited curiosity, or, at least, the direction of curiosity into definite channels.[10]

In 1886 Symons sent Pater a copy of his *An Introduction to the Study of Browning*, in which Pater's remarks on Browning in the essay on Winckelmann are quoted with approval. Symons's heroes were Browning, Meredith, and Pater, a fact he intended to convey to Pater on their first meeting. But although Pater invited him, by letter of December 2, 1886, to visit him at his London home, 12 Earl's Terrace, Kensington, no occasion arose for some time. Writing to James Dykes Campbell on January 8, 1887, Symons said of Pater:

> I have always been curious to know what sort of man he is, in the flesh: really I can scarcely conceive him as a man in the flesh at all, but rather an influence, an emanation, a personality, quite volatilised and ethereal![11]

In August 1887 Symons reviewed *Imaginary Portraits*, favorably enough except that he observed at some length that Pater couldn't, or wouldn't, create characters:

The result of Mr Pater's method is so charming that we have no right, I think, to complain that he gives us just, and only, what he does. At the same time it is quite obvious that neither Watteau, nor Denys, nor Sebastian, nor Duke Carl really lives, in so much as a finger-tip, with actual imaginative life; they are all ghosts, names, puppets of an artist and a philosopher who has evoked or constructed them for his purpose, but has not been able, or has not wished, to endow them with flesh and blood, with the breath of life.[12]

Pater thanked Symons for the review, "which I have read carefully and on the whole with much pleasure."[13] He didn't protest at Symons's assumption that the realistic novel was the only acceptable form of fiction, or remind him that there were several traditions of fiction which could readily accommodate the procedures of *Imaginary Portraits* and *Marius the Epicurean*.

On November 9, 1887, Pater returned the compliment of the review by reviewing Symons's book on Browning in *The Guardian*. "Certainly we shall not quarrel with Mr. Symons," he wrote, "for reckoning Mr. Browning, among English poets, second to Shakespeare alone." Specifically, the Browning of *Men and Women* and *Pippa Passes*. Perhaps he meant contemporary poets, and therefore ignored the claims of Chaucer, Spenser, Milton, Pope, and Wordsworth; if not, it is a bizarre assessment. Pater emphasizes Browning's modernity:

The world and all its action, as a show of thought, that is the scope of his work. It makes him pre-eminently a modern poet —a poet of the self-pondering, perfectly educated, modern world, which, having come to the end of all direct and purely external experiences, must necessarily turn for its entertainment to the world within.[14]

In that formulation, Browning looks like Pater, who wanted to believe that the world and all its actions are a show of thought and might be expressed by putting minds thinking in a sequence of shows. It didn't occur to Pater to wonder why his own work differed so much from Browning's but issued apparently from the same assumptions about life and thought.

A few weeks later, Symons sent two of his poems, "A Revenge" and "Bell in Camp," to Pater with a request that he look at them. Pater liked them, but urged Symons to devote himself to the art of prose:

> You know I give a high place to the literature of prose as a fine art, and therefore hope you won't think me brutal in saying that the admirable qualities of your verse are those also of imaginative prose; as I think is the case also with much of Browning's finest verse.[15]

Pater gave the same advice to any aspiring poet who consulted him.

Symons and Pater met at last in London on August 7, 1888. The next day, Symons wrote to Campbell:

> He is a curious personage—not at all unlike what one would expect him to be—a little difficult to talk with on account of his excessive complaisance, and the dainty way in which he holds an opinion, making it seem quite gross and rude to have ever ventured a difference. Nothing could have been kinder than his manner, or more flattering than his opinions about my pieces.[16]

Pater liked Symons's poems well enough to persuade George Macmillan to publish a volume of them, *Days and Nights* (1889). He allowed Symons to dedicate the book to him—"To Walter Pater in All Gratitude"— and with doubtful propriety he reviewed it in the *Pall Mall Gazette* on March 23, 1889:

> The finer pieces of this volume, certainly, any poet of our day might be glad to own, for their substance, their dramatic hold on life, their fine scholarship; and they have this eminent merit, among many fine qualities of style—readers need fear no difficulty in them. In this new poet the rich poetic vintage of our time has run clear at last.[17]

There is no sign of embarrassment. Pater thought that friends should support one another in this way, so he wrote in praise of Gosse, Raffalovich, and Bussell when occasions arose.

Symons, in return, went to the extremity of attending two of Pater's public lectures, two of only three lectures he confessed ever to have attended. On November 17, 1890, Pater lectured on Prosper Mérimée at the Taylor Institution, Oxford. On November 23 he gave a lecture on Wordsworth at Toynbee Hall, London, and the following night repeated the lecture on Mérimée at the London Institution. On August 2, 1892, he was supposed to give a University Extension lecture at Oxford on Raphael, but he switched to Leonardo at the last moment. Symons recalled hearing him lecture on Raphael at Toynbee Hall some-time in 1892:

> I never saw a man suffer a severer humiliation. The act of reading his written lecture was an agony which communicated itself to the main part of the audience. Before going into the hall at Whitechapel he had gone into a church to compose his mind a little, between the discomfort of the underground railway and the distress of the lecture-hall.[18]

Pater was easy with Symons, recognized in him a disciple, and was content to receive his tribute. In conversations with Arthur Galton, he kept babbling about Symons: how he was as deep as Browning, and better than Meredith. Symons was soon recognized as Pater's ephebe, especially when he published *The Symbolist Movement in Literature* (1899) and was understood, notably by Henry James, to have appropriated Pater's style. Symons didn't make such a claim. In fact, he never implied that he understood Pater, but that he saw whatever Pater could bring himself to disclose:

> In a room, if he was not among very intimate friends, Pater was rarely quite at his ease, but he liked being among people, and he made the greater satisfaction overcome the lesser reluctance.[19]

Symons was intimate enough with his master to see how fond he was of cats, how much pleasure he took in fairs and carousels, how odd he found it that French people liked to see wolves rather than tigers in traveling shows. Symons asked him, too, about his name, and was it Dutch:

> I once asked Pater if his family was really connected with that of the painter, Jean-Baptiste Pater. He said: "I think so, I believe so, I always say so."[20]

But the friendship cooled sometime in 1892. Pater's last known letter addressed to "My dear Symons" is dated June 24, 1891. Many letters

are lost or destroyed, but when Symons asked Pater for a favor—
probably to write something for the first number of the *Yellow Book*—
Pater's decorous refusal, dated January 17, 1894, was addressed to "My
dear Mr. Symons." It was a blatant rebuke.

Why the friendship ended, no one knows. Lawrence Evans, editor
of Pater's letters, thinks that Pater probably brought about the estrangement because he "disapproved of the frank, or decadent, eroticism
of Symons's poetry, and life."[21] It is true that Symons was, as Yeats
called him, "a scholar in music-halls," and that he spent most of his
evenings carousing with Dowson, Horne, and sundry chorus girls. If
chronology could be thwarted, I would guess that Pater was incensed
when Symons's "The Decadent Movement in Literature" referred to
Decadence as "really a new and beautiful and interesting disease": a
crude allusion to Pater's phrase, in "Poems by William Morris," about
"that whole religion of the middle age" as "but a beautiful disease or
disorder of the senses." It was a more venial fault of taste that Symons,
in the same essay, used without acknowledgment and in regard to
Mallarmé a sentence already famous from Pater's "A Prince of Court
Painters." Symons has been describing Mallarmé's *cenacle* in the Rue
de Rome:

> "A seeker after something in the world, that is there in no
> satisfying measure, or not at all," he has carried his contempt
> for the usual, the conventional, beyond the point of literary
> expression, into the domain of practical affairs.[22]

Symons repeated the quotation in a passage about Mallarmé in *The
Symbolist Movement in Literature* (1899). But the cooling had taken place
before "The Decadent Movement in Literature" appeared in November
1893. Not that it necessarily involved a row; if it had, Symons could
not have written to Pater for any reason.

After Pater's death, Symons continued to regard himself, and to
be regarded, as Pater's disciple. "I remember meeting Pater at your
house," he wrote to Raffalovich. "He who was then John Gray repeated
one of his poems. A certain expression passed over Pater's face and he
asked Gray to say it over again. 'The rest was silence.' " *Studies in the
History of the Renaissance* remained "to me perhaps the rarest book of
prose ever written."[23] Symons's "Christian Trevalga," in *Spiritual Ad-
ventures*, was his tribute to Pater's invention of the "imaginary portrait."

While it lasted, the friendship with Symons encouraged Pater to think that he was taking due part in London literary life. With Symons, Pater prescribed the tone of the relation, the precise degree of familiarity and distance. Symons understood the conditions if not the man who ordained them. In that respect he differed from George Moore. Moore wanted Pater's friendship, but he pushed too hard for it. They met in Mary Robinson's house in the summer of 1885. Moore was greatly taken with *Marius the Epicurean* and preparing to write about it in *Confessions of a Young Man* (1888). But in the meantime he wrote *A Mere Accident* (1887), a novel about a girl raped by a tramp on the Sussex downs. He asked Pater to review it in *The Guardian*, but Pater declined; the letter of refusal is lost, and Moore's several accounts of it vary in detail and emphasis. But it is clear that Pater couldn't see why anyone would want to write such a book, life being rough enough already. When Moore's *Confessions* appeared, he sent Pater a copy and elicited from him a reply of unusual vivacity:

> My dear, audacious Moore,
> Many thanks for the "Confessions," which I have read with great interest, and admiration of your originality—your delightful criticisms—your Aristophanic joy, or at least enjoyment, in life—your unfailing liveliness. Of course, there are many things in the book I don't agree with. But then, in the case of so satiric a book, I suppose one is hardly expected to agree or disagree.—What I cannot doubt of is the literary faculty displayed. "Thou com'st in such a questionable shape!" —I feel inclined to say, on finishing your book: "shape"— morally, I mean; not in reference to style.
> You speak of my own work very pleasantly; but my enjoyment has been independent of that. And still I wonder how much you may be losing, both for yourself and for your writings, by what, in spite of its gaiety and good-nature and genuine sense of the beauty of many things, I must still call a cynical, and therefore exclusive, way of looking at the world. You call it only "realistic." Still—!
> With sincere wishes for the future success of your most entertaining pen, . . .[24]

Pater was ready to enjoy Moore's impishness, provided he was not required to acknowledge it in *The Guardian* or elsewhere. His familiarity with Moore was not like Yeats's. Yeats and Moore were friends in the sense that Moore made fun of Yeats in print and Yeats wrote *Dramatis Personae* to punish Moore for insulting him and for printing lies about Lady Gregory. Yeats felt justified in noting that Moore had a coarse palate, that he lacked the style he claimed, and that he had written a long preface to prove he had a mistress in Mayfair. Pater kept well clear of such sordidness. Moore's gusto was worth reading, but there was no need to continue meeting it socially. In "Avowals" (August 1904) Moore claimed that he had wearied of Pater, tired of his shyness, his inability to meet a friend halfway; claimed, too, that Pater's taste was peccable, his purpled prose about the Mona Lisa and his fondness for the works of Burne-Jones being sufficient evidence.

In the end, Moore complained to Symons about Pater's reserve:

> He did not feel Pater to be reserved, he said. But was it that Pater was not reserved with Symons, or was it that Symons did not aspire to the same intimacy as I did?[25]

Moore's explanation was that Pater, though an agnostic, liked Protestantism and was inclined to accept traditional and formal procedures to escape "from the fretful." Besides, "in these modern days respect for ancient usages and traditions takes the place of faith."[26]

Pater paid off whatever debt he thought he owed Moore by reviewing *Modern Painters* in the *Morning Chronicle*, June 10, 1893. He liked the book and evidently if silently felt that it was in keeping with his own interests in the criticism of art, to discern, in a body of art, the quality unique to that artist:

> As a personal quality or power it will vary greatly, in the case of this or that work or workman, in its appeal to those who, being outsiders in the matter of art, are nevertheless sensitive and sincerely receptive, towards it. It will vary also, in a lesser degree, even to those who in this matter *really know*. But to the latter, at all events, preference in art will be nothing less than conviction, and the estimate of artistic power and product, in every several case, an object of no manner of doubt at all, such as may well give a man, as in Mr. Moore's own case, the courage of his opinions. In such matter opinion is, in fact, of the nature of the sensations one cannot help.[27]

The review was Pater's last word on Moore: it documents a relation decently allowed to lapse.

It is not clear why Pater wrote such things. Symons thought he wrote them because he didn't wish "altogether to miss his connection with the passing hour." Symons had the ballet, Pater *The Guardian*.[28] There is a more obvious reason: he wanted to put his friends under obligation. Remarkably sensitive to bad reviews of his books, Pater put himself at risk of humiliation to forestall them. Lionel Johnson is our witness to this extravagance. It is hard to establish the details of their relation. They met for the first time, according to Ian Fletcher, at Oxford in April 1888:

> I sat next Pater at luncheon: he was gracious and merciful, long suffering, and of great grossness. An ugly pig, though learned and charming too.[29]

In London, Johnson consorted with Horne, Selwyn Image, Simeon Solomon, Kegan Paul, Stenbock, and eventually with Pater. On March 30, 1889, he visited Pater in Kensington and three days later described the occasion to Arthur Galton:

> Pater was in radiant spirits, and most delightful. . . . He talked theology and praised Anglicanism for its "reverent doubt and sober mysticism": he also said much about his father, his own life and was very intimate. . . . Afterwards, we heard Benediction and Vespers at the Church of the Kensington Convent; . . . London transfigures him. He was especially kind, and solicitous, because I arrived at his house, in a shaken condition of nerves, with one crushed and bloody hand: the other having been upset in a hansom, which prostrated itself on the pavement outside the Brompton Oratory.[30]

Pater was then in his High Anglican phase, and Johnson was a Roman Catholic, so Benediction and Vespers were not bizarre.

In January 1890 Johnson reviewed *Appreciations* in Horne's magazine *The Century Guild Hobby Horse*. Pater didn't see the review when it came out, but Galton, who was assistant editor, told him about it. On February 18 Pater went to see Johnson, who then wrote to Galton:

Pater has just left me: your letter sent him round, insisting to
know what I had said of him: he was immensely agitated, coming
at nine in the morning.[31]

Nine was an unseemly time for visiting Johnson, who normally slept
off his drunken nights and arose only in time for dinner. Pater liked
the review, as well he should have, every word of it encomiastic. In
May 1890, when the second and revised edition of *Appreciations* appeared, Pater and Johnson met again. Johnson wrote to Horne:

This afternoon, I went for a walk with Pater, to my great surprise: he was very genial and amusing, and happy: all because
The Guardian has reviewed him favourably. He insisted on
giving me introductions to half a dozen editors, on the strength
of my notice of him. . . . He said, he suppressed his Aesthetic
Poetry essay, because "there were things in it"; which some
people, pious souls! thought profane, yes! profane.[32]

Johnson's punctuation, eccentric on principle, makes the report a little
difficult to construe, but the gist of it is clear. The "pious souls" included
Charles L. Graves, who said in his review of the first edition that "there
are certain passages—notably in the essay on Aesthetic Poetry—in
which Mr. Pater, without intending it, almost persuades the plain
person to be a Philistine."[33]

Johnson seems to have thought that Pater might turn Catholic, and
he wrote "A Friend" as a prayer for his conversion. The poem was
written, according to Lawrence Evans, in 1889, but was held over for
publication in Lord Alfred Douglas's *Spirit Lamp* in May 1893. As a
tribute, presumably, to the "White-Nights" chapter of *Marius the Epicurean* and to Pater's preoccupation elsewhere with whiteness, Johnson
writes:

> *His are the whitenesses of soul*
> *That Virgil had: he walks the earth*
> *A classic saint, in self-control,*
> *And comeliness, and quiet mirth.*
>
> *His presence wins me to repose:*
> *When he is with me I forget*

All heaviness: and when he goes,
The comfort of the sun is set.

But in the lonely hours I learn,
How I can serve and thank him best:
God! trouble him: that he may turn
Through sorrow to the only rest.[34]

The poem is modeled on George Herbert's "The Pulley," in which the soul is to be won to God's rest by trouble. Johnson gives Pater the tribute of using one of his favorite words "comeliness," and a concept long associated with him, self-control, *ascesis*.

Johnson returned to whiteness in "The Work of Walter Pater" (September 1894):

There is a strange purity of effect, the result of the refiner's fire, through which it has passed. The Welsh word for *white* means also something which is a combination of *holy, reverend, felicitous*; much in the sense of Herrick's "White Island." In the finer portions of Mr. Pater's work, there is a "whiteness," a "candour," indescribably felt, through this purity and cleanliness of it, as though there were "a sort of *moral* purity" in art of so scrupulous and dainty a distinction.[35]

And again in the later poem, "Walter Pater," published in the *Academy*, October 11, 1902; but this time, whiteness is the ethical criterion for both Pater and Johnson. The poem reads, in part:

Gracious God rest him, he who toiled so well
  Secrets of grace to tell
Graciously; as the awed rejoicing priest
  Officiates at the feast,
Knowing, how deep within the liturgies
  Lie hid the mysteries.
Half of a passionately pensive soul
  He showed us, not the whole:
Who loved him best, they best, they only, knew
  The deeps, they might not view;
That, which was private between God and him;
  To others, justly dim.

Calm Oxford autumns and preluding springs!
To me your memory brings
Delight upon delight, but chiefest one:
The thought of Oxford's son,
Who gave me of his welcome and his praise,
When white were still my days;
Ere death had left life darkling, nor had sent
Lament upon lament;
Ere sorrow told me, how I loved my lost,
And bade me base love's cost.
Scholarship's constant saint, he kept her light
In him divinely white[36]

The poem ends with a reference to Pater as "Hierarch of the spirit, pure and strong, / Worthy Uranian song"—one of the first printed allusions to his homoerotic disposition.

Pater's friendship with Johnson, while it lasted, was comparatively easy. Johnson didn't pester him or make him feel on edge, as Moore often did. His Catholicism, too, was congenial to Pater in the later years; not that Pater believed in Christianity, but he was now finding more and more reasons for respecting it and acknowledging the appeasing value of its rituals. Johnson's life was weird enough to interest Pater but not to make him afraid that he would be drawn into it.

This was the main worry in Pater's friendship with Wilde. In his first term at Magdalen College, Oxford, Wilde read *Studies in the History of the Renaissance*, "that book," as he later remarked, "which has had such a strange influence over my life."[37] It is possible that Pater's book, rather than Huysmans's *A Rebours* or another claimant, is the "yellow book" Wilde's Lord Henry sends to Dorian Gray, who imitates it in his progress to immorality. The chapters on Leonardo and Winckelmann are suggestive enough for that purpose. *Studies in the History of the Renaissance* became, Wilde said, "the golden book of spirit and sense, the holy writ of beauty"; he took the occasion to quote from Swinburne's sonnet on Gautier's *Mademoiselle de Maupin* and to make significant fellowship between four morally questioned writers. Wilde never changed his opinion, that Pater's prose in that book was far superior to Carlyle's and to Ruskin's. He kept extolling it to every qualified reader he met.

Wilde's career at Oxford began in October 1874 when he went up to Magdalen on a scholarship. Ruskin was then Slade Professor of Art, and Wilde attended his lectures. He even allowed Ruskin to persuade him to put their ostensibly shared socialism into practice. At Ruskin's request, Wilde joined a gang of undergraduate road-diggers to mend a road in Ferry Hinksey—an episode that Joyce recalled, in his essay on Wilde, by remarking that in Wilde's Oxford years a pompous professor named Ruskin was leading a crowd of Anglo-Saxon adolescents to the promised land of the future society, behind a wheelbarrow. For a time, Ruskin became Wilde's prophet, priest, and poet. After graduation, they kept in communication for a while. On November 28, 1879, they went together to the Lyceum to see Irving as Shylock and afterwards to a ball given by Millais and his wife to celebrate their daughter's marriage. In later years, Wilde recalled his time at Oxford mainly in association with Ruskin's lectures and the personality they displayed. But Ruskin's moral bearing was too much for Wilde in the long run. He gradually turned to Pater, having succumbed to his prose.

In July 1877 Wilde published an article on the Grosvenor Gallery in the *Dublin University Magazine* and sent a copy of it to Pater. A few references to Greek islands, handsome boys, and Correggio's paintings of adolescent beauty alerted Pater to the writer's disposition. He thanked Wilde for the article, praised the cultivated tastes it displayed, and invited him to make "an early call upon your return to Oxford." They met in late October. By November Pater was writing to "My Dear Wilde" and lending him Flaubert's new book, *Trois Contes*, a gathering of "Un Coeur simple," "La Legende de Saint Julien l'Hospitalier," and "Herodias"—the last of which greatly influenced Wilde's *Salome* (1893). Wilde sent Pater a few of his poems, and Pater urged him to change to prose: "prose is so much more difficult," he told Wilde, as he told everyone. It is probable that Pater came to regard Wilde as one of the young men upon whom a reading of the Conclusion to *Studies in the History of the Renaissance* might have a regrettable effect. If so, his misgiving was belated. By 1877, when Pater suppressed the dangerous pages, Wilde had already read them and accepted the way of life they implied.

The friendship flourished, but Pater never really liked Wilde; he thought his charm somewhat vulgar. In turn, Wilde thought Pater timid for not living up to the daring of his prose. They saw each other from time to time. Wilde introduced Pater to selected friends—Douglas Ainslie and, much later, Lord Alfred Douglas—during the years in which Pater was becoming more conservative. But Pater and Wilde did not write about each other's work till June 1887 when Wilde published an anonymous review of *Imaginary Portraits* in the *Pall Mall Gazette*. The review didn't amount to much, but it extolled Pater's mastery of prose and gave prominence to a sentence in "A Prince of Court Painters"—the study of Watteau—which became nearly as famous as Pater's aria on the Lady Lisa. Wilde said:

> The account of Watteau is perhaps a little too fanciful, and the description of him as one who was "always a seeker after something in the world that is there in no satisfying measure, or not at all" seems to us more applicable to him who saw Monna Lisa sitting among the rocks than to the gay and debonair *peintre des fêtes galantes*.[38]

Wilde complained that Pater's prose was sometimes laborious:

> Here and there one is tempted to say of Mr. Pater that he is "a seeker after something in language that is there in no satisfying measure, or not at all."[39]

But in the end Wilde was charmed by the writing: "when all is said, what wonderful prose it is. . . ."

On the strength of such praise, Pater felt himself justified, when *Appreciations* came out on November 15, 1889, in asking Wilde to write about it. "If I am intrusive in saying this," he told him, "I am sure you will forgive me. . . ." Wilde reviewed it under his own name in the *Speaker* on March 22, 1890, and drew attention to the essay on Wordsworth as the best thing in the book. But the most striking part of his review was its comparison of Pater with Newman: in each, we find "the union of personality with perfection." That Wilde doesn't make much of the comparison is of little account; his making anything of it is what matters.

But Wilde was even then working on "The Critic as Artist," a dialogue he published in the July and September 1890 issues of the *Nineteenth Century* and again in *Intentions* (1891). Here Pater's practice as a critic is the main justification for Wilde's theory of criticism as invention: the critic takes the work of art as starting-point for a new creation. Who cares whether Ruskin's views on Turner are sound or not, Wilde's Gilbert says to his Ernest:

Who, again, cares whether Mr. Pater has put into the portrait of Monna Lisa something that Lionardo never dreamed of? The painter may have been merely the slave of an archaic smile, as some have fancied, but whenever I pass into the cool galleries of the Palace of the Louvre, and stand before that strange figure "set in its marble chair in that cirque of fantastic rocks, as in some faint light under sea," I murmur to myself, "She is older than the rocks among which she sits; like the vampire, she has been dead many times, and learned the secrets of the grave; and has been a diver in deep seas, and keeps their fallen day about her; and trafficked for strange webs with Eastern merchants; and, as Leda, was the mother of Helen of Troy, and, as St. Anne, the mother of Mary; and all this has been to her but as the sound of lyres and flutes, and lives only in the delicacy with which it has moulded the changing lineaments, and tinged the eyelids and the hands." And I say to my friend, "The presence that thus so strangely rose beside the waters is expressive of what in the ways of a thousand years man had come to desire"; and he answers me, "Hers is the head upon which all 'the ends of the world are come,' and the eyelids are a little weary."[40]

Gilbert's further reflections, on beauty, form, music, and subjectivity, are applied Pater: illogical, indeed, since Pater's paragraph about Mona Lisa testifies to his own impression and should merely be the starting-point for anyone else's. Wilde's impression should be yet another flight of creativity, not a recitation of Pater's. But the passage has its propriety as one in which two people, Gilbert and his friend, make love by murmuring quotations to each other.

The friendship between Pater and Wilde virtually came to an end in the winter of 1891. While *The Picture of Dorian Gray* was still in manuscript and before he started serial publication of it in July 1890 in *Lippincott's Monthly Magazine*, Wilde showed it to Pater. The following March, he published the Preface to it in the *Fortnightly Review*: pure Pater, a celebration of music and the uselessness of art. It is not clear what part of the book Pater took exception to. If Wilde told the truth under Edward Carson's cross-examination in the first trial on April 3, 1895, he didn't delete any part of *The Picture of Dorian Gray* but made an addition to it. "In one case it was pointed out to me," Wilde said, "not in a newspaper or anything of that sort, but by the only critic of the century whose opinion I set high, Mr. Walter Pater—that a certain passage was liable to misconstruction, and I made an addition."[41] It is probable, as Donald Lawler has argued, that the passage in question is the one in which Basil Hallward refers to several young men whose lives have been ruined, allegedly, by their association with Dorian Gray. Wilde added a few sentences in which Dorian disclaims responsibility for introducing any of these men to vice or folly.[42]

Sometime in the autumn of 1891 Wilde introduced Lord Alfred Douglas to Pater. The meeting didn't lead to a friendship:

> Wilde had an immense opinion of Pater and spoke of him always with reverence as the greatest living writer of prose. I tried to appreciate Pater and he personally was kind to me, but quite apart from the fact that he had practically no conversation and would sit for hours without saying more than an occasional word, I never could bring myself to have more than a very limited admiration for his far-famed prose, which has always seemed to me artificial, finicking and over-elaborated to an exasperating degree. I have altogether livelier recollections of Mr., now the Reverend Dr., Bussell, Pater's most intimate friend at Brasenose College, for he was a fine musician and had a devotion to Handel and Bach. . . .[43]

Pater's sense of the relation between Lord Alfred and Wilde, added to common rumor about Wilde's sexual life, made him decide that minor textual changes in *Dorian Gray* were not enough. He could have avoided having anything further to do with the book. Instead, with unusual boldness, he arranged to review it and took the occasion to repudiate not only Lord Henry but his creator.

The review began with predictable gestures of praise for Wilde's cleverness, but Pater soon indicated where he diverged from him:

> A wholesome dislike of the commonplace, rightly or wrongly identified by him with the *bourgeois*, with our middle-class—its habits and tastes—leads him to protest emphatically against so-called "realism" in art. . . .[44]

It is strange to find Pater holding out the possibility that "the commonplace" might not be justly identified with the habits and tastes of the *bourgeoisie*. More than Arnold, Ruskin, or Newman, it was Pater who made this identification mandatory. Now that it has been appropriated by Wilde, he must dissociate himself from it. Pater assumes that Wilde's novel is designed to recommend "a dainty Epicurean theory" for the middle class. But it fails, according to the author of *Marius the Epicurean*:

> A true Epicureanism aims at a complete though harmonious development of man's entire organism. To lose the moral sense therefore, for instance, the sense of sin and righteousness, as Mr. Wilde's hero—his heroes are bent on doing as speedily, as completely as they can, is to lose, or lower, organisation, to become less complex, to pass from a higher to a lower degree of development. . . . Lord Henry, and even more the, from the first, suicidal hero, loses too much in life to be a true Epicurean—loses so much in the way of impressions, of pleasant memories, and subsequent hopes, which Hallward, by a really Epicurean economy, manages to secure.[45]

Once he has disowned Lord Henry, whom Wilde evidently intended to be recognizably Paterian, Pater can afford to be generous. Lord Henry is "the spoiler of the fair young man," but Dorian—though an unsuccessful experiment in Epicureanism—is "a beautiful creation." The moral of the story is that "vice and crime make people coarse and ugly." Ordinary readers should take the novel as if it were a story by Poe about doppelgänger, not of two persons but of a man and his portrait. A few more words of praise, and Pater regards himself as having done his duty.

No quarrel ensued, but the friendship lapsed. Even before the review appeared, Wilde was speaking harshly of Pater to Richard Le Gallienne. And then or later, Vincent O'Sullivan heard Pater say "something very severe about 'Mr. Wilde,' as he called him, which I prefer to leave in darkness."[46] But in February 1893 Wilde sent Pater a copy of *Salome*, presumably to remind him that in happier times Pater had given him Flaubert's stories and the idea for the play. There is no evidence that Pater acknowledged the gift.

When Wilde heard of Pater's death, he asked, according to Max Beerbohm, "Was he ever alive?"[47] But in July 1895 Wilde was allowed to choose fifteen books to be sent to him in prison: they included *The Renaissance*. Two months later he got *Greek Studies*, *Appreciations*, and *Imaginary Portraits*. Robert Ross, visiting Wilde in prison in May 1896, undertook to send him *Gaston de Latour* when it came out on October 6. A further list, submitted to the prison authorities on December 3, 1896, included Pater's posthumous *Miscellaneous Studies* (1895). In the long letter to Lord Alfred, written from Reading Jail at intervals between January and March 1897, Wilde had Pater in mind on several occasions. Recalling the passage in *Studies in the History of the Renaissance* where Pater says that our failure consists in forming habits, Wilde found himself guilty: his habit of giving in to Lord Alfred "had stereotyped my temperament to one permanent and fatal mood." Thinking of the distinction between contemplating the spectacle of life and engaging in life, Wilde quoted—inaccurately, placing it in *Marius the Epicurean* rather than in the essay on Wordsworth—Pater's remark that "to witness this spectacle with appropriate emotions is the aim of all culture." In the same letter, Wilde said of Christ that "his morality is all sympathy"—which is what Pater said of Botticelli. And Wilde recalled the passage in the book on the Renaissance in which Pater refers to Michelangelo as "one of those who incur the judgment of Dante, as having 'wilfully lived in sadness.' " Wilde tells Lord Alfred:

I remember during my first term at Oxford reading in Pater's *Renaissance*—that book which has had such a strange influence over my life—how Dante places low in the Inferno those who wilfully live in sadness, and going to the College Library and turning to the passage in the *Divine Comedy* where beneath the dreary marsh lie those who were "sullen in the sweet air," saying for ever through their sighs:

> *Tristi fummo*
> *nell' aer dolce che dal sol s'allegra.*

I knew the Church condemned *accidia*, but the whole idea seemed to me quite fantastic, just the sort of sin, I fancied, a priest who knew nothing about real life would invent. Nor could I understand how Dante, who says that "sorrow remarries us to God," could have been so harsh to those who were enamoured of melancholy, if any such there really were. I had no idea that some day this would become to me one of the greatest temptations of my life.[48]

Finally, in a letter of April 16, 1900, to Robert Ross, Wilde described a recent trip to Rome, where on Easter Sunday he attended vespers at the Lateran:

> music quite lovely: at the close a Bishop in red, and with red gloves—such as Pater talks of in *Gaston de Latour*—came out on the balcony and showed us the relics.[49]

Inaccurate, as Rupert Hart-Davis has noted. Wilde is thinking of the bishop in "Denys L'Auxerrois" who, "in vestments of deep red in honour of the relics, blessed the new shrine. . . . At last from a little narrow chest, into which the remains had been almost crushed together, the bishop's red-gloved hands drew the dwindled body."

The relation between Pater and Wilde was genuine, but there were limits to it. Whitman said, "He most honors my style who learns under it to destroy the teacher." Neither Hopkins nor Wilde honored Pater's style in that degree. Hopkins was not in any lasting sense Pater's pupil, schooled as he was in the academies of Keats, Newman, and Ruskin. Wilde learned whatever he needed from Pater, but unlike Pater he was a man of the theater and he delighted in greasepaint and first nights. Pater gave him metaphors and allusions, and he used them provocatively, but Wilde did not need to get rid of Pater to clear a space for himself. The essay on Winckelmann makes a case in point. Wilde read it at Oxford, and used it to develop his own thinking. He noted especially the suggestive passage in which Pater contrasts Greek sensuousness with Christian asceticism: the one is shameless and childlike, it does not fever the conscience; the other discredits the slightest touch of sense. The word "touch" stirs Pater's mind to further intimations of sensuous pleasure, and he immediately quotes without comment the passage from 1 Samuel 14 in which Jonathan says, "I did but taste a little honey with the end of the rod that was in my hand, and lo! I must die." I remind you that Jonathan's father, Saul, has ordained that none of his people will eat food till the Philistines are defeated; and Jonathan, who has not heard of the edict, dips his staff into a comb of honey and puts it to his mouth. When Saul learns of this, he determines that his son must be put to death. But the people protest, and Jonathan is pardoned. "My father has troubled the earth," Jonathan says. It is pertinent to mention that Jonathan has defied his father and persisted in his great friendship with David, a relation that many readers deem to be homosexual. So the taste of honey has often been taken as figurative and erotic. Pater's context, his essay on the notorious homosexual Winckelmann, makes these intimations emphatic. An association of imagery brings together Greek sensuousness, the artistic life, homosexual friendship, and transgression. Pater has to show Winckelmann released from the intoxication of that honey by being a pagan. "From this intoxication," he says, "Winckelmann is free: he fingers those pagan marbles with unsinged hands, with no sense of shame or loss."[50] "Fingers," not "looks at."

In the poem "Hélas!" Wilde recalls Pater's quotation of the passage from Samuel:

> To drift with every passion till my soul
> Is a stringed lute upon which all winds can play,
> Is it for this that I have given away
> Mine ancient wisdom and austere control?
> Methinks my life is a twice-written scroll
> Scrawled over on some boyish holiday
> With idle songs for pipe and virelay
> Which do but mar the secret of the whole.
> Surely there was a time I might have trod
> The sunlit heights, and from life's dissonance
> Struck one clear chord to reach the ears of God:
> Is that time dead? lo! with a little rod
> I did but touch the honey of romance—
> And must I lose a soul's inheritance?[51]

It is a poem of second thought in which Wilde alludes not only to Pater's "Winckelmann" and the drifting Conclusion to *Studies in the History of the Renaissance* but to the Coleridge of "The Aeolian Lyre." In Romantic literature the sounds of the wind through the lyre are generally heard as inspiration, the true voice of feeling as if it were verified by nature. But Wilde's poem emphasizes the dark side of drifting, yielding to every passion. It is ironic that what is lost is "austere control," since that phrase, too, is Paterian in his later emphasis on *ascesis*, the self-discipline required for the achievement of a style. The move from "scroll" to "Scrawled over" mimes the twice-written character of the life: the first, inscribed by God; the second, a boyish scrawl. In the last lines Wilde makes the association with Jonathan explicit, as if to say, "I didn't know that what I did was forbidden, and maybe the people who love my plays will demand that I be pardoned." To make way for the last line, the rhetorical question, Wilde changes the structure of Jonathan's sentence. In Samuel the sentence makes a strong ethical discrepancy between the minor quality of the act and its appalling consequence; the transition is effected by the exclamation "lo!". "I did but taste a little honey with the end of the rod that was in mine hand, and lo! I must die." In Wilde's poem the "lo!" is brought forward to anticipate the discrepancy it isn't called upon to enact; the littleness is given to the rod rather than to the amount of honey; and Jonathan's "I must die" is changed to refer to spiritual death, "And must I lose a soul's inheritance?" The poem uses the motifs that Pater has assembled—sensuousness, pleasure, art, homosexual friendship, pagan blitheness, the touch and taste of honey—but it recalls, to rebuke these, the Christian asceticism that Pater mentioned only to relegate. The teacher is not destroyed, but a lesson is recited different from his.

8

Last Years:
Mrs. Humphry Ward

PATER'S FRIENDSHIPS with writers and artists meant a good deal to him, especially in his London years, but he was not by nature cordial. He was always interested in meeting homosexuals, but toward other people he remained distant. He was ready to learn from anyone, and in that cause to put up with minor exacerbations. He learned from Swinburne, for instance, that the French writers to take special note of were Baudelaire, Gautier, and Flaubert, and that it was possible to do art criticism in a memorably grand style. For these gifts, he was ready to accompany Swinburne in a hansom cab to a social occasion, even though Swinburne was so drunk that on their arrival he fell to the pavement. But it is hard to believe that sober Walter and drunk Algernon were friends.

Mostly, Pater kept up an interest in writers because of shared preoccupations and opinions worth thinking about. In his later years the writer who, more than anyone else, impelled him to these exertions was Mrs. Humphry Ward. Granddaughter of Dr. Thomas Arnold, Mary Arnold married Humphry Ward in 1872. He had been one of Pater's pupils at Brasenose. He came up to Oxford in 1864 when Pater was a probationary Fellow at Brasenose. Twenty-two years old and

good-looking, he soon attracted Pater's attention. By the summer of
1867 their friendship was such that Ward accepted Pater's invitation
to spend a month with him by the seaside at Sidmouth, an experience
which, he recalled, "made us rather intimate."[1] When Ward married
Mary Arnold, they set up house in Bradmore Road, nearly opposite
Pater's. In *A Writer's Recollections*, Mary describes a dinner party at
which Pater, "pressed controversially beyond the point of wisdom,"
told a professor's wife, a woman of Anglican conviction, that no reasonable person could govern his life "by the opinions of a man who
died eighteen centuries ago."[2] The professor and his wife left in
agitation.

But by 1881, when the Wards moved to London, Pater was a
changed man: he had not returned to Christianity, but his affections
had begun to turn back to the faith. Mrs. Ward recalled:

> I once said to him in *tête-à-tête*, reckoning confidently on his
> sympathy, and with the intolerance and certainty of youth, that
> orthodoxy could not possibly maintain itself long against its
> assailants, especially from the historical and literary camps, and
> that we should live to see it break down. He shook his head and
> looked rather troubled. "I don't think so," he said. Then, with
> hesitation, "And we don't altogether agree. You think it's all
> plain. But I can't. There are such mysterious things. Take that
> saying, 'Come unto me, all ye that are weary and heavy laden.'
> How can you explain that? There is a mystery in it—something
> supernatural."[3]

In June 1885 Mrs. Ward reviewed *Marius the Epicurean* in *Macmillan's
Magazine*. She greatly admired the book, but was troubled by its timid-
ity: it seemed to her to recant the Conclusion to *Studies in the History
of the Renaissance* and to offer in its place a version of utilitarianism.
Marius's Epicureanism, or his Cyrenaicism, as Pater called it, is presented as an enthusiasm appropriate to young men much taken with
the beauty of the world and beset by the brevity of life. When the
glamour of youth fades, Cyrenaicism shows itself inadequate: seizing
the highly colored moments which are to pass away so quickly, it fails
to achieve a comprehensive sense of life. Mrs. Ward interpreted Pater
as saying that one should submit to Christianity, or at least act as if
one did: conform, make company with the faithful, and maintain one's
misgiving in privacy. She was not content with that. Contrasting Pater

with her father's friend Clough, she praised Clough's determination "to seek no personal ease or relief at the expense of truth, and to put no fairy tales knowingly into the place which belongs to realities."[4]

Pater was pleased with the review nonetheless and told Mrs. Ward that he must soon try to deal with the most serious of her objections. He probably meant: I must, in revising the book, find better reasons for sending Marius toward Christianity at the end. In the event, he made a few changes in the second edition, and several thousand local emendations in the third (1892), but none of these answered Mrs. Ward's complaint.

In December 1885 she sent Pater a copy of her translation of Amiel's *Journal Intime*. The book touched his concern with religious belief, a matter also explored in her Introduction. Pater thanked her, but took the occasion to clarify his own position:

> . . . I gather from your well-meditated introduction, that I shall think, on finishing the book, that there was still something Amiel might have added to those elements of natural religion, (so to call it, for want of a better expression,) which he was able to accept, at times with full belief, and always with the sort of hope which is a great factor in life. To my mind, the beliefs, and the function in the world, of the historic church, form just one of those obscure but all-important possibilities, which the human mind is powerless effectively to dismiss from itself; and might wisely accept, in the first place, as a workable hypothesis. The supposed facts on which Christianity rests, utterly incapable as they have become of any ordinary test, seem to me matters of very much the same sort of assent we give to any assumption, in the strict and ultimate sense, moral. The question whether those facts were real will, I think, always continue to be what I should call one of the *natural* questions of the human mind.[5]

Clearly a reply to Mrs. Ward's review of *Marius the Epicurean*, Pater's letter gave her notice that he would review *Amiel's Journal* at length, as he did on March 17, 1886, in *The Guardian*. The review anticipated the pattern of his review of *The Picture of Dorian Gray* in 1891: in each case he identified the author's moral or religious position and claimed that it was merely partial by comparison with the full account of life he had not the courage to adopt. Amiel was an unsatisfactory mixture of two personalities. One was the familiar adept of modernity, weary, self-conscious, issuing from "the culture of *ennui* for its own sake." The other and far stronger personality was "possessed of gifts, not for the renunciation, but for the reception and use, of all that is puissant, goodly, and effective in life, and for the varied and adequate reproduction of it; who, under favourable circumstances, or even without them, will become critic, or poet, and in either case a creative force; and if he be religious (as Amiel was deeply religious) will make the most of 'evidence,' and almost certainly find a Church."[6] Pater's belief at this point, which might have operated as a conviction if he had persuaded himself to act upon it, was that the case for crediting Christianity was no worse than that for crediting anything. In questions of morality, we live upon working hypotheses, and by working them to the bone. Amiel, according to Pater, shrank from the logic he disclosed:

> Assenting, on probable evidence, to so many of the judgments of the religious sense, he failed to see the equally probable evidence there is for the beliefs, the peculiar direction of men's hopes, which complete those judgments harmoniously, and bring them into connection with the facts, the venerable institutions of the past—with the lives of the saints. By failure, as we think, of that historic sense, of which he could speak so well, he got no further in this direction than the glacial condition of rationalistic Geneva. "Philosophy," he says, "can never replace religion." Only, one cannot see why it might not replace a religion such as his: a religion, after all, much like Seneca's.[7]

Amiel should have brought the Great Possibility, as Pater called it, within his plan.

On February 4, 1888, Mrs. Ward's *Robert Elsmere* appeared, a novel in three volumes; it was an immense popular success. The story of an Anglican minister who loses his faith, leaves his ministry, joins a group of Unitarians, and thereby causes his wife, Catherine, acute pain evidently caught the mood of its time. The origin of the book was a set of Bampton Lectures given by Rev. John Wordsworth—Pater's opponent—in March 1881. The lectures, under the title "The Present Unsettlement in Religion," were an attack, in effect, on Arnold, Jowett, Pater, Dean Stanley, Nettleship, Sidgwick, T. H. Green, and others who would not accept the doctrines of Christianity. Mary Ward attended the first of the lectures, and published a reply called "Unbelief and Sin: A Protest addressed to those who attended the Bampton Lecture of Sunday March 6." Rev. Wordsworth is clearly the preacher referred to in this passage in book VII, chapter XLVI of *Robert Elsmere*, where Catherine is shown moving a little in her husband's moral direction:

> She had, in fact, undergone that dissociation of the moral judg-
> ment from a special series of religious formulae which is the
> crucial, the epoch-making fact of our day. "Unbelief," says the
> orthodox preacher, "is sin, and implies it": and while he speaks,
> the saint in the unbeliever gently smiles down his argument,
> and suddenly, in the rebel of yesterday men see the rightful heir
> of to-morrow.[8]

Here as elsewhere Mrs. Ward was a little too pleased with herself as the smiling saint in the unbeliever: "formulae" is an insult, set against "moral judgment."

Pater's review of *Robert Elsmere* praised it in general and local terms as a novel in the tradition of Jane Austen, George Sand, and George Eliot, but he was dissatisfied with the presentation of Robert. The main issue of the "religious question," he insisted, was no longer where Mrs. Ward supposed it was; "it has advanced, in more senses than one, beyond the point raised by Renan's *Vie de Jésus*":

> Of course, a man such as Robert Elsmere came to be ought not
> to be a clergyman of the Anglican Church. The priest is still,
> and will, we think, remain, one of the necessary types of hu-
> manity; and he is untrue to his type, unless, with whatever
> inevitable doubts in this doubting age, he feels, on the whole,
> the preponderance in it of those influences which make for faith.
> It is his triumph to achieve as much faith as possible in an age
> of negation.[9]

Pater is referring to the ideal type of priesthood, not to Robert Elsmere as a failed exemplar of it:

> Doubtless, it is part of the ideal of the Anglican Church that,
> under certain safeguards, it should find room for latitudinarians
> even among its clergy. Still, with these, as with all other genuine
> priests, it is the positive not the negative result that justifies the

position. We have little patience with those liberal clergy who dwell on nothing else than the difficulties of faith and the propriety of concession to the opposite force.[10]

Pater has moved a long way, in this last sentence, from the tenderness he showed in *Studies in the History of the Renaissance* toward Abelard and other adepts of antinomianism:

Yes! Robert Elsmere was certainly right in ceasing to be a clergyman. But it strikes us as a blot on his philosophical pretensions that he should have been both so late in perceiving the difficulty, and then so sudden and trenchant in dealing with so great and complex a question. Had he possessed a perfectly philosophic or scientific temper he would have hesitated.[11]

And he should have persisted in hesitating, apparently, since the case for doubt is no stronger than the case for belief, in "a world so obscure, in its origin and issues, as that in which we live":

Robert Elsmere was a type of a large class of minds which cannot be sure that the sacred story is true. It is philosophical, doubtless, and a duty to the intellect to recognize our doubts, to locate them, perhaps to give them practical effect. It may be also a moral duty to do this. But then there is also a large class of minds which cannot be sure it is false—minds of very various degrees of conscientiousness and intellectual power, up to the highest. They will think those who are quite sure it is false unphilosophical through lack of doubt. For their part, they make allowance in their scheme of life for a great possibility, and with some of them that bare concession of possibility (the subject of it being what it is) becomes the most important fact in the world. The recognition of it straightway opens wide the door to hope and love; and such persons are, as we fancy they always will be, the nucleus of a Church.[12]

Elsmere's recourse to a pale Unitarianism, to Christ in his "purely human aspect," does not satisfy Pater: "it is the infinite nature of Christ which has led to such diversities of genius in preaching as St. Francis, and Taylor, and Wesley."

So the debate between Pater and Mrs. Ward ended. Neither in his review of the book nor in further correspondence did Pater indicate to Mrs. Ward that he recognized himself in the character of Edward Langham in *Robert Elsmere*, a victim of moral debility, endlessly hovering between this and that. In *The Case of Richard Meynell* she changed her mind on the religious issue and advocated that doubting clergy should stay in the Christian fold and work to improve it from within. When *The History of David Grieve*—a sequel to *Robert Elsmere* with a similar theme—was published in January 1892, Pater read it, liked it, and congratulated her but did not review it.

Pater's later years were preoccupied with the question he debated with Mrs. Ward, that of religious belief. In his quiet way he resolved to defend his position in a fiction, "an Imaginary Portrait of a peculiar type of mind in the time of Marcus Aurelius," as he described it to Violet Paget. Arnold's essay established Aurelius as a sage who could be alluded to. Early in December 1882 Pater set out by himself on a trip to Rome and Naples; he was abroad for about seven weeks, four of them in Rome. It was his first sight of the city. He didn't know Italy very well. Since his first visit to Florence, Pisa, and Ravenna with Shadwell in 1865, he had relied mostly upon the hearsay of Italian paintings and prints. Violet Paget gave him letters of introduction to her friends in Rome, but he didn't use them, preferring to visit the churches and galleries by himself.

The following summer he resigned his tutorship at Brasenose, but not his fellowship; he wanted to give all his time to *Marius the Epicurean*. Virtually everything he read he converted into that context. Finding in Violet Paget's "The Responsibilities of Unbelief" three positions represented—cultivated man of the Enlightenment, aesthetic pessimist, and atheist—he thought of Marius moving toward a fourth, that of slowly attained acquiescence in Christianity. He told Paget that such a "fourth sort of religious phase" was "possible for the modern mind," though he didn't further describe it to her.

His model for this achievement was Newman. Among Pater's manuscripts there is an essay on "The Writings of Cardinal Newman" which he didn't publish, probably because he couldn't decide whether Newman's position was feasible or not. At the beginning of the essay Pater says that Newman devoted his entire life "to the lost cause of his adoption," by which I assume he means Christianity, but he immediately saves part of the day by adding, "if indeed any cause which has at any time really represented a very complex interest of human nature can rightly be called lost."[13] As he proceeds, he enters more sympathetically into Newman's progress toward religious belief. He paraphrases Newman's arguments about development, assent, "the illative sense," and the validity of the act of faith even on imperfect evidence. Such thinking as Pater did, he did by commenting on the work of other writers, especially Plato, Montaigne, Pascal, Hobbes, Berkeley, Kant, Coleridge, Emerson, John Stuart Mill, Whewell, F. D. Maurice, and Newman. But in the later years Newman was particularly evident, an exemplary figure of possibility.

Not that Pater was bold enough to align himself in any public way with Newman. When he was still young Pater occasionally imagined the somber gratification of settling into the axioms of common sense and community, but he expressed these images indirectly, as in an early essay, "The Bacchanals of Euripides," when he thought of Euripides's old age. Pater did not live long enough to know such age, but he schooled himself in its demeanor:

> Writing in old age, he is in that subdued mood, a mood not necessarily sordid, in which (the shudder at the nearer approach of the unknown world coming over him more frequently than of old) accustomed ideas, conformable to a sort of common sense regarding the unseen, oftentimes regain what they may have lost, in a man's allegiance. It is a sort of madness, he begins to think, to differ from the received opinions thereon. Not that he is insincere or ironical, but that he tends, in the sum of probabilities, to dwell on their more peaceful side; to sit quiet, for the short remaining time, in the reflexion of the more cheerfully lighted side of things; and what is accustomed—what holds of familiar usage—comes to seem the whole essence of wisdom, on all subjects; . . .[14]

Marius the Epicurean was published on March 4, 1885. It was successful enough to make Pater set about improving its style for a new edition. With modest fame as incentive, he and his sisters moved up to London, settling upon a bashful little house, 12 Earl's Terrace, Kensington, near Holland House. Clara and Hester preferred London to Oxford, and so did he, at least while the publication of a new book made his public life stir itself. When Ruskin resigned the Slade Professorship of Art at Oxford, Pater let his name go forward, but he lost to Sir Hubert von Herkomer, founder of the Herkomer School of Art. In the event, he did not cut much of a dash in London: he mainly went to the National Gallery and diverted himself occasionally at the theater. Social life gratified him more in prospect than in proof; with few exceptions, the people he met he was content not to cultivate.

At least once, Pater accepted the duty of having an opinion on a matter of some public interest. In the autumn of 1886 there was much talk of establishing English literature as a subject at Oxford and Cambridge. The *Pall Mall Gazette* ran a series of articles on the matter. On November 27, Pater contributed a letter in response to an invitation from the editor. Normally, he would not have felt impelled to intervene, even on a question for which he deemed himself qualified. So far as I know, this was the sole occasion on which he broke silence: he never replied in public to a review of his books or to an editorial on any public issue. On the question of English, he said that Oxford had contributed to English literature mainly by "its abundant and disinterested devotion, in the face of much opposition, to Greek and Latin literature":

> I should, therefore, be no advocate for any plan of introducing English literature into the course of university studies which seemed likely to throw into the background that study of classical literature which has proved so effective for the maintenance of what is excellent in our own.[15]

Besides, "intelligent Englishmen resort naturally for a liberal pleasure to their own literature"; why confound that pleasure by drawing it into a system of examinations and cramming? If the motive for introducing courses in English literature was to provide a soft option for minds too lazy to rise to Greek and Latin, Oxford should have nothing to do with the plan:

> That is the last thing we require from the university, in an age already overloaded with the heavy, incondite, "brute matter" of knowledge, and too bustling in its habits to think of that just management of its material which is precisely what we admire in the Greek and Latin writers.[16]

Pater's advice was not taken. In 1893 Oxford established a School of English, while salving its conscience by making the subject arduously philological. First-year undergraduates were required to take courses in Anglo-Saxon language and literature, a subject transferred from the Antiquities of Northern Europe to add historical density to modern English.

There is no evidence that Pater was much troubled by Oxford's decision. He had higher considerations on his mind. In those years he resumed attending church, not habitually but when the spirit moved him. The spirit was mostly an aesthetic impulse: he attended service for the ritual, not the doctrine. When Rev. E. V. Eyre invited him, in June 1893, to come to a meeting in aid of the completion of his Church of the Holy Redeemer, Pater chose not to go as far as Clerkenwell, but he told Father Eyre how much he enjoyed the Sunday-morning service, how he prayed that God's blessing would be lavished upon the church, and how he sometimes thought that religion—in "such a Church as yours, so fair and cheerful and full of light"—was "the only way in which poetry can really reach the hard-worked poor."[17] The only difference his renewed affection for the Church made was that the young men he cultivated now had to be, like Richard C. Jackson in former years, not only good-looking but of a religious disposition, preferably Anglo-Catholic or, like Francis Fortesque Urquhart, Roman Catholic. There is no evidence that Pater's friendships with these men were especially close. Jackson told the biographer Thomas Wright that he was Pater's most intimate companion and the model for Marius; but Jackson was a fantasist, a self-consecrated Bishop of the Greek Orthodox church, self-appointed President of the "Blake Society of Arts and Letters," self-proclaimed friend of Dean Church, Dr. Pusey, Canon Liddon, Browning, and D. G. Rossetti. Some of his claims may be true, but it is unlikely that he consorted with Pater for many years without any of Pater's official friends knowing of the relation. Pater suffered fools gladly enough if they were handsome; besides, in his later years he liked to have someone to talk to about God. In these communications his favorite companion, but not his only one, was Lionel Johnson. When Newman died on August 11, 1890, Pater and Johnson went together to the Brompton Oratory to take part in the Requiem Mass for the repose of the Cardinal's soul.[18] On Sunday, January 4, 1891, Pater went to Mass with Sir Mountstuart Grant Duff:

> Mr. Pater spent the day with us. He and I went together to the little Catholic Chapel, and he remarked, as we talked about the Mass, on its wonderful wealth of suggestion.[19]

In *Marius the Epicurean* the Mass is described as "the greatest act of worship the world has seen."[20] Grant Duff's diary for December 11, 1892, records a conversation in which Pater told him that he was planning a theological work in three parts, *Hebrew and Hellene*, *The Genius of Christ*, and *The Poetry of Anglicanism*. None of these was ever written. After *Marius the Epicurean*, Pater thought of writing two further books dealing with similar ethical and religious questions, one to be set in sixteenth-century France, the other in England at the end of the eighteenth century. Evidently he assumed he would never die. The unfinished *Gaston de Latour* is the only remnant of that plan.

Instead, he wrote two chapters of a book he hoped to write on the great churches of France. In the summer of 1893 the Paters moved back to Oxford, taking the house at 54 St. Giles's. A few weeks later they made another trip to France, concentrating on Vézelay, Amiens, and Beauvais. As if he wanted to correct Ruskin again, Pater wrote as the first chapter of the book "Notre dame d'Amiens"; it was published in March 1894. "Vézelay" appeared in June. A third chapter, "Notre dame de Troyes," was drafted but left incomplete.

In the last week of February 1894 Pater met Mallarmé, who was giving the Taylorian Lecture at Oxford under the title "La Musique et les Lettres." His host was Frederick York Powell. "*L'excellent M. Powell a, tout le temps, été pour moi maternel*," Mallarmé wrote to his wife. The lecture went well: "he was delightful," Powell noted, "and we are as thick as thieves. . . . a charming man; beautiful manner and speech." Powell knew Pater quite well, but not well enough to know his taste. Once, when Powell was offered Rodin's bronze *The Man with the Broken Nose* on easy terms, he thought Pater would like the first refusal of it, so he brought it to him. Pater looked at it only long enough to shudder. Thanking Powell, he said, "I don't think I could *bear* to live with it." Powell reminded himself, belatedly, that Pater always thought of "the ideal of manly beauty as somewhere between nineteen and twenty-three." And free of a broken nose. Pater's paganism flourished upon the sight of beautiful men. In his last years, when like Marius the Epicurean he moved toward Christianity, he was susceptible to aesthetically pleasing images of its founder and the beauty of Anglican ceremonies.

Powell assumed that Pater would be pleased to meet Mallarmé, not only a great poet but an artist in prose. Perhaps he was pleased, but he did not converse with Mallarmé on the relation between music and literature or upon any other topic. Oliver Elton's biography of Powell has only this to say of the meeting:

> Mallarmé taught English in a *lycée*; Pater was deeply versed in French; but neither would venture on the language of the other master. They regarded each other in silence, and were satisfied, while Powell's voice was heard in alternate tongues. His French was good, rich, and instinctive, if not always formally right: he had the sense of the language as a fencer has "le sentiment du fer."[21]

Pater left no account of the meeting. He was in poor health, suffering from gout and low spirits. Five months later he died.

9

The Sisters

Aᴏᴛᴇʀ Pᴀᴛᴇʀ'ꜱ ᴅᴇᴀᴛʜ, his sisters left Oxford for London, to live in a small house, 6 Canning Place, off Gloucester Road, Kensington. Clara Ann, the younger one, survived till August 9, 1910; Hester Maria till August 5, 1922.

The sisters are hard to describe. Their education in Heidelberg hardly amounted to more than the qualifications of a governess. But they learned German. When they came back to England, their main occupation was to provide an agreeable home for their brother. If they resented this small destiny, they kept quiet about it. Pater sometimes invoked their opinion when he wanted to avoid the responsibility of enforcing his own. In March 1894 Sir William Rothenstein did a drawing of him and proposed to publish it. Pater thought it made him look like a Barbary ape, and he wrote to the publisher John Lane to prevent publication. He also told Rothenstein that Hester and Clara probably wouldn't like the drawing, "in which case I would rather not have it published."[1] Predictably, the sisters obliged him by disliking it. After his death they changed their opinion and agreed to publication.

There is no evidence that Pater felt misgiving about the constraints of their domestic duty. Society kept such women back, but Pater did not offer to release them. In "The Myth of Demeter and Persephone" he has a curious sentence about Demeter's domestic bearing:

> But the house of the prudent countryman will be, of course, a place of honest manners; and Demeter *Thesmophoros* is the guardian of married life, the deity of the discretion of wives. She is therefore the founder of civilised order.[2]

In the nineteenth century discretion was what women, more especially wives, were supposed to have. Husbands were not under such extreme obligation. In a typical episode of *Sense and Sensibility*, when Marianne has committed the impropriety of visiting Allenham with Willoughby in Mrs. Smith's absence, Elinor asks her, "do you not now begin to doubt the discretion of your own conduct?" Pater evidently shared this sentiment, and valued his spinster sisters for the civilized order they ensured while he entertained his undergraduates to hand-holding teas.

Hester's life was entirely domestic, embroidery her only visible distinction. A rather sour person, she seemed to most visitors formidably dismal. After her sister's death, Richard Jennings persuaded Henry James to join him in paying a call on Hester. Not a happy idea:

> The poor lady lived much alone. I fear that the visit was not a success. . . . Hester Pater glared at him and told him that she hated "horrid" ghost stories about children. This turn of the screw became so painful that we soon rose to go. On the doorstep of the tiny house, whence he was perfectly audible from within, James discriminated long and loud in this manner: "Pater? *Walter* Pater? Well, yes. Yes, well enough—after a fashion; that fashion being of a kind somehow prone—I might say calculated—to bring forth, to be conducive to, *legend*. Part of the legend survives in there; the old lady, I mean, survives. She looks *cross*. I suspect she *is* cross. May crossness explain her solitude?"[3]

Clara started out with more favorable prospects than her sister. She was better looking, indeed distinguished in that way, more intelligent, too. In Oxford she joined friends to arrange lectures and to further the higher education of women. She taught herself some Latin and Greek and retained enough German to make it possible, according to Pater, that she might do some translation work. In 1886, despite her lack of academic qualifications, she became Vice-Principal of Somerville, a new hall of residence for women students at Oxford which she helped to found. From 1887 to 1894 she was the first tutor in classics at Somerville. Vera Brittain has commented on the portrait of her that hangs in the college:

> The portrait of Clara Pater, adorning the secluded passage outside the private dining-hall of the Senior Common Room, shows a serious, oval face framed by smooth dark hair, and clearly defined brows above contemplative eyes. Like her brother, Miss Pater represented the quintessence of Oxford aestheticism; with other contemporaries who had been influenced by the Pre-Raphaelites, she was often to be seen in peacock-blue serge ornamented with crewel sun-flowers and an amber necklace. . . . The inevitable amber appears in her picture, decorating the neck of a demure white dress.[4]

Clara was occasionally of help to her brother in literary matters. She transcribed *Gaston de Latour*, like herself incomplete. In 1898 she taught Virginia Stephen (later Virginia Woolf) the rudiments of Latin and Greek, but not well enough to make them a secure possession.

In their later years the sisters faded quietly together and roused themselves only to refuse to have anything to do with Thomas Wright when he decided to write a biography of their brother. He went ahead, wrote the book, and had the gall to offer the sisters a copy of it. They refused, "as it has been written extremely against our wishes." A year later they allowed A. C. Benson to write a life of Pater. The fact that Gosse thought well of Benson made the difference. Clara and Hester shared with Benson the little they knew of their brother and the less they understood. He was now, as James said, a legend, and apparently as opaque to his sisters as to anyone else.

Part III

The Work

10

"Diaphaneitè"

I N "THE TRAGIC GENERATION" Yeats distinguishes two affiliations in nineteenth-century English poetry. He has been referring to the islands of Phaedria and Acrasia in *The Faerie Queene*:

In those islands certain qualities of beauty, certain forms of sensuous loveliness were separated from all the general purposes of life . . . I think that the movement of our thought has more and more so separated certain images and regions of the mind, and that these images grow in beauty as they grow in sterility. . . . Shakespeare leaned, as it were, even as craftsman, upon the general fate of men and nations, had about him the excitement of the playhouse; and all poets, including Spenser in all but a few pages, until our age came, and when it came almost all, have had some propaganda or traditional doctrine to give companionship with their fellows. Had not Matthew Arnold his faith in what he described as the best thought of his generation, Browning his psychological curiosity, Tennyson, as before him Shelley and Wordsworth, moral values that were not aesthetic values? But Coleridge of the "Ancient Mariner" and "Kubla

Khan," and Rossetti in all his writings, made what Arnold has called that "morbid effort," that search for "perfection of thought and feeling, and to unite this to perfection of form," sought this new, pure beauty, and suffered in their lives because of it.[1]

It is a contentious account of the matter, but suggestive, too. Allowing for many differences between the several writers, it is true that Wordsworth, Arnold, Browning, and Tennyson took reality where it appeared to be, in the public domain—the general purposes of life—and proposed only to make the best of it. Poets of the other affiliation did not. If we add Pater and Swinburne to Coleridge, Rossetti, Dowson, Symons, Lionel Johnson, Beardsley, and the early Yeats, we find that they indeed separated from the general purposes of life "certain images and regions of the mind." Those images "grow in beauty as they grow in sterility." The notion was Pater's before Yeats took it up. To grow in sterility is a contradiction in terms, but if we construe sterility in the sense in which Pater uses the word in his major essay on Wordsworth, where it means an intransitive condition or a state of beholding for the sake of beholding and nothing else, we see that this was a feasible choice, though a desperate one. Literature is the better for being in that sense sterile, for not engaging in the transitivity of getting public things done. The writers in Yeats's second tradition elected to live "beyond culture"—Lionel Trilling's phrase with a different generation in view —and they withdrew their credence from the images offered them by the general interests of society. They made for themselves an "adversary life" at a time when official life was deemed to be bourgeois, Protestant, imperial, male, and heterosexual. They did not dissent from these values in every particular, but they felt no loyalty toward the consensus the values implied. Yeats said of those writers that they "must make all out of the privacy of their thought," and that they "suffer from the terrors that pass before shut eyes."

Yeats's phrase in "Ego Dominus Tuus"—"dissipation and despair"—refers to the same writers, men who have "awakened from the common dream." The common dream means acceptance of the generally proposed purposes of life, the ordinary sense of reality as practiced in physical and mechanical work, the axioms of life as conveyed in newspapers and realistic novels. Yeats has in mind chiefly Dowson and Johnson as writers who have awakened from that dream. But if he were to extend his survey beyond these to the entire "tragic generation," he would allude to the antithetical culture denoted by magic, astrology, psychical research, opium-addiction, homosexuality, pornography, solipsism, and the internal capacities of a language freed from the duty of reference. Different indulgences, indeed, but they indicate some of the constituents of an adversary life in Pater's belated day and in the London of Yeats's early career. Not that Pater, Yeats, and their associates engaged in all or many of these practices; some did, some didn't. But they made their sentences and stanzas dally with these motifs, choosing images of desire from the diction they offered. Baudelaire and Gautier were their precursors in this respect, especially in scenes of imagined lesbian love, which provided many heterosexual writers with the bliss of fantasy, imaginary sexual and literary transgression.

Yeats had in mind two ways of being a writer. He found both in Spenser, at once Tudor propagandist and poet of the Bower of Bliss. But the names he attached to each affinity hardly matter; all the better if we think of them a little abstractly. In Victorian literature the Bower of Bliss was French. Writers who withheld credence from the common or civic sense of reality were much taken with French poetry and fiction, and especially with writers deemed to be irregular—Gautier, Baudelaire, Flaubert, Rimbaud. The literature we think of as modern—Mallarmé, Proust, Yeats, Eliot, Valéry, Pound, Joyce—arose not from the values embodied in the major orthodox writers but from those of "the tragic generation" and the writers, mainly French, whom they accepted as masters. Modernism is the art and literature of an adversary relation to the official purposes of late-nineteenth-century society. Its motto is "When in Rome, do as the Greeks."

Henry James's "The Next Time" is a variation on Yeats's theme—the antagonism between the stupid, broad-backed public and the writer who may to his disadvantage be a true artist. Ray Limbert tries, year by dreary year, to write a popular novel because he needs the money; the book must be coarse enough to please the commonest reader. He fails because his imagination will not let him bend low enough to succeed. In the end, and without realizing what he is doing, he turns away from the broad back and consults only his imagination. He gives himself over to the aesthetic imperative, ignoring every other claim upon him. The narrator reports of him in this last phase:

> The great thing was that he was immensely interested and was pleased with the omens. I got a strange stirring sense that he had not consulted the usual ones and indeed that he had floated

away into a grand indifference, into a reckless consciousness of art. The voice of the market had suddenly grown faint and far: he had come back at the last, as people so often do, to one of the moods, the sincerities of his prime. Was he really, with a blurred sense of the urgent, doing something now only for him-self? We wondered and waited—we felt he was a little confused. What had happened, I was afterwards satisfied, was that he had quite forgotten whether he generally sold or not. He had merely waked up one morning again in the country of the blue and had stayed there with a good conscience and a great idea. He stayed till death knocked at the gate.[2]

The novel on which Limbert is working at the end is aptly called *Derogation*; it remains a fragment. The country of the blue is whatever space an imagination consulting its own desires would invent. "The Next Time" is James's dream of not having to write for a living or to compete with journalists and popular novelists. It is not an unmediated vision but one in which the mediations—language, grammar, syntax, diction—don't count as impediments but as the means of one creative possibility after another. Limbert has turned away at the end from Grub Street, as James turned away from the theater and the coarse public that Wells, Shaw, and Bennett so lucratively beguiled.

"Diaphaneitè" was Pater's first country of the blue. He gave it as a talk to the Old Mortality in July 1864, but didn't publish it. He retained much of its spirit and several sentences of its detail for the essay on Winckelmann, a more important occasion, and for the last chapter of *Studies in the History of the Renaissance*. It was published post-humously in *Miscellaneous Studies* (1895), the volume prepared for the publisher by Shadwell.

Pater did not invent the word "diaphaneitè," he merely interfered with it by the eccentric placement of a grave accent, a gesture Shadwell didn't bother to correct. The word came into French in the fourteenth century and English in the seventeenth; in both languages it means the state of being pervious to light. Air, crystal, and shallow water are instances of it. David de Laura has shown that "Diaphaneitè" is much indebted to Arnold's *Essays in Criticism*. Each marks an attempt to develop the concept of culture toward certain images of its embodiment. But Pater is far more inventive than Arnold. Where Yeats needed two rival affiliations, Pater's "Diaphaneitè" distinguishes three types of char-acter. The first is worldly; it coincides with material interests and enjoys their success: it is the character of men who govern. Or, extending the type toward Yeats's discrimination in "The Tragic Generation," it marks the tradition of writers who retain the companionship of their fellows by sharing a common sense of reality. Pater's second type is alien to the first, but related to it by its alienation: it is exemplified by saint, artist, and sage. These people are "out of the world's order," but they work "in and by means of the main current of the world's energy." Their right to exist is readily conceded. Such people are useful to the world: "as if dimly conscious of some great sickness and weariness of heart in itself, it turns readily to those who theorise about its unsoundness." The second type speaks for the conscience of the first and is intermittently allowed to be audible. If it presented a serious risk of undermining the first, it would have to be suppressed. But there is no risk. So the writers in Yeats's "tragic generation" are given space in which to express themselves and to run amok if they wish. Pater says of his two types that in each "a breadth and generality of character is required," presumably because one type lives in the world and the other by the irony of rebuking it. The two are joined in contrast and conflict, statement and counter-statement, assertion and denial.

"Diaphaneitè" projects a third type. It is neither broad nor general but rare:

> It does not take the eye by breadth of colour; rather it is that fine edge of light, where the elements of our moral nature refine themselves to the burning point. It crosses rather than follows the main currents of the world's life.[3]

This is the first intimation of burning with a hard, gem-like flame. Pater protects the exemplars of this type by saying that the world "has no sense fine enough for those evanescent shades"; it cannot classify them or even contemplate them as it contemplates saints and thinkers, moral ideals. In "Winckelmann," "that fine edge of light" becomes "a sharp edge of light" and is ascribed not to the few but to "the supreme Hellenic culture."

This third type may seem to be merely the embodiment of Arnoldian disinterestedness, but it is not. Disinterestedness in Arnold's account is a quality of one's attention to images and objects at large. A good critic silences the dialogue of his mind with itself while he judges particular objects and actions in the light of the best ideas he can find. Arnold recommends this course in *Culture and Anarchy* and *Essays in*

Criticism. The critic should raise his mind above the bias of his standard interests and especially above his preoccupation with himself. He should pay attention to each object as it presents itself, and should discriminate one from another. Disinterestedness is the mark of one who is alert in the world, conscientious, responsible. But Pater's diaphanous type does not observe this duty; it is not concerned with the world, doesn't even prefer one part of life to another. It looks to a higher consideration and "seeks to value everything at its eternal worth." It tries to live *sub specie aeternitatis*. But "tries" is misleading. The distinctive moral quality of this type is simplicity: it is a happy gift of nature, such that it seems to issue from an order of grace; it comes "without any struggle at all." A person of this type treats life in the spirit of art and finds that as he comes nearer to the perfection of his type, "the veil of an outer life not simply expressive of the inward becomes thinner and thinner."

The passage I have quoted from "Diaphaneitè" is also homosexual code. Pater's syntax is peculiar. The subject of the sentence, "It," refers to "another type of character." The first clause is straightforward: "it does not take the eye by breadth of colour." But the next clause doesn't continue describing the type, it identifies it with "that fine edge of light, where the elements of our moral nature refine themselves to the burning point." "Refine themselves," not "are refined," as if this self-refining were spontaneous in the course of such a nature: the type is as elemental as light, and is indistinguishable from its supreme property, "that fine edge of light." But nothing is yet described. The light is not in nature or landscape; it comes into nature when the elements of our moral nature refine themselves to the burning point. Every detail from "that fine edge of light" through "refine themselves" to "the burning point" would be recognized by Pater's Oxford associates as an allusion to the flame of male homosexual love in Plato's *Symposium*. It is recommended by being associated with a grace of nature.

Why are there three types? To maintain difference while removing conflict. Two types or principles make for conflict, but the discrimination of three forces, in the ascending order of spirituality that Pater's triad discloses, permits a vocabulary of evanescence and refinement. "Those evanescent shades" fill up the blanks "between contrasted types of character." Yeats does something similar in "Byzantium," a poem of threes—miracle, bird, handiwork—and of gradations among the three:

Before me floats an image, man or shade,
Shade more than man, more image than a shade; . . .

The order in which we read the words, shade, then man, then image, then shade, is displaced by the different order of adjudication, image more than shade, shade more than man. There is no question of conflict.

"Diaphaneitè" is a difficult essay, mainly because it affronts one's common sense according to which more is better: more life, better life. In Pater's sense of life, more is vulgar. A life is better the more refined it is, the more it dispenses with what the mob deems enrichments. Pater takes a common adjective of plenitude, cancels it, and presents only its trace as supreme value. His terms of praise are lavished on one's readiness to do without: so we have "colourless," "unclassified," "sexless," "impotence," "ineffectual." (In "Winckelmann," "a kind of impotence" is deleted.) Pater is urging his fellows to live in the space between "neither" and "nor," as if they were relics from the classical age "laid open by accident to our alien modern atmosphere."

The type of diaphaneity is represented first by Dante's Beatrice, then by Raphael, "who in the midst of the Reformation and the Renaissance, himself lighted up by them, yielded himself to neither, but stood still to live upon himself. . . ." It is also embodied in the hermaphrodites of Greek sculpture: "the statues of the gods had the least traces of sex." But the strangest instance of the type is Charlotte Corday. Pater's source is the chapter given to her in Carlyle's *The French Revolution*. Hard to see her as diaphanous, but Carlyle presents her as complete, her energy "the spirit that will prompt one to sacrifice himself for his country." More to Pater's point, Carlyle describes Corday as "still": "of beautiful still countenance." Pater quotes the first part of this passage:

What if she, this fair young Charlotte, had emerged from her secluded stillness, suddenly like a Star; cruel-lovely, with half-angelic, half-daemonic splendour; to gleam for a moment, and in a moment be extinguished: to be held in memory, so bright complete was she, through long centuries!—Quitting Cimmerian Coalitions without, and the dim-simmering Twenty-five millions within, History will look fixedly at this one fair Apparition of a Charlotte Corday; will note whither Charlotte moves, how the little Life burns forth so radiant, then vanishes swallowed of the Night.[4]

Marat's assassin, brought out for execution, "wears the same still smile." Pater shows no interest in the deed, but he invokes Corday in Carlyle's image of her: entirely still, complete, her momentary gleam, her extinction, the afterimage of her in our memory. She appears to be the cause of herself.

Gerald Monsman has emphasized the influence of Fichte's transcendental idealism on this aspect of Pater's early work. To the idealist, as Fichte says in the "Second Introduction to the Science of Knowledge," the only positive quality is freedom: "existence, for him, is a mere negation of freedom." The self begins "by an absolute positing of its own existence."[5] To posit oneself and to be are one and the same. Fichte then declares that the self's mode of existence in the world is moral, its duty is to participate as finite being in the Absolute or Divine Idea. As if he anticipated Arnold's concept of culture and proposed an alternative to it, Fichte says:

> In every age, that kind of education and spiritual culture by means of which the age hopes to lead mankind to the knowledge of the ascertained part of the Divine Idea, is the Learned Culture of the age; and every man who partakes in this culture is a Scholar of the age. . . . The true-minded Scholar will not admit of any life and activity within him except the immediate life and activity of the Divine Idea; . . . he suffers no emotion within him that is not the direct emotion and life of the Divine Idea which has taken possession of him. . . . His person, and all personality in the world, have long since vanished from before him, and entirely disappeared in his effort after the realization of the Idea.[6]

This doesn't seem to differ much from Arnold's appeal, in *Culture and Anarchy*, to one's best self, but it does, because "best" in Arnold always means the best that public, historical life has ever produced; it refers to an accredited value, though one that is often forgotten or ignored. Fichte does not appeal to a civic or historical value. Nor does Pater, who retained Fichte's concept of culture and the exemplary character of "the scholar." The difference between Fichte and Pater is that Pater placed the Divine Idea within the self and declared its realization to be the achievement of diaphaneity. "Simplicity in purpose and act," Pater says, "is a kind of determinate expression in dexterous outline of one's personality." "Determinate" is Fichte's word: *Bestimmtheit*. Simplicity is the mark of one's self-culture. Pater speaks of "a mind of taste lighted up by some spiritual ray within." The diaphanous person recognizes by instinct the elements in the world which are his:

> It is just this sort of entire transparency of nature that lets through unconsciously all that is really lifegiving in the established order of things; it detects without difficulty all sorts of affinities between its own elements, and the nobler elements in that order.[7]

"Really" is Pater's answer to Arnold's claim in using the same word, that he always knows the difference between appearance and reality. "Nobler" introduces a rival principle of choosing the things in the world that should interest the scholar. Arnold is again alluded to and refuted. Not only the Arnold of *Essays in Criticism* but of "The Scholar Gypsy." Pater uses a phrase from the poem without naming it or its author. Having described the achievement of diaphaneity, he says, "This intellectual throne is rarely won." In "The Scholar Gypsy" Arnold writes,

> *And then we suffer! and amongst us one,*
> *Who most has suffered, takes dejectedly*
> *His seat upon the intellectual throne;*

Arnold urges the gypsy—who has sequestered himself, "with powers / Fresh, undiverted to the world without"—to remain apart from that world, "with its sick hurry, its divided aims." Pater's diaphanous type is his version of the scholar gypsy, with this difference: that he calls upon him to come into the world and maintain his autonomy there, as the perfection of standing still.

The virtue to be practiced is always stillness, held against the play of circumstances and "one's own confusion and intransparency." It is Pater's highest tribute that Raphael "stood still to live upon himself." Hence "the heroism, the insight, the passion, of this clear crystal nature." Nearly thirty years later, in a lecture at Oxford on August 2, 1892, Pater thought it worthwhile to mention that in the Blenheim Madonna in London, Raphael has given the Baptist "a staff of transparent crystal."[8] Charlotte Corday, too, stood still in her being. It appears not to matter that Raphael painted masterpieces and Corday knifed Marat to death.

But the most complete instance of diaphaneity is not mentioned in Pater's essay. When he came to read Winckelmann in the light of Hegel and Goethe, he noted the signs of his diaphaneity: his sense of affinity to Plato, his "happy, unperplexed dexterity," his "transparent nature, with its simplicity as of the earlier world," the instinctive certitude with which he knew himself. As if to prepare the reader to recognize Winckelmann as a Fichtean scholar, Pater quoted Corday's words before the Convention: one is always a poor executant of conceptions not one's own. *"On exécute mal ce qu'on n'a pas conçu soi-même."*[9] Twenty pages later, on Winckelmann:

> To the criticism of that consummate Greek modelling he brought not only his culture but his temperament. We have seen how definite was the leading motive of that culture; how, like some central root-fibre, it maintained the well-rounded unity of his life through a thousand distractions. Interests not his, not meant for him, never disturbed him. In morals, as in criticism, he followed the clue of instinct, of an unerring instinct.[10]

The source of Winckelmann's instinct is nature, the root-fibre; no point in inquiring further. Not only Winckelmann, but his interests, and the sculpture for which he felt such ardent affinity, speak of diaphaneity: the Panathenaic frieze as "the highest expression of the indifference which lies beyond all that is relative or partial," the Hellenistic bronze in Berlin—the *Boy Praying*—"Fresh, unperplexed, it is the image of man as he springs first from the sleep of nature, his white light taking no colour from any one-sided experience." The boy is "characterless, so far as *character* involves subjection to the accidental influences of life."[11]

The claim Pater makes for diaphanous people could hardly be larger: the world has no use for them till it needs a scapegoat, hero, or sacrificial victim:

> Poetry and poetical history have dreamed of a crisis, where it must needs be that some human victim be sent down into the grave. These are they whom in its profound emotion humanity might choose to send.[12]

The essay ends with a conceit:

> People have often tried to find a type of life that might serve as
> a basement type. The philosopher, the saint, the artist, neither
> of them can be this type; the order of nature itself makes them
> exceptional. It cannot be the pedant, or the conservative, or
> anything rash and irreverent. Also the type must be one dis-
> contented with society as it is. The nature here indicated alone
> is worthy to be this type. A majority of such would be the
> regeneration of the world.[13]

No writer is on oath in his last paragraph, but Pater can hardly expect
to see a society founded on diaphaneity. Yeats's equivalent of that
power, the *sprezzatura* he found described in Castiglione's *Book of the
Courtier*—recklessness, nonchalance—is attributed to a few heroes, aris-
tocratic free spirits, notably Kevin O'Higgins and Robert Gregory, the
Irish airman who foresaw his death and claimed "a lonely impulse of
delight":

> *Some burn damp faggots, others may consume*
> *The entire combustible world in one small room*
> *As though dried straw, and if we turn about*
> *The bare chimney is gone black out*
> *Because the work had finished in that flare.*[14]

But Yeats never envisaged those heroes as exemplars of a basement
type of life. What can Pater have in mind but a vision of human life
beginning again, founding itself on the order of nature as a diaphanous
person would interpret it, free of the dross of history?

"Diaphaneitè" anticipates "Winckelmann" as a defense of homosexuality; it is Pater's dream of a new life, based on superior instinct,
the companionship of beautiful young men, Hellenic in every tone,
each self its own divinity. But the essay may be read in more general
terms. There is a sentence in Edward Thomas's book on Pater which
may be helpful. Pater, Thomas says, "has no sense but vision, and he
can adapt to it all things presented to him."[15] In this light, Pater's three
types correspond to three experiences of seeing. In the first it is gratifying to find the eye brought to a temporary rest by seeing an object,
opaque, unquestionable. This is the rhetoric of realism, a procedure
legitimized by its reference. In the second the eye sees an object, but

equivocally: the relation between the object and the light around it is indeterminate. This is the rhetoric of irony, which establishes itself as superior to what it sees. Irony finds pleasure not in the object to be seen but in itself, the mind in its distancing stance, gathering its force. In the third experience, the order ascending in spirituality, the mind's eye is gratified by seeing things that offer little or no resistance. The eye sees through them: air, blue sky, crystal, clear water. The mind returns to itself after seeing such objects, and feels that the world is permeable. If blue is for James, Stevens, and other writers the color of the imagination, it is because the imagination, in one of its moods, is pleased to find its internal light pass through objects and return to its starting point. In "In Memory of Major Robert Gregory," Yeats claims that the mind by that act of vision returns to itself with doubled might.

In effect, Pater's essay is a plea to young men (Shadwell as supreme instance) to remain young, transparent, free in a world that resents their freedom. "Diaphaneity" is an aesthete's word for freedom of mind and body. Or rather for passion leading to what the broad-backed world calls sin. "Diaphaneitè" is the beginning of Pater's thought as "The Child in the House" is the first expression of his desire. The difference between "Diaphaneitè" and *Studies in the History of the Renaissance* is that in the first, Pater assumes with Fichte that unity of experience follows from the inaugural act of the self, its self-positing; in *Studies* he finds not unity of being or experience but the flow of dispersal and recuperation. Subject and object are vulnerable: we have no choice; we must take the mind as it appears to be, supposedly and for the moment, and the object is forever dissolving under our gaze. "Natural laws we shall never modify," Pater says in the essay on Winckelmann, "embarrass us as they may; but there is still something in the nobler or less noble attitude with which we watch their fatal combinations."[16] The "something" is not further explained, except that each of us finds it in himself and accounts it moral. "Something" is one of Pater's words for diaphaneity; it does not specify any object or quality, but it is still not nothing, it marks the site of a self-engendering. Meanwhile the pathos of "watch" is allowed to sigh. The supreme value is experience itself.

Pater does not consider, in "Diaphaneitè" or elsewhere, the social and political consequence of Fichtean self-positing. One of the lessons learned from *The Origin of Species* was that values could not be based upon a mere biological narrative of species. Darwin's metaphors of development, progress, and refinement could be "translated inward," ascribed to a mind or a spirit considered to some extent free of body. Progress could be ascribed to one's desire, even if not to one's wisdom: one could desire finer feelings and seek occasions for them. Pater found in the history of art, not in politics, instances of Fichtean self-positing, as in those visionary artists who refuse to transcribe the data before them and insist upon the privilege of their own vision. For a politics of self-positing we go to Yeats in one of his moods, with this difference: that Yeats is moved by the energy of self-positing rather than by its participation in a Fichtean Absolute Idea. In "The Statues" Pearse shares with Cuchulainn the energy of subject and will rather than an Idea to be appealed to in default of God.

11

Studies in the History
of the Renaissance

*I have not in these notes attempted the Paterine art of appreciation,
e.g., as in taking the perhaps sole readable paragraph of Pico Mirandola
and writing an empurpled descant.*
—Ezra Pound, "A Shake Down" (1918)

*"Edith," murmured Eeldrop, who had not been attending to this cat-
alogue, "I wonder what has become of her." "Not pleasure, but fulness
of life . . . to burn ever with a hard gem-like flame," those were her
words. What curiosity and passion for experience! Perhaps that flame
has burnt itself out by now. . . ."*

*"Just now you saw that bright flame burning itself out," said
Appleplex, "now you see it guttering thickly, which proves that your
vision was founded on imagination, not on feeling. And the passion for
experience—have you remained so impregnably Pre-Raphaelite as to
believe in that? What real person, with the genuine resources of instinct,
has ever believed in the passion for experience? The passion for experience
is a criticism of the sincere, a creed only of the histrionic."*
—T. S. Eliot, "Eeldrop and Appleplex" (1917)

I

ON THE FIRST PAGE of *Studies in the History of the Renaissance* and
before saying a word about the Renaissance, Pater dissociated
himself from Arnold and Ruskin without naming either of them. It

was not a mere gesture, least of all a gesture of disdain. It was the clearest token of his temper and his professional conduct. Arnold constantly named his opponents, challenged them to show cause why they should ever again be listened to. Ruskin, too, was pugnacious in exposition and debate. He often sounded as if the only concession he would make to an opponent would be to allow him to choose his weapons for the duel. But Pater never argued. He didn't even imply that the issue before him was a matter he would debate if he had more time. He simply made a space for himself a little apart from his opponents. He didn't so much as hint that posterity would decide the issue in his favor.

On this occasion, he forestalled any comparison of his work with Ruskin's by dismissing the attempt "to define beauty in the abstract, to express it in the most general terms," or "to find some universal formula for it." Pater thought the search for such an abstraction or a formula was vain. But he didn't say why, except that he associated it with the search, equally pointless, for a metaphysical principle. An aesthetic principle was just as clearly a will-o'-the-wisp as a religious doctrine. In default of Pater's reasons, I assume he thought that the only thing you could do with an abstract principle or a definition was to apply it on each occasion. The application might give you a sense of power, but it would suppress the differences between one object of interest and another, the crucial issue in criticism. Concern for principle would displace the only consideration worth thinking about, one's impression when looking at a beautiful object in art or nature. More specifically, by removing himself from Ruskin's interests, Pater alerted readers to note the several occasions, including the chapter on Michelangelo, when he would take a strikingly independent line. He had to declare his independence, because otherwise Ruskin occupied the whole space in the criticism of art and, more to the immediate point, enforced a morally contemptuous account of the Renaissance. In *The Stones of Venice* Renaissance art is the work of powerful men rotten with insolence. They forgot that art is justified only if it states a true thing or adorns a serviceable one. Pater knew that Ruskin was the enemy, and that the Slade Professor's appeal to social values and the usefulness of good art had already convinced many solid citizens. Ruskin was a formidable rhetorician. Pater did not tangle with him in Oxford or elsewhere. But he quietly repudiated the inquiry after principles of beauty that Ruskin conducted in *Modern Painters*. A principle, even if you settled for one, deflects you from the only evidence that counts, your experience of looking at a particular work of art. Ruskin was a nuisance, especially when he started denouncing "the 'aesthetic' folly," but you could not get rid of him merely by wishing him gone.

Pater had also to separate himself from Arnold, because Arnold's rhetoric was too strong to be engaged directly, even if Pater felt disposed to attempt it. This insouciant passage effected the separation without throwing down a gauntlet:

> "To see the object as in itself it really is," has been justly said to be the aim of all true criticism whatever; and in aesthetic criticism the first step towards seeing one's object as it really is, is to know one's own impression as it really is, to discriminate it, to realise it distinctly.[1]

The quoted phrase about seeing the object as in itself it really is comes from "On Translating Homer" (1862). Arnold thought well enough of it to repeat it in "The Function of Criticism at the Present Time" (1864). In fact, it simply endorses what Ruskin said in the third volume of *Modern Painters* about "the pathetic fallacy" as self-indulgence. In "Christabel" Coleridge has a red leaf that "dances as often as dance it can." Ruskin thought this a morbid notion, a false idea. Coleridge, according to Ruskin, fancies a life in the leaf, and will, which there is not. Not that Ruskin's intervention was decisive. He got himself into a philosophic mess by claiming that the word "blue" does not mean the sensation caused by a gentian on the human eye but rather the power of producing that sensation, a power always in the gentian whether or not anyone is there to experience it. German idealists disposed of that claim pretty effectively. It doesn't make better sense to ascribe power to a gentian than to the mind that engages with it. Arnold shared Ruskin's "objectivist" prejudice, but he did not present it as part of a serious philosophic argument. Pater pretended to think that he did. Arnold merely appealed to the common reader's assumption that what appears to be an object in the world is precisely what it appears to be. The main thing is to see it clearly and act upon that clarity. Arnold wasn't interested in philosophy unless it had particular bearing upon a moral or social conviction. He wasn't an epistemologist. But he regularly appealed to common sense, even though he knew that this sense was not self-evident and that it mainly arose from the general assumption that scientists knew what they were talking about. In the middle of the nineteenth century it was normally assumed that a thing was real and true if it appeared to present itself without human intervention. Objective truth was whatever didn't need to be further elucidated or interpreted. A real object was one that simply said *Voilà!* A plain style took advantage of this prejudice and pretended to deliver its meaning by saying *Voilà!* Scientific research was designed not only to discover the mysteries of the universe but meanwhile to add to the number of things that could be taken as self-evident. Arnold disputed with scientists, especially when they tried to influence public policy in the matter of education, but he practiced, as they did, the rhetoric of self-evidence. Pater knew how strong Arnold's position was and how effectively he seemed to claim to have no style and no need of one. Like Samuel Butler, Arnold developed a style that appeared to convince by being self-evident. They had scientists to thank for that felicity. Pater knew the rhetoric he had to deal with. In a late essay on Prosper Mérimée he says that Mérimée's style, "simple and unconcerned," keeps the eye "ever on its object"; it lends itself "to an almost phlegmatic discovery of the facts, in all their crude natural colouring, as if he but held up to view, as a piece of evidence, some harshly dyed oriental carpet from the sumptuous floor of the Kremlin, on which blood had fallen."[2] It was audacious of Pater nearly to repeat Arnold's phrase while surrounding it with words of low spiritual life—"unconcerned," "phlegmatic," "harshly"—and the routine rhetorical ploy of "as if he but held up to view. . . ."

In the passage I've quoted from *Studies in the History of the Renaissance* Pater pretended to think that Arnold was writing as a philosopher and implied that he was a naif in that role. His sentence is a quiet snub: "justly" is ironic, the repetition of "as it really is" is parody, "realise" claims to appreciate that the mind, far from coming upon real objects and assenting to their independence, brings into action whatever reality it can know. The displacement of "object" by "impression" is insolent. The "first step" is the only one Pater intends taking. Taking it, he declares every other direction null. He doesn't value the aim that Arnold assigns to knowledge. Notionally there may be a thing "in itself," but Pater doesn't believe that anyone can get behind the impression it has made on him, or rather, the impression his mind has delivered, incited to that activity by a semblance to which it has paid attention. He doesn't believe that anyone can know an object in an independent sense or find it bodied forth against the mind that engages it. He evades a difficult question by not saying "one's own impression *of the object*." As soon as one's mind has produced an impression, the source of the production becomes a minor issue. Even if there is a connection between a presumptive object and a certain impression, Pater doesn't feel enough piety toward the object to maintain its rights; supposedly there was an object, but he has lost interest in it. The mind is its own place. But it is ironic that Pater, having displaced "one's object" in favor of "one's own impression," treats the impression as if it were an object held in place by the attention of the verbs "to know," "to discriminate," and "to realise." "To see" is displaced by "to know," but the evidence for knowing is no better than for seeing. It is a further irony that the degree of realization proposed is a word of apparently objective status: "distinctly." We suppose that Pater, looking at an apparent object, becomes conscious of feeling a certain sensation. He gives it such attention that it becomes a virtual object, which he calls an impression. He stares at it long and hard enough to make it appear to exist. At that point it has superseded the object that provoked it to begin with, and it has fulfilled the mind that set the experience astir. Pater is not yielding up to Arnold the privileged vocabulary of knowledge, but he is disagreeing with him about the object to be seen and known.

The effect of Pater's swerve from Arnold is to define "aesthetic criticism" by releasing it from the criterion of truth and the rhetoric of *mimesis*. Arnold's purpose in trying to see an object "as in itself it really is" was to establish truth as the prime consideration. He deemed truth to be achieved by a mind that looked at an object and saw it clearly, without illusion or fantasy. It was a moral duty to look at it in that way. Pater didn't accept the duty. He consulted a different tradition from that of truth and *mimesis*. His master was Longinus, not Aristotle. He looked at an object under the sign of pleasure, not of truth. He found a particular pleasure in looking at an object, all the more if it was beautiful. His pleasure consisted in the incitement and expression of energy. It was more important to feel alive and free than to join with Arnold in establishing objects as true. Truth in Arnold's sense would have to find other servants.

Maybe Pater should have committed himself to a vocabulary of pleasure and defended it against Aristotelians by reintroducing knowledge and gravity as acts of discrimination, choosing among different pleasures as more or less worth seeking. Instead, he kept to the words of knowledge and consciousness, disputed what was there to be known, and saved the day by drawing each act of consciousness into a psychological context already prepared to receive it. Perhaps unwisely, he remained with the terms of epistemology and ontology and hoped to refine them to his subjective purpose. He was a relativist in this vocabulary, so he refused to deduce a morality, as Arnold did, from the determination to enforce the veridical status of objects. Just as serious as Arnold, Pater, too, is a moralist: how we look at things is an indication of our way of being present in the world. But the only evidence we have that there is an object to be seen is that we have apparently irresistible knowledge of the impression the act of looking at it has produced. Pater's moral sense depends, just as much as Arnold's, on his epistemology, but the only evidence he deems admissible in each case is his impression, not the thing that may be supposed to have provoked it. His morality is the gravity with which he tries to know each impression, as if his further life depended on it. Indeed it does, because he has no other mode of proceeding. Pater is modern, he is not a loyal son of the Enlightenment. He doesn't believe that the crucial project is to master natural processes by coming to understand them. He retains the official vocabulary of knowledge; he makes an issue of knowing, even though he insists that the only thing to be known is a projection of the mind that proposes to know. It is a constrained projection, not a freehand drawing, but even a drawing can't be explained by the character of the object attended to. "What you look hard at seems to look hard at you," Hopkins noted. But that seeming is an illusion of one's attention. Pater's chief concern was his pleasure in feeling alive. He derived his entire sensuous and intellectual life from the experiences that gave him this pleasure. For the moment, in the passage from *Studies in the History of the Renaissance*, Pater is content to make life harder for Arnold. Arnold's readers knew that he wasn't a professional philosopher, didn't need to be, and didn't work hard for precision in philosophic definitions. Pater affected to think that a major philosophic difference separated them, and that he had the better part of the argument. Arnold never pretended to such nicety, any more than his readers did. He has a politics, a morality, and in some loose sense an aesthetic. In the phrase quoted by Pater, Arnold is merely claiming that his morality depends upon his conviction that an object is truly independent of the mind that addresses it. Pater is showing off, making fun of Arnold's gullible character.

But Pater's own position is vulnerable. He thought he could rest upon the entire history of idealism since Descartes, so he never questioned the certitude Descartes claimed for the evidence of inner perception. In "The Idols of Self-Knowledge," Max Scheler made a formidable case against the assumption that the self-evident character of inner perception is superior to that of external perception. So far as I can judge, it did not occur to Pater to consider such a case or to question the self-certainty from which idealism starts. He wrote *Studies in the History of the Renaissance* upon this inherited axiom and also upon Winckelmann's authority, since Winckelmann's description of the Apollo Belvedere in 1764 freely projected his feelings upon the work of art under the guise of finding them there.

As Mrs. Pattison pointed out, Pater should not have called his book *Studies in the History of the Renaissance*. His sense of the Renaissance wasn't historical. He convinced himself that a change had taken place in the thought and feeling of Europe between the end of the twelfth century and the French Revolution. Italian art of the fifteenth century marked a crucial stage in that change. But what he saw was what he wanted to see. The change began as an antinomian assertion within the otherwise imperious orthodoxy of the Middle Ages: it was exemplified by the poetry of Courtly Love, the passion of Abelard and Eloise, the Albigensian heresy, and by any other instances of "the free play of human intelligence around all subjects presented to it." The Renaissance in fifteenth-century Italy indicated the emergence on a large scale of forces in consciousness which first asserted themselves in a few superior minds in the Middle Ages. Images of Greek art and myth gave Renaissance artists access to a far wider and more demanding range of feelings than those that issued from piety and the church.

Pater was interested in history for the images it offered and the feelings it inspired, but in the end the only history he cared about was that of someone's mind; it became historical by being representative of a certain type of feeling. Leonardo's mind was interesting because it was the supreme instance of the Leonardesque way of feeling, it invented a psychological type. The type, as a mode of being, is also a mode of knowledge. Indeed, Pater himself is the most thoroughgoing exemplar, in English writing, of modernity as the movement from "the appropriation of being by knowledge" to "the identification of being and knowledge," or, rather, the identification of being and thinking.[3] This was the only act of the mind that interested him. The great artists he admired were those who took responsibility for their lives and disregarded, so far as possible, what the orthodoxy of their time declared to be real. In the later years of the nineteenth century in England, orthodoxy declared that reality was well enough understood and managed by politics, economics, systems of communication, and the development of a modern industrial society. Pater didn't contest that assumption. But he lived by a different and separate prejudice, that his true life was private, an antinomian mode of being, a style as individual as his prose.

In the chapter on Winckelmann, Pater refers to "the development of the thoughts of man concerning humanity" and to "the growing revelation of the mind to itself."[4] He never doubted the development or that it was a revelation. He is modern because he thinks himself modern, a beneficiary of the growing revelation of the mind to itself. The modern mind knows only its own impressions, but upon that conviction it knows, better than any previous mind, what it can do. It can discover antithetical forms of itself, independent of the forms officially prescribed. "Aesthetic Criticism" is Pater's name for this capacity, when he sets it among the considerations that interest him. He practices it as a special concern for antithetical values, to protect them against the mob of officers.

In "The School of Giorgione," published in October 1877 and included in the third edition of *The Renaissance* (1888), Pater pursued the logic of aesthetics as an antinomian form of intelligence. "Art, then," he says, "is thus always striving to be independent of the mere intelligence, to become a matter of pure perception, to get rid of its responsibilities to its subject or material." The mere intelligence is evidently a rough-and-ready fellow, much like Arnold; attached to subject-matter as if attachment were the only honorable relation to it. Pure perception, on the other and finer hand, is gratified by the union of form and matter in objects that appear to exhibit it. That this union should appear to obtain is Pater's invariable proviso. Appearances are enough:

> . . . the ideal examples of poetry and painting being those in which the constituent elements of the composition are so welded together, that the material or subject no longer strikes the intellect only; nor the form, the eye or the ear only; but form and matter, in their union or identity, present one single effect to the "imaginative reason," that complex faculty for which every thought and feeling is twin-born with its sensible analogue or symbol.[5]

It was cheeky of Pater to use yet another of Arnold's phrases—"imaginative reason," from "Pagan and Medieval Religious Sentiment" (1864)—and to claim, implicitly, to be putting it to superior use, finding the complete union of form and matter in music. Hence "all art constantly aspires towards the condition of music"[6]:

> It is the art of music which most completely realises this artistic ideal, this perfect identification of matter and form. In its consummate moments, the end is not distinct from the means, the form from the matter, the subject from the expression; they inhere in and completely saturate each other; and to it, therefore, to the condition of its perfect moments, all the arts may be supposed constantly to tend and aspire. In music, then, rather than in poetry, is to be found the true type or measure of perfected art.[7]

Pater doesn't mean opera or program music, but pure music: Beethoven's last quartets, say. Music is the supreme art not because it produces the ideal unity of content and form but because it submits the claim of content to that of form. In music, whatever is meant by content has become form. That there is a form is far clearer than that there is or has been a content. The virtuality of art is most complete in a work of music. Every other art is in some degree committed to "mere intelligence": words to old meanings, visible forms to appearances. In music alone the displacement of content by form has been fully accomplished. Listening to music, we are released from our subjection to objects, released, too, from concepts, the imperatives of grammar and syntax. Our lives continue to be real, but that reality is freed from the ball-and-chain of time and place. We are exempted from the law.

The faculty of mind that escapes mere intelligence is reverie. It is day-dreaming only if we oppose it to night-dreaming: we are in control of the one but not the other. Bachelard's *The Poetics of Reverie* is its sufficient elucidation, Yeats's "Among School Children" its sufficient poetry. In any description it is the act of a mind that has released itself for the time being from its attachment to the given world. Pater finds it in Michelangelo's sonnets:

> It was just because Vittoria raised no great passion that the space in his life where she reigns has such peculiar suavity; and the spirit of the sonnets is lost if we once take them out of that dreamy atmosphere in which men have things as they will, because the hold of all outward things upon them is faint and

uncertain. Their prevailing tone is a calm and meditative sweetness. The cry of distress is indeed there, but as a mere residue,
a trace of bracing chalybeate salt, just discernible in the song
which rises like a clear, sweet spring from a charmed space in
his life.[8]

In reverie the mind goes into itself, resorts to desires thwarted in the
world, charms itself to make a space for further charms. It evades the
wear and tear of its worldly existence or the force of habit by diving
under them or musing beyond them: making a rival world of forms
elsewhere.

The aim of reverie is to enable the mind to enjoy its freedom. "To
set the spirit free for a moment" is Pater's phrase for it in the Conclusion,
and to secure that freedom he is willing to try nearly any device. In
"The School of Giorgione" he associates its happiness with play, as if
he were drawing Schiller's theory in the *Letters on the Aesthetic Education
of Man* into Giorgione's practices and forms:

> In these then, the favourite incidents of Giorgione's school,
> music or the musical intervals in our existence, life itself is
> conceived as a sort of listening—listening to music, to the read-
> ing of Bandello's novels, to the sound of water, to time as it
> flies. Often such moments are really our moments of play, and
> we are surprised at the unexpected blessedness of what may
> seem our least important part of time; not merely because play
> is in many instances that to which people apply their own best
> powers, but also because at such times, the stress of our servile
> everyday attentiveness being relaxed, the happier powers in
> things without are permitted free passage, and have their way
> with us.[9]

Pater's solipsism isn't so extreme that it denies the existence of those
"things without." We listen to music, or to the music of what happens,
but we don't claim to have composed it. It is enough for Pater that the
individual mind is necessary for the production of things, and that
"things without" come into presence—into one's presence—only when
that mind enables them by paying attention. Forms which we have not
invented are given to us, as if a grace in their appearance responded to
the grace of our disposition in waiting for them to appear. In the
Conclusion again:

Every moment some form grows perfect in hand or face; some
tone on the hills or the sea is choicer than the rest; some mood
of passion or insight or intellectual excitement is irresistibly real
and attractive to us,—for that moment only. Not the fruit of
experience, but experience itself, is the end.[10]

The means is the end, while the going is good. Play is Pater's name,
as it is Schiller's, for the mind in this state of greater freedom than
usual. For this satisfaction, absolute freedom is not required.

If art is the substitution of an image for being, it follows that the
substitution is effected even in a naturalistic novel, where it is not
perhaps intended and we least advert to it. A represented object, as
Levinas says, by the very fact of its becoming an image, is no longer
the object represented: this image is not a pipe or the tangle of Neiera's
hair. What it is, Pater finds difficulty in saying. At one point in the
chapter on Winckelmann he drives himself into the vain sublimity of
claiming that Greek sculpture, having removed from images of man
the mere accidents of his life, discloses his divinity:

> In proportion as the art of sculpture ceased to be merely dec-
> orative, and subordinate to architecture, it threw itself upon
> pure form. It renounces the power of expression by lower or
> heightened tones. In it, no member of the human form is more
> significant than the rest; the eye is wide, and without pupil; the
> lips and brow are hardly less significant than hands, and breasts,
> and feet. But the limitation of its resources is part of its pride:
> it has no backgrounds, no sky or atmosphere, to suggest and
> interpret a train of feeling; a little of suggested motion, and
> much of pure light on its gleaming surfaces, with pure form—
> only these. And it gains more than it loses by this limitation to
> its own distinguishing motives; it unveils man in the repose of
> his unchanging characteristics. That white light, purged from
> the angry, bloodlike stains of action and passion, reveals, not
> what is accidental in man, but the tranquil godship in him, as
> opposed to the restless accidents of life.[11]

Here the rhetorical kinship of "repose," "unchanging," "tranquil,"
"purged," and "white" enhances the felicity of a quiet life to the point
at which only one's godship, not one's humanity, can account for it.

In the later years of the nineteenth century the cult of Greek sculpture, especially when Arnold and other critics emphasized the repose of Greek forms and the control over experience to which that repose testified, encouraged many people to think of God as unchanging Man. If with Wallace Stevens we say that God and the imagination are one, who are we who say it, and by what vanity do we murmur the appeasing words?

At the end of the chapter on Winckelmann, Pater brings together several of these considerations. His theory of art—it is Bacon's theory, too, and Sidney's—is a theory of its fictiveness: the merit of a work of art is that for as long as we give our minds to it we are released from the pressure of worldly forces. Impressed by modern science, Pater asks, in effect, Is there freedom, despite Darwin? Or is there at least a feasible illusion of freedom, as in Goethe and Hugo?

Pater doesn't question or describe the status of that illusion. How valuable can it be, since we know it's an illusion? Another question he doesn't ask is, What can one's consciousness do, given that it appears to be unable to change anything in the world and can't even claim stability or identity for itself? But the question is implicit in the particular claim Pater makes: that the mind can appease itself by producing, as in art, images of desire and its satisfaction. In Pater's time, much thinking came to little more than this. Sharon Cameron has observed, in her *Thinking in Henry James*, that James is constantly complaining of being browbeaten by cultural forces so crude that they don't allow any room for consciousness; but, in fact, James embraces his embattled state so as to free himself of "the given, to banish it, and to substitute for what is there what is *wanted* to be there." But it doesn't follow, either in James or in Pater, that "power is a consequence of the ability of consciousness to dominate objects."[12] One's consciousness produces the illusion that it dominates objects, and the illusion lasts as long as one's attention holds. After that, the objects go their merry, crass way. Pater's claim to "deal with the conditions of modern life" means only that he evades their obduracy by seeming to rearrange them, making new semblances more congenial than the ones that beset us. What else can art do? Nothing, in sober fact. But the little that art can do is enough. It is foolish to make a grander claim for it.

It follows from Pater's theory of fictiveness that art is best when it minds its own business. It has no moral design upon us. Nor should we look for a message in it:

In its primary aspect, a great picture has no more definite message for us than an accidental play of sunlight and shadow for a few moments on the wall or floor: is itself, in truth, a space of such fallen light, caught as the colours are in an Eastern carpet, but refined upon, and dealt with more subtly and exquisitely than by nature itself.[13]

The value of a work of art is that it is itself and has become itself by an act of genius in the spirit of freedom. Toward the demands of the world, art declares itself neutral. Like those angels to whom Pater refers in his chapter on Botticelli, angels "who, in the revolt of Lucifer, were neither for God nor his His enemies," art doesn't take sides; it is content to declare its independence. In the same chapter Pater describes Botticelli in this aspect:

So just what Dante scorns as unworthy alike of heaven and hell, Botticelli accepts, that middle world in which men take no side in great conflicts, and decide no great causes, and make great refusals. He thus sets for himself the limits within which art, undisturbed by any moral ambition, does its most sincere and surest work.[14]

To work undisturbed by any moral ambition is itself a moral ambition. I return to this question later. Pater's position is consistent with his antinomianism: the artist is neither for nor against the law, he stands aside from it. (But there is more to be said on this theme.)

It may be useful to bring several considerations together at this point and indicate what form Pater's aesthetic takes. He starts with consciousness or imagination, which like a good idealist he takes to mean a form of surplus energy, the mind when it is free of any local or instrumental duty. The world the mind has to confront is material and requires a materialist description, but the mind is a spiritual capacity. The purpose of consciousness, in its creative or projective character, is to enjoy itself. It does this either by floating free of the given world or by displacing the apparent objects to which it pays attention. By doing this, it feels free, enjoys for a while the experience of being released from attendance upon mere subject-matter. Contemplation is one name for this experience. It is not passive; it does not take dictation from the object it contemplates. Its grammatical tense is the present, since the past is deemed to be gathered into the present. While there is no strong inclination to long for a future, the images the mind projects are deemed to be better than those in the world in front of it, and therefore correspond to hope and a hypothetical future in which it will be realized. Meanwhile the present tense is an archetype of experience, its duration need not be specified. It features *kairos*, the time of value and revelation, rather than *chronos*, one thing after another, in Yeats's phrase "the cracked tune that Chronos sings." The mind enjoys the conviction of its power in the conditions it has prescribed for itself. These are clarified by Freud's statement in *Totem and Taboo* that only in the realm of art has our culture accepted that consciousness is omnipotent—as in music, for Pater and Schopenhauer the ideal art, far purer than words. Music is content with acoustic presence, and with *ascesis* as its formal obligation.

Beauty, as Schiller says in the *Kallias Letters*, is "freedom in illusion." It follows that genius is an "alter deus," creator of an antinomian world, also that what the artist creates is itself to be inspected as if it had some of the qualities of the world it displaced. Pater's sentences ask to be read as if they wanted to be looked at, not merely to be understood. They, too, are in an antinomian relation to the truth they hardly bother to convey. The antinomian truth, evident in every phrase and clause, in every qualifying phrase that postpones conclusion, is the labor that went into their production; it is not the sense to which an impatient reader is inclined to reduce them.

II

A paragraph in the book on the Renaissance shows the three main motifs upon which Pater proceeds as an aesthetic critic:

> One of the strongest characteristics of that outbreak of the reason and the imagination, of that assertion of the liberty of the heart, in the middle age, which I have termed a medieval Renaissance, was its antinomianism, its spirit of rebellion and revolt against the moral and religious ideas of the time. In their search after the pleasures of the senses and the imagination, in their care for beauty, in their worship of the body, people were impelled beyond the bounds of the Christian ideal; and their love became sometimes a strange idolatry, a strange rival religion. It was the return of that ancient Venus, not dead, but only hidden for a

time in the caves of the Venusberg, of those old pagan gods still
going to and fro on the earth, under all sorts of disguises. And
this element in the middle age, for the most part ignored by
those writers who have treated it preeminently as the "Age of
Faith"—this rebellious and antinomian element, the recognition
of which has made the delineation of the middle age by the
writers of the Romantic school in France, by Victor Hugo for
instance in *Notre-Dame de Paris*, so suggestive and exciting—is
found alike in the history of Abelard and the legend of Tann-
häuser. More and more, as we come to mark changes and distinctions of temper in what is often in one all-embracing
confusion called the middle age, that rebellion, that sinister claim
for liberty of heart and thought, comes to the surface. The
Albigensian movement, connected so strangely with the history
of Provençal poetry, is deeply tinged with it. A touch of it makes
the Franciscan order, with its poetry, its mysticism, its "illu-
mination," from the point of view of religious authority, justly
suspect. It influences the thoughts of those obscure prophetical
writers, like Joachim of Flora, strange dreamers in a world of
flowery rhetoric of that third and final dispensation of a "spirit
of freedom," in which law shall have passed away.[15]

Antinomianism is crucial. I must stay with it. Pater had an interest in
finding, below the surface of an apparently unified society, intimations
of visionary dissent. In his own time, while he acknowledged that
official society moved on its metaled ways—imperial, expansionist,
mildly Christian, ardent for commerce and industry, the manly virtues,
heterosexuality, the containment of women in obedience—he hoped to
take the harm out of these certitudes by making them doubt themselves.
He had no thought of winning but of thwarting their complacency.

The second motif arises with Venus. Pater received from Gautier
and, through him, from Heine's essay "Les Dieux en exil" (1853), the
notion that the pagan gods, at the time of the triumph of Christianity
in the third century, took flight and hid themselves on earth under
various disguises. Some went to Egypt, "where for greater security
they assumed the forms of animals"; some to Germany, where they
hired themselves out as woodcutters. Apollo "seems to have been content to take service under graziers, and as he had once kept the cows
of Admetus, so he lived now as a shepherd in Lower Austria." Pater
recurs to this motif in several chapters of *The Renaissance*. He wrote two

stories, "Apollo in Picardy" (1893) and "Denys L'Auxerrois" (1886), to set his imagination playing further upon the survival of the pagan gods. In *Plato and Platonism* and other books he saw their survival as an instance of the transmigration of souls. The matter was of historical interest, too, since he presented Pico della Mirandola as one who tried "to reconcile Christianity with the ideas of paganism." In the *Doni* Madonna in the Tribune of the Uffizi, Pater notes, "Michelangelo actually brings the pagan religion, and with it the unveiled human form, the sleepy-looking fauns of a Dionysiac revel, into the presence of the Madonna, as simpler painters had introduced there other products of the earth, birds or flowers, while he has given to that Madonna herself much of the uncouth energy of the older and more primitive "Mighty Mother.'" The chief merit of the Italian Renaissance to Pater was that its masters remembered the gods of an older dispensation even while celebrating the emblems of Christianity. They did not forget the images of an antinomian force, defeated or not, while they took the patronage of popes and bishops and decorated the church of Christ.

The survival of the pagan gods and the rise, in the middle years of the nineteenth century, of the historic sense were compatible motifs to Pater. He was much interested, too, in German and English anthropology. These pursuits allowed him to believe that nothing is ever lost; no feeling, no desire that has been part of human life, is ever entirely forgotten. They also enabled him to think of modernity as a critical relation to all that has been. We need not feel oppressed by the accumulation of historic images; the historic sense lets us discriminate between them. The idea of the gods in exile, hiding themselves perhaps for centuries and then turning up, still disguised, in medieval or modern France or Italy was one of Pater's favorite fancies. Anthropology allowed him to entertain it. The historic sense came later, and disposed those images in categories. But Pater took pleasure in the idea that adepts of modernity could have recourse to the whole experience of seemingly gone times. That is why Leonardo's Lady Lisa is older than the rocks among which she sits and, like the vampire, has been dead many times and learned the secrets of the grave. She is a pagan god in exile. That is why her smile is as it is: because her knowledge, at every phase of its acquisition, has been antinomian to the official knowledge of its day, the knowledge that has acted as power in forming a society to enforce it. In her beauty, as Pater describes it, "all the thoughts and experience of the world have etched and moulded there, in that which they have of power to refine and make expressive the outward form, the animalism of Greece, the lust of Rome, the mysticism of the middle age with its spiritual ambition and imaginative loves, the return of the Pagan world, the sins of the Borgias."[16] This fancy is just as radical as Nietzsche's in "The Use and Abuse of History." The difference is that Nietzsche recommends that we seek a past from which we may spring, rather than that past from which we seem to have derived. He is more ardent for a future than Pater is. Pater is more concerned to posit an adversary knowledge, and therefore an adversary being, as a quiet rebuke to the certitude with which modern orthodoxy acts in the world.

This motif is sustained by another one, the reference to Joachim of Flora. The play of words from "Flora" to "flowery" is in doubtful taste, but Pater took Joachim very seriously. Whatever he knew of him—of Joachim of Fiore, to give him his proper name—he appears to have got from Michelet and Renan. Joachim (*circa* 1135–1202) had a triune theology of Father, Son, and Holy Ghost, but he was heretical in separating the three and giving each a distinctive historical and moral destiny. Michelet's *History of France* has this redaction of Joachimism:

There are three ages, three orders of persons among the faithful. The first have been called to the work of fulfilling the Law; the second, to the work of the Passion; the last, who come from both, have been elected for the Freedom of contemplation. It is that which Scripture attests to when it says: "Where the Spirit of the Lord resides, there is Freedom." The Father imposed the work of the Law, which is fear and servitude; the Son, the work of Discipline, which is wisdom; the Holy Spirit offers Freedom, which is love.

To this, Michelet adds on his own behalf:

This great teaching was the alpha of the Renaissance. It circulates from that time on as an eternal Gospel. Many were to teach it in flames. And Jean of Parma . . . boldly declared that "the doctrine of Joachim is better than the doctrine of Christ."[17]

More accommodating than the doctrine of Christ, certainly, because it allows for a fancied supersession of Father by Son and of Son by Holy Ghost, and a suave progression from Law through Discipline to Freedom, from fear through wisdom to love. Pater felt no misgiving in thinking of the official Middle Ages, under the doctrine of the church, as fear; of the Renaissance as the art of breadth, wisdom, reconciliation of pagan and Christian images; and of modernity as characterized by the relative spirit, the supersession of religion by art, and the emergence at least in vision of flawless humanity.

Marjorie Reeves and Warwick Gould have shown, in their *Joachim of Fiore and the Myth of the Eternal Evangel in the Nineteenth Century* (1987), that Pater's Joachimism is developed in *Marius the Epicurean*, but that the third dispensation, when Marius reaches it, leads beyond itself to Catholicism. Marius dies on the brink of that revelation.

12

"Leonardo da Vinci"

"*For OUR LADY OF THE ROCKS by Leonardo da Vinci*"

Mother, is this the darkness of the end,
   The Shadow of Death? and is that outer sea
   Infinite imminent Eternity?
And does the death-pang by man's seed sustained
In Time's each instant cause thy face to bend
   Its silent prayer upon the Son, while He
   Blesses the dead with His hand silently
To His long day which hours no more offend?

Mother of grace, the pass is difficult,
   Keen as these rocks, and the bewildered souls
     Throng it like echoes, blindly shuddering through.
    Thy name, O Lord, each spirit's voice extols,
     Whose peace abides in the dark avenue
Amid the bitterness of things occult.
               —Dante Gabriel Rossetti

Leonardo's almost unholy dame with the folded hands . . .
   —Henry James, *A Small Boy and Others*

DURING THE LONG VACATION of 1869 Pater applied himself to his essay on Leonardo: it was published in the *Fortnightly Review* on November 1. His method was the one he used in all his essays on artists: he recalled as vividly as possible the few paintings and drawings he had seen, and read whatever biographical and descriptive accounts of Leonardo he could find in the Bodleian, the Brasenose library, the

Queen's College library, and the Taylor Institution library. He was not learned in the history of art or in any of the subjects he took up —Greek myths, English poetry, Greek philosophy. He was not an original thinker: virtually every idea he expressed can be traced to a source in English, French, or German writers. He is a force in the criticism of these subjects because he devised a distinctive style of writing about them: the Pateresque, a new color in the palette. For the essay on Leonardo he resorted to Vasari, Amoretti, Goethe, Clément, Gautier, Michelet, Houssaye, Quinet, Rio, Shelley, Stendhal, and Swinburne, picking a notion here, an image there. He did not claim to be a scholar of art, but an "aesthetic critic" working upon art, mythology, and literature. So he took Vasari's word for the biographical account of Leonardo, starting with his apprenticeship to Verrocchio. He didn't remark the possibility, which John Pope-Hennessy has now considered, that Leonardo's first training was in Pollajuolo's studio and that he came to Verrocchio in full possession of his craft.

Nor was Pater a "practical critic," if we think of Eliot, Richards, Empson, Kenneth Burke, and R. P. Blackmur as exemplars of that form of attention. As an aesthete, Pater should have been a close reader, but he wasn't. He could hardly have been a formalist, because formalism entails describing a work of art as an autonomous object. To Pater, an object could not be autonomous, except notionally and to begin with. Consideration of a painting might start by granting it some degree of independence, as if the mind attending to it were disinterested, but gradually the mind exerted its power and the work of art had to appear to give up its claim to self-possession. The independence ascribed to the painting was merely hypothetical or heuristic, a starting-point from which Pater ranged more or less freely. The starting-point might appease ordinary readers and satisfy the claim of common sense, but such gratification was brief, as it always is when an idealist begins to write.

Pater concerned himself, then, not with objects, works of art, but with the types of feeling they embodied. If you looked at five or six or a dozen works by the same artist or from his studio, you would gradually recognize a distinctive mode of feeling, an unusual sense of life, a bias of consciousness. For you, that would be the meaning of the paintings and the significance of the artist. If art entails the substitution of an image for being, as Levinas has argued, it is possible to effect a further displacement, converting the image into the particular structure of feeling from which it has supposedly issued. Ontology is displaced by psychology. This is Pater's form of attention. Even if the painting he is looking at is not the artist's work but someone else's who felt the enchantment of his style, no matter. The type of feeling may still be recognized in the artist's vicinity. In the essay on Leonardo, most of the paintings Pater attributed to him are not his but arise within the range of his style and might be mistaken for his work. Pater suspected and sometimes knew that this was the case—that the *Madonna of the Balances* was not a Leonardo—but he was not perturbed; he was casual in putting like beside nearly like. He kept himself reasonably up to date with the scholars, but that didn't secure him against error, against thinking that the *Last Supper* was painted in oil, or that the *Medusa* in the Uffizi was Leonardo's work.

Pater had no ambition in scholarship. Referring to Leonardo, he says that "for others remain the editing of the thirteen books of his manuscripts, and the separation by technical criticism of what in his reputed works is really his, from what is only half his, or the work of his pupils." What remains for Pater is a loftier mission:

> But a lover of strange souls may still analyse for himself the impression made on him by those works, and try to reach through it a definition of the chief elements of Leonardo's genius.[1]

Through it, the impression; not through them, the paintings and drawings. The sentence would have been good enough without the insistent "through it," but "it," reaching back for "impression," relegates "those works" to the status of evidence or illustration. In "analyse" Pater claims not to be a mere impressionist but to apply quasi-scientific criteria to his perception. He examines what he is sure of, his feelings in the presence of certain paintings. But the phrase that identifies his whole activity in criticism is "a lover of strange souls." "Souls" doesn't imply a theology but a humanist claim to spiritual capacity. "Strange" is supposed to make the reader think of genius.

Or of one form of genius. In the middle of the nineteenth century Leonardo was widely regarded as a bizarre, compelling figure, site of conflicting impulses, the *Medusa* his most revealing work. Pater's description of that painting is brief, probably because he was anticipated by Shelley's poem "On the Medusa of Leonardo da Vinci," with its references to beauty and horror, "the agonies of anguish and of death." It is a subject, Pater says, "that may well be left to the beautiful verses of Shelley." But not until Pater has associated the painting with "the fascination of corruption" and described the color of Medusa's face:

> The hue which violent death always brings with it is in the features; features singularly massive and grand, as we catch them inverted, in a dexterous foreshortening, crown foremost, like a great calm stone against which the wave of serpents breaks.[2]

If the Medusa's forehead is like a stone—and Pater's addition of "calm" is excessive—it is difficult to see the snakes as making a wave. Their horror consists in the degree to which each of them is differentiated and the heaped repulsiveness of that differentiation. "About the dainty lines of the cheek a rabbit creeps unheeded," Pater thought in the *Fortnightly* essay, but he soon and rightly changed his mind, deleted the reference, and transferred his attention to the bat which in all later versions "flits unheeded."

But it was Swinburne, more than Shelley, Michelet, Taine, or Gautier, who showed Pater one of the styles in which an impression of Leonardo's paintings could be described. Swinburne brought together most of the intimations which constitute the French Leonardo of the nineteenth century, precursor to Gautier, Baudelaire, Huysmans, and the literature of Decadence. Fascination, the experience to which Baudelaire's essays and poems testify most memorably, is the word to which Pater keeps returning. Leonardo is mage, sorcerer, adept of occult practice and divination; during the years in Milan he is surrounded by "brilliant sins and exquisite amusements." Swinburne is Pater's mentor in this lurid emphasis. In July 1868 Swinburne published in the *Fortnightly Review* "Notes on Designs of the Old Masters at Florence," a report on his visit to the Uffizi and the Pitti in the spring of 1864:

> Of Leonardo the samples are choice and few; full of that indefinable grace and grave mystery which belong to his slightest and wildest work. Fair strange faces of women full of dim doubt and faint scorn; touched by the shadow of an obscure fate; eager and weary as it seems at once, pale and fervent with patience or passion; allure and perplex the eyes and thoughts of men.[3]

Thinking of Leonardo and Michelangelo, Swinburne says,

The least thought of these men has in it something intricate and enormous, faultless as the formal work of their triumphant art must be. All mysteries of good and evil, all wonders of life and death, lie in their hands or at their feet. They have known the causes of things, and are not too happy. The fatal labour of the world, the clamour and hunger of the open-mouthed all-summoning grave, all fears and hopes of ephemeral men, are indeed made subject to them, and trodden by them underfoot; but the sorrow and strangeness of things are not lessened because to one or two their secret springs have been laid bare and the courses of their tides made known; refluent evil and good, alternate grief and joy, life inextricable from death, change inevitable and insuperable fate.[4]

These unclashing opposites—good and evil, life and death, fears and hopes, grief and joy—do not apprehend anything in the world apart from the right Swinburne claimed to manage them. After a while the platitudes—change inevitable and insuperable fate—cease to disturb his distinctive tone. The sole idea in the passage, that Leonardo and Michelangelo deal with their themes by treading them underfoot, is enough to make a show of justification for the grandiloquence with which Swinburne recites his commonplaces. The rhythm calls out our irony and yet survives its attention. Pater acknowledged his debt to Swinburne's essay, but did not say what in it especially he admired.[5]

His own idea was the development of a commonplace which he shared with the neo-French image of Leonardo, especially with Shelley, Baudelaire, Gautier, and Swinburne:

Curiosity and the desire of beauty—these are the two elementary forces in Leonardo's genius; curiosity often in conflict with the desire of beauty, but generating, in union with it, a type of subtle and curious grace.[6]

The curiosity is directed upon nature—water and rock—and upon human faces. When it came in conflict with the desire of beauty, "it tended to make him go too far below that outside of things in which art really begins and ends."[7]

This is a surprising thing for Pater to say. He added the "really" in the last edition he prepared, that of 1893. So the general statement is retained from 1869 to the end of his life. It is hard to see how it is compatible with his insistence on the mind's productive role in experience, unless he means that while art begins and ends in "that outside of things," it may occupy the space between by pursuing more subjective interests. But this is implausible. A better explanation may be found in the essay on Winckelmann, where he has the same beginning and ending:

> But take a work of Greek art,—the Venus of Melos. That is in no sense a symbol, a suggestion, of anything beyond its own victorious fairness. The mind begins and ends with the finite image, yet loses no part of the spiritual motive. This motive is not lightly and loosely attached to the sensuous form, as its meaning to an allegory, but saturates and is identical with it. The Greek mind had advanced to a particular stage of self-reflexion, but was careful not to pass beyond it. In oriental thought there is a vague conception of life everywhere, but no true appreciation of itself by the mind, no knowledge of the distinction of man's nature: in its consciousness of itself, humanity is still confused with the fantastic, indeterminate life of the animal and vegetable world. In Greek thought, on the other hand, the "lordship of the soul" is recognised; that lordship gives authority and divinity to human eyes and hands and feet; inanimate nature is thrown into the background. But just there Greek thought finds its happy limit; it has not yet become too inward; the mind has not yet learned to boast its independence of the flesh; the spirit has not yet absorbed everything with its emotions, nor reflected its own colour everywhere. It has indeed committed itself to a train of reflexion which must end in defiance of form, of all that is outward, in an exaggerated idealism. But that end is still distant: it has not yet plunged into the depths of religious mysticism.[8]

But this, too, is odd. If the Greek mind found its happy limit, why did it commit itself to modern idealism and morbid self-consciousness? The limit can't have been as happy as Pater says if it forced the mental traveler to catch that expensive train. The insecurity of the argument is in the phrase about the defiance of form. Normally in Pater's writings form is what matter sometimes has the good fortune to become, as in a work of art or a beautiful face. In *Plato and Platonism*, considering Plato's novelty, Pater writes:

Nothing but the life-giving principle of cohesion is new: the new perspective, the resultant complexion, the expressiveness which familiar thoughts attain by novel juxtaposition. In other words, the *form* is new. But then, in the creation of philosophical literature, as in all other products of art, form, in the full signification of that word, is everything, and the mere matter is nothing.[9]

But in the essay on Winckelmann form is "all that is outward," the visible surface of a thing before it has caught the artist's attention.

Clearly, but not clearly enough, Pater is searching for his own happy limit, a dynamic accord of subject and object. Or better still, a state of feeling in which a distinction need not be adverted to between subject and object. Ideally, each of these words could be regarded as unnecessary or even factitious. Failing that, one might settle for the words but use them strategically, as if in bad faith. T. S. Eliot worked with this possibility in his early poems and, discursively, in his dissertation on F. H. Bradley. To describe immediate experience, as he put it, one should use words which offer only a surreptitious suggestion of subject or object:

> If we say presentation, we think of a subject to which the presentation is present as an object. And if we say feeling, we think of it as the feeling of a subject about an object. . . . It may accordingly be said that the real situation is an experience which can never be wholly defined as an object nor wholly enjoyed as a feeling, but in which any of the observed constituents may take on the one or the other aspect.[10]

So in "Preludes" the morning "comes to consciousness" because someone's feeling is an observed constituent of the experience.

Pater isn't as good a student as Eliot; he doesn't try to work such things out; he settles for subject and object and lets his mood confirm or confound the particular issue. Normally in the end he sacrifices the object to the subject, because he has an interest in seeing the object sublimed in form, and form as the visible sign of the mind's activity in that medium. But he wants to postpone the end. Meanwhile he responds most vividly to artists who, like Leonardo and Botticelli, play fast and loose with appearances. In the essay on Leonardo he remarks, conflating several comments by Clément, Taine, and Gautier, that the hair of the *St. John the Baptist* is a woman's hair, the face like that of a nearby Bacchus, and the whole painting a profane work:

> We recognise one of those symbolical inventions in which the ostensible subject is used, not as matter for definite pictorial realisation, but as the starting-point of a train of sentiment, subtle and vague as a piece of music. No one ever ruled over the mere *subject* in hand more entirely than Leonardo, or bent it more dexterously to purely artistic ends. And so it comes to pass that though he handles sacred subjects continually, he is the most profane of painters; the given person or subject, Saint John in the Desert, or the Virgin on the knees of Saint Anne, is often merely the pretext for a kind of work which carries one altogether beyond the range of its conventional associations.[11]

"Mere" and "merely" show that Pater is either dismissing the rights of subject-matter or endorsing Leonardo's high hand in dealing with it. As in the later essay on Style, there are disciplines to be observed, but genius is above the law; it keeps faith only with itself. In the sentence on the *St. John the Baptist*, Pater shows no misgiving in the word "bent"—"or bent it more dexterously to purely artistic ends"—nor does he allow us to feel that Leonardo might have thought twice about the force exerted. A great artist bends the visible world to his will. Things that happen to exist are valued, but not for their existence: it is their being available to the artist's attention that makes them valuable. They enjoy the privilege of having been looked at by a great will, a mind of genius. "And so it comes to pass" glances at a common phrase in the New Testament, but without the misgiving that might in another writer attend the glance.

Pater's essay has been mocked. George Moore made fun of its Mona Lisa, the *femme fatale* diving in deep seas. He said that Lisa's enigmatic smile was sufficiently accounted for by the foolish things she heard tourists in the Louvre say about her. Donald Stauffer once pretended to think that Pater hadn't seen the painting but only an engraving of it, and that he conflated his impression of the engraving with his recollection of Dürer's *Melancholia*. A joke, surely: Pater and his sisters spent most of the summer of 1864 in Paris; there is no reason to suppose that he avoided going to the Louvre or seeing a painting already famous. Valéry, too, turned his irony upon the smile. But his *Introduction to the Method of Leonardo da Vinci* is chiefly valuable as an introduction to the method of Paul Valéry; it has little to do with Leonardo. Freud's essay on Leonardo is a family romance, more informative about Freud than about Leonardo; but it refers to Pater's essay and develops the notion that the smile is Leonardo's tribute to his mother.

The most charming irony ever turned upon Pater's set piece is Joyce's. Start with this passage from 1 Corinthians 10:11:

> Now all these things happened unto them for ensamples: and they are written for our admonition, upon whom the ends of the world are come.

Now one of Pater's sentences about Lisa:

> Hers is the head upon which "all the ends of the world are come," and the eyelids are a little weary.

The change from "whom" to "which," with "head" for its reference, makes a mild obscenity possible. Pater doesn't intend such a thing. But in the "Lestrygonians" chapter of *Ulysses* Joyce has Leopold Bloom overhear the ethereal poet George Russell reporting what I assume was a dream to his disciple Lizzie Twigg:

> —Of the twoheaded octopus, one of whose heads is the head upon which the ends of the world have forgotten to come while the other speaks with a Scotch accent. The tentacles. . . .

Russell is as innocent as Pater. Poet, beard and bicycle with a listening woman at his side, passes by the gate of Trinity College and Bloom confounds phrases already self-confounded:

> What was he saying? The ends of the world with a Scotch accent. Tentacles: octopus. Something occult: symbolism.[12]

We are returned to Pater. Something occult, indeed.

13

"Botticelli"

"For Spring by Sandro Botticelli"

What masque of what old wind-withered New-Year
Honors this Lady? Flora, wanton-eyed
For birth, and with all flowrets prankt and pied:
Aurora, Zephyrus, with mutual cheer
Of clasp and kiss: the Graces circling near,
'Neath bower-linked arch of white arms glorified:
And with those feathered feet which hovering glide
O'er Spring's brief bloom, Hermes the harbinger.

Birth-bare, not death-bare yet, the young stems stand
This Lady's temple-columns: o'er her head
Love wings his shaft. What mystery here is read
Of homage or of hope? But how command
Dead Springs to answer? And how question here
These mummers of that wind-withered New-Year?
>   —Dante Gabriel Rossetti

A FRAGMENT ON SANDRO BOTTICELLI" was published in the *Fortnightly Review* on August 1, 1870. In a letter of November 28, 1881, to Henry J. Nicoll, Pater said he believed the essay was "the first notice in English of that old painter," and that "it preceded Mr. Ruskin's lectures on the same subject by I believe two years."[1] "By more than a year" would have been an accurate and sufficient claim. In 1883 Ruskin maintained, without justification or delicacy, that he had been the first to discern and teach the greatness of Turner, Tintoretto, Luini, Botticelli, and Carpaccio. In fact, as Donald L. Hill has noted, Botticelli had already received decent appreciation in Crowe and Cavalcaselle's *A New History of Painting in Italy* (1864). But the significance of the attention Pater gave Botticelli was that he compared him with Ingres and, in 1873, placed him in the company of Luca Della Robbia, Michelangelo, and Leonardo da Vinci. It was not necessary to insist on the qualitative differences between these: sufficient that Botticelli was given the status of their fellowship.

The essay is brief, taking up only six pages of the *Review*. It was written under difficulties. Pater had little to work on. He had Vasari, as usual, and now Crowe and Cavalcaselle, but there were few paintings to be seen. Pater saw *The Birth of Venus* on his first visit to Florence in the summer of 1865. Several of the paintings long attributed to Botticelli, including the Palmieri altarpiece, are no longer thought to be his. Pater didn't know the drawings, illustrations of *The Divine Comedy*, that were then in Hamilton Palace. Nor had he any secure means of distinguishing between the several Madonnas, some of them by Botticelli, some not.

There has been much dispute about *The Birth of Venus* since Aby Warburg's *Sandro Botticelli's Birth of Venus and Spring* (1893). Several scholars have related it to neo-Platonism. E. H. Gombrich has made the relation more specific by associating it with Ficino and quoting a passage from the commentary on Plato's *Philebus* in which Ficino says that the divine spirit pours itself into the soul and matter, which is the sea. The soul, upon being fertilized, creates Beauty within itself. This creation, its birth from the soul, is called Venus. In a letter to Botticelli's patron, Lorenzo di Pierfrancesco—who eventually owned the *Primavera*—Ficino says that Venus means Humanitas, "a nymph of excellent comeliness born of heaven and more than others beloved by God All-Highest." Venus's soul and mind are Love and Charity, her eyes Dignity and Magnanimity, the hands Liberality and Magnificence, the feet Comeliness and Modesty." The whole, according to Ficino, "is Temperance and Honesty, Charm and Splendour."[2]

Pater is not concerned, as Gombrich, Panofsky, Lightbown, and other scholars have been, with the meaning of *The Birth of Venus*, its narrative affiliations. But a passing reference to Botticelli's "new readings of his own of classical stories" indicates that Pater sensed in the paintings a novel relation to their sources. He assumes that the novelty was Botticelli's; he doesn't mention the poet Angelo Poliziano, whose *Stanze* is now thought to have shown Botticelli how to combine, in the *Primavera*, Greek, Roman, and modern Florentine motifs. In *The Portrayal of Love* (1992) Charles Dempsey interprets the *Primavera* as a rustic calendar of the Roman Republic, April being Aphrodite's month and May Mercury's. Pater is not concerned with such matters or with the relation of paintings to the history of ideas. He is content to assume that *The Birth of Venus* presents the winds, Zephyr and Chloris, wafting the newborn Venus on a shell toward the shore, where she is to step forth and to be clothed by a nymph, the Hora of Spring. Lightbown has noted that the painting does not deal with the birth of Venus, her issuing from the foam of the castration of Uranus. Nor does the painting propose to re-create the *Venus Anadyomene* of Apelles; it deals rather with Venus's first step upon the shore at Cythera or at Paphos. Pater does not bother with meanings that may be established by scholarship. He doesn't say anything about Venus's pose or the disposition of the several figures. It has been suggested that Botticelli took the arrangement from the traditional group attending the baptism of Christ, a scene associated with the manifestation of the Holy Ghost. No thought of these matters disturbs Pater's prose:

> An emblematical figure of the wind blows hard across the grey water, moving forward the dainty-lipped shell on which she sails, the sea "showing his teeth," as it moves, in thin lines of foam, and sucking in, one by one, the falling roses, each severe in outline, plucked off short at the stalk, but embrowned a little, as Botticelli's flowers always are. Botticelli meant all this imagery to be altogether pleasurable; and it was partly an incompleteness of resources, inseparable from the art of that time, that subdued and chilled it. But his predilection for minor tones counts also; and what is unmistakable is the sadness with which he has conceived the goddess of pleasure, as the depository of a great power over the lives of men.[3]

That kind of prose brings readers into art galleries. To Pater, Venus is not Ficino's Humanitas but pleasure and love and the burdensome character of their bearing upon our lives. He speaks of her not as if she were to land on the earth and assume her responsibilities but as if, foreseeing them, she would prefer to let them pass into other hands.

This predicament and the tone it has produced in the painting are Pater's concern. As always, he believes that the purpose of art is to offer the distressed soul release, however temporary; as he says in the essay on Style, "a sort of cloistral refuge, from a certain vulgarity in the actual world."[4] A great artist discovers and reveals in his work a particular mode of feeling. He may or may not have felt anything of the kind in his own behalf. We need only assume that the artist was especially gifted in imagining such a feeling and devising a form for it. Pater's aim as a critic was to indicate the particular feeling he divines in Botticelli's paintings:

> I have said that the peculiar character of Botticelli is the result of a blending in him of a sympathy for humanity in its uncertain condition, its attractiveness, its investiture at rarer moments in a character of loveliness and energy, with his consciousness of the shadow upon it of the great things from which it shrinks. . . .[5]

Pater finds this emotion even in Botticelli's colors: he speaks of them as if they shrank from the responsibility of being their official selves. The color in *The Birth of Venus*, he says, is "cadaverous or at least cold":

> And yet, the more you come to understand what imaginative colouring really is, that all colour is no mere delightful quality of natural things, but a spirit upon them by which they become expressive to the spirit, the better you will like this peculiar quality of colour.[6]

Pater's friend Herbert Horne, who became the most authoritative scholar of Botticelli, dismissed Pater's comments on the coloring. The color of *The Birth of Venus* appears cadaverous or cold, he said, partly because "the medium, the glair and yolk of egg, with which the pigments were tempered, has much deteriorated in consequence of the canvas on which the picture is painted not having afforded it the same projection as a panel, and partly because the painting has not been varnished, which is a great preservative against the action of the atmosphere, and particularly against damp, from which it appears to have suffered." The painting has also suffered from overcleaning and, in parts, from retouching.[7]

But the most revealing detail of the sentence from Pater just quoted is the word "spirit," which he uses to refer both to the color of natural things and to the quality in the artist which is to be expressed through

his attention to those things—"a spirit upon them by which they become expressive to the spirit." In the last phrase, "spirit" refers first to
the artist's vitality and, in only smaller measure, to our own when we
look at the painting. It is typical of Pater to refer to apparently natural
and objective things with words that are already or incipiently subjective. Spirit began as breath, and in *A Tale of a Tub* Swift made gross
play with the fact that breath is merely wind. But when Pater uses the
word "spirit," he has nothing in view but spirituality as the supreme
human development. Using it to refer to the color of natural objects,
he means that they are not to be thought of as utterly independent of
us. "Expressive" in Pater's sentence is the word, apparently descriptive
of these objects, which corresponds to "impression" in our minds when
we look at them. Both words are subjective.

In "The Myth of Demeter and Persephone" Pater writes again of
spirit: it is vitality common to natural processes and to us who feel
them as if they were also our own. Modern science, he says, explains
changes of the natural world by the hypothesis of certain unconscious
forces; the sum of these forces makes the scientific conception of nature.
But, alongside this mechanical conception, "an older and more spiritual,
Platonic, philosophy has always maintained itself." This is a philosophy
of instinct rather than of understanding: it starts not with "an observed
sequence of outward phenomena" but with "some such feeling as most
of us have on the first warmer days in spring, when we seem to feel
the genial processes of nature actually at work; as if just below the
mould, and in the hard wood of the trees, there were really circulating
some spirit of life, akin to that which makes its energies felt within
ourselves." The entire paragraph is a murmur of "feeling" and "spirit":

> Starting with a hundred instincts such as this, that older un-
> mechanical, spiritual, or Platonic, philosophy envisages nature
> rather as the unity of a living spirit or person, revealing itself
> in various degrees to the kindred spirit of the observer, than as
> a system of mechanical forces. Such a philosophy is a syste-
> matised form of that sort of poetry (we may study it, for instance,
> either in Shelley or in Wordsworth), which also has its fancies
> of a spirit of the earth, or of the sky,—a personal intelligence
> abiding in them, the existence of which is assumed in every
> suggestion such poetry makes to us of a sympathy between the
> ways and aspects of outward nature and the moods of men.[8]

The translation of "spirit" as "personal intelligence" is bold, but Pater's context impels him to it; he is among the sentiments and fancies of Greek myth, and of modern poets to whom such intimations come agreeably. "Genial" shows that he has Wordsworth and Coleridge in mind, as well as Shelley; poets who give him authority to use a subjective vocabulary in speaking of a relation between man and the natural world. "Personal intelligence" carries that authority beyond the strict letter permitted by Romantic poets.

If we revert to the distinction which Pater makes between Botticelli as visionary painter and Giotto as dramatic painter, we find a more elaborate account of spirit, but this time without use of the word. Giotto, "the tried companion of Dante, Masaccio, Ghirlandajo even," merely transcribes "the outward image." Such artists are "almost impassive spectators of the action before them." They seem merely to take dictation from the nature they address. "Impassive" dominates Pater's account of them, and might just as well be "passive." The choice he offers is between the impassive artist and the visionary. The visionary starts with an external object to be painted, but he never finds it sufficient to his desire. No degree of being-in-itself could make up for the penury of a mind that is permitted merely to bear witness to objects. Botticelli becomes a visionary painter by feeling that objects are not enough and that their objectivity is not what he cares about. The genius of which Botticelli is the type "usurps the data before it as the exponent of ideas, moods, visions of its own; in this interest it plays fast and loose with those data, rejecting some and isolating others, and always combining them anew." Pater may have recalled Keats's description of the egotistical or Wordsworthian sublime. To Botticelli, as to Dante,

> the scene, the colour, the outward image or gesture, comes with all its incisive and importunate reality; but awakes in him, moreover, by some subtle law of his own structure, a mood which it awakes in no one else, of which it is the double or repetition, and which it clothes, that all may share it, with visible circumstance.[9]

Pater can explain Botticelli's deportment only by giving it a sequential form. The artist begins with the object before him, allows it to make at least a local claim for its objectivity—"with all its incisive and importunate reality." Soon, however, this claim "awakes" another: the apparent reality of the object is answered by some subtle law of the artist's own structure. Law and structure can hardly be set aside, even though they seem to insist only to the extent of establishing a certain mood in the artist. Or a certain disposition: the artist is already a visionary, even before he takes up his brush. "Mood" is not as concessive as it appears. It displaces the object, the scene, the outward image or gesture, making it merely the double or repetition of the mood "which it clothes, that all may share it, with visible circumstance." "Clothes" means that the clothing is secondary; what is primary is the "mood" it covers but doesn't conceal. It makes the mood public, but at the cost of its independence; it is reduced, by this service, to visible circumstance. The whole process is one by which objects are brought to attend upon minds, and in the end to yield to them. "Usurps" has set the tone for everything that follows.

14

"Winckelmann"

THE LONGEST CHAPTER of *Studies in the History of the Renaissance* was first published in the *Westminster Review* for January 1867 as a review of two books, Winckelmann's *The History of Ancient Art among the Greeks* and Otto Jahn's biography of Winckelmann. Its remote origin was "Diaphaneitè," from which Pater transcribed several sentences and a young man's dream of other men. The point of this economy was that he regarded Winckelmann as a complete exemplar of diaphaneity: ". . . that transparent nature, with its simplicity as of the earlier world. . . ." Pater associates diaphaneity with the beauty and autonomy of youth, and writes of Winckelmann as if he had remained changelessly young till his death by murder on June 8, 1768, at the age of fifty. He also associates him with a particular style of sculpture:

> If one had to choose a single product of Hellenic art, to save in the wreck of all the rest, one would choose from the "beautiful multitude" of the Panathenaic frieze that line of youths on horses, with their level glances, their proud patient lips, their chastened reins, their whole bodies in exquisite service. This colourless unclassified purity of life, with its blending and in-

terpenetration of intellectual, spiritual, and physical elements, still folded together, pregnant with the possibilities of a whole world closed within it, is the highest expression of that indifference which is beyond all that is relative or partial. Everywhere there is the effect of an awaking, of a child's sleep just disturbed. All these effects are united in a single instance—the *Adorante* of the museum of Berlin, a youth who has gained the wrestler's prize, with hands lifted and open in praise for the victory. Naive, unperplexed, it is the image of man as he springs first from the sleep of nature; his white light taking no colour from any one-sided experience, characterless so far as character involves subjection to the accidental influences of life.[1]

In "The Age of Athletic Prizemen" (1894) Pater reverts to "the *Adorante* of Berlin, Winckelmann's antique favorite, who with uplifted face and hands seems to be indeed in prayer, looks immaculate enough to be interceding for others."[2]

The main structural quality of the long passage I've quoted is the repeated "with"; a preposition of neutral proximity, doing the work, such as it is, of a descriptive adjective. Of all the prepositions in English, this "with" makes the least claim upon the collocations it effects. Pater's use of it keeps the claim as small as possible by dispersing the energy it appears to gather. The relations it establishes are without consequence. In its first use it places in the vicinity of the line of youths on horses four adjectival phrases, referring in sequence to glances, lips, reins, and bodies. But these phrases draw attention to the adjectives they contain rather than to the nouns these adjectives qualify. The points of light in the phrases are "level," "proud," "patient," "chastened," and "exquisite." These form a single meta-adjective describing diaphaneity rather than the Hellenic youths on horses. In the second sentence, "with" effects the least possible relation between one abstraction, "purity of life," and two more, "blending and interpenetration." Two further adjectival phrases intervene before the noun, "purity," finds its verb, "is." The process resembles metaphor as Hegel describes that figure in the *Philosophy of Fine Art*:

The metaphor, in fact, is always an interruption to the logical course of conception and invariably to that extent a distraction, because it starts images and brings them together, which are not immediately connected with the subject and its significance, and for this reason tend to a like extent to divert the attention from the same to matter cognate with themselves, but strange to both.[3]

Pater capitalizes upon this interruptive quality, and uses "with" to distract the reader's attention from the considerations it ostensibly raises. His paragraph is like the Old Mortality, a web of hypothetically erotic relations which may or may not come to anything but in the meantime desultorily occupy the same space. Potential conflicts are dispersed through the phrases by drawing the reader's attention away from the officially privileged relations between noun and verb. Conflicts are voided by the mere fact of expression, in which motives are distracted among the grammatical particles.

This style of willed distraction is a sign of Pater's prejudice against the axioms of being. He always wanted to see a thing becoming something else. In *The Renaissance* he speaks of "the *ennui* which ever attaches itself to realisation" and the necessity, in that case, of having some conflict grieve the existing harmony so as to obtain a profounder music. In *Plato and Platonism* he takes evident pleasure in Heracliteanism, associating Heraclitus with Hegel and with Darwin, Darwinism being the science "for which 'type' itself properly *is* not but is only always *becoming*." In the essay on Winckelmann, Pater's favorite development is that by which "the claim of Greek religion is that it was able to transform itself into an artistic ideal."[4] In later editions "claim" was changed to "privilege." In the same spirit Pater was pleased to assert that the broad foundation for all religions is a universal pagan sentiment which is altered by whatever forces modify one's life. In Renaissance art, paganism and Christianity are not rightly opposed; the deeper view preserves the identity of European culture. The Renaissance itself "was an uninterrupted effort of the middle age." It was because Winckelmann understood these mobilities that he was a great scholar of his subject.

In the essay, as in "Diaphaneitè," words for lack are transvalued so that they become, in a different order of merit, words for abundance: colorless, unclassified, indifference, naive, white, characterless, immaculate. "Indifference" is like James's "grand indifference," a condition in which one does not have to care for common opinion. The process of transvaluation corresponds to the one by which a character becomes "ideal," drawn away from its apparently objective being by force of the mind that perceives it.

Pater refers to Robert Browning's poems as instances of this process.

Browning takes a character often of little interest "and throws it into some situation, apprehends it in some delicate pause of life, in which for a moment it becomes ideal." The pause is necessary, I assume, so that the character may be seen apart from the accidental influences which keep him in the mode of character. That is the point of "for a moment":

> Take an instance from "Dramatis Personae." In the poem en-
> titled "Le Byron de nos Jours" we have a single moment of
> passion thrown into relief in this exquisite way. Those two jaded
> Parisians are not intrinsically interesting; they only begin to
> interest us when thrown into a choice situation. But to discrim-
> inate that moment, to make it appreciable by us, that we may
> "find it," what a cobweb of allusions, what double and treble
> reflections of the mind upon itself, what an artificial light is
> constructed and broken over the chosen situation—on how fine
> a needle's point that little world of passion is balanced![5]

The interest Browning's poem has for Pater is that of seeing one thing evanescing into another, a choice instance of the mind's conversion of accident to experience. The four exclamatory phrases, starting with "what a cobweb of allusions," are so opulent that we hardly notice that the first two lack a verb; the third—"what an artificial light is constructed and broken over the chosen situation"—discourages us from asking what the force of "broken" is, and the fourth chooses not to say what the needle's point is or why it is especially fine. It is a style of association which turns the space of a paragraph into a tissue of im-plication from which no particular action is supposed to arise.

The essay on Winckelmann has several examples of this process. One is a conceit. Pater imagines what would have happened if Winck-elmann and Goethe had met. It is a homosexual fantasy, "Diaphaneitè" as realized in a supreme conjunction of genius, art, beauty, and scholarship:

> Goethe, then in all the pregnancy of his wonderful youth, still
> unruffled by the press and storm of his earlier manhood, was
> awaiting Winckelmann with a curiosity of the noblest kind. As
> it was, Winckelmann became to him something like what Virgil
> was to Dante. And Winckelmann, with his fiery friendships,
> had reached that age and that period of culture at which emo-

tions, hitherto fitful, sometimes concentrate themselves in a vital unchangeable relationship. German literary history seems to have lost the chance of one of those famous friendships the very tradition of which becomes a stimulus to culture, and exercises an imperishable influence.[6]

Winckelmann's fiery friendships were all with young men. Curiosity is a crucial attribute of Pater's Romanticism. Culture, as he uses the word, is a quality of the individual and of the little group around him rather than of the entire English society that Arnold hopes to redeem. The loss is not sustained by "German literary history," which can hardly feel it, but by the fellowship of homosexuals from Plato's academy to Pater's Brasenose.

15

Greek Studies

Michelangelo's David is the presiding genius of Florence. . . . The Tuscan pose—half self-conscious all the time. Adolescent. Waiting. The tense look. No escape. The Lily. Lily or iris, what does it matter? Whitman's Calamus, too . . . Dionysus and Christ of Florence. A clouded Dionysus, a refractory Christ. Dionysus, brightness of sky and moistness of earth: so they tell us is the meaning. Giver of riches. Riches of transport, the vine. Nymphs and Hamadryads, Silenus, Pan and the Fauns and Satyrs: clue to all these, Dionysus, Iacchus, Dithyrambus. David?—Dionysus, source of reed-music, water-born melody. "The Crocus and the Hyacinth in deep grass"—lily-flowers. Then wine. Dew and fire, as Pater says. . . . The soul that held the fire and the dew clipped together in one lily-flame, where is it? David. Where is he? Cinque-Cento, a fleeting moment of adolescence. In that one moment the two eternal elements were held in consummation, forming the perfect embodiment of the human soul. And then gone. David, the Lily, the Florentine—Venus of the Scallop-Shell—Leonardo's John the Baptist. The moment of adolescence—gone. The subtle, evanescent lily-soul. They are wistful, all of them: Botticelli's women; Leonardo's, Michelangelo's men: wistful, knowing the loss even in the very moment of perfection.

—D. H. Lawrence, "David"

As a poet, Mr. Murray is merely a very insignificant follower of the pre-Raphaelite movement. As a Hellenist, he is very much of the present day, and a very important figure in the day. This day began, in a sense, with Tylor and a few German anthropologists; since then we have acquired sociology and social psychology, we have watched the clinics of Ribot and Janet, we have read books from Vienna and heard a discourse of Bergson; a philosophy arose at Cambridge; social emancipation crawled abroad; our historical knowledge has of course increased; and we have a curious Freudian-social-mystical-rationalistic-higher-critical interpretation of the Classics and what used to be called the Scriptures. . . . All these events are useful and important in their phase, and they have sensibly affected our attitude towards the Classics; and it is this phase of classical study that Professor Murray—the friend and inspirer of Miss Jane Harrison—represents. The Greek is no longer the awe-inspiring Belvedere of Winckelmann, Goethe, and Schopenhauer, the figure of which Walter Pater and Oscar Wilde offered us a slightly debased re-edition. And we realize better how different—not how much more Olympian—were the conditions of the Greek civilization from ours. . . .

—T. S. Eliot, "Euripides and Professor Murray"

I

IN 1857 CERTAIN MARBLES were discovered in the sacred precinct of Demeter at Cnidus. Charles Newton's *A History of Discoveries at Halicarnassus, Cnidus, and Branchidae* explained the significance of the find. Pater was then eighteen, intellectually precocious if not especially diligent. But he was assiduous enough to develop from Cnidus an interest in mythology, comparative religion, linguistics, anthropology, and the art of Greece and Rome. Before *Studies in the History of the Renaissance* was published, Heinrich Schliemann was excavating Troy. When Pater became a don, he turned his attention not only to the classics but to Greek philosophy and mythology. Between 1875 and 1889 he prepared as lectures or essays a series of studies of Greek religion, literature, and art. His themes were the myths of Dionysus, Demeter, and Persephone, the *Bacchanals* of Euripides, and the origins of Greek sculpture. Much of his information came from Pausanias's *Description of Greece*, and he supplemented it from the work of Grote, Overbeck, and other scholars, many of them German. He planned a book on Dionysus and cognate myths, but in the end dropped the idea. A year after his death, Shadwell collected the published essays into a book called *Greek Studies*.

In broad terms there are two traditions in modern interpretations of Greek art and thought. Both are opportunisms, in the sense that they find in Greece mainly what they require for their own local purposes. To each, Greece is a parable to be recited for its modern bearing. The first tradition, mainly drawn from Winckelmann, Lessing, Hegel, Herder, Humboldt, and Goethe, culminates for English society in Arnold. According to this interpretation, the culture of Greece between the sixth and fifth centuries B.C. featured childlike innocence, ideal beauty, nobility, equanimity, and reserve. Victorian public schools maintained Greek and Latin at the center of the curriculum, despite the positivist claim of science, so that those values might be inculcated. They were supposed to form a moral empire, and to thrive in just relation to the values of the Empire without. The parable, as Arnold recited it, spoke of turbulence finally overcome, passion not merely spent but converted to wisdom. A certain tone is sign that the conversion has been achieved. This tone issues, he maintained, from the best experience that human life has ever given, so its phrases elicit a perennial, hard-won serenity. Arnold regarded modern Britain as in need of the intelligent poise he found in the classics of Greece. Perhaps Homer never existed, or might have been a woman, as Butler proposed, but the poems existed and a culture manifested itself in their diction and cadence. The culture was there to be discovered again as a supreme achievement. The touchstones of poetry which Arnold quoted in the second series of *Essays in Criticism*, from Homer, Dante, Shakespeare, and Milton, testified to a changeless human spirit, to the highest sense of life as such. It might be thwarted or perverted by local forces, beginning with the Sophists, but in some sense it was independent of historical contingency. "It is this chiefly which gives to our spirits what they can rest upon." In *On Translating Homer* (1861), Arnold attacked Francis Newman's translation of the *Iliad* not merely because he deemed it sordid but because Newman's declared sense of Homer's style as "quaint, garrulous, prosaic, and low" tended to undermine the *Iliad* as a force in English cultural life. There was no merit in retaining the *Iliad* if Newman's sense of it was all it came to. "Search the English language for a word which does not apply to Homer," Arnold said, "and you could not fix on a better than *quaint*, unless perhaps you fixed on one of the other three." So his assault on Newman had the same motive as *Culture and Anarchy* and *Essays in Criticism*, to bring over from other cultures, especially from Greece, Rome, Germany, and France, the particular values which modern Britain lacked, notably sweetness and light, the continuous application of intelligence to the matter in hand. Even in Celtic literature, he found a quality of mind which Britain could well emulate. Translations were crucial in the middle years of the century as means of getting for English society the best that had ever been thought in the world: in Greece, to begin with.

Arnold's sense of Greek culture proved immensely persuasive and was only defeated in the long run, like much else besides. Disputes between scientists and humanists, moderns and ancients, such men as John Stuart Mill, Darwin, Huxley, and Sidgwick, proceeded with independent verve, but Arnold was always there to speak up for the possibility of producing a civil society along with the more evident production of factories, smoke, and rancor. Some writers received Arnold's general sense of Greek culture and converted it into their own vocabularies. The idea of disinterestedness, for example. Arnold took control of the word and gave it his tone, but Henry James, no classicist, translated it into a particular style of blankness. In chapter 28 of *The Portrait of a Lady* we find Isabel Archer saying good-bye to Lord Warburton in the Capitoline Gallery in Rome. Alone then, among the shining antique marbles, "she sat down in the middle of the circle of statues, looking at them vaguely, resting her eyes on their beautiful blank faces; listening, as it were, to their eternal silence." James's narrative comments:

> It is impossible, in Rome at least, to look long at a great company of Greek sculptures without feeling the effect of their noble quietude. It soothes and moderates the spirit, it purifies the imagination. . . . Isabel sat there a long time, under the charm of their motionless grace, seeing life between their gazing eyelids and purpose in their marble lips.[1]

But "blank" has special provenance in James. There is a blankness before perception or in default of it, and for that state there is no good to be said. The other blankness, coming after perception and constituting its late achieved value, is a state for which everything good is to be said. As in *A Small Boy and Others*, where James describes his sense of hanging about the Rue des Vieillards:

> The name of the street was by itself of so gentle and intimate a persuasion that I must have been ashamed not to proceed, for the very grace of it, to some shade of active response. And there was always a place of particular arrest in the vista brief and blank, but inclusively blank, blank *after* ancient, settled, more

and more subsiding things, blank almost, in short, with all Matthew Arnold's "ennui of the middle ages," rather than, poorly and meanly and emptily, before such states, which was previously what I had most known of blankness.[2]

The faces of the Greek statues are blank in that better sense; their noble quietude is an accomplishment, spiritual, moral, a condition of complete simplicity, as Eliot wrote parenthetically of another spiritual state, "(costing not less than everything)."

The second tradition of interpretation is a revision of the first. Nobility and equanimity are acknowledged as supreme qualities of Greek culture, but revisionists also point to the forces which constantly threaten this stability. Not that they complain of the threat. The question they ask is: Were the forces merely destructive as if on deadly principle, or did the encounter with them produce an even greater culture than the placid one Arnold cherished? In *The Tyranny of Greece over Germany*, E. M. Butler shows that it was Heine who most vigorously challenged mid-Victorian notions about Greece and its culture. He mocked the Olympian shibboleth of "noble simplicity and serene greatness" by calling it rigid and lifeless. In *Studies in the History of the Renaissance* Pater confused the issue by presenting Winckelmann, the first adept of Greek calm, as entirely high-souled. He took Goethe's word for this, and ignored Winckelmann's naivete. But in the essays on Greek mythology he distanced himself not only from Winckelmann's sense of Greek culture but from the rhetoric of disinterestedness and nobility he found in Arnold. Burckhardt, Pater, Nietzsche, Frazer, Gilbert Murray, E. R. Dodds: these revisionist writers, differing as they do in tone and emphasis, interpret Greece as the site of turbulence, ferocity, and sorrow, not merely of wisdom. They make at least as much of Dionysus as of Apollo. Dionysus, as Pater says, is a Chthonian god, "and, like all the children of the earth, has an element of sadness; like Hades himself, he is hollow and devouring, an eater of man's flesh—*sarcophagus*—the grave which consumed unaware the ivory-white shoulder of Pelops."[3] Simone Weil's *La Source grecque* and in particular her essay on the *Iliad* as poem of force—the force that "does not kill just yet"—are part of this tradition, too. She refused to be merely consoled.

Pater did not take public command of his subject, the culture of Greece, as Arnold, Grote, and Jowett did. He was always shy in intellectual matters and shrank from engaging on equal terms with the personages of scholarship and rhetoric. He remained the don who got a poor second. But among the English writers it was Pater who most eloquently expressed the revisionist view of Greece. In "The Marbles of Aegina" and *Plato and Platonism* he argues that Greek sculpture, reflecting the larger movements of Greek history, exhibits a dynamic relation between two opposing tendencies, centrifugal and centripetal, Ionian and Dorian, Asiatic and European, Dionysian and Apollonian:

> There is the centrifugal, the Ionian, the Asiatic tendency, flying from the centre, working with little forethought straight before it, in the development of every thought and fancy; throwing itself forth in endless play of undirected imagination. . . . It is this centrifugal tendency which Plato is desirous to cure, by maintaining, over against it, the Dorian influence of a severe simplification everywhere, in society, in culture, in the very physical nature of man. An enemy everywhere to *variegation*, to what is cunning or "myriad-minded," he sets himself, in mythology, in music, in poetry, in every kind of art, to enforce the ideal of a sort of Parmenidean abstractness and calm.[4]

It is a continuous conflict of types: Hephaestus and Apollo, Heraclitus and Parmenides. Not quite the same as the polarity between Arnold's Hebraism and Hellenism, because in that a simple choice may resolve the issue.

But Pater's account of these conflicting forces makes sense only in relation to his general theory of myth. A myth is a story told for the benefit of the community to which it is addressed: its purpose is to make sense of the life those people live. A seafaring community will have myths quite different from those told to a community living among mountains and forests. Such myths spring up spontaneously in many minds from the conditions that surround them, and they represent to them, in sensibly realized images, all they know, feel, or fancy of those conditions. But Pater is unwilling to represent the situation as one in which a set of external factors provokes a response, by way of an explanatory or appeasing story, in the minds of the community. It is a mark of the infirmity of language that one is obliged to speak of one factor and then of another. In an ideal language, as in a painting, the several constituents of an experience would be expressed simultaneously. Philosophic idealism is constantly beset by this constraint. But Pater brings the response so close to its provocation that they are virtually simultaneous. An instinct nearly anticipates what it has to meet, as if it had a vocation for that and exerted a prejudice in its favor.

Pater hoped to find in mythology good reasons for thinking that feelings are innate, as if inscribed in human bodies before the need of them. Local conditions activate one feeling rather than another, but the relation between the feeling and the conditions it has to meet is primordial consanguinity. You could almost start with the feeling and derive the conditions from it. In a myth, this feeling tries to discover for itself a narrative destiny, a story, personal through and through. Whatever we mean by development, so long as we sway to this rhythm of response and embodiment, it can't be mechanical or unconscious; it must extend into larger narrative sequences a personal vocabulary, sure of itself in what the world calls error. The act of imagination and figure required for this purpose is personification: What else can the spirit do but give names to wind and wave, the seasons in their change, the forces of loss and lack and death, the coming back of spring? Pater interpreted personification in the Greek myths as evidence not that neo-Platonism was true but that it was especially congenial to people who felt that the visible and audible world exhibited "the unity of a living spirit or person." So the sky in its unity and variety and the sea in its unity and variety were named Zeus, Glaucus, Poseidon. The earth in its changes, the growth and decay of all earthly things, was apprehended in the story of Demeter, of the earth as mother. Personification, the naming of natural forces, drew toward a personal vocabulary agencies in the world which, but for the naming, would have remained arbitrary and opaque. People who passed their lives among vines, as Pater says, their days beside the winepress, developed their experience into a complete religion, an adequate "story of the night," its god Dionysus:

> Dionysus, as we see him in art and poetry, is the projected expression of the ways and dreams of this primitive people, brooded over and harmonised by the energetic Greek imagination; the religious imagination of the Greeks being, precisely, a unifying or identifying power, bringing together things naturally asunder, making, as it were, for the human body a soul of waters, for the human soul a body of flowers; welding into something like the identity of a human personality the whole range of man's experiences of a given object, or series of objects—all their outward qualities, and the visible facts regarding them—all the hidden ordinances by which those facts

and qualities hold of unseen forces, and have their roots in purely visionary places.[5]

By making for the human body a soul of waters, and for the human soul a body of flowers, the Greeks under the sign of Dionysus gathered their entire experience of life into a personal form. They brought together, simultaneously active, the forces which a later philosophy haplessly set apart by calling them subject and object. They made Dionysus the spiritual form of fire and dew, god of trees, the vine, music of the reed.

In another place, Dionysus gave form to a more dreadful structure of experiences. The people of Thrace made him Dionysus Zagreus, the hunter:

> This transformation, this image of the beautiful soft creature become an enemy of human kind, putting off himself in his madness, wronged by his own fierce hunger and thirst, and haunting, with terrible sounds, the high Thracian farms, is the most tragic note of the whole picture, and links him on to one of the gloomiest creations of later romance, the werewolf, the belief in which still lingers in Greece, as in France, where it seems to become incorporate in the darkest of all romantic histories, that of Gilles de Retz.[6]

And in the *Bacchanals* of Euripides Pater finds his revisionist parable, a play "almost wholly without the reassuring calm, generally characteristic of the endings of Greek tragedy."[7]

The origins of Pater's ideas on myth are not important. He found whatever he needed, and made himself from the finding. Most of the ideas he took from Tylor's account of animism and the vocabulary of survival in the first volume of *Primitive Culture* (1871). Animism, as Tylor described it, "the deep-lying doctrine of Spiritual Beings, which embodies the very essence of Spiritualistic as opposed to Materialistic philosophy," appealed to Pater as a description of the ways in which an ostensibly outworn creed is still retained. Belief, Tylor admitted, "can propagate itself without reference to its reasonable origin, as plants are propagated from slips without fresh raising from the seed." It was also of moment to Pater that Tylor allowed for "the change from passive survival to active revival"[8] when conditions favoring its recurrence arise. Tylor seemed to give scientific support to the idea of the gods in exile returning under favorable conditions in medieval and modern life. We cannot say for sure that any sentiment is lost. Whatever has been vital may recover its life in ways and places no one can predict. Pater held to this idea of recursive possibility, his unofficial sense of being. He was not daunted by the fact that forces he did not care for had apparently won. Nor did he approach ancient religion, as Frazer did in *The Golden Bough*, on the assumption that the people who gave themselves to those beliefs and practices suffered from the disability of not being Victorian scholars and gentlemen. The European Enlightenment did not disprove or in any respect invalidate certain primitive beliefs for which there is no rational support. Pater always consulted the feeling from which certain acts and sufferances ensued. It was sufficient for him to understand that a particular feeling requires its destined form and will be appeased by no other. It is of no account to him whether the form is officially accredited or not. So in "The Myth of Demeter and Persephone" he gives the word "survival" in inverted commas; it is a reference to Tylor just as clearly as the preceding reference is to Blake:

> If some painter of our own time has conceived the image of *The Day* so intensely, that we hardly think of distinguishing between the image, with its girdle of dissolving morning mist, and the meaning of the image; if William Blake, to our so great delight, makes the morning stars literally "sing together"—these fruits of individual genius are in part also a "survival" from a different age, with the whole mood of which this mode of expression was more congruous than it is with ours. But there are traces of the old temper in the man of to-day also; and through these we can understand that earlier time—a very poetical time, with the more highly gifted peoples—in which every impression men received of the action of powers without or within them suggested to them the presence of a soul or will, like their own—a person, with a living spirit, and senses, and hands, and feet; which, when it talked of the return of Kore to Demeter, or the marriage of Zeus and Hera, was not using rhetorical language, but yielding to a real illusion; to which the voice of man "was really a stream, beauty an effluence, death a mist."⁹

The cognitive status of that illusion is a question. By calling it a real illusion Pater is claiming that as an illusion it can't be refuted; its being an illusion is conceded, but no further concession is offered. Similarly, such propinquity obtains between voice and stream, beauty and effluence, death and mist that again only the infirmity of language separates each of these companions.

In the development of a myth, Pater distinguishes three phases. There is first "its half-conscious, instinctive, or mystical, phase, in which, under the form of an unwritten legend, living from mouth to mouth, and with details changing as it passes from place to place, there lie certain primitive impressions of the phenomena of the natural world." Emphasis falls on the impressions rather than on the phenomena. The second phase is conscious, poetical, or literary: it is one "in which the poets become the depositories of the vague instinctive product of the popular imagination, and handle it with a purely literary interest, fixing its outlines, and simplifying or developing its situations." This is presumably its aesthetic phase, though Pater does not yet call it that; it is the one in which narrative forms are ordained to appear as if they had their origin in human freedom. The imagination finds pleasure in its unhindered activity. Thirdly, as Pater says, "the myth passes into the ethical phase, in which the persons and the incidents of the poetical narrative are realised in abstract symbols, because intensely characteristic examples, of moral or spiritual conditions."[10]

His example is the myth of Demeter and Persephone. In the first phase, changes in physical things, the occult order of summer and winter, for which no scientific explanation was available, is told through the invention of Demeter and Persephone at first in confused union. At some point they are separated, their powers recognized as distinct. The myth tells of the stealing of Persephone and the wanderings of Demeter in search of her. In the second phase, the poets take possession of the two and produce them as we know them in art and poetry, with copious incident and well-established relationships. Lastly, "these strange persons—Demeter and Persephone—these marvellous incidents—the translation into Hades, the seeking of Demeter, the return of Persephone to her,—lend themselves to the elevation and correction of the sentiments of sorrow and awe, by the presentment to the senses and the imagination of an ideal expression of them."[11]

Some parts of the theory are not clear to me. Pater says nothing about the naming; he evidently assumes that the names are always adequate. Or that with each addition to the story the name becomes more comprehensive. Persephone is the sum and burden of everything that happens to her. But I recall from "Notes Toward a Supreme Fiction" the passage in which Stevens says,

> *Phoebus is dead, ephebe. But Phoebus was*
> *A name for something that never could be named.*
> *There was a project for the sun and is.*[12]

It is as if Stevens resented that a name should be interposed between one's mind and the sun, or rather, between one's mind and the idea of the sun, an idea projected by one's mind. We are to see the sun again "with an ignorant eye / And see it clearly in the idea of it." Stevens's idealism is for the moment even more extreme than Pater's. Pater allowed for the name, was content to think that the poets named Phoebus in the second phase of a community's need, and that the name was adequate. If there is something that never could be named, it is hard to see how it could be loved or appeased. We murmur the name and respect the force of it.

I don't understand, either, why Pater distinguishes the ethical phase of the myth of Demeter and Persephone as the one in which they "lend themselves to the elevation and correction of the sentiments of sorrow and awe, by the presentment to the senses and the imagination of an ideal expression of them." Demeter, Pater says, "cannot but seem the type of divine grief." Persephone is "the goddess of death, yet with a promise of life to come." Pater appears to say that only when these figures are construed as types can they enter the general understanding of human life—of life as such, not just in Greece or Thrace. Maybe he is thinking, as Kierkegaard thought, of a distinction between the being of aesthetic man and the becoming of ethical man. But he has talked himself into saying that an incident becomes significant only when it is construed as part of a more inclusive story. In *The Burning Fountain* Philip Wheelwright defines the archetypal imagination in similar terms; it sees "the particular as somehow embodying and expressing a more universal significance—that is, a 'higher' or 'deeper' meaning than itself."[13] But even that doesn't entail Pater's emphasis on elevation and correction, which implies that the events have to sacrifice something of themselves as the cost of entering an ethical mode of understanding. Eliot's review of *Ulysses* says this in effect when he claims that Joyce's use of the Homeric myth "is simply a way of controlling, of ordering, of giving a shape and a significance to the immense panorama of futility and anarchy which is contemporary history."[14] An event is merely a fragment of that chaos until it is redeemed by being drawn into a larger perspective in which it may be thought to play a part, its penury now redeemed. I take it that "elevated" and "corrected" are Pater's words for some such enhancement. I think I understand Eliot's insistence and Joyce's practice, but I wonder why Pater, so tender toward feelings and actions he values "for their own sake," should here hold out for an ulterior value, as if feelings, images, and stories were not enough.

It is unusual of Pater to appeal beyond the apparent level of the image he is describing. He does not normally locate its meaning either above or below the appearances that tell of it. The artist may indeed be construed as a type and in that respect his significance is abstracted somewhat from the images he has projected, as the psychological whole is superior to every particle it has produced. But we are moving from one consideration to another, not comparing like with like. Normally, Pater's descriptions celebrate and distinguish the image before him by invoking, so far as he can, the particular imagination that created it. But he is content to propose its significance descriptively or comparatively and to let the meaning of the images consist entirely of the resonance they set astir. Or if he goes beyond this consideration, it is to glance at an alternative possibility within the artist's experience, not to rebuke the image in the light of an abstract figure.

His account of the *Discobolus*, in "The Age of Athletic Prizemen," is a case in point. The bronze statue by the Athenian sculptor Myron of a stooping discus thrower was made famous by descriptions of it in Pliny and Quintilian. A marble copy of it was discovered on March 14, 1781, at the Villa Palombara on the Esquiline Hill, a property of the Massimo family. Restored by Angelini, it was placed in Palazzo Massimo delle Colonne. It is possible that Pater saw it there; he spent the month of December 1882 in Rome. The palaces of the Massimo family were not open to ordinary tourists, but a gentleman of Pater's quality would not have been turned away. In the last years of the nineteenth century the statue was moved to the palace in Via dei Coronari of the extinct Lancellotti family, whose title had been assumed by a branch of the Massimi. Pater writes of the replica as if he knew it well, but he was not scrupulous in such matters. He often wrote of things he hadn't seen, confident that he could divine them from copies and other evidence. He may only have seen a good replica of the *Discobolus*. He made a final trip to Italy with his sisters in August 1891, and they spent some time in Florence, but there is no sign of Rome in their itinerary. The *Discobolus* was already famous, and it has retained its allure. Leni Riefenstahl featured it in her film of the 1936 Olympic Games. In 1937 Hitler started trying to acquire it, and he succeeded on May 18, 1938, when the Italian minister for foreign affairs, Galeazzo Ciano, sold it to him. It was brought to Germany within a month and put on display in the Glyptothek, Munich. Returned to Italy on November 16, 1948, it was placed in the Museo Nazionale on April 2, 1953. The copy that Pater saw in the British Museum is a replica found at Tivoli in 1791 and acquired for Charles Townley.[15]

Pater's account of Myron's *Discobolus* is a phantasm of it. He starts, as he must, with Pliny and Quintilian, and adds his own sense of a sculptor's development toward the subject of athletic men:

> And when he came to his main business with the quoit-player, the wrestler, the runner, he did not for a moment forget that they too were animals, young animals, delighting in natural motion, in free course through the yielding air, over uninterrupted space, according to Aristotle's definition of pleasure: "the unhindered exercise of one's natural force."[16]

One sentence from Pliny's *Historia Naturalis* is responsible for this flourish. Myron, Pliny says, "only cared for the physical form and did not express the sensations of the mind, and his treatment of the hair of the head and of the pubes continued to betray an archaic want of skill."[17] Myron is known to have sculpted a dog, a heifer, a Perseus, sawyers, a Satyr, a cicada, an Apollo, and a locust. "He was apparently the first to multiply truth," Pliny says, *"primus hic multiplicasse veritatem videtur"*—meaning that he sculpted things he saw in the natural world which had not been depicted before. But Pater chose to associate him with the depiction of young men who have nothing in view but the free exercise of their bodies:

> It is of the essence of the athletic prizeman, involved in the very ideal of the quoit-player, the cricketer, not to give expression to mind, in any antagonism to, or invasion of, the body; to mind as anything more than a function of the body, whose healthful balance of functions it may so easily perturb;—to disavow that insidious enemy of the fairness of the bodily soul as such.[18]

It is a confused sentence, as Pater tries to resolve the privileging of body over mind by calling body, in the end, the bodily soul. His feelings about beautiful young men on the playing fields in Oxford and London have perturbed his prose. In this mood he complains with justice that the intrusion of mind upon the bodies of such men causes them "to be no longer youthful." Besides, as a work of art the *Discobolus* is "a thing to be looked at rather than to think about." The statue seems so natural that it makes him exclaim, "the natural is ever best!":

> Perhaps that triumphant, unimpeachable naturalness is after all the reason why, on seeing it for the first time, it suggests no new view of the beauty of human form, or point of view for the regarding of it; is acceptable rather as embodying (say, in one perfect flower) all one has ever fancied or seen, in old Greece or on Thames' side, of the unspoiled body of youth, thus delighting itself and others, at that perfect, because unconscious, point of good-fortune, as it moves or rests just there for a moment, between the animal and spiritual worlds.[19]

"Perfect, because unconscious": Pater's meaning is clear, but how he brought himself to say it, we can only guess, unless it is that every intellectual has moods in which he wishes he were a professional athlete, his mind indistinguishable from the instinct of his limbs. Pater put all his trust in consciousness because he couldn't think of anything better to do with his time, but when he saw young men bathing or playing cricket, he could not be sure that he had made the right choice.

In "The Age of Athletic Prizemen" he allows his ardor to maintain itself through a comparison of two versions of the discus thrower:

> The face of the young man, as you see him in the British Museum for instance, with fittingly inexpressive expression, (look into, look at the curves of, the blossomlike cavity of the opened mouth) is beautiful, but not altogether virile. The eyes, the facial lines which they gather into one, seem ready to follow the coming motion of the *discus* as those of an onlooker might be; but that head does not really belong to the *discobolus*. To be assured of this you have but to compare with that version in the British Museum the most authentic of all derivations from the original, preserved till lately at the Palazzo Massimi in Rome. Here, the vigorous head also, with the face, smooth enough, but spare,

and tightly drawn over muscle and bone, is sympathetic with, yields itself to, the concentration, in the most literal sense, of all beside;—is itself, in very truth, the steady centre of the *discus*, which begins to spin; as the source of will, the source of the motion with which the *discus* is already on the wing,—that, and the entire form.[20]

Richard Payne Knight's *Specimens of Antient Sculpture* (1809) told the embarrassing truth about the Townley version: the head does not belong and is wrongly turned. But the critical discrimination of the two versions is entirely Paterian. His labored breathing in the first parenthesis and again toward the end—"is sympathetic with, yields itself to"—is typical of him when he knows what he has to say but is not sure that it is enough. A scruple in some occult relation to his feelings results in this stress of reiteration, its heavy stopping upon the prepositions lest they resolve the matter prematurely by accepting the offer of the noun.

Pater has much more to say of the *Discobolus*, but he interrupts himself to ask the question that sends us back to the issue of type:

> Was it a portrait? That one can so much as ask the question is a proof how far the master, in spite of his lingering archaism, is come already from the antique marbles of Aegina. Was it the portrait of one much-admired youth, or rather the type, the rectified essence, of many such, at the most pregnant, the essential, moment, of the exercise of their natural powers, of what they really were? Have we here, in short, the sculptor Myron's reasoned memory of many a quoit-player, of a long flight of quoit-players; as, were he here, he might have given us the cricketer, the passing generation of cricketers, *sub specie aeternitatis*, under the eternal form of art?[21]

Elevation, correction, and now "the rectified essence." Rectified, according to the *O.E.D.*, comes mainly from chemistry and religion in zeal for purity. Perhaps it is enough to say that in "The Age of Athletic Prizemen" Pater is cherishing his beloved images and beginning the process of making an ethic of them, or at least a style in communion with them. Stevens says in "The Noble Rider and the Sound of Words" that the poet must be able "to abstract himself, and to withdraw with him into his abstraction the reality on which the lovers of truth insist."[22]

That is Pater's effort, though Stevens would not be willing to call it an ethic. In Pater, it is as if he could justify the cherishing of such images only by having them somewhat subdued. But he is going back, too, to his essay on Lucca della Robbia in *Studies in the History of the Renaissance*:

> *Allgemeinheit*—breadth, generality, universality—is the word chosen by Winckelmann, and after him by Goethe and many German critics, to express that law of the most excellent Greek sculptors, of Phidias and his pupils, which prompted them constantly to seek the type in the individual, to purge from the individual all that belongs only to the individual, all the accidents, feelings, actions of a special moment, all that in its nature enduring for a moment looks like a frozen thing if you arrest it, to abstract and express only what is permanent, structural, abiding.
>
> In this way their works came to be like some subtle extract or essence, or almost like pure thoughts or ideas; and hence that broad humanity in them, that detachment from the conditions of a particular place or people, which has carried their influence far beyond the age which produced them, and insured them universal acceptance.[23]

But the matter could not be allowed to end in that Arnoldian spirit.

Pater wrote "The Age of Athletic Prizemen" virtually at the same time as "Apollo in Picardy." In the first he imagines Myron's *Discobolus* as a work of achieved poise, of rest between two movements:

> We have but translations into marble of the original in bronze. In that, it was as if a blast of cool wind had congealed the metal, or the living youth, fixed him imperishably in that moment of rest which lies between two opposed motions, the *backward* swing of the right arm, the movement *forwards* on which the left foot is in the very act of starting. The matter of the thing, the stately bronze or marble, thus rests indeed; but the artistic form of it, in truth, scarcely more, even to the eye, than the rolling ball or disk, may be said to rest, at every moment of its course,—just metaphysically, you know.[24]

But in "Apollo in Picardy," Apollyon, playing with his son Hyacinthus, takes the discus and sets it wheeling:

> How easily it spins round under one's arm, in the groove of the bent fingers, slips thence smoothly like a knife flung from its sheath, as if for a course of perpetual motion! *Splendescit eundo*: it seems to burn as it goes.[25]

It burns as it goes, and Apollyon throws it for the last time. Pater's sometimes violent imagination asserting itself, the discus "is itself but a twirling leaf in the wind, till it sinks edgewise, sawing through the boy's face, uplifted in the dark to trace it, crushing in the tender skull upon the brain."

II

Pater's sense of "the other Greece" is elaborated in two companion stories, "Denys L'Auxerrois" (1886) and "Apollo in Picardy" (1893).

He found the idea for "Apollo in Picardy" in an engraving of Domenichino's painting of Apollo and Hyacinth. In the story, the sun-god appears in medieval France as Apollyon, a beautiful young man, a shepherd hired by the monastery of Notre-Dame de-Pratis. Prior Saint-Jean, on a long visit to the monastery for the sake of his health, first sees Apollyon, asleep, a harp and a bow nearby. The priest is writing a book in several volumes on the application of mathematics to astronomy and music. Instinctively, he distrusts the shepherd, but as he proceeds with his work he finds himself discovering, as if by his sensory capacity alone, truths supposedly the province of systematic reasoning, "matters no longer to be reasoned upon and understood, but to be seen rather, to be looked at and heard":

> Did not he *see* the angle of the earth's axis with the ecliptic, the deflexions of the stars from their proper orbits with fatal results here below, and the earth—wicked, unscriptural truth!—moving round the sun, and those flashes of the eternal and unorbed light such as bring water, flowers, living things, out of the rocks, the dust?[26]

But when he tries to apply himself to his writing, he finds his hand driven beyond itself into extravagances of imagery:

> If he set hand to the page, the firm halo, here a moment since, was gone, had flitted capriciously to the wall; passed next through the window, to the wall of the garden; was dancing back in another moment upon the innermost walls of one's own miserable brain, to swell there—that astounding white light!— rising steadily in the cup, the mental receptacle, till it over-flowed, and he lay faint and drowning in it. Or he rose above it, as above a great liquid surface, and hung giddily over it— light, simple, and absolute—ere he fell. . . . Prior Saint-Jean slept, or tried to sleep, or lay sometimes in a trance without food for many hours, from which he would spring up suddenly to crowd, against time, as much as he could into his book with pen or brush; winged flowers, or stars with human limbs and faces, still intruding themselves, or mere notes of light and dark-ness from the actual horizon.[27]

This secret knowledge eventually causes the prior to sink into madness and die. The whole episode is interpreted by the narrator as an example of "a cold and very reasonable spirit disturbed suddenly, thrown off its balance, as by a violent beam, a blaze of new light, revealing, as it glanced here and there, a hundred truths unguessed at before, yet a curse, as it turned out, to its receiver, in dividing hopelessly against itself the well-ordered kingdom of his thought."[28] After Hyacinth's death, Apollyon leaves as mysteriously as he had arrived.

In "Denys L'Auxerrois," Dionysus appears in the Middle Ages in Auxerre, born to a local girl, mistress to the Count of Auxerre. He grows up handsome and charming, working in the fields, his element the trees and vines, water, and wind music. Soon he starts turning the villagers toward idleness, freedom, and license. Gradually the people begin to suspect him of sorcery. He enters a monastery. But when the time of carnival comes round and the people have a pageant "in which the person of Winter would be hunted blindfold through the streets," they set upon Denys:

> And it happened that a point of the haircloth scratched his lip deeply, with a long trickling of blood upon the chin. It was as if the sight of blood transported the spectators with a kind of

mad rage, and suddenly revealed to them the truth. The pretended hunting of the unholy creature became a real one, which
brought out, in rapid increase, men's evil passions. The soul of
Denys was already at rest, as his body, now borne along in
front of the crowd, was tossed hither and thither, torn at last
limb from limb. The men stuck little shreds of his flesh, or,
failing that, of his torn raiment, into their caps; the women
lending their long hairpins for the purpose.[29]

Dionysus the wine-god, Dionysus Zagreus the hunter; the hunter
hunted.

To moralize these stories somewhat: in each, a god appears, far
from his old dispensation and in another country, another time. He is
still a force of nature and is hardly acculturated despite his having a
name and a body not palpably different from bodies around him. As
a force of nature, he drives people beyond or beneath themselves. He
becomes a scandal when social or cultural values reassert themselves.
The arcane knowledge he brings is exciting, and at first the people are
charmed to receive it. But after a while they begin to suspect that he
is alien. They associate him with strange occurrences, an unexplained
death, perhaps a murder. In the end they turn upon him, to destroy
him or at least to expel him.

In one of the passages I've quoted from "Apollo in Picardy," the
light is personified to the degree to which it may be said to have glanced
here and there. But it remains a natural force and is therefore deemed
to be exempt from social or moral adjudication. In its own setting, a
natural force must be appeased or otherwise drawn into the sociality
of narrative. In Pater's stories the god enters surreptitiously upon a
new setting, conceals his identity for a while, but is finally recognized
as still a force of nature, not of culture. Such a force is what defeats
one's consciousness in the end: it is one's death. Meanwhile, according
to Pater's fictions, one may enjoy the practice of consciousness in converting forces of nature to oneself, or having the sentiment of the
conversion. One's consciousness makes these forces appear to agree to
become social and domestic. We call these appearances culture and
place a high value upon them. Pater takes pleasure in these acts of
conversion, even though he says in "Apollo in Picardy" that the prior,
on vacation at the monastery, "certainly did not reflect how much we
beget for ourselves in what we see and feel, nor how far a certain

diffused music in the very breath of the place was the creation of his own ear or brain."[30]

In Pater's stories the conflict is not precisely Nietzsche's, between Apollo and Dionysus. It is between Apollo and Dionysus Zagreus: between one's consciousness and every force in the world that refuses to submit to it. The stories tell against Pater's idea of aesthetic criticism, a theory that makes every claim for one's consciousness and admits defeat only in the end and because there it must. The stories concede that there is always something that refuses to be converted into ourselves. It is a mark of our imagination, our "violence within," that it tries to expunge the indissoluble element. That is what the attempt to make consciousness account for the whole of one's experience comes to. It is a desperate device, even though one fails only at last.

16

"The Child in the House"

Voilà, *the germinating, original, source,*
specimen, of all my imaginative *work.*[1]
—Walter Pater

ON APRIL 17, 1878, Pater sent George Grove, editor of *Macmillan's Magazine*, an "imaginary portrait" called "The House and the Child." He wanted it to be published anonymously, presumably because it was more personal than the essays he normally signed, but Grove persuaded him to let it go forward with his name. It was published in the August issue with the title changed to "The Child in the House." Pater told Grove that he meant it to be complete in itself and the first of a series, "with some real kind of sequence in them." He called it a portrait and expected readers, "as they might do on seeing a portrait, to begin speculating—what came of him?"[2] But when he published *Imaginary Portraits* on May 24, 1887, he didn't include "The Child in the House." He told William Sharp that he found "it would need many alterations, which I felt disinclined to make just then." He revised it in April or May 1894 for publication by a private press at Oxford, but the *Macmillan's* text was used for its first appearance in a trade edition, the *Miscellaneous Studies*, published on October 18, 1895, after Pater's death.

The portrait is of a boy during his first twelve years, living with his family in an old house somewhere in the south of England. His father has been in India and dies there. At the end, the family moves away. The portrait painter is the boy thirty years on, living a life we are told virtually nothing about. The story is often thought to be autobiographical, and there are some points of convergence between Pater's childhood and the boy's. Pater made much ado about houses as settings for the feelings that arise in them and therefore as tokens of a relation between outer and inner experience. A comparison with Proust has often been considered. Pater also thought a good deal about memories in their later configurations, but he was never as explicit on the theory of memory as Rilke was in *The Notebooks of Malte Laurids Brigge*:

> And still it is not yet enough to have memories. One must be able to forget them when they are many and one must have the great patience to wait until they come again. For it is not yet the memories themselves. Not till they have turned to blood within us, to glance and gesture, nameless and no longer to be distinguished from ourselves—not till then can it happen that in a most rare hour the first word of a verse arises in their midst and goes forth from them.[3]

Rilke means, I assume, that by the time memories have become indistinguishable from ourselves, they have blended with more recent experience and can't be separated from it even by analysis. Pater often speculated about the process by which apparently external events and objects are drawn toward the mind that engages them: as impressions, it is their destiny to become that mind in a larger figure of itself. He also thought about the decision by which one isolates for special attention some part of one's life. In "Poems by William Morris" he has a striking passage about this. The composite experience of all the ages is part of each of us, he says, and it is futile to live as though this were not the case. We can't become children again:

> But though it is not possible to repress a single phase of that humanity, which, because we live and move and have our being in the life of humanity, makes us what we are; it is possible to isolate such a phase, to throw it into relief, to be divided against ourselves in zeal for it, as we may hark back to some choice space of our own individual life.[4]

I take this to mean: we may be divided against ourselves in zeal for some phase of our lives, childhood for instance, because other considerations suggest that we should keep on living without even glancing back. William Empson once wrote that it doesn't even help one's understanding to stop living in order to understand. One reason why Pater wasn't much of a novelist was that, divided against himself in zeal for his subject, he never overcame the division. Trying to write fiction, he couldn't really believe in the existence of feelings other than his own, so his characters look as if they were seen through water. His criticism was homework in learning that there might be feelings quite different from his own and that at least when they issued from a genius they should decently be recognized.

Some parts of his own childhood may have blended with matter of a later date and other things he contrived to imagine, but there is little merit in claiming to distinguish the parts. An autobiographical reading of the story is therefore no good. Pater never lived in such a house, his father didn't die abroad, the actual moves from Stepney to Enfield and later to Canterbury didn't at all resemble the move in the story. There is far more of Canterbury in Pater's "Emerald Uthwart" (1892) than of Enfield in "The Child in the House." Several episodes in the story are such that Pater is more likely to have invented them, even though his power of invention was slight, than to have lived them. Some details were drawn from his early essays and not otherwise from life. For instance: the boy Florian Deleal notes "the shadowy changes wrought on bare wall or ceiling—the light cast up from the snow, bringing out their darkest angles."[5] In an essay published in August 1870 Pater remarked the distinctive light on the face of Botticelli's Madonnas: "The white light on it is cast up hard and cheerless from below, as when snow lies upon the ground, and the children look up with surprise at the strange whiteness of the ceiling."[6]

The story begins as if it were a parable. One day Florian, now grown up, helps a poor old man and that night receives, "like a reward for his pity," a dream of the old house in which he lived as a boy. The dream "did for him the office of the finer sort of memory, bringing its object to mind with a great clearness, yet, as sometimes happens in dreams, raised a little above itself, and above ordinary retrospect." It is memory in the comparative degree, like Pater's favorite form of the adjective. He calls it memory, though he might just as well have called it the mind in its enhancing or transfiguring character. The walls and doors appear as in a dream, free of empirical duty. In the "Essay

Supplementary to the Preface" of 1815 Wordsworth says that "the appropriate business of poetry (which, nevertheless, if genuine is as permanent as pure science), her appropriate employment, her privilege and her *duty*, is to treat of things not as they *are*, but as they *appear*; not as they exist in themselves, but as they *seem* to exist to the *senses* and to the *passions*."[7] Giving appearances such privilege, a poet asserts the constitutive power of the mind in the production of experience. As in the sixth book of *The Prelude*:

> *But to my conscious soul I now can say—*
> *"I recognise thy glory": in such strength*
> *Of usurpation, when the light of sense*
> *Goes out, but with a flash that has revealed*
> *The invisible world, doth greatness make abode.* . . . .

Pater is more timid. He likes to have evidence, even when he flouts it. The purpose of memory in his fiction is not to recall an old experience but to create a new one, acting upon the *fiat* of dreams, visions, fears, desires, absolute because personal. The house and "the gradual expansion of the soul which had come to be there" make one experience, "inward and outward being woven through and through each other into one inextricable texture—half, tint and trace and accident of homely colour and form, from the wood and the bricks; half, mere soul-stuff, floated thither from who knows how far."[8] What soul-stuff is, Pater doesn't say. He gives it a material form, but only because language is poor in names for spiritual entities.

It doesn't make any difference to Pater whether one's feelings arise from occasions of nature or of culture. The Muse doesn't bother with such a distinction. A landscape may set a mind thinking or dreaming; so may a house. Some vague system of correspondence is operating, but there is no need to analyze it or to be dainty in considering how it works. Artists are not under any obligation to represent the objects in nature or culture that have set their minds astir: such debts need not be paid.

As children, Pater says in the spirit of Wordsworth, "we see inwardly" because of an innate desire for beautiful appearances. But a child's sense of beauty is not dependent upon any choiceness or special fineness in the objects at large:

. . . the child finds for itself, and with unstinted delight, a difference for the sense, in those whites and reds through the smoke on very homely buildings, and in the gold of the dandelions at the road-side, just beyond the houses, where not a handful of earth is virgin and untouched, in the lack of better ministries to its desire of beauty.[9]

A difference for the sense is the child's version of the transfiguring power of mind. Seeing inwardly is the best way of seeing; a pity it has to change and children have to grow up. But the change is tolerable if there is some residual consanguinity, however occult, between children and the world in which they grow. They must continue to be able to find a difference for the sense in what it confronts. If they can do this, they retain the things that surround them, rooms and landscapes, as sanctuaries of their feeling.

Pater makes much of these shapes, voices, accidents, and rooms, but he thinks of them in the end as "parts of the great chain wherewith we are bound." He appears to be slighting our ability to convert such things to ourselves. It is not clear why he insists on the chain, but he gives a show of reason in his essay on Pascal. He worked on it during the last weeks of his life:

There are moments of one's own life, aspects of the life of others, of which the conclusion that the will is free seems to be the only—is the natural or reasonable—account. Yet those very moments on reflexion, on second thoughts, present themselves again, as but links in a chain, in an all-embracing network of chains. In all education we assume, in some inexplicable combination, at once the freedom and the necessity of the subject of it.[10]

An all-embracing network of chains isn't quite as harsh as the chain that merely binds. Pater may only mean: at every moment of my life I felt free to choose what I would do, but now on second thought it seems to have been all necessity.

There is another possibility, that the chain is the insistence of one's senses rather than the proliferation of external objects and events demanding attention. There is a passage in *The Prelude* which speaks to this sentiment—Wordsworth is Pater's shade in this story as elsewhere—and clarifies the issue:

> *for I had an eye*
> *Which in my strongest workings, evermore*
> *Was looking for the shades of difference*
> *As they lie hid in all exterior forms,*
> *Near or remote, minute or vast, an eye*
> *Which from a stone, a tree, a wither'd leaf,*
> *To the broad ocean and the azure heavens,*
> *Spangled with kindred multitudes of stars,*
> *Could find no surface where its power might sleep,*
> *Which spake perpetual logic to my soul,*
> *And by an unrelenting agency*
> *Did bind my feelings, even as in a chain.*[11]

The child's eye insists on finding difference in objects apparently the same; can't stop doing this, even when the objects on view, like the stars, can't well be questioned; and imposes this logic upon the feelings, "even as in a chain." But at least the external world can't be blamed for the chain.

In Florian's early life necessity takes the form of two insistences. Sensory images speak to him of beauty and of death. Some of these seem to be accidental, like the chance by which one evening a garden gate, usually closed, stood open:

> and lo! within, a great red hawthorn in full flower, embossing heavily the bleached and twisted trunk and branches, so aged that there were but few green leaves thereon—a plumage of tender, crimson fire out of the heart of the dry wood.[12]

The tree is felt as blessing but as disturbance too; the excitement caused by such images is so compelling that he half longs to be free of it:

> A touch of regret or desire mingled all night with the remembered presence of the red flowers, and their perfume in the darkness about him; and the longing for some undivined, entire possession of them was the beginning of a revelation to him, growing ever clearer, with the coming of the gracious summer guise of fields and trees and persons in each succeeding year, of a certain, at times seemingly exclusive, predominance in his interests, of beautiful physical things, a kind of tyranny of the senses over him.[13]

In Pater, as in Wordsworth, the chief tyrant is the sense of sight. As a result in later years, Florian was never willing to think of soul "but as in an actual body, or of any world but that wherein are water and trees, and where men and women look, so or so, and press actual hands."[14]

The second tyranny is the fear of death, "the fear of death intensified by the desire of beauty." Intimations of mortality crowd upon Florian: in later life the morgue in Paris, a cemetery in Munich, in childhood a graveyard with a freshly dug grave readied for a child. In one paragraph the narrator's mind, speaking for Florian's, can hardly release itself from the syllables of finality:

> Also, as he felt this pressure upon him of the sensible world, then, as often afterwards, there would come another sort of curious questioning how the last impressions of eye and ear might happen to him, how they would find him—the scent of the last flower, the soft yellowness of the last morning, the last recognition of some object of affection, hand or voice; it could not be but that the latest look of the eyes, before their final closing, would be strangely vivid; one would go with the hot tears, the cry, the touch of the wistful bystander, impressed how deeply on one! or would it be, perhaps, a mere frail retiring of all things, great or little, away from one, into a level distance?[15]

It is typical of Pater's narrator to end the meditation not with a high tragic note but with a trailing off, a dying fall into the level distance.

Talk of ghosts and revenants issues in Florian's sense of a dead spirit taking form beside him:

> Afterwards he came to think of those poor, home-returning ghosts, which all men have fancied to themselves—the *revenants*—pathetically, as crying, or beating with vain hands at the doors, as the wind came, their cries distinguishable in it as a wilder inner note. But, always making death more unfamiliar still, that old experience would ever, from time to time, return to him; even in the living he sometimes caught its likeness; at any time or place, in a moment, the faint atmosphere of the chamber of death would be breathed around him, and the image with the bound chin, the quaint smile, the straight, stiff feet,

shed itself across the air upon the bright carpet, amid the gayest company, or happiest communing with himself.[16]

It seems important here that the revenants, having lived in ordinary social worlds, now express themselves as a force of nature, the wind, and differ from its common form only in their greater intensity, the "wilder inner note" of it. They have returned not only to the places they lived in but to the natural world from which they first came. Responsive to such intimations, Florian finds the house of thought becoming the house of religion, inhabited for him by some "ideal, hieratic persons." Seen things are in correspondence with the unseen:

> Sensibility—the desire of physical beauty—a strange biblical awe, which made any reference to the unseen act on him like solemn music—these qualities the child took away with him, when, at about the age of twelve years, he left the old house, and was taken to live in another place.[17]

On the last day of the story Florian runs back to the house to look for a pet bird he has neglected to bring with him:

> But as he passed in search of it from room to room, lying so pale, with a look of meekness in their denudation, and at last through that little, stripped white room, the aspect of the place touched him like the face of one dead; and a clinging back towards it came over him, so intense that he knew it would last long, and spoiling all his pleasure in the realisation of a thing so eagerly anticipated.[18]

Whiteness, here as elsewhere in Pater, is beauty on the face of death, the prospect of death in a beautiful body, the color of Greek marble alive in the form in which it tells of death. The corpse is pale and meek, like a child wise enough to know that dying is in the nature of things and the best one can hope for is to stay childlike about it. In Pater and in the decadence he and Huysmans gave warrant for, the price one pays for extreme achievements of refinement is that there is no return from them, even as a vacation exercise, to common forms of existence. There is only further refinement, the last curiosity. In the passage I've quoted, the notable feature is the abruptness with which the narrator, still speaking for Florian, translates the empty rooms into personal terms; we come upon "lying so pale" before we know where we are or what is lying, what is pale. Only gradually as we go through the sentence do we divine that the rooms are waiting to become revenants in their due time, especially the stripped white one.

17

Marius the Epicurean

IT IS HARD TO KNOW what its first readers saw in *Marius the Epicurean*. Most of the reviewers concerned themselves with Pater's account of Epicureanism and the conviction with which he sent Marius beyond that Bower of Bliss toward Christianity. Or with doubts about Pater's accuracy as a historian of Rome in the early years of the second century. Lay readers presumably received the book as one of several fictions about early Christianity, like Kingsley's *Hypatia* and Newman's *Callista*. Comparisons between the age of the Antonines and the Victorian age were common if not commonplace: ages of transition, both. But *Marius the Epicurean* is more a spiritual romance than a novel. Its sketches of ancient Rome and Pisa are perfunctory; it shows no interest in the density or variety of ordinary life. Pater hardly even tried to imagine characters who would have a semblance of existence apart from Marius's interest in them. As usual, he acted on his prejudice that the only history worth reciting is the history of someone's consciousness, the succession of a hero's mental and spiritual states. He was not willing to imagine anything that might, because of its independent claim upon the reader's attention, put the privilege of Marius's ideas and sensations at risk. Marius is not an imagined person but a system of thoughts encountering objects, events, people, and places as further systems of thought. And, in the end, as extensions of his own. He never comes upon a system that is not a system of thought. Contingency is internalized as a crisis, a scruple by which the system is agitated to turn aside from its official direction. So the book is not a historical novel. Comparisons with Scott, Balzac, Stendhal, and Tolstoi, or even with lesser historical novelists, are beside whatever point *Marius* has. In the historical novel characters are bodied forth against the societies they have to meet, and it is understood that genuine conflicts are entailed. In principle, this is as true of *Flaubert's Parrot*, *Chatterton*, and *The Last Station* as of *La Chartreuse de Parme*. The societies in these novels are not merely picturesque; they have values just as producible if not as refined as the hero's. But Marius's only obligation is to move like a tourist through certain scenes: the scenes are not given any intrinsic character, they are contexts of ideas, but their frail images set the structure of his mind and conscience astir.

It is clear that Pater started thinking of writing such a book shortly after he had suppressed the Conclusion for the 1877 edition of *The Renaissance*. On that occasion he did what had to be done, but he kept in view the possibility of eventually finding a place for the sentiments he had to sacrifice. His essays on Greek mythology, "The Myth of Demeter and Persephone" and "A Study of Dionysus," apparently enabled him to imagine feelings beyond his own, though not entirely other than his own. The possibility of retaining such feelings and removing them to the safe distance of an earlier time suggested a form new to him, the "Imaginary Portrait," in which mildly invented characters would mingle with real ones. What he intended in *Marius the Epicurean* was "an Imaginary Portrait of a peculiar type of mind in the time of Marcus Aurelius."[1] Arnold's essay on Aurelius made Stoicism a current interest, consistent with a wise Empire and a morality of self-discipline. In 1876 Pater's tutor, W. Wolfe Capes, published *The Roman Empire of the Second Century or the Age of the Antonines*, a study of Rome from the murder of Domitian and the rise of Nerva to the death of Marcus Aurelius in A.D. 180. Capes's book indicated to Pater the sources he needed: Dion Cassius, Pliny, Fronto, Eusebius, Philosostratus, Epictetus, Plutarch, and Lucian. It was a help, too, that Capes was so well disposed to Marcus Aurelius. Pater had something he could revise.

He had large ambitions. He planned three volumes on much the same issue of philosophy and belief, the historical circumstances alone changing from one to the next:

I may add that "Marius" is designed to be the first of a kind of trilogy, or triplet, of works of a similar character; dealing with the same problems, under altered historical conditions. The period of the second of the series would be at the end of the 16th century, and the place France: of the third, the time, probably the end of the last century—and the scene, England.[2]

In the event, he didn't finish the second of these, *Gaston de Latour*, or even start the third.

Marius the Epicurean was a successful if not quite a popular book. We are not dealing with *Ben-Hur* or *I, Claudius* but with a book that seemed to go out of its way to avoid attracting readers but still got a fair number of them. It was published in an edition of one thousand copies on March 4, 1885. A second edition of two thousand copies, with some minor corrections and one major one, appeared on November 12, 1885. When a third edition was called for, Pater made about six thousand textual changes, mostly local niceties of phrasing, to make the book accord with the criteria he set himself in his essay "Style," published in December 1888. This version, the last he supervised, was published in an edition of two thousand copies on August 10, 1892. The book was cordially reviewed, and it sold reasonably well. It has continued to have a shadowy life as a classic few feel themselves stirred to read.

The only textual change of any importance Pater made was for the second edition. He deleted a remarkably cruel passage describing an episode in which a cat is nearly burned to death. That he should have thought of writing such a passage is hard to explain. He was tender to animals and especially fond of cats. I can only conjecture that he imagined the episode in a moment of moral aberration and included it because of an association in his mind between modern novel-reading and the pleasure pagan Romans took in the cruelties of the amphitheater. In the chapter called "Manly Amusements" he remarked:

The time had been, and was to come again, when the pleasures of the amphitheatre centered in a similar practical joking upon human beings. What more ingenious diversion had stage manager ever contrived than that incident, itself a practical epigram never to be forgotten, when a criminal, who, like slaves and animals, had no rights, was compelled to present the part of Icarus; and, the wings failing him in due course, had fallen into a pack of hungry bears? For the long shows of the amphitheatre were, so to speak, the novel-reading of that age—a current help provided for sluggish imaginations, in regard, for instance, to grisly accidents, such as might happen to one's self; but with every facility for comfortable inspection.[3]

If Pater felt strongly, because justly, about such spectacles, it is odd that he presented to the reader's comfortable inspection an incident such as might happen to one's favorite cat. Evidently Pater, on second thought, found it odd.

The technique of the book is debonair. Pater doesn't indulge himself in what James called "the muffled majesty of authorship." He doesn't claim omniscience as a formal or epistemological principle. He simply establishes a narrator, a modern witness, lets him say "I" as often as he likes, gives him the capacity to enter anyone's mind and report what he finds there. From time to time the narrator draws the reader's attention to something in Defoe, Swift, or Gautier, and takes it for granted that what he says about the Rome of Aurelius will bear a modern application:

> That age and our own have much in common—many difficulties and hopes. Let the reader pardon me if here and there I seem to be passing from Marius to his modern representatives—from Rome, to Paris or London.[4]

With the same nonchalance, the narrator leaps over sixteen centuries and pretends that the reader is there beside him:

> To an instinctive seriousness, the material abode in which the childhood of Marius was passed had largely added. Nothing, you felt, as you first caught sight of that coy, retired place,— surely nothing could happen there, without its full accompaniment of thought or reverie.[5]

You? Pater might as well have said "I," as he does in the passage that follows, a meditation, one of several, on whiteness, the excuse for it being that Marius's home is called White-Nights, *Ad Vigilias Albas*. Pater doesn't expect us to believe that Marius thought in this fashion about whiteness, or about white as the color of after-thoughts and after-images, the stronger color, as of red roses, having come first. Whiteness is Pater's motif, variously bleached with considerations of candor as a condition one reaches by self-denial after turbid feelings. The narrator suffuses Marius's mind with whiteness, to show him characteristically in nights "not of quite blank forgetfulness, but passed in continuous dreaming, only half veiled by sleep."[6] Again, Marius is not to be construed as thinking these thoughts, but we are to find them an illuminating setting for him. He is the portrait, these motifs the frame.

The action of the book is simple. Marius starts out from the inherited pagan religion of Rome, grows up, moves into the world of ideas—Heraclitus, Aristippus, Aurelius, Cornelius Fronto, Lucian—and gradually learns to discriminate between one value and another. The main claimants are Stoicism and Cyrenaicism, each of them to be found inadequate. In the end he meets a group of Christians and, while he remains a pagan connoisseur and is not formally converted, he dies in their arms, as if baptized by desire. T. S. Eliot thought the book incoherent, "a number of fresh starts," forgetting that his own poetry exhibited the same method and made a virtue of it. The only requirement of a method is to get convincingly from beginning to end through a plausible sequence of transitions. By that test there is no fault in Pater's. Fault arises when he forgets about Marius and thinks only of himself and of the personal reasons for writing the book.

The main reason was to refute the charge, leveled against *Studies in the History of the Renaissance*, that he was a hedonist, an epicurean, and—the implication was clear—that he instructed his undergraduates at Brasenose to live for pleasure alone. *Marius the Epicurean* attacks both Epicureanism and Stoicism; each is shown as partial, morally limited, an exaggeration of one element in an ideally comprehensive philosophy. Aurelius's Stoicism, in Pater's account of it, is high-minded but morally obtuse. There is much more to be said for Epicureanism, and Pater can hardly say enough for it, since whatever its defects, it is a philosophy of the senses and of the body. The advice to eat, drink, and be merry, as he says, depends upon the quality of the person who sits down to the table. But in the end Epicureanism—or Cyrenaicism, as Pater calls it—is inadequate, a philosophy for youngsters:

And we may note, as Marius could hardly have done, that Cyrenaicism is ever the characteristic philosophy of youth, ardent, but narrow in its survey—sincere, but apt to become one-sided, or even fanatical. It is one of those subjective and partial ideals, based on vivid, because limited, apprehension of the truth of one aspect of experience (in this case, of the beauty of the world and the brevity of man's life there) which it may be said to be the special vocation of the youth to express.[7]

The implication is that the Conclusion to *Studies in the History of the Renaissance* was appropriate to its moment and to its readers at the time. Unfortunately, boys can't stay boys. Pater escapes from the charge of hedonism by saying that, alas, it is merely a phase one passes through. One grows out of it and away from it simply by getting older; it is not necessary to get wiser. Even at the stage represented by Marius's "new Cyrenaicism," he is being directed beyond himself and his partiality:

> Not pleasure, but fulness of life, and "insight" as conducting to that fulness—energy, variety, and choice of experience, including noble pain and sorrow even, loves such as those in the exquisite old story of Apuleius, sincere and strenuous forms of the moral life, such as Seneca and Epictetus—whatever form of human life, in short, might be heroic, impassioned, ideal: from these the "new Cyrenaicism" of Marius took its criterion of values.[8]

To strengthen his defense, Pater assigns to Flavian the qualities he himself was accused of having. Flavian is a pagan, a Euphuist, an egotist, and a sensualist. Not surprisingly, Pater kills him off with fever, victim of a plague, before the book has well begun. Marius is left to make the most of his experiences and to find them at last fulfilled on the brink of Christianity.

The merit of Pater's method is that it enables him to include virtually anything that comes to his mind, or may be attracted to its orbit, without having to show much cause for its being there. The story of Cupid and Psyche, to which Capes draws attention, occupies thirty pages of an early chapter, translated from book 4 of *The Golden Ass*, for no reason except that Marius and his friend Flavian are supposedly reading it. Flavian becomes the author of the "Pervigilium Veneris," a freedom Pater takes because no other poet is known to have written it. Near the end of the book a long Platonic dialogue is composed merely because the writer Lucian comes to Rome and meets Marius's Stoic friend Hermotimus on the Via Appia. These items inhabit the book for two reasons: they show us what Marius has been thinking about and what we should be thinking about to merit his company.

But what I have said about *Marius* doesn't at all indicate its tone. The book is indeed a revision of the Conclusion to the *Studies* of 1873, a "white" after-life of that red. But the motto of both books might well be the same: death is the mother of beauty. In the fourth chapter of *Marius* the narrator breaks into one of many cadenzas, this one on the aim of higher education:

> He was acquiring what it is the chief function of all higher education to impart, the art, namely, of so relieving the ideal or poetic traits, the elements of distinction, in our everyday life—of so exclusively living in them—that the unadorned remainder of it, the mere drift or *debris* of our days, comes to be as though it were not.[9]

"Relieving" is not clear to me, unless he means it in a military sense, to relieve a position by guarding it against the enemy, relieving the elements of distinction in our everyday lives by fending off the characterless or mundane elements. If we make the most of our days, the unadorned remainder will come to appear not to matter. The answer to the inevitability of death is the possibility of beauty, making the most, aesthetically, of the interval we are given between two eternities. This is Pater's rebuke to Aurelius, whose Senate speech on the world, life, and death sounds glib. Aurelius makes himself invulnerable to suffering by not feeling at all. Pater couldn't approve of anyone who, like Aurelius, despised the body even to the degree of allowing suicide, tolerated evil, and permitted savagery as an entertainment in the amphitheater. Translating a passage from the *Meditations*—II.12 in the Loeb edition—Pater mischievously has Aurelius using one of Arnold's most famous phrases, the ancient M.A. quoting the modern one, his critic, sage of Oxford. It is the same phrase that Pater showed up as spurious on the first page of *Studies in the History of the Renaissance*. The Loeb translation of Aurelius's Greek reads,

> [Think] . . . what it is to die, and that if a man look at death in itself, and with the analysis of reason strip it of its phantom terrors, no longer will he conceive it to be aught but a function of Nature,—but if a man be frightened by a function of Nature, he is childish.[10]

Pater's irony upon Arnold reads:

Consider what death is, and how, if one does but detach from it the appearances, the notions, that hang about it, resting the eye upon it as in itself it really is, it must be thought of but as an effect of nature, and that man but a child whom an effect of nature shall affright.[11]

The first result of this is to diminish Arnold by having Aurelius speak in his name. But then there is a further implication, that death is the only thing in the world which, because it is opaque to consciousness, may be seen as in itself it really is.

I remark on this little episode because it corresponds to a peculiarity in Pater's narrative habit, that he invariably represents someone's dying as an arbitrary event. Flavian dies of the plague. Pater never tries to give reason or to make a dying probable; he is indifferent to the showing of cause, when death is in question. If death is opaque to consciousness, it doesn't matter when or how it occurs.

The best that can be said for *Marius the Epicurean* is that it is an achievement of style. But style is nearly all that the literature from Pater to Stevens claims to achieve; it must not be deemed to count for nothing. It counts for a distinctive possibility of living mostly by ruses, by circumventing the standard terms which modern societies offer as the means of living. Pater's sentences, like those passages in "Notes Toward a Supreme Fiction" which are fully themselves and about nothing, are practices, utopian exercises, fictions so pure that everything in them is bleached, turned white. Everything exists to end up in a style—Marius, too, who is a mode of language trying to explore its limits. Otherwise put, Marius is a textual subject reaching toward textual objects which, as soon as come upon, become further phrases of himself. If this seems to amount to nothing, I have described it poorly. Marius lives by producing more sentences; so did Pater. The production of sentences, in Pater's case as first of the modernist writers, is the means of living an antinomian life. To use a notion I find in Michel de Certeau's *The Practice of Everyday Life*, in a culture of consumption, the feints and ruses of Pater's sentences, without ceasing to consume, become "another production." It is as true of Pater in *Marius the Epicurean* as of Stevens in "The Comedian as the Letter C," that— in Fredric Jameson's formulation—"one never meets anything but contents of the same order."[12] The only consideration that makes these ruses and feints tolerable is the oppressiveness of the social practice they are devised to evade.

18

Imaginary Portraits

He is very much interested in the life of the seeress of Prevorst, and in all the phenomena of the middle nature, and here, where most of all the sweetness and resoluteness of soul have power, he seems to seek in a fictitious world, but how different from that in which Watteau (in Pater's happy phrase) may have sought, both with a certain characteristic inconstancy, what is found there in no satisfying measure or not at all.
—James Joyce, "James Clarence Mangan" (1907)

THE BOOK OF THIS TITLE was published on May 24, 1887; it gathered together four stories or portraits already published: "A Prince of Court Painters" (October 1885), "Denys L'Auxerrois" (October 1886), "Sebastian van Storck" (March 1886), and "Duke Carl of Rosenmold" (May 1887). Pater thought of including "The Child in the House" (April 1878) but decided against it; it would have needed too many alterations.

The "imaginary portrait" is hardly a genre in itself, it is a mixture of genres. Pater was impressed by Landor's *Imaginary Conversations* and by Hawthorne's romances of New England. Not by the historical novel, evidently. He didn't want to feel responsible for the depiction of an age, a historical configuration, a particular moment in the emergence of a social formation. Or to subject his heroes to pressure from their assumed contexts. He wanted to practice a form of fiction in which he might freely allude to historical events and personages without incurring an obligation, least of all an obligation to regard reality as primarily historical. In "A Prince of Court Painters" the family party makes a trip to Cambrai and sees Fénelon in the cathedral, but the event receives no further attention. In the matter of historical fact Pater also took liberties, so many that it is a pity he did not derive more satisfaction from them. He has Watteau elected to the French Academy in 1712, not in the true 1717. He lets the narrator of "A Prince of Court Painters" read *Manon Lescaut* in October 1717, though the book wasn't published till 1731. By playing loose with easily verified facts, he released himself from their importunity and told his readers that he was doing so. He didn't consider that historical events deserved any particular respect by virtue of their merely having come to pass.

Pater never wrote a theory of fiction or anything comparable to the Preface to *The House of the Seven Gables*, in which Hawthorne claims a romancer's right to present "the truth of the human heart" under circumstances "to a great extent of the writer's own choosing or creation." Pater didn't make this claim but he acted upon it. In "Duke Carl of Rosenmold" he has the duke somewhat ingenuously study the history of the Middle Ages without any sense of the fictive element in such history, but he adds an admonition to this effect:

> Surely, past ages, could one get at the historic soul of them, were not dead but living, rich in company, for the entertainment, the expansion, of the present: and Duke Carl was still without suspicion of the cynic afterthought that such historic soul was but an arbitrary substitution, a generous loan of one's self.[1]

The duke is hardly to be looked to for consistency. To the slight extent to which he knows his mind, he thinks he is engaged in a project to summon Apollo to come to Germany and inspire a new Enlightenment. He has found in a fifteenth-century *Ars Versificandi* by Conrad Celtes a Sapphic ode "To Apollo, praying that he would come to us from Italy, bringing his lyre with him." In a rush to the head he thinks it would be possible to recover Apollo by studying "the vast accumulated material of which Germany was in possession." Where to begin? In one's self, apparently. Pater sends the duke off to look for "a deeper understanding of the past, of nature, of one's self—an understanding of all beside through the knowledge of one's self."[2]

Pater had no good reason to think that these notions would issue in good stories. The fact that he called them portraits suggests that he mainly wanted to continue to write as he had started, in *Studies in the History of the Renaissance*. The chapters on Renaissance artists in that book are portraits of certain great types of being, with just enough veridical matter to keep them in their frames. Pater imagined what Leonardo was like, on the authority of a few pictures in the vicinity of the name, and he drew a portrait of the artist, or at least a sketch. In three of the four imaginary portraits he used the same procedure, except that he did not claim that Carl, Sebastian, and Denys had ever existed. But then he was not disposed to make much of the difference between someone who lived and someone who didn't.

The aim of fiction is to express, as Pater wrote in "A Prince of Court Painters," one's "dream of a better world than the real one." Literature itself is turned toward a better life. But Pater could imagine such a life only by having his sentences imply another world a little aside from the one in power. He could not deduce a better life from any possibilities he discerned in this one. The visible forms of the world, which exerted such a claim upon George Eliot and Balzac and even upon Hawthorne, were of merely picturesque interest to Pater. He paid attention to them now and again, but only for the impressions and vibrations that might bless the attention.

It may be said that there can't have been much wrong with Pater's method if it was also Hawthorne's. But the motive of romance in Hawthorne was tested and certified by having to make its way against Hawthorne's sense of the ordinary world and his incorrigible sense of evil and sin. He did not consult a merely subjective obligation. He released himself from the mimetic duty of realism. When he referred to "a very minute fidelity, not merely to the possible, but to the probable and ordinary course of man's experience," he did not undertake to practice it. But fidelity to appearances meant more to him than his theory of fiction entailed: it made common cause with other fidelities, historical, moral, and theological, to the extent of their nearly amounting to a cause. In "Young Goodman Brown" we are not allowed to think that the hero's initiation into the infernal forest is a conceit on Hawthorne's part or a delusion on Brown's, or that Brown's meeting with his wife Faith near the end is chimerical. The force of the story does not depend upon the probable but upon the glare of abysmal possibilities. Their being felt as possible is sufficient to make them count as irrefutable. James, who exaggerated the lightness and airiness of Hawthorne's stories, was yet sensitive to his spiritual power, his conviction of "a life of the spirit more complex than anything that met the mere eye of sense."[3]

There is nothing of this conviction in Pater's imaginary portraits. Here the life of the depicted spirit is merely of psychological interest and interesting or not in that way. We don't feel that there is pressure of a different kind which threatens the psychological nicety of the portrait to the point of refuting its terms. The portraits don't issue from anything more exacting than the tendency of psychological attributes to gather themselves into types, there to invite a static because unquestioned description.

Some of the types are bizarre and might even have been productive if Pater had found for them anything to do. Sebastian has the interest of a fanatic, a philosophic idealist so extreme that he has removed every impediment to his logic. He craves to achieve a *tabula rasa* according to the axiom that "all was but conscious mind." In a few sentences Pater describes the *ennui* of his being consistent:

> And at length this dark fanaticism, losing the support of his pride in the mere novelty of a reasoning so hard and dry, turned round upon him, as our fanaticism will, in black melancholy.[4]

In the end, Sebastian can only refute himself by a spontaneous act of self-sacrifice. He dies while saving a child's life.

Pater's most serious defect as a writer of fiction, even as a writer of romance, is that he thinks a character may be sustained by the ideas he or she is given to hold. And while he can imagine what it would be like to hold an idea, he can't imagine any consequence of holding it, the difference it would make. In his sense of the world at large it makes no difference, because he gives this world such tenuous acknowledgment. In the life within, it makes only the difference between having an idea and not having one. The hero's mind is occupied, or it isn't. He is sad, or not. Pater is in the position that the novelist Mark Ambient, in "The Author of 'Beltraffio,' " ascribes to his own work. "I've always arranged things too much," he says, "always smoothed them down and rounded them off and tucked them in—done everything to them that life doesn't do." Pater's imaginary portraits, especially those of Sebastian and of Carl, are arduously smoothed, rounded, and tucked, and in the end they are frigid parables. He deals with ideas and notions but forgets the feelings from which they arose, of which they are only the congealed residue.

The best of the portraits is "A Prince of Court Painters." Pater liked to think that he was a descendant of Jean-Baptiste Pater, French painter of *fêtes galantes* and a protégé of Watteau's. He may have seen in the museum at Valenciennes two relevant paintings, Jean-Baptiste

Pater's *Portrait of the Artist's Sister* and Watteau's *Portrait of M. Pater*, Jean-Baptiste's father and Watteau's godfather. The story is told in extracts from a journal kept by Jean-Baptiste's elder sister. All of the extracts are concerned with Watteau; it gradually becomes clear that the diarist is in love with him and that he has only a friend's feeling for her. He is entranced by success in Paris and the adulation he receives. He dies at the age of thirty-seven.

The interest of the story is diverse. As a description of Watteau's paintings, it is as good as any of the chapters of *Studies in the History of the Renaissance*. But that is a minor consideration. More to the point, the story is a finely imagined series of transitions. The simplest is from Valenciennes to Paris. At the beginning of the eighteenth century, Valenciennes was a part of Flanders newly acquired by France. Watteau quickly makes the transition from Dutch values to the French practice of doing without any. The diarist remains Dutch and therefore despises the falsity she ascribes to Paris. She thinks of herself as "a tame, unambitious soul." "I find," she writes, "a certain immobility of disposition in me, to quicken or interfere with which is like physical pain." Watteau she finds "so brilliant, petulant, mobile!" As the years drag their slow length along, she maintains her conviction that Watteau's success hasn't made him happy and that he still lacks "that quietude of mind, without which, methinks, one fails in true dignity of character."

Meanwhile she puts up with Watteau's triumphs by telling herself that he really despises the subjects that have ensured it:

> If I understand anything of these matters, Antony Watteau paints that delicate life of Paris so excellently, with so much spirit, partly because, after all, he looks down upon it or despises it. To persuade myself of that, is my womanly satisfaction for his preference—his apparent preference—for a world so different from mine. Those coquetries, those vain and perishable graces, can be rendered so perfectly, only through an intimate understanding of them. For him, to understand must be to despise them; while (I think I know why) he nevertheless undergoes their fascination. Hence that discontent with himself, which keeps pace with his fame. It would have been better for him—he would have enjoyed a purer and more real happiness —had he remained here, obscure; as it might have been better for me![5]

She deals with her resentment by consigning it to her journal, attaching it to "that gallant world, those patched and powdered ladies and fine cavaliers."

The most telling transition is from Watteau's unfinished portrait of the diarist to the finished thing it might have been. He has required her to wear a fashionable dress:

> My own portrait remains unfinished at his sudden departure. I sat for it in a walking-dress, made under his direction—a gown of a peculiar silken stuff, falling into an abundance of small folds, giving me "a certain air of piquancy" which pleases him, but is far enough from my true self. My old Flemish *faille*, which I shall always wear, suits me better.[6]

Three years later, the portrait—"my own poor likeness"—remains on the easel as it was.

Pater's method in the story is to approach his main themes obliquely. We are never told directly that the diarist is in love with Watteau or that he has rejected her. The lethal word is used not about her love of him but about his having cast off her brother Jean-Baptiste, his pupil:

> Jean-Baptiste! he too, rejected by Antony! It makes our friend-ship and fraternal sympathy closer. And still as he labours, not less sedulously than of old, and still so full of loyalty to his old master, in that *Watteau* chamber, I seem to see Antony himself, of whom Jean-Baptiste dares not yet speak,—to come very near his work, and understand his great parts. So Jean-Baptiste's work, in its nearness to his, may stand, for the future, as the central interest of my life. I bury myself in that.[7]

The transition here is remarkable. Watteau has rejected Jean-Baptiste, but the sister, establishing her brother's work as the central interest of her life, conjures the figure of Watteau to stand sympathetically beside it. She summons him to appear, as in the rhetorical figure of proso-popoeia. Jean-Baptiste's work then becomes the force of mediation between her and Watteau. It could remain in that posture for the rest of her life. But the last sentence gives the show away: "I bury myself in that." Not even: "I shall bury myself in that." It is the continuous present tense, and as lethal as the other verb of rejection.

19

Gaston de Latour

L IKE RONSARD'S *Franciade* to which it alludes, *Gaston de Latour* is unfinished. After the success of *Marius the Epicurean*, Pater planned two further volumes in which a man with preoccupations similar to Marius's would deal with them in different historical conditions. He started with *Gaston de Latour*, "a sort of *Marius* in France, in the 16th century,"[1] as he called it. He published the first five chapters in successive numbers of *Macmillan's Magazine* from June to October 1888. The sixth remained in manuscript, but after Pater's death Shadwell deemed it publishable and included it in *Gaston de Latour: An Unfinished Romance*, which appeared on October 6, 1896. Chapter 7, "The Lower Pantheism," is complete; a short version of it was published as "Giordano Bruno" in the *Fortnightly* in August 1889. Fragmentary manuscript of a further six chapters has survived, but not in presentable form.

In his Preface dated July 1896 Shadwell said of the book:

> The work, if completed, would have been a parallel study of character to "Marius the Epicurean," the scene shifted to another age of transition, when the old fabric of belief was breaking up, and when the problem of man's destiny and his relations to the

unseen was undergoing a new solution. The interest would have centred round the spiritual development of a refined and cultivated mind, capable of keen enjoyment in the pleasures of the senses and of the intellect, but destined to find its complete satisfaction in that which transcends both. Something of the same motive appears in some of the Imaginary Portraits, such as Sebastian Van Storck, and Duke Carl of Rosenmold, undertaken about the same time. How Mr. Pater would have developed the story we can only guess: from the fragmentary state in which he has left it, it seems not impossible that he was himself dissatisfied with the framework which he had begun, and that he deliberately abandoned it.[2]

The remote origin of the book is the chapter on du Bellay in *Studies in the History of the Renaissance*, especially the passage in which Pater says of the poetry of du Bellay, Ronsard, and other writers of the *Pleiad* that "it was once poetry *à la mode*." This poetry is "part of the manner of a time, a time which made much of manner, and carried it to a high degree of perfection."[3] Du Bellay's claim that modern French could hold its own against Greek and Latin allows Pater to associate himself with modernity—as if the dispute between Ancients and Moderns were still going on—and with the privilege of young men in their possession of modern life.

The story, such as it barely is, traces a pattern common to most of Pater's fictions. A young man finds, as he moves out into the world, that the values on which he has lived are in conflict with his new experience. He must resolve the conflict in one of three possible ways: by holding a difficult balance of interests, by settling for the new force of attraction against the old, or, a remote possibility, by discovering a higher system of values that transcends the conflict. This was Pater's "one story and one story only." It was also a version of his own life as a young man. But this coincidence does not allow us to reduce his work to its autobiographical germ.

Gaston de Latour, born in the Château of Deux-manoirs at La Beauce, "the great corn-land of central France," grows up to become a cleric at the Cathedral of Chartres. It is the middle of the sixteenth century, the years of the religious wars in the reign of Charles IX. One chapter deals with the siege of the cathedral by an army of Huguenots. Gaston has three friends: Jasmin, who is likely to become a poet; Amadée, who appears destined for the army; and Camille, who is turned toward the law. Jasmin gives Gaston a present, a copy of Ronsard's *Odes*, and Gaston finds the poems an apt expression of "the truant and irregular poetry of his own nature":

> Here was a poetry which boldly assumed the dress, the words, the habits, the very trick, of contemporary life, and turned them into gold. It took possession of the lily in one's hand, and projecting it into a visionary distance, shed upon the body of the flower the soul of its beauty. Things were become at once more deeply sensuous and more deeply ideal . . . the visible was more visible than ever before, just because soul had come to its surface.[4]

The narrator recognizes that such poetry, with its "intimate fitness to the mind of its own time," is neglected as soon as that time has passed and a new version of modernity asserts itself. It can't be helped. For the moment, Gaston is exhilarated to find himself expressed, and he moves easily into a mood in which sensory and moral considerations seem to be benignly indistinguishable:

> And his new imaginative culture had taught him to value "surprises" in nature itself; the quaint, exciting charm of the mistletoe in the wood, of the blossom before the leaf, the cry of passing birds at night. Nay! the most familiar details of nature, its daily routine of light and darkness, beset him now with a kind of troubled and troubling eloquence. The rain, the first streak of dawn, the very sullenness of the sky, had a power, only to be described by saying that they seemed to be *moral* facts.[5]

But before the chapter is over, Gaston is worrying about the conflict between his early piety and his new religion, the worship of physical beauty. Pater has been reading Baudelaire on Gaston's behalf:

> Might that new religion be a religion not altogether of goodness, a profane religion, in spite of its poetic fervours? There were "flowers of evil," among the rest.[6]

Gaston speculates that there may be, "in some penetrative mind in this age of novelties," a scheme to harmonize the sacred and profane loves.

But if there isn't, he will choose, "to his pacification," the profane.

It is not enough for Gaston and his friends to read Ronsard's poems. They must pay the great man a visit at Croix-val. He gives Gaston a letter of introduction to his friend Montaigne. Gaston sets out for La Rochelle, delivers the letter, and accepts Montaigne's hospitality for nine months. He wishes to eat the fruit not only of the Tree of Knowledge but of all the trees in the garden. Montaigne's essays seem to justify this appetite. Pater recalls Arnold and reports of Montaigne:

> For him, as for Plato, for Socrates whom he cites so often, the essential dialogue was that of the mind with itself. . . .[7]

Montaigne is another great exemplar of modernity in his sense of "the diversity, the undulancy, of human nature"; he is the philosopher of difference, not only of the difference between one person and another but between one self and another domiciled in the same body, "the many men who keep discordant company within each one of us." Gaston, like Montaigne and Pater, takes pleasure in mobility, "the healthful pleasure of motion, of thoughts in motion." Always on the understanding that the evidences of truth are one's own productions:

> Whatever truth there might be, must come for each one from within, not from without. To that wonderful microcosm of the individual soul, of which, for each one, all other worlds are but elements,—to himself,—to what was apparent immediately to him, what was "properly of his own having and substance": he confidently dismissed the inquirer. His own egotism was but the pattern of the true intellectual life of every one. "The greatest thing in the world is for a man to know that he is his own."[8]

But it isn't, for Montaigne, Gaston, or Pater, a question of knowledge. In *Montaigne en mouvement* (1982), Jean Starobinski notes that "it is to *feeling* that Montaigne shifts the burden of *knowing*." The role of the body is always recognized:

> To be sure, it is also a proper function of the mind to feel, intuitively, by means of one of the faculties attributed to the "spiritual sense." *Sensation*, in the broad sense, refers to the perception of thoughts as well as of modifications of the body. But to know oneself "through sensation" is to do so without

the aid of discursive reason: "I *judge* myself only by *actual sen-sation*, not by reasoning." Feeling is a necessary condition of judgment—this is Montaigne's first topic. . . .[9]

Montaigne is therefore a heretic, if one has the effrontery to judge him upon doctrinal grounds. So the episode in which Gaston seeks him out leads, after an interval of one chapter, to his hearing a lecture by a more resolute and more decisively punished heretic, Giordano Bruno (1548–1600).

The interval is called "Shadows of Events," an allusion I suppose to Bruno's *De umbris idearum* (1582), a treatise on magic, memory, and hermetic secrets. The title has its local bearing. Gaston is in Paris, living with Colombe, a woman he doesn't take seriously or much care for, who is pregnant with his child. Summoned back to the Château of Deux-manoirs, where his grandfather is dying, he leaves Colombe. While he is away, on the Eve of St. Bartholomew, August 23, 1572, there is a massacre in Paris. Thousands are killed. When he hears of it, Gaston hurries back to search for Colombe, doesn't find her, and lives on with the guilt of having abandoned her.

It is typical of Pater not to describe the massacre. As in Brueghel's *Icarus*, Auden's "Musée des Beaux Arts," and W. C. Williams's "Land-scape with the Fall of Icarus," the big things are done offstage; the splash is quite unnoticed. Pater likes to keep aloof. When he takes possession of a lily, he projects it into a visionary distance, removing its importunity. Much as he claimed that all art constantly aspires toward the condition of music, his own aspired toward the condition of tapestry. His mind took more seriously than other minds Marcus Aurelius's saying that "whatever may happen to you was prepared for you from all eternity; and the implication of causes was from eternity spinning the thread of your being." The thread of life was more than a metaphor to Pater, but he thought of it not only as something inev-itably cut but as material in the meantime for a woven picture. In the "Modernity" chapter he describes the three friends visiting Gaston:

> Threads to be cut short, one by one, before his eyes, the three would cross and recross, gaily, pathetically, in the tapestry of Gaston's years; and, divided far asunder afterwards, seemed at this moment, moving there before him in the confidential talk he could not always share, inseparably linked together, like some complicated pictorial arabesque, under the common light, of

their youth, and of the morning, and of their sympathetic understanding of the visible world.[10]

Arabesques, like Raphael's in the Vatican, introduce the motion of
living beings into an otherwise static object. The motion has been
stilled, but we know it has been stilled, and we can restore its moving
value by a flick of mind. Pater's theme is never one thing in itself; it
is always the "common light" in which the relations between the thing
and other values are interpreted, and moved by being interpreted. In
this passage, the light he begins with is figurative ("of their youth"),
then literal ("of the morning"), and finally moral ("of their sympathetic
understanding of the visible world"). Formally, the theme is light, but
Pater doesn't merely look at it. The variousness of the available relations
is what he's after.

Sometimes the relations are equable; they merely issue from another
way of looking at things, a different but not exacting perspective. In
the first chapter of *Gaston de Latour*, for instance, the scene is the church
at La Beauce, the young Gaston is being received into orders as a cleric:

> Seen from the incense-laden sanctuary, where the bishop was
> assuming one by one the pontifical ornaments, La Beauce, like
> a many-coloured carpet spread under the great dome, with the
> white double house-front quivering afar through the heat,
> though it looked as if you might touch with the hand its distant
> spaces, was for a moment the unreal thing. Gaston alone, with
> all his mystic preoccupations, by the privilege of youth, seemed
> to belong to both, and link the visionary company about him
> to the external scene.[11]

The company (which, by the way, is unlikely to have been the source
of Hart Crane's lines in "The Broken Tower": "And so it was I entered
the broken world / To trace the visionary company of love. . . .") is
merely the gathering of priests and clerics in the church on that morning. The company is the company as Gaston sees it, now that he feels
himself participant in two worlds, either of which might on occasion
seem unreal, the other real. It doesn't matter, because in such seemings
all things are.

In the "Shadows of Events" chapter, the dominant relations are
sinister. Nature seems to have malice in mind. The most pressing
relation is between public and private actions: the massacre in Paris

and Gaston's betrayal of Colombe, the malign obscurity of the causes of each. Pater's choice paradigm of such obscurity is the battle over the corpse of Patroclus in the *Iliad*:

> We all feel, I suppose, the pathos of that mythic situation in Homer, where the Greeks at the last throb of battle around the body of Patroclus find the horror of supernatural darkness added to their other foes; feel it through some touch of truth to our own experience how the malignancy of the forces against us may be doubled by their uncertainty and the resultant confusion of one's own mind—blindfold night there too, at the moment when daylight and self-possession are indispensable.[12]

"Blindfold" makes the darkness not only supernaturally prescribed but social and cultural, the malignancy entered upon historical life. In a passage of Gaston's brooding upon his guilt, we read that his betrayal "owed its tragic significance there to an unfriendly shadow precluding knowledge how certain facts had really gone. . . ." "Unfriendly" assimilates to human life a force otherwise impersonal, like the weather. Gaston's feelings swirl back and forth between guilt and a protest of helplessness:

> And more and more as he picked his way among the direful records of the late massacre, not the cruelty only but the obscurity, the accidental character, yet, alas! also the treachery, of the public event seemed to identify themselves tragically with his own personal action. Those queries, those surmises were blent with the enigmatic sense of his own helplessness amid the obscure forces around him, which would fain compromise the indifferent, and had made him so far an accomplice in their unfriendly action that he felt certainly not quite guiltless, thinking of his own irresponsible, self-centered, passage along the ways, through the weeks that had ended in the public crime and his own private sorrow.[13]

"Not quite guiltless" and "sorrow" amount to a pretty venial sentiment after all the brooding. Pater's aesthetic of mobility has this consequence: his mind is so fluid in its attention to outer and inner correlations that it is possible to dissolve in high sentences the otherwise dourly insistent forces of responsibility. At one point in the chapter he allows Gaston to think of blaming poor Montaigne:

Delirium was in the air already charged with thunder, and laid hold on Gaston too. It was as if through some unsettlement in the atmospheric medium the objects around no longer acted upon the senses with the normal result. Looking back afterwards, this singularly self-possessed person had to confess that under its influence he had lost for a while the exacter view of certain outlines, certain real differences and oppositions of things in that hotly coloured world of Paris (like a shaken tapestry about him) awaiting the Eve of Saint Bartholomew. Was the "undulant" philosophy of Monsieur de Montaigne, in collusion with this dislocating time, at work upon him, that, following with only too entire a mobility the *experience* of the hour, he found himself more than he could have thought possible the toy of external accident![14]

Not that Gaston, or indeed Pater, had ever sought an "exacter view of certain outlines, certain real differences and oppositions of things." Differences, yes, but not oppositions. Even these were produced most often by a sense of place and of the *genius loci* rather than by an exacting sense of morality. In a fair copy of the unpublished chapter 13—fair, because in Clara Pater's hand—Gaston visits the cemetery of the Innocents in Paris, enters a nearby church, and feels himself "once more the creature of the influences of his consecrated boyhood." The one place in which a moral judgment is not made is in an apparently stable self, bodied forth against what surrounds it.

As a result, Pater's typical sentences allude to disparate considerations but keep them far enough apart to avoid conflict. His mind takes promiscuous pleasure in recognizing differences, but it doesn't like to set them out in ranks or make distinctions which require a choice. Antithesis is alien to him, though he risks the embarrassment of producing occasions for it; as in this one about Gaston watching his grandfather dying:

A religious pretext had brought into sudden evidence all the latent ferocities of a corrupt though dainty civilisation, and while the stairways of the Louvre, the streets, the vile trap-doors of Paris, run blood, far away at Deux-manoirs Gaston watches as the light creeps over the silent cornfields, the last sense of it in those aged eyes now ebbing softly away.[15]

In another writer, this survey of the massacre in Paris and the ebbing scene at Deux-manoirs would make an irony, enforced by their presence in one sentence. Pater's syntax turns the other cheek. "And while" smooths the discrepancy, the object of Gaston's watching is postponed by a relative clause—"as the light creeps over the silent cornfields"—and when it arrives it is a much diminished thing, "the last sense of it."

20

Appreciations

Hic. *And I would find myself and not an image.*
Ille. *That is our modern hope, and by its light*
     We have lit upon the gentle, sensitive mind
     And lost the old nonchalance of the hand;
     Whether we have chosen chisel, pen or brush,
     We are but critics, or but half create. . . .
        —W. B. Yeats, "Ego Dominus Tuus"

I

*A*PPRECIATIONS: WITH AN ESSAY ON STYLE appeared from Macmillan on November 15, 1889. The book had a dedication: "To the Memory of My Brother William Thompson Pater who quitted a useful and happy life, Sunday April 24, 1887: Requiem Eternam Dona ei Domine et Lux Perpetua luceat ei."

Pater culled material for the book mostly from his essays in the *Fortnightly*, the *Westminster*, and *Macmillan's*. An essay on Style and another on Romanticism enclosed three groups: one on Wordsworth, Coleridge, and Lamb; the second on Shakespeare and Browne; the third on Aesthetic Poetry. For this last, he reached back twenty years to his early review-essay on Morris, reprinting with significant changes the first fifteen paragraphs of it. All the changes were in the cause of prudence.

For instance, near the beginning of the essay Pater attributed the sweetness of Morris's *The Defence of Guenevere* to its mixture of Arthurian legend and Christianity, "the strange suggestion of a deliberate choice between Christ and a rival lover":

> That religion shades into sensuous love, and sensuous love into religion, has been often seen; it is the experience of Rousseau as well as of the Christian mystics. The Christianity of the middle age made way among a people whose loss was in the life of the senses only by the possession of an idol, the beautiful idol of the Latin hymn-writers, who for one moral or spiritual sentiment have a hundred sensuous images. Only by the inflaming influence of such idols can any religion compete with the presence of the fleshly lover.[1]

Revising this, Pater removed the three idols, the inflaming influence, and the fleshly lover:

> The Christianity of the Middle Age made way among a people whose loss was in the life of the senses partly by its aesthetic beauty, a thing so profoundly felt by the Latin hymn-writers, who for one moral or spiritual sentiment have a hundred sensuous images.[2]

Provençal love-poetry, according to Pater in 1868, was a rival religion to Christianity: "the rejection of one idolatry for the other is never lost sight of." In 1889 "idolatry" is muted to "worship." In the next paragraph "the idolatry of the cloister" becomes "the devotion of the cloister." Pater's association of the church with magic—"Quite in the way of one who handles the older sorceries, the Church has a thousand charms to make the absent near"—becomes not "quite" anything but a metaphor separated from its subject: "But then, the Church, that new Sibyl, had a thousand secrets to make the absent near."

The most offensive sentence in the early review was diminished, in *Appreciations*, to a postponed simile. "That whole religion of the middle age was but a beautiful disease or disorder of the senses" became "That monastic religion of the Middle Age was, in fact, in many of its bearings, like a beautiful disease or disorder of the senses." In a book dedicated to his brother's memory and asking the Lord to give him eternal rest and let perpetual light shine upon him, Pater could not have darkened that prayer by repeating this passage:

The modern poet or artist who treats in this way a classical story comes very near, if not to the Hellenism of Homer, yet to that of the middle age, the Hellenism of Chaucer. No writer on the Renaissance has hitherto cared much for this exquisite early light of it. Afterwards the Renaissance takes its side, becomes exaggerated and facile. But the choice life of the human spirit is always under mixed lights, and in mixed situations; when it is not too sure of itself, is still expectant, girt up to leap forward to the promise. Such a situation there was in that earliest return from the overwrought spiritualities of the middle age to the earlier, more ancient life of the senses; and for us the most attractive form of classical story is the monk's conception of it, when he escapes from the sombre legend of his cloister to that true light.[3]

The last phrases are insolent in their charge that the light of Hellenism is what Christianity falsely claims to have. Pater recanted enough to refer to the monk escaping "from the sombre atmosphere of his cloister to natural light." The monk could achieve that, presumably, by going for a walk in the garden.

"Poems by William Morris" is Pater's most daring essay. It is not surprising that he later divided it in two, prepared a different house for each part, revised each while failing to note its effrontery, and suppressed each after its first publication in a book. The part that became "Aesthetic Poetry" in the first edition of *Appreciations* is Pater's theory of art for art's sake.

His exemplars of aesthetic poetry are Morris and D. G. Rossetti, but Morris even more than Rossetti. Pater starts the essay by taking him at his poetic word. In the first stanza of *The Earthly Paradise*, Morris acknowledges that "Of Heaven or Hell I have no power to sing." Not only does he lack Dante's genius and Milton's, but he cannot say anything to mitigate the conditions of our lives:

> *Of Heaven or Hell I have no power to sing,*
> *I cannot ease the burden of your fears,*
> *Or make quick-coming death a little thing,*
> *Or bring again the pleasure of past years,*
> *Nor for my words shall ye forget your tears,*
> *Or hope again for aught that I can say,*
> *The idle singer of an empty day.*[4]

We have here the gist and the provocation of Aestheticism. Idle and empty are what the world calls art. Morris takes the description without much ado. Yeats deals with a similar feeling in "Adam's Curse," defensively, since he knows that poets work their poems by stitching and unstitching, and women their beauty by labor just as hard: "Yet now it seems an idle trade enough." Morris is, I think, Yeats's example as he is Pater's, quoting precedents out of beautiful old books. If we are genial about this, we take idle to mean agreeably detached and empty to mean emptied of all the interests commonly accepted as real. An aesthete is an artist who considers what he can do by standing aside. What he does has its adversary merit in relation to the Victorian consensus on the moral value of work.

Morris's apology is predicated upon a condition nearly universal: there is nothing to be done, except for the little nothings an artist in this condition might attempt in his own terms. But the condition was also local to Morris and Pater. John Lucas has argued that in the middle years of the nineteenth century English writers started finding England, and especially English cities, unknowable, opaque. Even those who thought they had an irresistible claim to speak for the whole country started doubting that they could cope with such heterogeneity. *Bleak House* is profoundly concerned with this opacity.[5] Lucas's point might be developed. People in an industrial society have to learn to be indifferent to whatever they don't understand and therefore can't control. Max Weber has described the process by which, in the later years of the nineteenth century, people started handing over large parts of their lives to experts: bankers, priests, economists, politicians. Most of them seem to have done this reluctantly, and they took some of the harm out of it by persuading themselves that they lived their true lives in the privacy of their feelings. Those who had some leisure and a little spare money resorted to music, literature, and painting to revive their sense of the missing or abandoned parts of their lives. Or of modes of life still to be imagined. They convinced themselves that their silences were numinous, to be enjoyed in an art gallery, a library, a concert hall. As late as *Howards End*, the really fateful events happened at a concert or in a garden, contemplating a house, old trees. The problem was: how to intuit a sense of the whole, while learning to ignore or yield up to others much of what was there. Not that writers calmly gave up the attempt to understand the whole. The realistic novel is the major Victorian genre because novelists had more success than poets or dramatists in developing a relatively unburdened language capable of responding to the new forces they had to deal with. Aestheticism was one expression of the premonition, sad indeed, that most of life, in the forms in which it presented itself, could not be understood and yet must be lived. Morris's Aestheticism seems hard to reconcile with his socialism, but it expresses the motives his socialism couldn't use up, the sense that a day apparently full was also irrefutably empty. In *The Earthly Paradise* he justifies his singing " 'of names remembered' / Because they, living not, can ne'er be dead." Pater might have made the same claim for *Marius the Epicurean*, but by then English fiction was preoccupied with semblances of living people. Other forms of fiction were thought to be romances, sports, or conceits, the sort of thing Poe and Hawthorne wrote. *Marius* should have been a long poem, like *The Ring and the Book* and *Aurora Leigh*, not a work in competition with *Middlemarch*.

Morris's aim in *The Earthly Paradise*, *The Life and Death of Jason*, and *The Defence of Guenevere*—the books to which Pater referred—was to intuit an alternative world, good while the reading lasted, by singing of fictive names remembered. Pater was delighted with the aim and charmed by the poems. He praised Morris for gathering into the nineteenth century so much of what was essential in Greek mythology and medieval poetry. Morris's poems, according to Pater, embodied a certain sequence in relation to ordinary life. The sequence defines Aestheticism.

There is, to begin with, the ordinary world of sight and sound. Pater doesn't choose to be subtle about it or even to kick stones in its favor. Above that world, there is a secondary state which he finds in poetry:

> Greek poetry, mediaeval or modern poetry, projects above the realities of its time a world in which the forms of things are transfigured.[6]

"Above," because the movement is toward more and more spiritual states; "the forms of things" are not allowed to impose themselves. The poet's will is taking command, even though the ordinary world of sight and sound is alluded to. But Pater then posits a third state and finds it in Morris's poems. Of the secondary state, Morris's poetry takes possession, "and sublimates beyond it another still fainter and more spectral, which is literally an artificial or 'earthly paradise.' " This third creation, Pater says, "is a finer ideal, extracted from what in relation to any actual world is already an ideal."[7] Morris started with the actual, transcended it in a secondary ideal, and then created an even finer one, chemically purer than the other, as Johnson remarked that the heat of Milton's mind might be said to sublimate his learning. The learning is already a play of mind apart from the nature to which it alludes. Heat is the third force: it sets astir Pater's favorite sequence, ushering in a state of purity and refinement that cannot be found in nature. It is, he says, like some strange second flowering after date, and "it renews on a more delicate type the poetry of a past age, but must not be confounded with it." Type: it issues not from nature but from a formal anticipation of itself. There is no need to fend off the trace of type as in printing; in print, Morris's poems merit a more delicate type or font than the common ones.

Pater's essay recites many versions of this triad. One of them involves Christianity, which starts from the ordinary world of sight and sound only to withdraw from it and to deny its authority. Pater regards the cloister as this secondary place, the monk its exemplar. But in this early essay he thinks, by a remarkably brash prejudice, that it is the supreme felicity of a religion, having spiritualized its doctrines, to develop into an art. "Who knows whether, when the simple belief in them has faded away, the most cherished sacred writings may not for the first time exercise their highest influence as the most delicate amorous poetry in the world?" As an art, religion returns to the world, but now it is the world imagined, in Pater's terms as in Stevens's "the ultimate good." The monk becomes a pagan:

> The *Defence of Guenevere* was published in 1858; the *Life and Death of Jason* in 1867; and the change of manner wrought in the interval is entire, it is almost a revolt. Here there is no delirium or illusion, no experiences of mere soul while the body and the bodily senses sleep or wake with convulsed intensity at the prompting of imaginative love; but rather the great primary passions under broad daylight as of the pagan Veronese. This simplification interests us not merely for the sake of an individual poet—full of charm as he is—but chiefly because it explains through him a transition which, under many forms, is one law of the life of the human spirit, and of which what we call the Renaissance is only a supreme instance. Just so the monk in his cloister, through the "open vision," open only to the spirit, divined, aspired to and at last apprehended a better daylight,

but earthly, open only to the senses. Complex and subtle interests, which the mind spins for itself may occupy art and poetry or our own spirits for a time; but sooner or later they come back with a sharp rebound to the simple elementary passions—anger, desire, regret, pity and fear—and what corresponds to them in the sensuous world—bare, abstract fire, water, air, tears, sleep, silence—and what De Quincey has called the "glory of motion."[8]

But to come back to the simple elementary passions is not the same experience as that of never having left them. It is to open one's senses to daylight, "the better daylight," after a night of dream or delirium. According to Pater's rhetoric this "late" condition feels like a new first one:

Everywhere there is an impression of surprise, as of people first waking from the golden age, at fire, snow, wine, the touch of water as one swims, the salt taste of the sea. And this simplicity at first hand is a strange contrast to the sought-out simplicity of Wordsworth. Desire here is towards the body of nature for its own sake, not because a soul is divined through it.[9]

We begin again, if only to fail better. It is a world, Pater says, "in which the centaur and the ram with the fleece of gold are conceivable." Trying again, in a gorgeous sentence: "the song sung always claims to be sung for the first time." As Stevens, remembering Hopkins's poems, writes in "Notes Toward a Supreme Fiction":

> But the difficultest rigor is forthwith,
> On the image of what we see, to catch from that
>
> Irrational moment its unreasoning,
> As when the sun comes rising, when the sea
> Clears deeply, when the moon hangs on the wall
>
> Of heaven-haven. These are not things transformed.
> Yet we are shaken by them as if they were.
> We reason about them with a later reason.[10]

This essay of Pater's on Morris anticipates the passage I have quoted from Yeats's *Autobiographies* about the two traditions in nineteenth-century English poetry. Yeats's tenderness toward the second one because of its dependence upon images separated from the general purposes of human life rhymes with Pater's sense of the vulnerable character of "aesthetic poetry." In the essay on Morris, aesthetic poetry speaks of Courtly Love, its place is the château, its voice the fleshly lover's:

> Hence a love defined by the absence of the beloved, choosing to be without hope, protesting against all lower uses of love, barren, extravagant, antinomian.[11]

The adjectives refer to Provençal passion, not to mundane love. "Barren," as in Yeats's "for a barren passion's sake"; "extravagant," of course; "antinomian," because its *sprezzatura* is autonomous. Such love is "incompatible with marriage"; it is love of the absent chevalier, "of the serf for the chatelaine, the rose for the nightingale, of Rudel for the Lady of Tripoli." Provençal poetry sings of vassalage:

> To be the servant of love, to have offended, to taste the subtle luxury of chastisement, of reconciliation—the religious spirit, too, knows that, and meets just there, as in Rousseau, the delicacies of the earthly love. Here, under this strange complex of conditions, as in some medicated air, exotic flowers of sentiment expand, among people of a remote and unaccustomed beauty, somnambulistic, frail, androgynous, the light almost shining through them, as the flame of a little taper shows through the Host. Such loves were too fragile and adventurous to last more than for a moment.[12]

These poets of Provence make a rival religion with a new rival cultus. "Coloured through and through with Christian sentiment, they are rebels against it." Like Abelard and Heloise.

II

"Poems by William Morris" is also the most English of Pater's essays, even more so than "The Child in the House," "An English

Poet," and "Emerald Uthwart." But Pater's England is not the country as given: on that, he has little purchase. Here as elsewhere he invents a place responsive to his desires, calls it England, and has the panache to take Wordsworth for its minstrel. Morris's sense of English scenery is "from an eye well practised under Wordsworth's influence, in the song of the brown river-bird among the willows, the casement half opened on summer-nights, the noise of bells, such as in moonlit lanes rings from the grey team on the market night." One image inciting another, and with the fourteenth book of *The Life and Death of Jason* open before him, Pater murmurs the names of English birds as if for practice:

> Nowhere but in England is there such a nation of birds, the fern-owl, the water-hen, the thrush in a hundred sweet variations, the ger-falcon, the kestrel, the starling, the pea-fowl; birds heard from the field by the townsman down in the streets at dawn; doves everywhere, pink-footed, grey-winged, flitting about the temple, troubled by the temple incense, trapped in the snow. The sea-touches are not less sharp and firm, surest of effect in places where river and sea, salt and fresh waves, conflict.[13]

Morris's poem, Pater implies, gathers to itself the legend of Jason, the Golden Fleece, the Argonauts, the Sirens, the garden of the Hesperides, Medea, and the death of Pelias; then enriches this legendry with intimations of Courtly Love. In the end, the romance of this poetry opens upon the landscapes, transfigured indeed, of modern England. "The composite experience of all the ages," Pater says, "is part of each one of us." Greece and Rome, the Middle Ages, the Renaissance: these and other episodes constitute our experience. But we are not merely the sum of historical forces. One's particular consciousness works upon those and makes of them, within unofficial reason, what it wills. The same consciousness can make much of one phase and little of another, for no clear cause:

> But though it is not possible to repress a single phase of that humanity, which, because we live and move and have our being in the life of humanity, makes us what we are; it is possible to isolate such a phase, to throw it into relief, to be divided against

ourselves in zeal for it, as we may hark back to some choice
space of our own individual life.[14]

Not as simple as it appears. The first phrases, surrounding the allusion
to the *Acts of the Apostles*, make a claim nearly universal, though it would
be possible to reduce it to the statement that we modern people are
heirs to all the ages, our historical sense being what it is. Of course we
can repress any phase of humanity by not paying attention to it. That
is a consideration too sordid for Pater. It is more congenial to him to
press the opposite possibility, that we can write some parts of our lives
in italics. Childhood, as a clear instance, Wordsworth in attendance.
Or, with Morris in view, the moments in which we imagine paradise
and require it to be earthly, as in the extravagance of being in love.
Or, if we are aesthetes, the moments in which we imagine a country
of the blue and yearn to live in it.

I recite again two phrases set apart in Pater's essay. "Desire here is
towards the body of nature for its own sake, not because a soul is
divined through it." That's one. The other is ". . . to be divided against
ourselves in zeal for it." There is tension between them. Pater loves to
speak the phrase "for its own sake," as if to guard against violation
some precious sentiment. He is a witness to the charm of the intrinsic,
of a state of being or feeling that proposes to be itself, responsible for
its own mobility. He is so well disposed to the intrinsic that he is
willing to set aside as extraneous even the consideration that "a soul is
divined through it," a consideration we would expect him to value. In
the *Philosophy of Spirit* Hegel says that spirit, as distinct from matter,
is that which has its center in itself; it is free by virtue of the self-
contained mode of its existence. So with Pater's phrase: "To be divided
against ourselves in zeal for it" marks his scruple, the misgiving he feels
in projecting certain forms and images and giving them his undivided
attention. That, too, is a feature of Aestheticism.

It is not surprising that the aesthetic experience lasts for a moment
only and must be renewed under later incitement or happy coincidence.
"Such loves were too fragile and adventurous to last more than for a
moment," Pater says of Courtly Love. Consciousness, intensity, pulsations: no frame could endure their action for long. Think of the
glimpse in Baudelaire's poems, the deathly charm to Emily Dickinson
of things just going out of sight, Arthur Symons's saying of a certain
dance that it lasted only long enough to have been there, and Eliot's
"Burnt Norton":

Sudden in a shaft of sunlight
Even while the dust moves
There rises the hidden laughter
Of children in the foliage
Quick now, here, now, always—
Ridiculous the waste sad time
Stretching before and after.[15]

It would be splendid if such moments could be relied upon or extended at will or imagined afresh, but no writer since Wordsworth has counted upon this felicity. Aestheticism was designed to provide a setting for them, a scene of motifs and images sequestered from our given world: the scene was such as to conjure momentary illuminations into existence, by force of one's desire that they should appear.

21

"Style"

BEFORE HE SETTLED upon *Appreciations* as the title, Pater intended to call the book *On Style, with Other Studies in Literature*. "Style," published in the *Fortnightly Review* on December 1, 1888, is his best known but not his best essay; it is desultory work. The context of the essay is Pater's concern with Flaubert as supreme embodiment of a distinctive type, the modern artist as martyr in the cause of style. In the *Pall Mall Gazette* for August 25, 1888, Pater reviewed the first volume of Flaubert's *Correspondance*, and in the *Athenaeum* for August 3, 1889, the second. "Style" issued from Pater's preoccupation with style as mark of aesthetic virtue.

The essay starts with an absurd attack on Dryden. There is no merit, Pater says, in distinguishing sharply between prose and poetry, as Dryden did, his protest against the confusion of the two "coming with somewhat diminished effect from one whose poetry was so prosaic":

In truth, his sense of prosaic excellence affected his verse rather than his prose, which is not only fervid, richly figured, poetic, as we say, but vitiated, all unconsciously, by many a scanning line. Setting up correctness, that humble merit of prose, as the central literary excellence, he is really a less correct writer than he may seem, still with an imperfect mastery of the relative pronoun.[1]

After this display of hauteur, Pater comes to one of his main subjects. "Imaginative prose," he says, is "the special art of the modern world," the medium most responsive to the variety and complexity of modern experience. Pater goes on to distinguish between fact and a particular writer's sense of fact; the latter, since it respects above all the artist's vision, is the force that makes writing a fine art rather than a serviceable one. How a fact escapes being anyone's particular sense of it, Pater doesn't explain, but in saying that fact can be transcribed he supposes that the transcript is objective, independent of the transcriber. He then makes a distinction between soul and mind, but it is the standard one in the context of Romanticism between imagination or vision and reason. Repeating what he wrote in "The School of Giorgione," Pater says that, among the fine arts, music is superior in its unity of form and matter. Literature strives toward this unity, seeking "the absolute correspondence of the term to its import."[2] If it achieves this correspondence, it is good literature. If in addition the matter the literature informs is great, then the literature is great. Flaubert's search for *le mot juste* is the paradigm of the artistic spirit in the modern world.

None of these matters is clarified by Pater's attention to it. The theory of language as correspondence between word and thing is useless. The word "table" doesn't, in any of its attributes, correspond to or resemble an article of furniture; only a certain social and linguistic convention associates them. The idea of correspondence represses the convention and implies that the reference of table to a piece of furniture is sanctioned by an English-speaking nature. Flaubert worked for his style and practiced *ascesis*, but there is no evidence that his search for *le mot juste* is animated by a theory of correspondence: it makes more sense to assume that the particular *mot*, when found, is *juste* to the other words in its vicinity rather than to an object in the world waiting to be named and summoned. Pater's consideration of form and content retains a distinction many nineteenth-century critics tried to get rid of, though I concede that his description of a successful literary structure is eloquent. When such a structure is complete, "all becomes expressive." The house the writer has built "is rather a body he has informed."[3] This is a strong version of the claim that the structure the artist has labored over, as if it were entirely objective, turns out to be expressive, too, of his spirit. But Pater's brisk discrimination of good content and great content is vain. Apparently concerned with style, he doesn't quote so much as a line of verse or a sentence of prose to illustrate his argument. Nor a word of Flaubert's fiction. Pater is content to provide a biographical context, Flaubert's correspondence, for the notion of style in relation to work and self-discipline. What he says of Flaubert in one essay and two reviews amounts to what Henry James said of him in a sentence: "His case was a doom because he felt of his vocation almost nothing but the difficulty."

"Style" does not clarify its themes, but it shows the extent to which Pater in his last years moved from a vocabulary of pleasure to one of morality. David de Laura has shown, in *Hebrew and Hellene in Victorian England*, that Pater wrote "Style" with Newman's "Literature" at his hand.[4] Newman's emphasis on style as signature, a writer's personal mark or bearing, enabled Pater to move between Newman and Flaubert as his diverse masters. Newman's own style remembered not only the classical past, Greece and Rome, but the Latin of the Catholic church and the English of Anglicanism. Flaubert's "martyrdom" to *le mot juste* was the modern, secular correlative to an earlier martyrdom to faith: his means of grace was the labor of working a recalcitrant language. Pater's sense of style held Newman and Flaubert in tense relation. Literature, like the other fine arts, gives its readers, Pater said, "a sort of cloistral refuge, from a certain vulgarity in the actual world." The motive of literature is not hedonistic. The artist finds in his conscience an answerable morality. He is a scholar among words. As often before, Pater takes the word "scholar" and some of its resonance from Fichte's essays on the subject. The scholar is the ideal student, instructor of mankind, its conscience in the task of self-realization. Emerson's "The American Scholar" offers a similar challenge. In Pater, the scholar's terms of reference are at once sensuous and severe, *ascesis* his commandment. Wallace Stevens received the word from Emerson and Pater, making it refer to the imagination in the aspect of its morality. A scholar belongs to a clerisy of language, learned, monastic. The clerics are men, and their readers have the attributes of educated men, as Pater explains:

> The literary artist is of necessity a scholar, and in what he proposes to do will have in mind, first of all, the scholar and the scholarly conscience—the male conscience in this matter,

as we must think it, under a system of education which still to so large an extent limits real scholarship to men. In his self-criticism, he supposes always that sort of reader who will go (full of eyes) warily, considerately, though without consideration for him, over the ground which the female conscience traverses so lightly, so amiably.[5]

Supposedly, women in Pater's England have a conscience, but not an educated or trained one. Henry James used the same words, "light" and "amiable," in condescending to Jane Austen's novels. Pater is thinking of his sisters, but he is not forgetting that much of the best nineteenth-century English literature was written by women. Presumably they were great writers to the extent to which they imagined what it would be like to be, by education and training, a man. Pater did not think of George Eliot's novels in any patronizing way; they were written, it appears, by a woman who was capable of imagining herself having a man's artistic conscience. She was in Pater's sense a scholar. It was also possible for an uneducated man to be a scholar as if by nature or desire. In another essay in *Appreciations* Pater ascribes to Charles Lamb "the true scholar's way of forgetting himself in his subject." And in a late essay on Raphael, Pater not only tells us that Raphael was a scholar, but keeps murmuring the word throughout. He associates scholarship with "the enthusiastic acquisition of knowledge for its own sake," Raphael's studying with Perugino and Pinturicchio, and the scholar's last reward, "a purely cerebral strength—the strength, the power of an immense understanding."[6] Purity of heart, in a scholar, is apparently to love one thing, the precise word. The scholar, like the artist, hates surplusage, is recognized by his "tact of omission," self-restraint. The aim of art is truth, but the truth for which Pater feels most tenderness is the artist's respect for his own sense of fact, the "vision within."

The most revealing passages in "Style" are concerned with details. Pater says of Flaubert's letters:

Writing to Madame X., certainly he does display, by "taking thought" mainly, by constant and delicate pondering, as in his love for literature, a heart really moved, but still more, and as the pledge of that emotion, a loyalty to his work. Madame X., too, is a literary artist, and the best gifts he can send her are precepts of perfection in art, counsels for the effectual pursuit of that better love.[7]

It cost Pater nothing to claim that a man's love of art is better than his love of a woman. But he reaches "that better love" by submitting himself to the force, as we have already come upon it, of the comparative degree of adjectives. "A heart really moved, but still more," is one version of this submission. Another is the sentence in which he claims that "the better" coincides with "the later":

> And so it happens, to its greater credit, that the better interest even of a narrative to be recounted, a story to be told, will often be in its second reading.[8]

There is no difference between "a narrative to be recounted" and "a story to be told," but the second has for Pater the merit of postponing the conclusion of the sentence, making delay a sign of scruple. It corresponds to the enacted effortfulness of another sentence: "But still, after all, with Flaubert, the search, the unwearied research, was not for the smooth, or winsome, or forcible word, as such, as with false Ciceronians, but quite simply and honestly, for the word's adjustment to its meaning." Three phrases postpone the arrival of the subject, "the search": a second thought produces "the unwearied research." The verb tells what the search was not for. What it was for is further postponed by two rhyming phrases, "as such, as with false Ciceronians" and by a judgment in advance, "but quite simply and honestly." What "the word's adjustment to its meaning" means, Pater doesn't say: if adjustment is required, a different word should evidently be sought. The context of these second thoughts is Pater's affection for Late Latin, his special feeling for writings of the Silver Age—one of the marks of a sensibility hesitating upon the decadence it prefigures.

But the strangest device in Pater's essay is his use of "does but" where the context requires no such extravagance. "Pedantry being only the scholarship of *le cuistre* (we have no English equivalent) he is no pedant, and does but show his intelligence of the rules of language in his freedoms with it. . . ." This is itself pedantic. *Le cuistre* combines the senses of caddishness and pedantry, but only a pedant would think the English language defective in lacking one word for the combination of those two. The rhetorical violence of "does but" makes a pointless show of difference. Pater means, "He shows his knowledge of the rules of language in the freedoms he takes with them." Then we have: "For in truth all art does but consist in the removal of surplusage." Surely not in truth. The claim in "does but" is a conceit. Pater shouldn't say more than: "one of the signs of artistic genius is the removal of surplusage." Two pages later:

> The otiose, the facile, surplusage: why are these abhorrent to the true literary artist, except because, in literary as in all other art, structure is all-important, felt, or painfully missed, everywhere? —that architectural conception of work, which foresees the end in the beginning and never loses sight of it, and in every part is conscious of all the rest, till the last sentence does but, with undiminished vigour, unfold and justify the first. . . .[9]

The rhetorical flourish of "why . . . except" smacks of *le cuistre*. The otiose, the facile, and surplusage are abhorrent to the literary artist for several reasons; no exception is entailed. But it is implausible that the function of the last sentence of a passage, or of an entire work, is solely to unfold and justify the first. The insertion of "with undiminished vigour" delays the verbs and makes the assertion still more extreme. On the same page, in reference to Henry L. Mansel:

> An acute philosophical writer, the late Dean Mansel (a writer whose works illustrate the literary beauty there may be in closeness, and with obvious repression or economy of a fine rhetorical gift) wrote a book, of fascinating precision in a very obscure subject, to show that all the technical laws of logic are but means of securing, in each and all of its apprehensions, the unity, the strict identity with itself, of the apprehending mind.[10]

Pater's sentence would lose nothing but its rhetorical surplusage if "but" were to be deleted. It would lose only an impression of accepted doom if it gave up the postponement of its subject and started: "The late Dean Mansel, an acute philosophical writer whose works. . . ." On the attributes of soul:

> . . . it is still a characteristic of soul, in this sense of the word, that it does but suggest what can never be uttered. . . .[11]

Delete "does but," and we have an acceptable claim. Retain it, and we have a supererogatory claim, that the only thing soul does is suggest what can never be uttered—absurd, if Pater is right in taking Blake as chief exemplar of soul.

"Style" is significant more for what it shows of Pater than for what it tells of style. It shows the sad steps with which he reached a conclusion, that the morality of writing must be sought not necessarily where Newman found it, in Christian theology, but in a writer's intuition of rectitude within the language he uses. Style is Pater's word for the achievement, the production in practice, of that intuition. The public context of the essay is the assumption that just as the purest English poetry was displayed in Palgrave's *Golden Treasury*, the possibilities of prose as a fine art could be seen not only in Flaubert but in various anthologies culminating, long after Pater's death, in Logan Pearsall Smith's *A Treasury of English Prose*. Prose, in the sense of an art not merely of communication, is not confined to the elegant consideration of nothing; its value, disclosed in the end, is the degree to which it displays the writer's labor and skill. The matter it considers is instrumental to that end. Anthologies of prose are displays of skill in negotiating sentences. The mind takes the risk of elaboration, qualification, postponement, only to intensify the satisfaction of negotiating them. The satisfaction is seen as the mark of virtue, a difficult art.

Rhetorically, Pater's essay claims to make a virtue out of conditions amounting to labor. It should be as difficult to write prose as to conduct a scientific experiment and communicate its results. In Victorian England the scientist was widely honored for his pursuit of truth: he was deemed to be a man of integrity, selfless, concentrated in purpose. The virtues recommended in Pater's "Style" are those of a scientist: *ascesis*, the removal of surplusage, the tact of omission—a favorite phrase Pater first used in "A Prince of Court Painters." These virtues amount to an ethic, because we are meant to feel the force of the temptations the writer has denied himself in order to achieve such probity. He has had to set aside the luxury of *copia*, a multitude of gypsy phrases, flourishes of the pen. The only pleasure he is permitted is the satisfaction of living in good faith with himself. Style is the name of that pleasure, a word that returns to the writer like a signature: it marks the conscientiousness with which he works.

In rhetorical terms, the appropriate figure is *amplificatio*, by which the writer works his material, as a scientist but also as any laborer or lover. The true artist alternates a "blithe, crisp sentence" with a "long-contending, victoriously intricate" one. Some sentences are instances of "the productive ardour"; they come upon possibilities, contingencies, negligencies, and take them up. Pater allows this, provided the writer is willing to go over his first thoughts and be ready to prefer his second. Some sentences go as straight as they can to the meaning. The literary artist, "somewhere before the end comes, is burdened, inspired, with his conclusion, and betimes delivered of it, leaving off, not in weariness and because he finds *himself* at an end, but in all the freshness of volition." The work of writing is like childbirth in Pater's imagining of that: all inspiration and labor and burden till just before the delivery, when the mother recovers the freshness of her volition. Perhaps it is true. The last few moments of the writing seem to achieve themselves. The writer "finishes the whole up to the just proportion of that ante-penultimate conclusion, and all becomes expressive." The last moment doesn't seem to have to be worked for.

The merit of Pater's description is that it presents writing as hard work, even if Adam's curse is sometimes removed. In that emphasis, Pater is with James, Conrad, Yeats, and Eliot: the language is recalcitrant, the writer can do only so much with it, there is always a defect. But Pater has talked himself into the comfort of murmuring these care-laden words. That he should want to make the case is more persuasive than the case made. His talk of surplusage and the tact of omission shows how his concept of style internalized the morality he was too diffident otherwise to declare. He takes upon his sentences and silently upon himself the curse of labor and sweat. It is edifying, I suppose. But when we read, for instance, Troilus's speech

> *Tell me, Apollo, for thy Daphne's love,*
> *What Cressid is, what Pandar, and what we:*
> *Her bed is India, there she lies, a pearl. . . .*

we look in vain for evidence that surplusage has been removed or tact employed in omitting a gaudy possibility.

22

"Shakespeare"

IN HIS ESSAY on D. G. Rossetti in *Appreciations* Pater says that poetry exercises two distinct functions:

> . . . it may reveal, it may unveil to every eye, the ideal aspects of common things, after Gray's way (though Gray too, it is well to remember, seemed in his own day, seemed even to Johnson, obscure) or it may actually add to the number of motives poetic and uncommon in themselves, by the imaginative creation of things that are ideal from their very birth.[1]

Rossetti wrote poetry of both kinds, but he was most inventive in the second: he added to poetry "fresh poetic material, of a new order of phenomena, in the creation of a new ideal." Presumably this second kind is independent of common things; it is a pure projection, an act of the mind in creation. "It must be abstract," as Stevens says. The difference between the essay on Rossetti and the one on Morris is that in the Rossetti "common things" are acknowledged in the first kind of poetry but not the second; in the essay on Morris these things are the existents from which first an essence and then (in Morris) a quintessence are derived.

The difference might be worth clarifying in other contexts, but in regard to *Appreciations* we need to note only the direction of Pater's interest: he always wants to go from common things to various refinements which either remove the commonness or establish themselves in an antinomian relation to it. In the essays on Shakespeare, for example, Pater concentrates on showing how Shakespeare gives us cause to sympathize with the most refined embodiment of an activity or a sentiment, especially in its defeat. In *Love's Labour's Lost* "what is a vulgarity in Holofernes, and a caricature in Armado, refines itself with him (Biron) into the expression of a nature truly and inwardly bent upon a form of delicate perfection, and is accompanied by a real insight into the laws which determine what is exquisite in language, and their root in the nature of things."[2] The claim in that last phrase is considerable; "root" in the vicinity of "exquisite" and referring back to "laws" asserts that there is natural continuity ("in the nature of things") between existence, essence, and quintessence. The poet's imagination acts to fulfill this continuity and to produce its most refined extracts. *Measure for Measure* starts from a rough story, Cinthio's *Promos and Cassandra*, as Shakespeare found it in Whetstone's version:

> Out of these insignificant sources Shakespeare's play rises, full of solemn expression, and with a profoundly designed beauty, the new body of a higher, though sometimes remote and difficult poetry, escaping from the imperfect relics of the old story, yet not wholly transformed, and even as it stands but the preparation only, we might think, of a still more imposing design.[3]

Pater refers to "that artistic law which demands the predominance of form everywhere over the mere matter or subject handled." The supreme version of that law of refinement in *Measure for Measure* is the transformation of Isabella from her "cloistral whiteness" into "a fiery, revealing eloquence." "The swift, vindictive anger leaps, like a white flame, into this white spirit. . . ." Pater's recollection of "Orcagna's fresco at Pisa," the *Triumph of Death* fresco attributed to Orcagna in the Camposanto, which he saw on his visit with Shadwell in 1865, is his imaginative response to death as a force in the play:

In places the shadow deepens: death intrudes itself on the scene, as among other things "a great disguiser," blanching the features of youth and spoiling its goodly hair, touching the fine Claudio even with its disgraceful associations. As in Orcagna's fresco at Pisa, it comes capriciously, giving many and long reprieves to Barnardine, who has been waiting for it nine years in prison, taking another thence by fever, another by mistake of judgment, embracing others in the midst of their music and song.[4]

This recollection goes along with Pater's concern for the "poetical justice" of the play, and for seeing it realized; true justice being, he says, not an affair of rights but "in its essence a finer knowledge through love."

In the third and most elaborate essay, "Shakespeare's English Kings," Pater recalls Charles Kean's performance of *Richard II* which he saw in London in 1858—"In the hands of Kean the play became like an exquisite performance on the violin"—to enrich his sense of comparable refinement. Acknowledging "the popularity, the showy heroism of Henry the Fifth," Pater draws the consideration of Shakespeare's history plays toward the figure of Richard II, most touching in defeat and the undoing of himself in the mirror scene. The play belongs with *Romeo and Juliet* to a small group of plays in which "by happy birth and consistent evolution, dramatic form approaches to something like the unity of a lyrical ballad, a lyric, a song, a single strain of music." Refinement ever in view, Pater thinks of these plays as aspiring toward the condition of music:

> It follows that a play attains artistic perfection just in proportion as it approaches that unity of lyrical effect, as if a song or ballad were still lying at the root of it, all the various expression of the conflict of character and circumstance falling at last into the compass of a single melody, or musical theme.[5]

It is the theory of poetic drama as we later find it in Eliot, musical form its paradigm. But in Pater, more than in Eliot, it is the culmination of a rhetoric of development and refinement.

"Shakespeare's English Kings" defines a certain tradition in the reception of Shakespeare's plays. Pater did not directly oppose the idea that Shakespeare celebrated the Tudor victory, but he claimed that Shakespeare's imagination favored the defeated cause. Ford Madox

Ford argues, in his book on Provence, that the better cause has invariably been defeated. It may be true. In any case, Pater started a little fashion of saying that Shakespeare's imagination was ashamed of its duty and insisted on giving the defeated kings the most touching lines. When Yeats went to Stratford-on-Avon to see the history plays, he had Pater's essay in mind and proposed that Shakespeare's deepest poetic instinct contradicted his sense of Tudor duty. The plays, Yeats argued in "At Stratford-on-Avon," do not endorse Henry V and the rough, successful heroes. John Butler Yeats's letters to Edward Dowden and Pater's essay on the kings convinced Yeats that Shakespeare's deepest sympathy went out to the defeated Richard II, "that unripened Hamlet," rather than to Henry V, "that ripened Fortinbras." Ostensibly, Yeats's essay is about Shakespeare, but it is really a plea for Yeats's contemporaries who seemed to have been defeated mainly because they had a cause too fine for common appreciation. Yeats was thinking, as always, of Pater, Wilde, Johnson, Dowson, Symons, Beardsley, and indeed of himself. Pater was his Richard II, Arnold and Ruskin his composite Henry V.

23

"Wordsworth"

The Greeks painted the eyes of marble statues and made out of enamel or glass or precious stones those of their bronze statues, but the Roman was the first to drill a round hole to represent the pupil, and because, as I think, of a preoccupation with the glance characteristic of a civilization in its final phase. . . . When I think of Rome I see always those heads with their world-considering eyes, and those bodies as conventional as the metaphors in a leading article, and compare in my imagination vague Grecian eyes gazing at nothing, Byzantine eyes of drilled ivory staring upon a vision, and those eyelids of China and of India, those veiled or half-veiled eyes weary of world and vision alike.

—W. B. Yeats, *A Vision*

PATER WROTE ABOUT WORDSWORTH several times, but his most concentrated efforts were an essay in the *Fortnightly Review*, April 1874, and a revision of it, fifteen years later, for *Appreciations*. This latter is the one to read.

The early essay is more daring than it looks. If it had been noticed in 1874, only a few months after the publication of the scandalous *Studies in the History of the Renaissance*, it would have given further offense. Pater begins innocuously, reciting the familiar distinction between Fancy and Imagination, but he takes little stock in it. He tended to think that a proposed distinction of kind was really one of degree between fundamentally cognate values. So he quickly replaces the distinction between Fancy and Imagination with one between "higher and lower degrees of intensity in the poet's perception of his subject, and in his concentration of himself upon his work."[1] As a Darwinian and in certain moods a Hegelian, Pater prefers to distinguish two or more degrees of one force than to separate two forces and give each a name. The distinction is never allowed to be a sharp one. Pater's imagination was not dramatic: he took no pleasure in seeing life as a conflict of values. Wordsworth was his model in this respect—as in the first "Essay upon Epitaphs," in which Wordsworth refers to "the best feelings of our Nature" as "feelings which, though they seem opposite to each other, have another and a finer connection than that of contrast." It is a connection "formed through the subtle process by which, both in the natural and the moral world, qualities pass insensibly into their contraries, and things revolve upon each other."[2] This is congenial to Pater because it respects transition more than disjunctions and antitheses; it regards one's best life as a tone poem in which beginning and end are related by association, and moment by moment the affections work as their own justification. Music was Pater's ideal form of expression because it transcended or resolved conflict and implied unity of being which there was no need to distinguish from unity of expression. It follows that Pater, associating Wordsworth with "a large element in the complexion of modern poetry," defines that element in philosophically idealist terms: "an intimate consciousness of the expression of natural things, which weighs, listens, penetrates, where the earlier mind passed roughly by." The earlier mind is the composite mind of eighteenth-century literature, which Pater like most of his contemporaries mistook for an age of dead reason, Blake being the sole exception to a prosaic rule. The "intimate consciousness" Pater links with "those pantheistic theories which locate an intelligent soul in material things." The theories are explained by reference to "the gods in exile," Heine's motif again. Translating the notion of the return of the pagan gods into Tylor's anthropological vocabulary of survival, Pater explains Wordsworth's sense of a life common to nature and man:

> It was like a "survival," in the peculiar intellectual temperament of a man of letters at the end of the eighteenth century, of that primitive condition, which some philosophers have traced in the general history of human culture, wherein all outward objects alike, including even the works of men's hands, were believed to be endowed with animation, and the world was "full of souls"—that mood in which the old Greek gods were first begotten, and which had many strange aftergrowths.[3]

Wordsworth was one of those after-growths, his participation in the *Zeitgeist* being modified by his susceptibility to a *vie antérieure*, his best poems "the instinctive productions of earlier life." Pater doesn't underline the motif of the gods in exile as clearly here as in *Studies in the History of the Renaissance*, but he has no other means of explaining how a modern writer can escape his *Zeitgeist* or observe it with misgiving: it is the only source of that antinomian energy which enables a writer to dissent from the axioms of his time without directly challenging them.

Wordsworth's method, according to Pater, was to start with natural life and "ennoble" it by ascribing to it a semblance of human passion and thought:

> Human life, indeed, is for him, at first, only an additional, accidental grace on an expressive landscape.[4]

More specifically:

> By raising nature to the level of human thought he gives it power and expression: he subdues man to the level of nature, and gives him thereby a certain breadth and coolness and solemnity.[5]

"Subdues," not the expected "lowers," presumably because man does not suffer a loss or reduction of his nature by these Wordsworthian gestures. Pater is using the word in much the same sense as Newman when he said that a man is subdued by his religion. Newman meant calmed, not overwhelmed or defeated. Wordsworth takes his bearings from the world apparently external to him and regards his life as an extension of natural life. Pater's description up to this point is straightforward; it is a development of Wordsworth's own account of his procedure as he outlined it in the Preface to the 1815 edition of his *Poems*. Wordsworth explains how he brought together, in "Resolution and Independence," images of stone and sea-beast and related them to the Old Man. It follows that the poet, as Pater says, "was attracted by the thought of a spirit of life in outward things, a single, all-pervading mind in them, of which man, and even the poet's imaginative energy, are but moments—that old dream of the *anima mundi*, the mother of all things and their grave, in which some had desired to lose themselves, and others had become indifferent to the distinctions of good and evil."[6] Pater is being lurid here. On the rare occasions on which a sentence of his moves swiftly, something surreptitious is going on: he is administering values which readers might be inclined to see administered differently. It takes panache to start with a spirit of life in outward things and end with indifference to the distinctions of good and evil. Pater is rushing from "spirit" through "mind" and "energy" to "*anima mundi*," lest he admit the responsibility of explaining what he takes these words to mean. Keeping to an idealist vocabulary, he brings the rush to a strikingly antinomian conclusion.

Pater claims that when Wordsworth concentrates his mind on this sentiment his language becomes faultless, the poet burning with a hard gem-like flame:

> In him, when the really poetical motive worked at all, it united, with absolute justice, the word and the idea; each, in the imaginative flame, becoming inseparably one with the other, by that fusion of matter and form which is the characteristic of the highest poetical expression.[7]

Not that this explains anything. Word and idea don't admit a valid distinction, because the idea can't exist apart from the word. The case isn't helped by talk of flame and fusion, Pater's favorite metaphors when he wants to declare that unity has been achieved but can't say how. What he needs here is the capacity that Wordsworth sometimes claimed for himself of being able to work with values he couldn't define. In *The Structure of Complex Words*, Empson quotes a passage from the first book of *The Prelude*:

> *and after I had seen*
> *That spectacle, for many days, my brain*
> *Work'd with a dim and undetermin'd sense*
> *Of unknown modes of being. . . .*

The large claim is in "work'd." There is a suggestion here, as Empson says, from the pause on "sense" at the end of the line, that Wordsworth had not merely "a feeling of" these unknown modes but something like a new "sense" which was partly able to apprehend them—"a new *kind* of sensing had appeared in his mind."[8] One of the strengths of Wordsworth's language is that he doesn't need impeccably stable words: he can take words which would be too vague for ordinary efficient use—Empson's case in point is "sense"—and give them an air of meaning more, though not necessarily more precisely, than they have undertaken to mean; and then claim that he has developed a new capacity in himself by doing this. Pater has a notion that this is going on, but he hasn't a convincing way of indicating it.

What he is sure of, however, is that the Wordsworth he reveres isn't the poet in common view. The point of his essay is to separate his poet from the Wordsworth presented by Mill and Arnold, guardian of common life, a poet social, domestic, and familial. Pater is willing to emphasize Wordsworth's sensitivity to the world of sight and sound, but as the essay goes on he makes even more of those passages in which that world seems to dissolve, displaced by the poet's imagination in its most daring autonomy:

> Sometimes as he dwelt upon those moments of profound, imaginative power, in which the outward object appears to take colour and expression, a new nature almost, from the prompting of the observant mind, the actual world would, as it were, dissolve and detach itself, flake by flake, and he himself seemed to be the creator, and when he would the destroyer of the world in which he lived—that old isolating thought of many a brain-sick mystic of ancient and modern times.[9]

As usual, Pater prepares quietly for the production of his own Wordsworth. He does not say that Arnold is wrong, or that Mill's Wordsworth is only a minor version of the poet. "The office of the poet is not that of the moralist," he says, "and the first aim of Wordsworth's poetry is to give the reader a peculiar kind of pleasure." Hardly a controversial claim. But Pater joins it to another one more implicative:

> Contemplation—impassioned contemplation—that, is with Wordsworth the end-in-itself, the perfect end.[10]

It seems innocent, but it leads to a paragraph in which Pater reflects severely on those who live by *doing*, not content with *being*:

> Meantime, to higher or lower ends, they move too often with something of a sad countenance, with hurried and ignoble gait, becoming, unconsciously, something like thorns, in their anxiety to bear grapes; it being possible for people, in the pursuit of even great ends, to become themselves thin and impoverished

in spirit and temper, thus diminishing the sum of perfection in the world, at its very sources.[11]

Evidently the world is too much with such people, late and soon. Consider rather the lilies of the field. Speaking for the contemplative mode, Pater protests against the reduction of life to a mechanical relation between means and ends. Such reduction, he says, "covers the meanness of men's daily lives, and much of the dexterity and the vigour with which they pursue what may seem to them the good of themselves or of others; but not the intangible perfection of those whose ideal is rather in *being* than in *doing*—not those *manners* which are, in the deepest as in the simplest sense, *morals*, and without which one cannot so much as offer a cup of water to a poor man without offence—not the part of 'antique Rachel,' sitting in the company of Beatrice. . . ."[12]

Here rapidity of transition is supposed to make argument unnecessary. Pater's association of being with manners depends on an acoustic after-image, linking manners and manner. The transition from manners to morals appropriates morality, too, on behalf of being, the giving of a cup of water to a poor man counting for beautiful behavior before it is also seen to be moral. The reference to Rachel and Beatrice alludes in the first instance to the *Inferno*, canto 2, "*con l'antica Rachele*" and then to the *Paradiso*, canto 32, where the seating arrangements in Paradise have Rachel sitting beside Beatrice: "*siede Rachel di sotto da costei / con Beatrice.*" What counts for Pater is the image of Rachel for the time being doing nothing, saying nothing, silent in contemplation.

In the next paragraph, Pater refers, without naming the author or the book, to the chapter in the *Autobiography* in which Mill tells how his reading of Wordsworth's poems released the feelings which his education had congealed. But that reference is the only concession he makes to the Wordsworth commonly revered for imagining what other people have inarticulately felt. The main emphasis of the essay is on Pater's quiet refusal to allow a free choice between being and doing; instead, he gathers into being the good of doing and discards the remainder:

> That the end of life is not action but contemplation—*being* as distinct from *doing*—a certain disposition of the mind: is, in some shape or other, the principle of all the higher morality. In poetry, in art, if you enter into their true spirit at all, you touch this principle, in a measure: these, by their very sterility, are a

type of beholding for the mere joy of beholding. To treat life in the spirit of art, is to make life a thing in which means and ends are identified: to encourage such treatment, the true moral significance of art and poetry. Wordsworth, and other poets who have been like him in ancient or more recent times, are the masters, the experts, in this art of impassioned contemplation.[13]

The claim in the first sentence is outrageous. Imagine what Albert Schweitzer or Mother Teresa would say of it. Pater doesn't define the "higher morality" or say who its exemplars are, or upon what authority he claims that its end is contemplation. It is enough for him that it is the higher morality and that he appropriates it for the privilege of being. Sterility, in this account of it, makes another contentious claim. The word denotes the quality of certain states of being by which they find their value in themselves and not in any further end they may be thought to seek. Pater thinks art and literature all the better for having no end in view beyond their self-sustaining existence. The *O.E.D.* doesn't recognize this valuation of sterility, but Pater's special sense of the word caught Yeats's attention, as I have noted. In "The Tragic Generation," he refers with notable tenderness to images separated from the general purposes of human life, images which "grow in beauty as they grow in sterility." To treat life in the spirit of art is to make life a thing in which means and ends are identified, or, rather, in which the temporal difference between means and ends is removed, and the end is always now, the privileged moment.

Pater's essay is, as usual, a dispute with Arnold and with Ruskin. Not that Pater and Arnold differed much in their understanding that Wordsworth wrote many weary poems and a sufficient number of decisive ones to make him a master. If Pater had prepared a selection of Wordsworth's best poetry, as Arnold did in 1879, it would have coincided with Arnold's choice, I don't doubt. But Pater's sense of the author of those few supreme poems differs from Arnold's and is meant to be recognized as antithetical to his. Arnold is not named in the body of the essay; a footnote to the revised version acknowledges that Arnold's choice of Wordsworth's poems has been made "with excellent taste." As usual, too, Pater starts from ostensibly Arnoldian assumptions, only to veer from them. Arnold's Wordsworth is the poet of human acknowledgment: if you read him well, you become a better neighbor, a better person. You appreciate Wordsworth's grasp of "local truth." It might seem, Arnold says, that Nature not only gave Wordsworth the matter for his poems but wrote them for him. "He has no style," he doesn't need one, he has only to keep his distance from Milton's style. Pater doesn't accept that version of Wordsworth, or of poetry as a social art. He presents Wordsworth as an exponent of art for art's sake, withdrawing from the world so as to contemplate it in universal form, to meditate upon life as such rather than upon its accidental manifestations.

Pater also argues silently with Ruskin. The ground of argument is a famous passage in the *Nicomachean Ethics*, book 10, chapter 8, where Aristotle says that perfect happiness is "some form of contemplative activity." His reason for this is that he ascribes to God "the activity of contemplation."[14] Obviously you could emphasize one of these values more than the other: "the activity of *contemplation*" or "the *activity* of contemplation." Ruskin and Wilde emphasized *contemplation* (*theoria*) and recommended it as a mode of mind transcending the tyranny of the senses. This spiritual contemplation, ethically informed, could then become the ground of a social theory, diversely but not contradictorily expressed by Ruskin, Morris, and Wilde. In his revision of *Modern Painters*, Ruskin made this choice the justification for his attack on art for art's sake: he denounced it as hedonist and utilitarian, and took the occasion to diminish "aesthesis" to mean "mere sensual perception of the outward qualities and necessary effects of bodies."[15] Pater emphasized rather the *activity* of contemplation, making much of its *energeia*. In this he followed, as Frank Turner has shown, Sir Alexander Grant's interpretation, in his edition of the *Ethics*. Consciousness is an active power, a flame of being, an end in itself. To appropriate Wordsworth, of all poets, as the exemplar of *energeia* was yet another instance of Pater's quiet audacity.

It could even have been worse. There is a good deal of evidence that Pater included the essay on Wordsworth in the batch of essays he sent to Macmillan on June 29, 1872, for publication as *Studies in the History of the Renaissance*. If so, it was the essay he withdrew a few months later. Macmillan agreed to cancel it, although it was also set up in print. The matter is not settled. Lawrence Evans thinks the canceled essay was a first version of "The School of Giorgione." But the reason Pater gave for withdrawing it was that he wanted to embody parts of it in the Preface. The Preface indeed contains a passage about Wordsworth, referring to his "strange mystical sense of a life in natural things, and of man's life as a part of nature."[16] It is innocuous. But if Pater had included in the book the entire essay on Wordsworth which he published in the *Fortnightly Review* on April 1, 1874, it would have entailed associating England's greatest modern poet with the survival of pagan or animistic feelings, not merely with one or two charming notions from Plato. Robert Crawford has shown that Pater draws upon Andrew Lang's essay on the *Chanson de Roland*.[17] Lang read Tylor's *Primitive Culture* (1871) in March 1872, and he was closely enough in touch with Pater to give him the gist of Tylor's theory of the survival of paganism in Christianity. Tylor and Lang were both Darwinists, though Lang felt uneasy about enclosing the whole of human history in one story of evolution. In 1871 English anthropology was a tendentious field. Pater was keenly interested in it because of his dealings with Greek art and mythology. He could have read Tylor's book then for himself, but I have no evidence that he did. I think he felt awkward about drawing Wordsworth's poems, in a book apparently about Renaissance art, into the acrimonies of biology, anthropology, mythography, and religion. In a separate essay on Wordsworth for the *Fortnightly* he could say what he liked.

In 1874 no one appears to have noticed that Pater was trying to kidnap Wordsworth and to attach him to an antinomian or dissenting tradition in Victorian society. In 1879 Arnold was troubled that Wordsworth might have been ousted by Tennyson, but he didn't consider the possibility that Pater had drawn Wordsworth into dubious fellowship with Poe, Gautier, and Baudelaire. In 1889 and 1890, reviewers of *Appreciations* thought the essay on Wordsworth the best part of the book, but they were mainly taken with its sympathy, its responsiveness, the passages in which Pater delineated a Wordsworth not entirely his own. Wilde recognized what Pater was doing, and disapproved of it. Transcribing a sentence of the essay into his commonplace book, he added to his supply of phrases for use in "The Critic as Artist"; but on the issue at hand, the social value of art, he was at that early stage closer to Ruskin than to Pater. He already delighted in Pater but saw no reason to become his disciple. That relation could be postponed.

Much depends on the passages in Pater's essay one chooses to emphasize. There is something in it for everyone. When Pater speaks of Wordsworth as poet of Nature, of its sights and sounds, the poet "Of joy in widest commonalty spread," he endorses the common Victorian image of Wordsworth. Quiet allusions to Wordsworth in that sense of him occur in virtually every work of Pater's. But on that theme he can't match Arnold's authority or the force of Mill's testimony. When he speaks of the other Wordsworth, exemplar of consciousness at the expense of natural being, he is more persuasive, perhaps because he speaks from a corresponding ambition in himself. We have been hearing a lot about this Wordsworth, poet of subjectivity to the degree of self-invention, blood brother of Milton's Satan and Byron's Cain. The critical tradition which emphasizes this image of Wordsworth starts with Hazlitt, Keats, and Hopkins and continues in Willard Sperry, Harold Bloom, Paul de Man, and Geoffrey Hartman. According to that tradition, Wordsworth was of Blake's party without knowing it and he leads to the self-inventions of Valéry and Stevens. I cannot think that Pater would approve of such a one-sided reading or be pleased to find the satanic Wordsworth so peremptorily displacing the poet of the Lake District. But he has himself to blame for those vertiginous passages of the essay in which Wordsworth becomes yet again witness to the egotistical sublime.

24

"Postscript"

F OR THE LAST CHAPTER of *Appreciations* Pater reached back to an early essay called "Romanticism" which he published in *Macmillan's Magazine* in November 1876. He still thought well of distinguishing between Classicism and Romanticism as tendencies. Classicism is a tendency toward order in beauty, measure, perfection of form. Romanticism is an antinomian impulse; it involves the addition of strangeness to beauty, "and the desire of beauty being a fixed element in every artistic organisation, it is the addition of curiosity to this desire of beauty, that constitutes the romantic temper."[1] But not too much strangeness or too much curiosity, since that excess would make the work grotesque.

Pater agreed with the standard notion that in England the eighteenth century was classical in tendency, and the nineteenth century romantic. Modern romanticism came into French literature with Rousseau, and in some sense its clearest manifestation is still French rather than German or English. But Pater was persuaded by Sainte-Beuve and Stendhal that it was best to think of "classical" and "romantic" as denoting two perennial types of feeling, either or both of them liable to occur in any period or any artist. The *Odyssey* is more romantic than the *Iliad*, Aeschylus more romantic than Sophocles. There are born classicists and born romanticists. But Pater was convinced, or at least charmed, by Stendhal's theory that all good art was romantic in its day.

This has consequences for literary history, but Pater leaves them dangling. If Stendhal's theory holds, it means that art begins with a genius of a certain disposition, strange, peremptory, daring; it then develops toward excess, at which point either the artist or his audience recurs to discipline, *ascesis*, at some cost. Pater gives one version of this phase:

> On the other hand, there are the born romanticists, who start with an original, untried *matter*, still in fusion; who conceive this vividly, and hold by it as the essence of their work; who, by the very vividness and heat of their conception, purge away, sooner or later, all that is not organically appropriate to it, till the whole effect adjusts itself in clear, orderly, proportionate form; which form, after a very little time, becomes classical in its turn.[2]

The only change of any significance in that passage between 1876 and 1889 is the emphasis on *matter*. The change announces that the theme is the relation of matter and form. "Organically" is required to do a lot of work here; Pater is still doing chemistry. The artist takes un-formed matter, heats it to the point at which it becomes susceptible to his vision; heats it further, purges away its excrescences, shapes it till it appears to him at once to satisfy his desire and to exhibit the destined form of itself to which it may be fancied as having aspired. The form is organic, or appears to be. At that point the artist's will has discovered its true fulfillment in the created object. The form, once recognized and established, "becomes classical in its turn." The only future it has is dismal, to become congealed in its certitude, and at that point there is urgent need of a new impulse, the next romantic force.

Pater made a few changes in the essay which are of biographical and ideological interest. He deleted Whitman's name from one passage: in 1889 Whitman was thought to be bad company. For the same reason he deleted Baudelaire's name three times, and in two of these replaced it by Victor Hugo's, a safe allusion. He removed one of his references to Gautier. Then he added, at the end of the essay, a new paragraph to say that there is no merit in starting a quarrel between classical and romantic motives. The urgent need is to induce order "upon the contorted, proportionless accumulation of our knowledge and experience, our science and history, our hopes and disillusion." In effecting this, we should "do consciously what has been done hitherto for the most part too unconsciously, to write our English language as the Latins wrote theirs, as the French write, as scholars should write." We live in an eclectic time, so it is reasonable to cultivate the excellences of diverse literary types; in literature as in other matters we should unite as many diverse elements as may be:

> To discriminate schools, of art, of literature, is, of course, part of the obvious business of literary criticism: but, in the work of literary production, it is easy to be overmuch occupied concerning them. For, in truth, the legitimate contention is, not of one age or school of literary art against another, but of all successive schools alike, against the stupidity which is dead to the substance, and the vulgarity which is dead to form.[3]

The last sentence is as far as Pater was willing to go in pursuit of Arnoldian vivacity.

25

Plato and Platonism

I

"THE LECTURES of which this volume is composed," Pater wrote of
Plato and Platonism, published on February 9, 1893, "were written
for delivery to some young students of philosophy, and are now printed
with the hope of interesting a larger number of them." He gave the
lectures at Brasenose in the Hilary Term, 1891, and concentrated on
Plato's vision of the ideal state. It was a severe topic for undergraduates,
but he mitigated its harshness by referring occasionally to other matters.
He took it for granted that a young man even mildly interested in Plato
would extend his curiosity to general considerations of art and literature
and would not object to hearing from time to time the names of Raphael,
Veronese, and Thackeray.

Pater's method of exposition seemed straightforward, but it concealed a prejudice. He explained what he understood philosophy to be
and described Plato's position in relation to that project. His tone was
consistently urbane, as if the grinding of an ax were the last thing he
intended. But the tone was rhetorically chosen not only for lucidity of
exposition but for a darker purpose that he kept postponing. At the
end he was in a position, consulting his own interests, imperceptibly

to take back much that he had given. He started concessively with the aim of philosophy:

> To realise unity in variety, to discover *cosmos*—an order that shall satisfy one's reasonable soul—below and within apparent chaos: is from first to last the continuous purpose of what we call philosophy.[1]

If that were true, Pater would have to disqualify himself from the practice of philosophy. He had no interest in finding a principle of unity subsuming the variety of human experience. Plato's particular aim, the reduction of "the Many" to "the One," seemed to Pater a vain endeavor, though he didn't say as much. He was not a Platonist; he did not allow his sense of "the particular presentations of our individual experience" to be submitted to the authority of "general forms." He granted that Plato favored this submission, and he explained why without indicating that he exercised forbearance in doing so. He didn't rebuke Plato as he rebuked Coleridge for the same ambition, that of finding a principle to which the various particles of one's life might be referred. But in the lectures he was biding his time. When he had done well enough by Plato's doctrine of ideas, he started undermining it from within. He did this by noting that of the three methods available to the criticism of philosophy—the dogmatic, the eclectic or syncretic, and the historic—the historic method was the most persuasive; it proposed to understand doctrines or systems in relation to the conditions in which they were first produced. The aim of *Plato and Platonism* is to see Plato "as a result from antecedent and contemporary movements of Greek speculation."

Plato had three great precursors, Pythagoras, Parmenides, and Heraclitus. By showing his relation to each, Pater presents him as a sage of far more diverse affiliations than would otherwise appear. He admits that Plato's relation to Heraclitus was mainly one of antagonism. Any philosophy of motion, mutability, and flux was alien to Plato, who maintained that motion is a token of unreality in things and of falsity in our thoughts of them. Plato sought the One, the universally active principle. But he had at least to entertain the Heraclitean prejudice before dismissing it. He was much more inclined to accept the Pythagorean theory of numbers, especially in the form of music, movement not as flux but as disciplined sound, "a formal development of purely numerical laws." From Parmenides he accepted with every sign of gratitude a prejudice in favor of impassivity, the static calm that rewards the conviction that thought and being are the same. Pater refers to "the old Eleatic teacher who had tried so hard to close the bodily eye that he might the better apprehend the world unseen."

Pater's account of these three philosophic positions, and of Plato's relation to each, introduces difference where there has seemed to be only repetition of the same. He displaces the interests of a philosopher by introducing those of an anthropologist: the aim is not to discover *cosmos* but to recognize differences of human feeling, the plurality of desires and fulfillments. He introduces difference again in describing how a great personality, a genius, without escaping from conditions, to some degree converts them to himself. How such a personality came about and settled in one body rather than another Pater doesn't say, but he notes that the historic method of criticism doesn't cover the case of genius. A complete criticism has to go beyond historical explanation:

> In the evolution of abstract doctrine as we find it written in the history of philosophy, if there is always, on one side, the fatal, irresistible, mechanic play of circumstance—the circumstances of a particular age, which may be analysed and explained; there is always also, as if acting from the opposite side, the comparatively inexplicable force of a personality, resistant to, while it is moulded by, them. It might even be said that the trial-task of criticism, in regard to literature and art no less than to philosophy, begins exactly where the estimate of general conditions, of the conditions common to all the products of this or that particular age—of the "environment"—leaves off, and we touch what is unique in the individual genius which contrived after all, by force of will, to have its own masterful way with that environment.[2]

This passage gives the characteristic rhythm of Pater's commentary. He acknowledges that there are limiting conditions governing any exercise of mind; on the other hand there is genius, force of personality which can be recognized but not accounted for. The work of art or philosophy manifests a particular relation between these values, but the relation is in the end occult.

From time to time Pater makes more of the constraints than of the freedoms a genius contrives to take with them:

For in truth we come into the world, each one of us, "not in nakedness," but by the natural course of organic development clothed far more completely than even Pythagoras supposed in a vesture of the past, nay, fatally shrouded, it might seem, in those laws or tricks of heredity which we mistake for our volitions; in the language which is more than one half of our thoughts; in the moral and mental habits, the customs, the literature, the very houses, which we did not make for ourselves; in the vesture of a past, which is (so science would assure us) not ours, but of the race, the species: that *Zeitgeist*, or abstract secular process, in which, as we could have had no direct consciousness of it, so we can pretend to no future personal interest.[3]

In this version of tradition, Wordsworth's "clouds of glory" amount only to belatedness: what I trail into my life is the residue of other lives. What I say is what the language I speak allows me to say. It is a wonder that anything new can be done. But Pater has only to express this sense of lateness and he reacts against the expression, asserting now that much is still possible, given force of personality to the degree of genius. The notes of the score are definitive, but a musician interprets them as he pleases within that large constraint.

Besides, there are forms available for the practice of every mode of philosophic thought, and each allows for certain liberties: three especially, the poem, the treatise, and the essay. These are genres of discourse rather than discourses. The poem expresses "enthusiastic intuitions"; the treatise "scholastic all-sufficiency," the array of premise and conclusion; the essay is appropriate to interventions of doubt and skepticism, Montaigne being its supreme exemplar:

It provided him with precisely the literary form necessary to a mind for which truth itself is but a possibility, realisable not as general conclusion, but rather as the elusive effect of a particular personal experience; to a mind which, noting faithfully those random lights that meet it by the way, must needs content itself with suspension of judgment, at the end of the intellectual journey, to the very last asking: *Que scais-je?* Who knows?—in the very spirit of that old Socratic contention, that all true philosophy is but a refined sense of one's ignorance.[4]

Pater has only to associate the essay with the Platonic dialogue and he is well on the way to making Plato appear as variously skeptical as Montaigne. Socrates is found wandering about, questioning his supposed scholars, questioning himself. There is no sign of finality or of abstract principle.

Pater does reasonably well by Plato's metaphysics and his politics, but he is evidently in a hurry to come to his aesthetics. Not surprisingly, Plato is appropriated as one who "anticipates the modern notion that art as such has no end but its own perfection,—'art for art's sake' ":

> And accordingly, in education, all will begin and end in "music," in the promotion of qualities to which no truer name can be given than symmetry, aesthetic fitness, tone. Philosophy itself indeed, as he conceives it, is but the sympathetic appreciation of a kind of music in the very nature of things.[5]

For the moment, Pater takes aesthetics to mean the theory of the attention one pays to "all productions in which the *form* counts equally with, or for more than, the *matter*." Plato supposes in people generally, he says, susceptibility to "the aspects and other sensible qualities of things and persons." He also supposes "some close connexion between what may be called the aesthetic qualities of the world about us and the formation of moral character, between aesthetics and ethics." This is too much supposing. It implies that if I lived in a beautiful place I would without further ado live a morally impeccable life. For the moment, Pater is thinking of Plato in his relation to Pythagoras, as in the third and tenth books of *The Republic*, which are impelled by ideas of harmony. He is also making a great deal of the faculty of imitation, how we imitate "what we see and hear, the forms, the sounds which haunt our memories, our imagination." But to turn Plato into an aesthete and then to have him mark an unargued connection between aesthetic and moral values, Pater has to claim that what people imitate is the form of the work of art rather than its matter or content:

> It is not so much the *matter* of a work of art, what is conveyed in and by colour and form and sound, that tells upon us educationally—the subject, for instance, developed by the words and scenery of a play—as the *form*, and its qualities,

concision, simplicity, rhythm, or, contrariwise, abundance, variety, discord.[6]

Training is required if young people are to respond to these qualities:

> And if art, like law, be, as Plato thinks, "a creation of mind, in accordance with right reason," we shall not wish our boys to sing like mere birds.[7]

Hence the bearing of aesthetics upon ethics and education.

Pater's argument suffers from the embarrassment of having to separate form and matter. Form is what remains when the matter is forgotten or has been displaced by other interests. At that point the qualities he lists as issuing from the form may be drawn upon for ethical and other educational purposes. He might have avoided the embarrassment by defining form not as that which survives the death of its matter but as the completion of matter. In *The Aesthetic Dimension*, Marcuse speaks of form as achieved content. The content is raw material, the bit of wood or stone with which a sculptor works; form is achieved matter, its destiny embodied at last.

But the separation of form and matter is worth the embarrassment it causes Pater, because it gives him another instance of the dispersal of Plato into his attributes. Every attribute, every affiliation, makes him appear not an implacable adept of the One but a witness, reluctant or not, to the Many. We see Plato as he was never willing to see himself, given over to moods and weathers. The first dispersal is effected by describing Plato's three very different precursors and his leaning for a while toward one or another; the next by implying that his form, the dialogue, the trajectory of question and answer, is wiser than he is, more responsive to the motion of life, more mercurial. In fact, the mode of question-and-answer isn't at all like the essay: the formulation of a question rules out any other divagations for the time being. Montaigne didn't ask questions, or answer questions asked by anyone else. Pater chose to ignore this difference. He enforced further dispersal by pointing to the ideal character of Plato's republic, that it is chiefly an emanation from one notable mood of the mind that has proposed it. The aesthetic consideration completes the story. A philosopher who supposedly looks for unity comes upon forms that have long forgotten their contents and appear to be doing well enough without them. At that point Plato becomes our contemporary, our Montaigne.

We have reached this point in the lectures without even adverting to the itinerary by which we have reached it. Pater has been leading us toward it surreptitiously. He appears to have been expounding Plato's philosophy as if it simply offered itself to be recited. But by emphasizing one aspect and ignoring another, he has turned Plato into a relativist, a Heraclitean despite many of his inclinations. We hardly notice what he has done, except that he has made Plato encounter Montaigne's *Essays* on the way. Any metaphysical position, according to Pater, even one that seems hopelessly perverse, can be found to be "realisable enough as one of many phases of our so flexible human feeling." But if we agree that our feeling is as flexible as that, we have to remove the aim, the search for an immutable principle, and remove the yearning for it. As Emerson says in "Circles," "Our moods do not believe in each other." They don't need to believe in each other, so long as the posited character of human life is deemed to be mobile, under the double sign of Heraclitus and Montaigne. In the end, Pater's Plato, like his Wordsworth, resembles Pater himself, anthropologist of caprice and difference.

II

In "Houseboat Days," John Ashbery appropriates two sentences from *Plato and Platonism* for his own rhetoric of mobility. He finds both in the chapter on Plato and the Sophists. Here is the first one:

> There is an every-day 'sophistry' of course, against which we have all of us to be on our guard—that insincerity of reasoning on behalf of sincere convictions, true or false in themselves as the case may be, to which, if we are unwise enough to argue at all with each other, we must all be tempted at times.[8]

Before giving the second passage, I should quote an earlier one, fifty pages back, from which it arises. Pater has been reciting the theory of metempsychosis in relation to the growing boy:

> Ancient, half-obliterated inscriptions on the mental walls, the mental tablet, seeds of knowledge to come, shed by some flower

of it long ago, it was in an earlier period of time they had been laid up in him, to blossom again now, so kindly, so firmly!⁹

Now the second one:

> For the essence of all artistic beauty is expression, which cannot be where there's really nothing to be expressed; the line, the colour, the word, following obediently, and with minute scruple, the conscious motions of a convinced intelligible soul. To make men interested in themselves, as being the very ground of all reality for them, *la vraie vérité*, as the French say:—that was the essential function of the Socratic method: to flash light into the house within, its many chambers, its memories and associations, upon its inscribed and pictured walls.¹⁰

Ashbery's poem is Pateresque in the sense that it turns a project of knowledge into one of feeling and blithely watches while one cognitive act is displaced by another:

> *The mind*
> *Is so hospitable, taking in everything*
> *Like boarders, and you don't see until*
> *It's all over how little there was to learn*
> *Once the stench of knowledge has dissipated, and the trouvailles*
> *Of every one of the senses fallen back.*

The mind in that mood is enjoying what Pater called, some pages back in *Plato and Platonism*, its "throwing itself forth in endless play of undirected imagination." Or the mood that James in *The Ambassadors* ascribes to Strether at the theater with Maria Gostrey, his mind "given over to uncontrolled perceptions." What a mind in that state comes upon is not an aim but one trouvaille and then another and another, as in a painting by Klee.

The "he" in Ashbery's next lines is Pater, or rather Pater under Ashbery's ascendancy:

> *Really, he*
> *Said, that insincerity of reasoning on behalf of one's*
> *Sincere convictions, true or false in themselves*

As the case may be, to which, if we are unwise enough
To argue at all with each other, we must be tempted
At times—do you see where it leads? To pain,
And the triumph over pain, still hidden
In these low-lying hills which rob us
Of all privacy. . . .

The pain follows, I assume, from one's determination to be sophistical, to live for winning and to suffer losing, to be irregularly at a loss, to win again in a rigmarole of such winnings, such losses. Always meeting one's double "through the chain of cigar smoke." Like Pater, Ashbery on this occasion doesn't "set much stock in things / Beyond the weather and the certainties of living and dying." The rest is optional:

To praise this, blame that,
Leads one subtly away from the beginning, where
We must stay, in motion. To flash light
Into the house within, its many chambers,
Its memories and associations, upon its inscribed
And pictured walls, argues enough that life is various.
Life is beautiful. He who reads that
As in the window of some distant, speeding train
Knows what he wants, and what will befall.[11]

There is more, but this is enough for my occasion. The motif of praise and blame comes from *The Republic*, the relevant passage of which Pater has quoted in the same chapter. The argument is that the real sophists were the Athenians at large, shouting and clapping, praising and blaming: the professional Sophists merely worked out the laws of winning and losing. Ashbery, like Pater, wants to turn away from this mess. In "Houseboat Days" the poet, like Pater, like Wordsworth, wishes to stay "in the beginning" and to make the beginning beautifully various, flashing his various light upon it, making it seem different moment by moment. It is a poem against the Sophists, against the routines of praising and blaming—except that it is quietly in praise of motion, as in *Plato and Platonism*, and of the emancipation of images.

III

But this chapter of *Plato and Platonism* isn't as simple as it looks. Not that "Houseboat Days" makes it look simple, but then Ashbery's relation to Pater's argument is opportunistic, he takes two sentences of it as if they landed on his private beach like driftwood. Pater has to be more prosaic. His duty in the chapter on the Sophists is to explain why Plato was so hostile to them. The argument seems easy. Sophists are pretenders to wisdom; they are professional, well-paid hacks, ghostwriters for better men. There are a few really wise men who know the truth of a matter, but Sophists merely mimic this truth. They teach well-off people the knack of pleasing a mob. In the *Gorgias* and the *Sophist*, Plato separates philosophy from rhetoric: one discovers knowledge by authentic processes (*tekhne*); the other plays upon public opinion by various tricks (*empeiria*). Sophists get rich because Athens is trivial:

> The great sophist was indeed the Athenian public itself, Athens, as the willing victim of its own gifts, its own flamboyancy, well-nigh worn out now by the mutual friction of its own parts, given over completely to hazardous political experiment with the irresponsibility which is ever the great vice of democracy, ever ready to float away any-whither, to misunderstand, or forget, or discredit, its own past.[12]

Sophists teach Athenians what they already know but don't know that they know, how to command a mob by obeying its lowest impulses.

Plato's most comprehensive objection to sophistry was that "for it no real things existed." Real things existed for Plato. Pater seems to be decisive on this point and entirely with Plato, but when he comes to say what these apparently real things are, he calls them things that are an end in themselves. These are what Plato knows, not matters on which he may merely have an opinion. But Pater's example, here and in other books, of a thing that is an end in itself is a work of art, considered in the spirit of art for its own sake. It's hard to see how this could activate Plato's main interest, the promulgation of an ideal state, its civic form.

There is also a strange reference to Heraclitus:

Protagoras, the chief of sophists, had avowedly applied to ethics the physics or metaphysics of Heraclitus. And now it was as if the disintegrating Heraclitean fire had taken hold on actual life, on men's very thoughts, on the emotions and the will.

That so faulty natural tendency, as Plato holds it to be, in the world around them, they formulate carefully as its proper conscious theory: a theory how things must, nay, ought, to be. "Just that," they seem to say—"Just that versatility, that mutable spirit, shall become by adoption the child of knowledge, shall be carefully nurtured, brought to great fortune. We'll make you, and your thoughts, as fluid, as shifty, as things themselves. . . ."[13]

A bizarre passage, and lest we miss the point, Pater a few pages later refers to "the sense in which sophistry is a reproduction of the Heraclitean flux." In Pater's general vocabulary, versatility, mutable, fluid, and flux are terms of praise. His pupil Hopkins was not alone in thinking of nature as a Heraclitean fire and man "her clearest-selvèd spark." Plato, too, was susceptible to the Heraclitean flux, as Pater has shown. In the passage I've quoted, motion, "that mutable spirit," is to become by adoption the child of knowledge: not a true-born child, apparently, but of doubtful provenance and fit only to be reared toward "great fortune." In "Plato's Pharmacy" Jacques Derrida has much to say about *logos* as a son who needs his father, who "would be destroyed in his very *presence* without the present *attendance* of his father."[14] Only *logos* as living discourse, not as writing, can have a father: the *logoi* are the children. Written words are orphans, according to Socrates in the *Phaedrus*. But in the passage from *Plato and Platonism*, the mutable spirit as the adopted child of knowledge is to be retained, nurtured, but only for an ignoble end: not a true end in itself but in something else, wealth, fame. The adopted child is not a true child but, Athens being the irresponsible state it is, may well come to make a bigger noise in the world than the true child makes.

On this theme in *Plato and Platonism* Pater veers from his common practice. Normally he ascribes a position to Plato and then quietly undermines it. On the question of sophistry he ends up with a blunt assertion. Plato "was no scholar of the Sophists as he understood them, but is writing of what he really knows." The change from past to present tense is awkward. "Scholar" is virtually a technical term in Pater, meaning an adept, one who knows a subject and sympathizes with the position it entails. How Plato came to "really know" anything is not clear, unless we forget Montaigne and everything Pater has sympathetically written of the *Essays*. The chapter ends so bluntly that we are left wondering what happened to Pater's urbane tone: it is as if he were forcing himself to side with Plato in the officious end. But we have not forgotten Heraclitus, all that flux, that fire.

26

"Amiens" and "Vézelay"

PATER SPENT MOST of September 1893 in France, visiting the old churches. By the following January he had written "Notre-Dame d'Amiens," "the first of a series, to be ready at intervals, on 'Some Great Churches of France,' " he told James T. Knowles, editor of *Nineteenth Century*.[1] It was published there in March. A second essay, "Vézelay," followed in the June number. A third, "Notre-Dame de Troyes," exists only as an unfinished manuscript.

Not for the first time, Pater was preceded by Ruskin. Between 1880 and 1885 Ruskin published a series of little guides, designed for children, to thirteenth-century Christendom as it was embodied in the cathedral at Amiens. In 1885 he made a book of them, *The Bible of Amiens*. He chose that church because he thought it the purest Gothic in France, a judgment Pater accepted and took as his starting point for "Notre-Dame d'Amiens." He also accepted Ruskin's description of St. Bernard of Clairvaux as "the first of the noble Puritans."[2] He approved, too, as Ruskin did, popular devotion to the Virgin. But he didn't acknowledge any of these debts to Ruskin. Proust was shocked by this neglect. In notes to his translation of *The Bible of Amiens*, he transcribed a few of Ruskin's phrases about Gothic—"Of Gothic, mind you;

Gothic clear of Roman tradition, and of Arabian taint: Gothic pure, authoritative, unsurpassable, and unaccusable;—its proper principles of structure being once understood and admitted"—and marked "the development of these ideas" in Pater's essay. "I do not know why Ruskin's name is never once mentioned," he complained.[3]

Both of Pater's published essays are acts of mitigation. Even as he recognized the form and character of a church, he looked for signs of its not being completely or authoritatively itself. He took pleasure in finding that it was not as self-possessed as it appeared to be or that over many centuries it had weathered into a state finer than its original form. If a church or any other object were completely itself, it seemed stolid, impenetrable, opaque to the imagination. Pater liked to find its certitude a little ashamed of itself and willing to entertain at least an occasional doubt or misgiving. He wanted the imagination to have a chance of gaining access to any matter.

Notre-Dame d'Amiens, "the greatest and purest of Gothic churches," illustrates, Pater says, "a characteristic secular movement of the beginning of the thirteenth century." He meant secular as distinct from monastic: it is a church of the people, issuing from "the local and municipal life of the commune," in reaction against the feudal authority. The Gothic style, with its pointed arches, concurred "with certain novel humanistic movements of religion itself at that period, above all with the expansion of what is reassuring and popular in the worship of Mary, as a tender and accessible, though almost irresistible, intercessor with her severe and awful Son."[4] But the Gothic buttress, while it secures light and grace, "is not a restful architectural feature." Pater associates this restlessness, "consolidation of matter naturally on the move," with the Catholic religion "in the thirteenth century still in natural movement in every direction." At Amiens the architecture speaks of energy the more impressive for not being entirely under control. The observer infects the observed with his own mobility, Beckett says in his book on Proust. No doubt: but in Pater's Amiens restlessness in the Gothic disturbs the observer. Even as a disinterested visitor, "you are conscious restlessly of that sustained equilibrium of oblique pressure on all sides, which is the essence of the hazardous Gothic construction, a construction of which the 'flying buttress' is the most significant feature."[5] Equilibrium is achieved, but you feel that it might not have been, or that it could still be lost. In those last years of his life Pater wanted to see evidence of order wherever he looked, but he retained some of his early feeling for doubt, change, and heresy, enough to modify the élan of certainty. The argument for belief was just as strong as the argument against it, he thought during those years. There was much in favor of orthodoxy, if only because it ensured one's fellowship with other people. Rest was a formidable quality, but it was the better for being not quite sure of itself.

At Vézelay, on the other hand, "the Gothic spirit" loses or gives up its restlessness: "amid the heavy masses of the old imperial style, it breathes the very genius of monastic repose."[6] But "breathes" and "genius" are enough to make the repose a little wary. The Madeleine of Vézelay is typically the church of a monastery, it is Romanesque, the style of the Cluniac order. But here the Romanesque architecture seems to have been studied not from Roman basilicas or temples but from arenas and triumphal arches. Vézelay is "this iron place"; it seems to remember the Roman imperium:

> In contrast to the lightsome Gothic manner of the last quarter of the twelfth century . . . the Cluniac church might seem a still active instrument of the iron tyranny of Rome, of its tyranny over the animal spirits. As the ghost of ancient Rome still lingers "over the grave thereof," in the papacy, the hierarchy, so is it with the material structures also, the Cluniac and other Romanesque churches, which most emphatically express the hierarchical, the papal system.[7]

Describing the southern aisle of the nave at Vézelay, "a nave of ten bays, the grandest Romanesque interior in France, perhaps in the world," Pater says that "in its mortified light the very soul of monasticism, Roman and half-military, as the completest outcome of a religion of threats, seems to descend upon one."[8] "Descend": as if even a mere visitor lived for the time being under its threat. The light is mortified, as if it were pinched or pressed in the service of death, subdued to mortality; it knows nothing of the open air and has forgotten its access to the sky. This version of Romanesque has, "at least for English eyes, something of a Saracenic or other Oriental character." At Vézelay, Pater says, "the Romanesque of Burgundy, alike in the first conception of the whole structure, and in the actual locking together of the big stones, its masses of almost unbroken masonry, its *inertia*, figures as of more imperial character, and nearer to the Romans of old, than its feebler kindred in England or Normandy."[9]

One senses how reluctant Pater was to use the italicized *inertia*, how alien it was to his feeling for mobility and for the readiness of structures to let themselves be changed. Ruskin disposed of the matter more trenchantly. He didn't like Vézelay. When he visited it again on his grand tour of France, Switzerland, and Italy in the summer and autumn of 1892—he went to Rheims, Troyes, Sens, Châlons, Avallon—he noted in his diary about Vézelay:

> More disappointed than ever with anything, but the interior is still typical Romanesque in the nave, and extremely pure and melodious Early English or French in apse. Note generally that the early churches have only three lights round apse, and that no interior can be perfect with less than five. I do not know if there are good examples of seven. The mimicked "Last Judgment"—M. Viollet-le-Duc's—is very carefully vile, and the whole west front the ugliest and most characteristically barren I ever saw in an old building.[10]

The more Pater acknowledges the imperial character of Vézelay, short of calling anything in the church ugly or carefully vile, the more he looks for reason to mitigate its inertia. He interprets the sculptures on the capitals of the nave, which offended Bernard, as indication that the sculptors felt "delight in the power of reproducing fact, curiosity in it, but little or no sense of beauty." He doesn't say which carvings he has in view. One of the most compelling is of Satan's lyre, and beside Satan we see a larger figure stroking a woman's breast. "The demon of impurity caresses a woman," the guidebook says. The demon is the stuff of nightmare with its huge head and eyes, its deformed mouth, and wild standing hair. Beautiful, perhaps not, but it can't be written off as an instance of the sculptor's pleasure in reproducing fact. No such fact exists; it is a fiction imagined by a sculptor equally happy to carve a gargoyle or a Madonna's hand. Yet here and without further ado, as Pater says, and surrounded by these fantastic carvings, "the Pointed style, determined yet discreet, makes itself felt." It is felt in Vézelay for the first time, according to Viollet-le-Duc, from whom Pater happily takes instruction. In fact, the transition from Romanesque to Gothic did not occur at Vézelay, although one can see both forms there simultaneously. Vézelay's narthex and nave were built about 1105, and its choir about 1170. Between these constructions, the first truly Gothic structure, St. Denis, was made circa 1135–44. Pater didn't trouble himself about historical facts; he took Viollet-le-Duc's word for them. "Here at last," Pater says, "with no sense of contrast, but by way of veritable 'transition,' and as if by its own matured strength, the round arch breaks into the double curve, *les arcs brises*, with a wonderful access of grace."[11] Pater swoons with pleasure to see the Romanesque style changing before his eyes and "with no sense of contrast" into the Gothic. Instead of recalling the might of Rome and the power, hardly less, of the papacy, the imagination in the Gothic style "is stirred to present one with what belongs properly to it alone." Pure Architecture, Pater seems to say, by analogy with Pure Poetry and Pure Music. In the end, he comes back to the Romanesque of Vézelay and admits that it is the preeminent style of a monastic church that has turned its back upon common life and "jealously closed inward upon itself." But in the meantime he watches for any sign of a more accommodating disposition.

This explains why, in the essay on Vézelay but before reaching that church, Pater writes two long paragraphs on the Cistercian church at Pontigny. He wants to speak of the reaction against monasticism with its "imperious but half-barbaric splendours." The abbey church at Pontigny is so simple that you might think it merely a large farm-building. The site which "the sons of Saint Bernard" chose is only a patch of pastureland "in the midst of a heady wine-district":

> Within, a heavy coat of white-wash seems befitting to the simple forms of the "Transition," or quite earliest "Pointed," style, to its remarkable continence of spirit, its uniformity, and cleanness of build. The long prospect of nave and choir ends, however, with a sort of graceful smallness, in a *chevet* of seven closely packed, narrow bays. It is like a nun's church, or like a nun's coif.[12]

Three sentences trace an arc of desire, as if in advance of his occasion at Vézelay Pater couldn't bear to let it be thought that his subject was given over entirely to military power, Rome, the Crusades, idiom of masters and slaves. The transitional words are continence, uniformity, cleanness; with smallness, the second sentence already has in view, at the end of nave and choir, the nun. But even then, the simile is too bold, too masculine, for Pater's mood: it is as if the word "church" were still too Roman to be borne. He concentrates the simile further, effecting with five more monosyllables an image of contained desire, "or like a nun's coif." No wonder the word "winsome" occurs in the

next paragraph, Pontigny still the theme. As always, Pater is tender
to minor life and kindred somewhat feeble.

Bernard of Clairvaux is the transitional figure. In 1146 Pope Eugene
chose Vézelay as the preaching center of the second crusade, and on
Good Friday—or, some say, Easter Sunday—Bernard preached the
crusade in the Pope's name. In his contest with Abelard, as Pater notes,
Bernard showed a temper hierarchic and reactionary. He thought, as
many did, that Abelard had the arrogance of a logician and that he
treated Holy Scripture as if it were dialectics rather than the revealed
Word of God. Bernard had his own arrogance of faith, and was ready
to believe in the theologian's trinity of Father, Son, and Holy Ghost
if he were permitted day by day to take it as a mystery and to practice
alongside it the domestic trinity of Father, Mother, and Child. But
Bernard can be interpreted to nearly any purpose, as Pater and other
readers recognize. "You would lose hold of everything actual," Henry
Adams says, "if you could comprehend in its contradictions the strange
mixture of passion and caution, the austerity, the self-abandonment,
the vehemence, the restraint, the love, the hate, the miracles, and the
scepticism of Saint Bernard":

> The Cistercian Order, which was founded in 1098, from the
> first put all its churches under the special protection of the
> Virgin, and Saint Bernard in his time was regarded as the apple
> of the Virgin's eye. Tradition as old as the twelfth century,
> which long afterwards gave to Murillo the subject of a famous
> painting, told that once, when he was reciting before her statue
> the "Ave Maris Stella," and came to the words, "Monstra te
> esse Matrem," the image, pressing its breast, dropped on the
> lips of her servant three drops of the milk which had nourished
> the Saviour. The same miracle, in various forms, was told of
> many other persons, both saints and sinners; but it made so
> much impression on the mind of the age that, in the fourteenth
> century, Dante, seeking in Paradise for some official introduction
> to the foot of the Throne, found no intercessor with the Queen
> of Heaven more potent than Saint Bernard.[13]

So in "Vézelay" Pater makes Bernard the transitional figure between
Pontigny and Vézelay and back again, the early Gothic of the one, the
threatening Romanesque of the other. Bernard preached at Vézelay,
but he denounced its ornament: "what is the use of those grotesque

monsters in painting and sculpture?" He preached the second crusade in that church, but he might have wept, as Pater says, "at the sight of the doomed multitude (one in ten, it is said, returned from the Holy Land), as its enthusiasm, under the charm of his fiery eloquence, rose to the height of his purpose."[14] It is the rhetorician of the crusade who leads Pater up the hill to the Madeleine.

One of the limitations of Pater's essay on Vézelay is that he knew virtually nothing about the iconography of church architecture. The interpretation of the central tympanum in the narthex of Vézelay, to take just one feature of the church, has long been disputed. Emile Mâle related the tympanum to the events on the day of Pentecost: the central scene is of the descent of the Holy Ghost, with Christ distributing the rays of heavenly grace to his apostles. Abel Fabre construes the scene as representing the mission that Christ gave to his apostles immediately before his Ascension. Adolf Katzenellenbogen has conflated these two interpretations and concluded that the central tympanum features prophecies of the Old Testament, their first fulfillment in the mission of the apostles, their second in the new mission of the second crusade. Katzenellenbogen also believes that it was the great theologian Peter the Venerable, once Prior of Vézelay and in 1122 Abbot of Cluny, who gave the sculptors the program for the central tympanum. Pater says nothing of this. In 1899 he was turning sympathically toward religion, but he did not show much interest in the detail of iconographic interpretation.

Preceded by Ruskin, Pater was succeeded by Henry Adams, who studied the old churches of France with different interests and metaphors. On August 18, 1895, Adams was at Notre-Dame d'Amiens with his friends Henry and Anne Cabot Lodge. He knew the church well and visited it often in well-qualified company, once with the sculptor Saint-Gaudens. In the same inquiring spirit he examined with John LaFarge the stained glass in the cathedral at Chartres. He saw most of the churches that Pater saw, and took notes: Amiens, Mont-Saint-Michel, Le Mans, Sens, Autun, Vézelay, Arles, Coutances. Like Pater, he read Viollet-le-Duc and kept up with the church historians. But his interest in the churches differed from Pater's. Exasperated with twentieth-century chaos and multiplicity, Adams went to the Middle Ages in France for proof of unity. Not for the intrinsic value of the proof, but for the possibility of bringing the Virgin of Chartres of the twelfth century to exert critical and moral pressure on modern chaos. He warmed to every occasion of conflict and contrast. Unlike Pater, he took no satisfaction in motifs of transience, mobility, deliquescence. Adams wanted to recite a moral lesson and to sharpen the contrasts for the sake of verve. The fact that the lesson would be lost on those most in need of it was dismal, but Adams could not stop to weep over it. "Eight or ten years of study," he reported, "had led Adams to think he might use the century 1150–1250, expressed in Amiens Cathedral and the Works of Thomas Aquinas, as the unit from which he might measure motion down to his own time, without assuming anything as true or untrue, except relation."[15] The relation in which he took particular interest was that between one force and another. He was indifferent to persons and their personalities, and derided any philosophy of will, based on the acts of great men.

Adams wasn't even much concerned with Mary's personality, except as force. The oldest problem of philosophy, religion, and science, he thought, was the attempt to bridge the chasm between multiplicity and unity, "but the flimsiest bridge of all is the human concept, unless somewhere, within or beyond it, an energy not individual is hidden; and in that case the old question instantly reappears: What is that energy?" Concepts were merely the trivial deposit of logic. At Chartres, energy not individual was embodied in the Virgin, and devotion to her made her an individual in some danger of displacing, as mother, the theologian's trinity of Father, Son, and Holy Ghost. Her force was not individual. "As far as a superficial student could follow," Adams said, "the thirteenth century supposed mind to be a mode of force directly derived from the intelligent prime motor, and the cause of all form and sequence in the universe—therefore the only proof of unity."[16] In *Mont-Saint-Michel and Chartres* the Virgin is loved and praised, but love and praise are incidental to the recognition of force in her. In *The Education of Henry Adams* women are worshiped not because of their beauty—or, if so, because of that incidentally—but because of their force:

Every one, even among Puritans, knew that neither Diana of the Ephesians nor any of the Oriental goddesses was worshipped for her beauty. She was goddess because of her force; she was the animated dynamo; she was reproduction—the greatest and most mysterious of all energies; all she needed was to be fecund.[17]

Speaking of the labor of building the church at Chartres, Adams writes,

> Of course, the Virgin was actually and constantly present during all this labour, and gave her assistance to it, but you would get no light on the architecture from listening to an account of her miracles, nor do they heighten the effect of popular faith. Without the conviction of her personal presence, men would not have been inspired; but, to us, it is rather the inspiration of the art which proves the Virgin's presence, and we can better see the conviction of it in the work than in the words. [18]

In the nineteenth century, according to Adams, people gave up being interested in what they didn't understand; in the thirteenth, people were interested only in the incomprehensible, and in adoring the force of it.

To mark further the difference between Adams and Pater: in the France of 1150–1250 Adams finds a value, which he called unity, embodied in an institution, the church, and having as its greatest force of attraction and reverence the Virgin of Chartres. He speaks of her as if she were a force of nature before she became a force of love and intercession and supplication. The Virgin, her church, her saints and sinners, made the unity Adams kept extolling while he denounced multiplicity and claimed not to understand it. When he had recited the moral of the story for the hundredth time, he kept staring at Chartres and shaking his head over the world he otherwise inhabited, Washington, the United States of Grant and Roosevelt, folly and chaos at large.

Pater's interest in the churches of France had nothing directly to do with politics and little with morality. If he shuddered at the half-barbaric quality of the Romanesque at Vézelay, we cannot conclude that the shudder marked also his sense of the half-barbaric character of the British Empire or the French, Belgian, and German empires. He visited the churches for the same reason that he looked at paintings and sculptures, to remind himself of the variety of human life, even of those forms of it which as a general rule he preferred to take on trust. Looking at naves and apses, he adverted to their historical and political values, but glancingly, since that was not his first concern. He construed the architectural features as evidence of mentality, though he was not

French enough to call it *mentalité*. Populaces held his attention because they consisted of individual people, and while he had nothing to say about the respects in which crowds differed from the individuals who added up to them, he assumed that a descriptive psychology would be adequate even then.

Part IV

27

Modernity: Arnold and Pater

Change has come suddenly, the despair of my friends in the 'nineties part of its preparation. Nature, steel-bound or stone-built in the nineteenth century, became a flux where man drowned or swam; the moment had come for some poet to cry "the flux is in my own mind."
—W. B. Yeats, Introduction to
The Oxford Book of Modern Verse 1892–1935 (1936)

"A kind of a morbid modernity? There is that," she dimly conceded.
—Mrs. Brookenham to Mr. Mitchett, in Henry James,
The Awkward Age

IN THE PREFACE to *Poems* (1853) Arnold explains why he has not included the poem "Empedocles on Etna":

I intended to delineate the feelings of one of the last of the Greek religious philosophers, one of the family of Orpheus and Musaeus, having survived his fellows, living on into a time when the habits of Greek thought and feeling had begun fast to change, character to dwindle, the influence of the Sophists to prevail. Into the feelings of a man so situated there entered much that we are accustomed to consider as exclusively modern; how much, the fragments of Empedocles himself which remain to us are sufficient at least to indicate. What those who are familiar only with the great monuments of early Greek genius suppose to be its exclusive characteristics, have disappeared: the calm, the cheerfulness, the disinterested objectivity have disappeared; the dialogue of the mind with itself has commenced; modern problems have presented themselves; we hear already the doubts, we witness the discouragement, of Hamlet and of Faust.[1]

From the representation of such a predicament, Arnold says, no poetical enjoyment could be derived; from a situation "in which the suffering finds no vent in action; in which a continuous state of mental distress is prolonged, unrelieved by incident, hope, or resistance; in which there is everything to be endured, nothing to be done."

On November 14, 1857, Arnold returned to his consideration of "the modern." The occasion was his inaugural lecture as professor of poetry at Oxford. The lecture was supposed to be the first in a series "on the modern element in literature," but Arnold gave them up when he decided that on several aspects of the question he was inadequately prepared. In the first lecture he spoke of the demand for "an intellectual deliverance":

> The demand arises, because our present age has around it a copious and complex present, and behind it a copious and complex past; it arises, because the present age exhibits to the individual man who contemplates it the spectacle of a vast multitude of facts awaiting and inviting his comprehension. The deliverance consists in man's comprehension of this present and past. It begins when our mind begins to enter into possession of the general ideas which are the law of this vast multitude of facts. It is perfect when we have acquired that harmonious acquiescence of mind which we feel in contemplating a grand spectacle that is intelligible to us; when we have lost that impatient irritation of mind which we feel in presence of an immense, moving, confused spectacle which, while it perpetually excites our curiosity, perpetually baffles our comprehension.[2]

Modernity, then, is a certain paradigm of experience: a complex spectacle, and the discovery of the point of vantage from which it becomes comprehensible. The virtue entailed by this situation Arnold calls adequacy. The aim of his lecture is to show that adequacy was more completely achieved in the age of Pericles than in that of Elizabeth. Thucydides was adequate to the one; Raleigh was not adequate to the other. Sophocles, Pindar, Aeschylus, and Aristophanes were adequate, but not Menander, because he expressed a moment in the history of

Greece when its spiritual life lacked a material basis in political and practical force. The only evidence Arnold produces for this is that the Athenian expedition to Syracuse failed and the Peloponnesian War turned out badly for Athens. The moral of the story is that the British Empire must ensure that its expeditions won't fail. The chief defect of modern Britain, as Arnold insists in "The Literary Influence of Academies" and *Culture and Anarchy*, is that its citizens are indifferent to ideas. Just as good law controls the society it addresses, and a great mind finding the right point of view comprehends the otherwise heterogeneous spectacle before it, so ideas bring calm to an otherwise fretful social scene. An adequate idea is the law of the turbulence it offers to control. The analogy at work is that of the art of landscape. When Wordsworth, Constable, and Turner look at a landscape and divine the otherwise occult law of its coherence, they are adequate. When we participate in their works, we share that adequacy; we are delivered from fever and fret.

Arnold's confidence in ideas as the social means of overcoming modern anxiety is strange to us. The excitement with which he sees ideas at large in France is an emotion we have difficulty appreciating. The loss of confidence in ideas, or the rejection of them because of the complacency the possession of them induces, is easily explained: ideas have not saved us. T. S. Eliot's essay on Baudelaire is an accurate account of that disappointment. He speaks of the middle years of the nineteenth century as a time rampant with ideas, notions, and programs, with revolutions that changed nothing. He despised ideas because he regarded them as congealed feelings, loose change passed without thought from mind to mind, newspaper to newspaper. It was his supreme tribute to Henry James to say that James had a mind so fine that no idea could violate it, and to contrast that mind with Chesterton's, a mind swarming with ideas but "I see no evidence that he thinks." Eliot means that James had an extraordinary power to imagine feelings long before they have been congealed as ideas.

Pater is with Eliot in this matter. He had no interest in ideas as the socially accredited forms of energy. Nor did he take his bearings from the analogy of landscape. The dialogue of the mind with itself is Arnold's phrase for a predicament he dreaded, one in which the social movements of energy are thwarted and minds are morbidly driven back upon themselves. Pater didn't feel this as a predicament but as an opportunity for the exercise of self-consciousness. He valued works of art not because they discovered the law of the apparent heterogeneity they surveyed, but because they provoked one's mind into a further dialogue with itself. They gave the mind not something to think about but something to think with. From time to time Pater felt misgiving: the dialogue of the mind with itself might be a sign of one's imprisonment. But more often he felt that it would bring about a certain state of feeling, healthy skepticism, rich in sensation, a pleasure in itself.

Pater is most explicit on modernity in his early essay on Coleridge and in the chapter of *Gaston de Latour* called "Modernity." The essay on Coleridge is precocious work, impelled by certitude possible only in a young man. Pater invokes a Darwinian *Zeitgeist* as if it were self-evidently the everlasting gospel. The chapter in *Gaston de Latour* is more decorous.

Modern thought is distinguished from ancient, according to Pater, "by its cultivation of the 'relative' spirit in place of the 'absolute.' " Ancient philosophy "sought to arrest every object in an eternal outline, to fix thought in a necessary formula, and types of life in a classification by 'kinds' or genera." To the modern spirit "nothing is or can be rightly known except relatively under conditions." The idea of "the relative" has been enriched in modern times by the sciences of observation:

> These sciences reveal types of life evanescing into each other by inexpressible refinements of change. Things pass into their opposites by accumulation of undefinable quantities. The growth of those sciences consists in a continual analysis of facts of rough and general observation into groups of facts more precise and minute. A faculty of truth is a power of distinguishing and fixing delicate and fugitive details. The moral world is ever in contact with the physical; the relative spirit has invaded moral philosophy from the ground of the inductive sciences. There it has started a new analysis of the relations of body and mind, good and evil, freedom and necessity. Hard and abstract moralities are yielding to a more exact estimate of the subtlety and complexity of our life. Always as an organism increases in perfection the conditions of its life become more complex. Man is the most complex of the products of nature.[3]

When it suits him, Pater is ready to appeal to "nature" or to "life," but not to ground a philosophy on those values. Nature, he says, "which by one law of development evolves ideas, moralities, modes of inward life, and represses them in turn, has in this way provided that the earlier growth should propel its fibres into the later, and so transmit the whole of its forces in an unbroken continuity of life." On the other hand, the dominant tendency of life "is to turn ascertained truth into a dead letter—to make us all the phlegmatic servants of routine." Here Pater anticipates Beckett's essay on Proust with its attack on habit as our second nature which prevents us from realizing our first. Why ascertained truths—Arnold's cherished ideas—become dead letters Pater doesn't say. But he implies that we have produced "the relative spirit" by analogy with nature's rhythm of evolving and suppressing. The relative spirit, "by dwelling constantly on the more fugitive conditions or circumstances of things, breaking through a thousand rough and brutal classifications, and giving elasticity to inflexible principles, begets an intellectual finesse, of which the ethical result is a delicate and tender justness in the criticism of human life." Our sense of the relative spirit should defeat habit and keep values mobile. Coleridge's idea of art as organic form is unacceptable. The artistic process must not be thought of as innate, a natural movement of energy; it is a human process of will and desire.

The relative spirit, according to Pater in *Plato and Platonism*, was invented "in the Renaissance of the sixteenth century." Montaigne's *Essays* was its first manifestation. The skeptical philosopher of Bordeaux, as Pater calls him, "does but commence the modern world, which, side by side with its metaphysical reassertions, from Descartes to Hegel, side by side also with a constant accumulation of the sort of certainty which is afforded by empirical science, has had assuredly, to check wholesomely the pretensions of one and of the other alike, its doubts."[4]

Pater rebukes Coleridge, then, as for a similar reason in *Studies in the History of the Renaissance* he silently rebukes Ruskin, for trying to establish principles, "to fix one mode of life as the essence of life." Even if it were possible to devise principles, they should not be allowed to control or to explain sensory experience. Instead of trying to establish one mode of life as its essence, we should consider the differences between one principle and another and regard the differences as charming. Then comes, Pater says, "the spectacle of the reserve of the elder generation exquisitely refined by the antagonism of the new." The new is bound to win, since it carries "the current of new life." These advancing forces "detach the highest minds from the past by pressing home its difficulties and finally proving it impossible." Such, Pater says, "is the charm of Julian, of St. Louis, perhaps of Luther; in the narrower compass of modern times, of Dr. Newman and Lacordaire;

it is also the peculiar charm of Coleridge." There is special felicity, apparently, in seeing a man of great soul fighting for a cause he hasn't recognized as lost.

The source of Pater's bravado in this early essay is his conviction that he is the rhetorician of the winning side. He has the word. Or rather, the words, of change, evanescence, growth, development, evolution. So he treats Coleridge as a gifted child who, wrong through and through, will not be bidden. "The perfect flower of any elementary type of life," Pater says, "must always be precious to humanity, and Coleridge is the perfect flower of the romantic type." Specifically:

> More than Childe Harold, more than Werther, more than René, Coleridge, by what he did, what he was, and what he failed to do, represents that inexhaustible discontent, languor, and home-sickness, the chords of which ring all through our modern literature.

The question of Coleridge's adequacy, in Arnold's sense, is not raised. It is enough that he is charming, exemplar of a doomed condition.

It doesn't occur to Pater that we who think ourselves on the winning side will in our turn lose to the next victor. Pater invokes the historic sense as if it were the mark of the perfection his age has reached. He sees modernity gathering up the choice images of former civilizations, examining them judicially by examining them historically. Setting Coleridge straight, he says:

> Theology is a great house, scored all over with hieroglyphics by perished hands. When we decypher one of those hieroglyphics, we find in it the statement of a mistaken opinion; but knowledge has crept onward since the hand dropped from the wall; we no longer entertain the opinion, and we can trace the origin of the mistake. Dogmas are precious as memorials of a class of sincere and beautiful spirits, who in a past age of humanity struggled with many tears, if not for true knowledge, yet for a noble and elevated happiness. That struggle is the substance, the dogma only its shadowy expression; received traditionally in an altered age, it is the shadow of a shadow, a mere γοίγου εἴδωλον, twice removed from substance and reality.

It follows that "the true method then in the treatment of dogmatic theology must be historical."

It is strange that Pater does not hear a false note in a sentence that so dogmatically dismisses the claim of dogma, or in the asserted "true" and "must be," or the claim to know where the "substance and reality" are to be found despite shadows beyond shadows. He continues on the historic method:

> Englishmen are gradually finding out how much that method has done since the beginning of modern criticism by the hands of such writers as Baur. Coleridge had many of the elements of this method: learning, inwardness, a subtle psychology, a dramatic power of sympathy with modes of thought other than his own. Often in carrying out his own method he gives the true historical origin of a dogma, but with a strange dulness of the historical sense, he regards this as a reason for the existence of the dogma now, not merely as reason for its having existed in the past. Those historical elements he could not envisage in the historical method, because this method is only one of the applications, the most fruitful of them all, of the relative spirit.

But the relative spirit, otherwise known as skepticism, doesn't guard Pater against claiming to know what he is talking about. T. S. Eliot once remarked the astonishing number of things Bertrand Russell believed: far more than Augustine. Pater's essay on Coleridge is rotten with beliefs, axioms, unargued hypotheses.

In *Studies in the History of the Renaissance* and in *Gaston de Latour* Pater retains these prejudices but subdues them in consideration of the possibility that he, too, like Coleridge, might be in error. In *Gaston de Latour* he refers to "our modern idea, or platitude, of the *Zeit-geist*," and at least allows for the possibility that some of its ascertained truths have become dead letters. The exhilaration he ascribes to Gaston is now found not in truths but in interests and pleasures for which no permanence is claimed. Gaston emerges, like Constantin Guys in Baudelaire's "The Painter of Modern Life," a connoisseur of appearances and glimpses:

> It was the power of "modernity," as renewed in every successive age for genial youth, protesting, defiant of all sanction in these matters, that the true "classic" must be of the present, the force

and patience of present time. He had felt after the thing, and here it was,—the one irresistible poetry there had ever been, with the magic word spoken in due time, transforming his own age and the world about him, presenting its everyday touch, the very trick one knew it by, as an additional grace, asserting the latent poetic rights of the transitory, the fugitive, the contingent.[5]

In *Studies in the History of the Renaissance*, Pater talks not of truth but of freedom, or rather, of the possibility of feeling free. Impelled by Hegel and Winckelmann, he thinks it splendid that Greek religion "was able to transform itself into an artistic ideal." He is still enjoying the rhetoric of evanescence and development. But he doesn't claim that appearances found to be pleasurable must also be found to be true:

What modern art has to do in the service of culture is so to rearrange the details of modern life, so to reflect it, that it may satisfy the spirit. And what does the spirit need in the face of modern life? The sense of freedom. That naive, rough sense of freedom, which supposes man's will to be limited, if at all, only by a will stronger than his, he can never have again. The attempt to represent it in art would have so little verisimilitude that it would be flat and uninteresting. The chief factor in the thoughts of the modern mind concerning itself is the intricacy, the universality of natural law even in the moral order. For us necessity is not as of old an image without us, with whom we can do warfare; it is a magic web woven through and through us, like that magnetic system of which modern science speaks, penetrating us with a network subtler than our subtlest nerves, yet bearing in it the central forces of the world. Can art represent men and women in these bewildering toils so as to give the spirit at least an equivalent for the sense of freedom?[6]

Pater is moving into a different vocabulary: of art, pleasure, freedom, passion, consciousness.

28

Art for Art's Sake

I

IT WOULD NOT BE NECESSARY to say anything about "art for art's sake" if readers still held the view of art and literature that A. C. Bradley elucidated in his inaugural lecture as professor of poetry at Oxford in 1901. According to Bradley, the phrase "Poetry for Poetry's Sake" implies that the experience of reading a poem proceeds, or should proceed, under these three assumptions:

> First, this experience is an end in itself, is worth having on its own account, has an intrinsic value. Next, its *poetic* value is this intrinsic worth alone. Poetry may have also an ulterior value as a means to culture or religion; because it conveys instruction, or softens the passions, or furthers a good cause; because it brings the poet fame or money or a quiet conscience. So much the better: let it be valued for these reasons too. But its ulterior worth neither is nor can directly determine its poetic worth as a satisfying imaginative experience; and this is to be judged entirely from within. And to these two positions the formula would add, though not of necessity, a third. The consideration of ulterior ends, whether by the poet in the act of composing

or by the reader in the act of experiencing, tends to lower poetic value. It does so because it tends to change the nature of poetry by taking it out of its own atmosphere. For its nature is to be not a part, nor yet a copy, of the real world (as we commonly understand that phrase), but to be a world by itself, independent, complete, autonomous; and to possess it fully you must enter that world, conform to its laws, and ignore for the time the beliefs, aims, and particular conditions which belong to you in the other world of reality.[1]

That chapter of *Oxford Lectures on Poetry* seems to me a persuasive description of the state of mind I should try to maintain, against other considerations, in reading a poem. I am aware that the position Bradley takes is vulnerable. It would be difficult to defend it against an opponent who said something along these lines: "I don't accept the privilege accorded to intrinsic values or the sequestering of ulterior values. The idiom of within and without is self-serving. I don't know what gives him the right to invoke 'the nature of poetry,' or to claim that a due sense of it ought to compel me to obedience, conforming to some laws apparently internal to the poems. I don't recognize such laws. Finally, 'the atmosphere of poetry' is an empty phrase." It would be difficult to rebut these charges. But Bradley's sense of poetry seems to me superior to that of the reader I have summoned to put the contrary case.

Within a few years after Bradley's lecture, it became commonplace to dislodge intrinsic values in favor of ulterior ones: religion, ethics, politics. Let me give a formidable example. In 1927 T. S. Eliot was confirmed in the Church of England. Three years later he published one of his most acerbic essays, "Arnold and Pater." The relation between these events is clear. As a Christian, Eliot was convinced that his first public duty was to serve the church by whatever means, in essays, lectures, reviews, poems, and plays; just as, when the war started in 1939, he thought his first duty as a writer was to serve the composite institution which he deemed to consist of Britain, Europe, and Christendom. He was also convinced during those years that literary criticism, as he said in "Religion and Literature," should be completed by criticism from a definite ethical and theological standpoint. These considerations explain the severity of his reflections on Arnold and Pater: he now regarded them as nuisances.

Before 1930, he veered in his sense of Pater. In May 1917 he published in the *Little Review* "Eeldrop and Appleplex," a Laforguian fiction in which Eeldrop is permitted to remember an acquaintance called Edith or Scheherazadee by the simple device of adding a phrase from *Marius the Epicurean*—"Not pleasure, but fulness of life"—to one from the Conclusion to *Studies in the History of the Renaissance*—"To burn always with this hard gem-like flame." The addition, in its personified form, is given "curiosity and passion for experience" sufficient to require fulfillment by recourse to a Russian pianist in Bayswater. The moral of the little story is that no real person, as distinct from a devotee of Pre-Raphaelite art, has ever believed in the passion for experience:

> The passionate person is passionate about this or that, perhaps about the least significant things, but not about experience. But Marius, des Esseintes, Edith. . . .[2]

Edith appears to have read Pater only to the extent of taking literally his recommendation: "Not the fruit of experience, but experience itself is the end." It is her punishment to be remembered without passion by Eeldrop—"Nothing ever happens to her; everything that happens is her own doing"—and to be seated for her portrait by Appleplex, who loses interest upon pronouncing her not tragic but dissatisfied. Pater belongs, we assume, to the world of J. Alfred Prufrock, Gerontion, and the personage anatomized in "Portrait of a Lady."

A sentence from Eliot's essay on *Hamlet* is evidence for this view. He has been claiming that "the most dangerous of critics" is the one who pays attention to the character Hamlet rather than to the play *Hamlet*. This is "the critic with a mind which is naturally of the creative order, but which through some weakness in creative power exercises itself in criticism instead." Such critics "often find in Hamlet a vicarious existence for their own artistic realization." Goethe and Coleridge are Eliot's examples: the one turned Hamlet into a Werther, the other into a Coleridge. "We should be thankful," Eliot concluded, "that Walter Pater did not fix his attention on this play."[3]

The snub is delivered with personal animus, as if Eliot were diagnosing, in his reference to Pater, an ailment he finds in himself as clearly as in Hamlet, an excess of emotion over the cause of it. Eliot's early poems are attempts to find objective correlatives for emotions he had good reason to fear. His early criticism attacks other writers for their failure to maintain a strict relation, in the expression of emotion, between cause and effect. In April 1921 he compared "what Pater tries to do in prose" with "what Swinburne often does in verse: to arouse indefinite evocation, depending as much upon literary association as upon the beauty of the rhythm":

> "This is the head upon which all the ends of the world have come, and the eyes are a little weary." Compare this whole passage about La Gioconda with the last chapter of Ecclesiastes, and see the difference between direct suggestiveness by precise reference, and the meretricious suggestiveness of vague literary association. There is more essential poetry in Turgenev's "Sportsman's Sketches," even in translation, than in the whole of Sir Thomas Browne or Walter Pater.[4]

In an essay on prose and verse, the "prose-poem" and "poetic prose," Eliot should have quoted Pater accurately: "Hers is the head upon which all 'the ends of the world are come,' and the eyelids are a little weary." No matter. He denounced in Pater what he saw in himself. He was just as susceptible as Pater was to vague invocation and incantation: precise reference is not the mark of his poems. He was not immune to the acoustic attractions of Poe, Tennyson, Edward Lear, and Swinburne. But in *The Criterion* for October 1924 Eliot was much more considerate to Pater, associating him with Arnold, Newman, and F. H. Bradley as "amongst the names which carry the most promise of future power"; against the popular successes, Carlyle, Wells, and Shaw.[5]

Eliot's purpose in the essay on Arnold and Pater, he said, was "to indicate a direction from Arnold, through Pater, to the 'nineties, with, of course, the solitary figure of Newman in the background." This entailed his showing, or rather asserting, that Arnold's intellectual confusion, further compounded by Pater, caused serious damage in the nineties and thereafter. Arnold was a scandal to Eliot because he encouraged readers to think that they could enjoy the emotions of Christianity without the labor of believing its doctrine. "The total effect of Arnold's philosophy," he wrote, "is to set up Culture in the place of Religion, and to leave Religion to be laid waste by the anarchy of feeling."[6] It was Arnold who did the first mischief, separating religion from thought, not foreseeing that the divorce would result in *Marius the Epicurean* and *De Profundis*. Pater's view of life, Eliot said, was merely a permutation of Arnold's. Each of them was a moralist trying to disguise himself as something else: literary critic, connoisseur, art critic, poet. Pater's view of art "impressed itself upon a number of writers in the 'nineties, and propagated some confusion between life and art which is not wholly irresponsible for some untidy lives." It was churlish of Eliot to rebuke Pater and to claim the right of speaking on behalf of tidy lives. But Yeats, too, much as he revered Pater, thought that he may have had a bad influence. In "The Tragic Generation" he speculated that *Marius the Epicurean*, "the only great prose in modern fiction," may have "caused the disaster of my friends":

It taught us to walk upon a rope tightly stretched through serene air, and we were left to keep our feet upon a swaying rope in a storm.[7]

Eliot pressed the issue further by quoting throughout from the first edition of *Studies in the History of the Renaissance*. He knew that the offensive parts of the Conclusion had been written "even before the 'seventies" but not that they had been published in "Poems by William Morris." He ignored the fact that in later editions Pater toned down several phrases: that he changed "some abstract morality," in a passage Eliot quoted, to "some abstract theory." From Pater's essay on Wordsworth, Eliot quoted this sentence:

To treat life in the spirit of art, is to make life a thing in which means and ends are identified: to encourage such treatment, the true moral significance of art and poetry.

But he didn't quote from the same essay Pater's assertion that "the office of the poet is not that of the moralist." It is odd, too, that having attacked Arnold, Eliot brought Arnold's criteria to tell against Pater. When we read Pater on Leonardo or Giorgione, Eliot said, we feel that his preoccupation with "whatever is morbid or associated with physical malady" is "coming between him and the object as it really is." Primarily a moralist, Pater "was incapable of seeing any work of art simply as it is." For similar reasons and with much the same vocabulary, Eliot isolated for rebuke, in "Shakespeare and the Stoicism of Seneca," the mentality he saw in Othello. Quoting Othello's great speech to the senators—"Soft you; a word or two before you go"—Eliot said that Othello was trying to cheer himself up by adopting an aesthetic rather than a moral attitude to his life, dramatizing himself against his environment; resorting to *bovarysme*, "the human will to see things as they are not."[8] Reviewing Yeats's *The Cutting of an Age*, he made the same complaint, that in Yeats's chapters on his friends and associates we never see them as they were, but always as projections of Yeats's own feelings.

But Eliot's main attack was directed against Pater's endorsement of "art for art's sake":

> His famous dictum: "Of this wisdom, the poetic passion, the desire of beauty, the love of art for art's sake has most; for art comes to you professing frankly to give nothing but the highest quality to your moments as they pass, and simply for those moments' sake," is itself a theory of ethics; it is concerned not with art but with life. The second half of the sentence is of course demonstrably untrue, or else being true of everything else besides art is meaningless; but it is a serious statement of morals.[9]

The wisdom Pater is talking about is that of getting as many pulsations as possible into our brief lives. The second part of his sentence is not demonstrably untrue. If Pater thinks that the concentration of one's mind upon a work of art is the type or paradigm of human life at its best, giving "the highest quality" to one's moments as they pass, and simply for those moments' sake, it is up to Eliot to demonstrate that he is in error:

> The theory (if it can be called a theory) of "art for art's sake" is still valid in so far as it can be taken as an exhortation to the artist to stick to his job; it never was and never can be valid for the spectator, reader or auditor. . . . The right practice of "art for art's sake" was the devotion of Flaubert or Henry James.[10]

Eliot might have acknowledged that in "Style" Pater names Flaubert as the most complete exemplar of the discipline of style. Sticking to one's job meant, in Eliot's case, writing for the church, an excellent motive but not to be required of everyone. "Ash-Wednesday" is a poem as well written as Eliot could make it, but it is first a work of devotion which happens also to be a superb poem. Readers who are not Christians may enjoy the poem either by imagining, while reading it, what it would be like to say these prayers and experience these feelings, or by taking pleasure in the poem as a coherent formal achievement. It would be hard to distinguish this latter from a reader's engagement for the time being in the rhetoric of art for art's sake.

Eliot's denunciation is extravagant. Pater's docrine (if it is that) is merely a claim that there are some experiences which are best approached on the assumption that their value is intrinsic. There is no merit in looking before or after. There are occasions, too, on which the mind, concentrated upon an object, delights also in its own capacity. If you are listening to a Beethoven quartet, you do well not to be thinking of anything else, even of sin, expiation, redemption, and God. I wish the doctrine could be given a second chance, now that we are admonished to regard a work of art as merely a disguised ideological formation and to attend to it as a detective interrogates a suspect.

II

Thomas Mann said of Aestheticism that it was "the first manifestation of the European mind's rebellion against the whole morality of the bourgeois age." Nietzsche's denial of intellect in favor of the beauty, strength, and wickedness of life was "the self-lashing of a man who suffered profoundly from life."[11] Only as aesthetic phenomena, Nietzsche said in *The Birth of Tragedy*, are life and the world eternally justified. We have art so that we may not perish of truth. I quote these familiar aphorisms merely to point to the adversary sense of life upon which art for art's sake depends. Art is beautiful, as Adorno says, "by virtue of its opposition to mere being."[12]

Kierkegaard has noted that Aestheticism gratifies a particular form of attention to its object, that of finding it "interesting." The quality of this attention is such that the aesthete doesn't feel under obligation to specify the interest or to consider its relations to discursive categories such as ethics and politics. To find something interesting is to assent to its being thus and not other; it is found interesting in itself, not because it sustains some other consideration or value. In the *Philosophy of History* Hegel invokes this intrinsic quality to justify his distinction between matter and spirit. Matter has its essence out of itself, the essence of spirit is freedom, its being free is the quality of its self-contained existence. I would add: in the experience of finding an object interesting in itself, I exert my own freedom and participate in the freedom of the object. The object is free because it has not accepted the responsibility of being other than it is or of furthering some extraneous aim. This explains why objects of aesthetic interest are thought to be more spiritual than material even when, as in a painting, they are palpably material. It also explains why materialists resent the spiritual form commonly ascribed to works of art.

Kierkegaard uses the concept of the aesthetic, as Adorno has noted, in three senses. The first is the common one, the realm of works of art and the theory of their production. The second is more pointed: the aesthetic in me is that by which I am immediately what I am, as distinct from the ethical, by which I become what I become. In *A Portrait of the Artist as a Young Man* Stephen tells Lynch that the aesthetic emotion is static and that the aesthetic image, temporal or spatial, is first "luminously apprehended as selfbounded and selfcontained upon the immeasurable background of space or time which is not it."[13] The fact that Stephen has Aristotle and Aquinas to thank, rather than Kierkegaard, is beside the present point. Kierkegaard's third sense of the concept, found only in the *Concluding Unscientific Postscript*, refers to the form of subjective communication:

> The subjective thinker is an existing individual essentially interested in his own thinking, existing as he does in his thought. His thinking has therefore a different type of reflection, namely the reflection of inwardness, of possession, by virtue of which it belongs to the thinking subject and to no one else.[14]

It follows, according to Kierkegaard, that aesthetic man is enslaved to the moment and can escape from this prison only by becoming ethical. Kierkegaard's direction is from aesthetic to ethical man, from poetic to religious experience, from the aesthetic moment to a leap beyond it.

But Kierkegaard's *angst* darkens the subject unnecessarily. It is possible to remain within the category of aesthetic man, taking pleasure in the sequence of its intrinsic interests. In Borges's "The Wall and the Books" we are encouraged to feel that "all forms have their virtue in themselves and not in any conjectural 'content.' " The aesthetic does not look beyond itself. Croce's concept of aesthetic form and Pater's assertion that all the arts constantly aspire to the condition of music prompt Borges to think of the aesthetic state as arrested in its own being:

> Music, states of happiness, mythology, faces belaboured by time, certain twilights and certain places try to tell us something,

or have said something we should have missed, or are about to say something: this imminence of a revelation which does not occur is, perhaps, the aesthetic phenomenon.[15]

It is like the figures on Keats's Grecian urn, their love "forever warm, and still to be enjoyed." In Borges the aesthetic quality depends upon being in the vicinity of communications, short of receiving them: if they reached us, we would have to act upon them. Action is a different mode of being alive. English Aestheticism begins with Keats and Lamb. But why does Borges's list include "faces belaboured by time"? Perhaps because they are so weathered that they may blithely remain where they are, set apart from their first purposive selves.

Mann regarded Nietzsche, Bergson, and Kierkegaard as exemplars of "a movement of intellectual revolt against the classical faith in reason of the eighteenth and nineteenth centuries." The movement, he thought, had done its work. What remained to be done was "the reconstitution of human reason upon a new basis, the achievement of a concept of humanity of greater profundity than the complacently shallow view of the bourgeois age." A new Aestheticism wouldn't suffice, he thought, because Aestheticism, "under whose banner freethinkers turned against bourgeois morality, itself belonged to the bourgeois age." To move beyond this age entails stepping out of an aesthetic era into a moral and social one. Mann implies that the Enlightenment was a naive exercise because it ignored the demonic elements in human nature and pretended that man was in every respect a reasoning animal.

The question is still contentious. For a time it seemed that we could deal with it locally by keeping politics apart from aesthetics. We had the bad examples of Pound and Yeats, who judged societies by criteria mainly aesthetic and ignored, amid the neo-Nietzschean clatter, the price exacted by heroes from victims. "The logical result of Fascism," Walter Benjamin said, "is the introduction of aesthetics into politics." Again: "All efforts to render politics aesthetic culminate in one thing: war." From the same essay, "The Work of Art in the Age of Mechanical Reproduction":

Fiat ars—pereat mundus, says Fascism, and, as Marinetti admits, expects war to supply the artistic gratification of a sense perception that has been changed by technology. This is evidently the consummation of *"l'art pour l'art."* Mankind, which in Homer's time was an object of contemplation for the Olympian

gods, now is one for itself. Its self-alienation has reached such
a degree that it can experience its own destruction as an aesthetic
pleasure of the first order. This is the situation of politics which
Fascism is rendering aesthetic. Communism responds by poli-
ticizing art.[16]

Benjamin's essay was published in 1936. The defeat of Mussolini's
Fascism and Hitler's Nazism has not reduced the force of the argument.
But we are again in a phase of critical theory according to which a
work of art is merely an illustration of a certain ideological formation.
The part of Aestheticism which should now be recovered, I suggest,
is its concern for the particularity of form in every work of art. Pater
seemed to imply this concern in *Studies in the History of the Renaissance*
when he referred to the virtue of every object of attention, the particular
quality by which it is that thing and no other. Unfortunately, he
thought of that virtue in psychological rather than in formal terms, and
hoped to come upon it by describing the impression a particular work
of art, or several works attributed to the same artist, made on him.
The impression turns out to mark a certain consanguinity of temper
which is embodied when one mind, under sensory stimulation, imagines itself in the vicinity of another.

Pater's aim in the exercise of mind was the pleasure of the activity
itself. He believed that thinking could proceed without being subjected
at every point to the drastic criteria of knowing. Even if you couldn't
know anything for sure, you could still keep your mind astir, you could
brood upon the sensations provoked by trying to know. It was Pater's
embarrassment to discover that consciousness couldn't account for the
whole of his experience. The next-best consideration was that he could
work his consciousness hard enough to produce the most intense moments of that experience, and settle for those exaltations in default of
continuous splendor.

Those moments are often compared to Joyce's epiphanies. But there
is a difference. Joyce's were found in the world at large. There is a
girl, her skirts kilted up, on Dollymount Strand. Stephen sees her.
The conjunction of mind and what it perceives is a revelation, a certain
style of language its enabling expression. Pater's epiphanies are internal.
In sublime moments he discovers that his mind has certain powers
beyond prediction.

Wilde practiced much the same assumption, but he kept his thinking
external, put his circus animals on show. In his plays, speaking dares

to be as free as the thinking that precedes it. The shock of his paradoxes and conceits is that they are audible. What Pater merely thought, in private, and wrote out in sentences for initiates, Wilde turned into *coups de théâtre*. He displaced the ethical interests of the theater by the production of appearances, sufficiently accredited by the free play of the mind that conjured them. It is sufficient that they are found interesting, as photographs and other glimpses are interesting in respects that don't call for elucidation. Pater and Wilde scorned Arnold's morality because it was founded primarily upon respect for objects, and only secondarily upon respect for the mind that attended to them.

It is a complication in Pater's version of art for art's sake that the object of attention need not be a work of art; it could just as well be a work of nature. Ostensibly writing of aesthetic objects, he doesn't distinguish between a picture, a landscape, or "a fair personality in life or in a book." The object doesn't matter; what matters is the mind's experience of pleasure in lavishing attention upon it. Work of the artist's hands, or the face of one's friend: there is no need to make a distinction.

Adorno has argued that Aestheticism had its hour and its place—the modern history of cities:

> It is there, like artificial street lighting, in the twilight of incipient despair, that this strange, dangerous, and imperious form emits its beam to eternalize, garishly, life as it slips away.[17]

But the aesthetic moment can be recovered at any time by reciting a few commonplaces that are often derided. I don't deride them. They are so evidently commonplaces that it is unnecessary to ascribe them to their putative authors, but they are none the worse for that consideration. A short list includes the following. A work of art is an object added to the world. Its relation to the world is not that of an adjective to the noun it qualifies. The relation is more likely to be utopian than referential. Art is art because it is not nature. The work discloses a fictive possibility, like Heidegger's flute-playing centaur. Art is always striving to be independent of the mere intelligence and to be rid of its responsibilities to its subject or material. In an achieved work of art we find a certain light we should seek in vain upon anything real. Poetry must resist the intelligence almost successfully. The work does not take any civic responsibility; it does not accept the jurisdiction of metaphysics, religion, morality, politics, or any public institution. As Susanne Langer says in *Feeling and Form*, a work of art is an object offered only or at least chiefly for perception: its mode is not real but virtual. It is the virtuality of the work of art that should protect it—but rarely does—from the rough strife of ideologues.

III

Among Pater's unpublished manuscripts at the Houghton Library in Harvard there is an incomplete essay called "The Aesthetic Life." It may have been the basis of some lectures. Pater takes the occasion to say that in the subversive light of modern empirical philosophy it may be prudent to hold by the only indubitable experience, "the domain of sense," the "unsophisticated presentations of eye and ear." Man does well to acquiesce "in the sensible world as the ascertained utmost limit of his horizon." It may then be feasible to construct "an 'aesthetic' formula of conduct," to deduce an ethic from a sense of beauty. But will it be possible for the aesthete, "this supposed son of the age," to find "in the world now actually around us sufficient congruity, sufficient sustenance or opportunity to make the aesthetic life practicable or worthwhile?" Is it sagacious "to develop further capacities already so much at a loss, which must be so constantly checked in contact with the bourgeois generation amid which after all we have to live?" In London, for instance. Pater refers to its "hideousness," which he mitigates to "ugliness." Anyone who wishes to "prosecute the life of aesthetic culture" in London will have to select the things to see, and to practice "a fine habit of ignoring or forgetting." Still, the son of the age "has had the privilege of the elder brother in becoming a scholar and possessing the touchstones, the authorities, the critical instincts of his scholarship, its sense of periods and their affinities." He has the advantage of "the historic sense" and much to choose from, the inherited art of many centuries. He appreciates the affinity between medieval art and Japanese art, the "likeness in Giotto to the Greeks and to William Blake." He has Wren's steeples to admire, and the modern art of Burne-Jones, Whistler, Corot's landscapes:

> For what an interesting period, after all, is this we live in!, admitted the ugliness of its material residence how interesting its soul![18]

The particular qualities that Pater ascribes to the aesthete are predictably like his own:

> It is part of his tact, his finely educated sense of fitness, to dissimulate his interests, to say less than he really feels, to carry about with him in self-defence through a vulgar age a habit of reserve, of irony it may be, this again becoming in its turn but an added means of expression.[19]

At this point the manuscript, like the argument, drifts away.

In his later years and most clearly in the essay on style, Pater reneged on art for art's sake. Or rather he acknowledged moral considerations substantively, not merely as deduced from a sense of beauty. In "Style," moving from a description of "good art" to "great art," he made the wretched concession of saying that good art depends on its form, but great art depends on its matter. Certain qualities are necessary if the work is to be art, but these are not sufficient to make it great. Thackeray's *Henry Esmond* is greater art than *Vanity Fair* because of "the greater dignity of its interests":

> Given the conditions I have tried to explain as constituting good art;—then, if it be devoted further to the increase of men's happiness, to the redemption of the oppressed, or the enlargement of our sympathies with each other, or to such presentment of new or old truth about ourselves and our relation to the world as may ennoble and fortify us in our sojourn here, or immediately, as with Dante, to the glory of God, it will be also great art. . . .[20]

Eliot need not have worried. But he assumed that the Conclusion to *The Renaissance* was more insidiously remembered than the little essay on style.

29

His Style

ONE OF THE EARLIEST and most hostile accounts of Pater's style is in Edward Thomas's *Walter Pater*. But the book is a job of journeywork. By the time it was published in 1913, Thomas had ceased to care for Pater and chosen to be exasperated instead. He wrote it because Pater was there to be written about: he was a name, as Maeterlinck, Swinburne, Borrow, Lafcadio Hearn, Keats, and the Duke of Marlborough were names. Thomas turned out a book on each. But Pater irritated him. Thomas thought it a grievous fate to be self-conscious, as Pater was, but then Pater should have worked his fate to the point of making it seem his choice. He "did not carry his self-conscious labours far enough":

> On almost every page of his writing words are to be seen sticking out, like the raisins that will get burnt on an ill-made cake. It is clear that they have been carefully chosen as the right and effective words, but they stick out because the labour of composition has become so self-conscious and mechanical that cohesion and perfect consistency are impossible. The words have

only an isolated value; they are labels; they are shorthand; they are anything but living and social words.[1]

The telling consideration is "social." In his youth, Thomas was much influenced by Pater's style, so he later dissociated himself from it with due violence. It was not, he now chose to discover, a social or a sociable style; it did not come from ordinary life or acknowledge it at any point. Frost's style did, bleak as its sociability often was. Pater would have written in the same style if he had had no readers. It was an entirely personal style, the raisins sticking out. Besides, the personality it expressed was timid. Thomas thought it too dainty to be admired. There were several matters which Pater's style could not or would not treat: in "Hippolytus Veiled" he called dung *sordes* even though the animal in the case was a sheep.

Thomas didn't raise the question of decadence. It was said of Pater that he gave a separate manuscript page to each sentence and that this was a sign of decadence. He didn't, but he left plenty of space between the lines for second thoughts, and he thought the proper unit of prose was a sentence. Linda Dowling has shown in her *Language and Decadence in the Victorian Fin de Siècle* that the standard attributes of decadence included a cult of Late Latin as correlative to Modernity, fondling attention to belatedness—"this late day"—brooding fascination with the decline and fall of the Roman Empire as type of the fate inevitably attending the British one, and a sense of desperate epiphanies. Dowling has also clarified the meaning of decadence as it was defined in Désiré Nisard's *Etudes de moeurs et de critique sur les poètes latins de la décadence* (1834) and developed by Nietzsche in *Der Fall Wagner*. Paul Bourget brought the definition into common understanding, and Havelock Ellis in an essay on Bourget made it still more popular. A style of decadence, Ellis wrote, "is one in which the unity of the book is decomposed to give place to the independence of the page, in which the page is decomposed to give place to the independence of the phrase, and the phrase to give place to the independence of the word."[2] Such a word —the fondled "girlish" in Stephen Dedalus's vicinity in *A Portrait of the Artist as a Young Man*—finds its place not in the world but in a Mallarméan book.

Pater's way with a sentence may be consulted in "A Study of Dionysus." He has been writing about Dionysus and his companions:

Quite different from them in origin and intent, but confused with them in form, are those other companions of Dionysus, Pan and his children. Home-spun dream of simple people, and like them in the uneventful tenour of his existence, he has almost no story; he is but a presence; the *spiritual form* of Arcadia, and the ways of human life there; the reflexion, in sacred image or ideal, of its flocks, and orchards, and wild honey; the dangers of its hunters; its weariness in noonday heat; its children, agile as the goats they tend, who run, in their picturesque rags, across the solitary wanderer's path, to startle him, in the unfamiliar upper places; its one adornment and solace being the dance to the homely shepherd's pipe, cut by Pan first from the sedges of the brook Molpeia.[3]

It is not one of his famous paragraphs, but a more typical one than those. The first sentence is inverted, adjectival phrases coming at once and accommodating a strong disjunction—"in origin and intent," as distinct from "in form"—before we are told to whom the disjunction applies. This information is further postponed by an adjectival phrase—"those other companions of Dionysus"—before we hear the subject of the sentence. We are to be delayed at every point. The rhythm of postponement governs the second sentence, too: it begins with an unattached nominative phrase, impeded further by having an adjectival phrase added to it—"and like them . . ."—before we are told that Pan has almost no story. The drift from story to presence and beyond is stopped by Blake's phrase, *"spiritual form,"* which Pater glosses, twenty pages later:

> . . . its *spiritual form*, to use again the expression I have borrowed from William Blake—form, with hands, and lips, and opened eyelids—spiritual, as conveying to us, in that, the soul of rain, or of a Greek river, or of swiftness, or purity.[4]

We have then by my count six nominative phrases, separated by semi-colons, grammatically attached to "Arcadia" only by the reiterated "its." The one about children and goats is a freehand drawing, such that when we come to the next "its" we are likely to have forgotten the Arcadia from which it depends. These several phrases are nominatives, but they are so far from adhering to their Arcadian reference that they have the character of vocatives. The sentence sounds like an ode, except that it doesn't begin with "O." The whole paragraph is French Symbolism, its procedure a series of digressions from a kernel sentence; Pan is the spiritual form of Arcadia.[5] What Pater makes of this is prose nearly independent of syntax. The long sentence is a show of its aureate diction. Pater deploys the coordinate phrases with such confidence in the evocative power of each that he hardly cares whether we retain the kernel sentence or not. We are entangled in a web of associations rather than allowed to speed from subject through verb to object. We are to feel, while reading the sentence, that we are in space but not in time; or, if we insist on being in time, that we are held in a prolonged present tense. Pater will decide the matter: how many coordinate phrases to include, and the expressive latitude of each. The phrases are variations on the character of Arcadia, and it matters to the rhythm of the sentence but not to its meaning otherwise that they come in one order rather than another. Much the same applies to another neo-Symbolist work, Stevens's "Notes Toward a Supreme Fiction": the order in which we receive the stanzas hardly matters. In Pater's sentence the delays, hoverings, and qualifications control the pace of the reading and therefore the conditions under which we are to reflect upon the apparent subject, Pan. Variations occur within the variations, as in the last phrase about the dance, "its one adornment and solace," where a flick of attention moves the reader's mind from adornment, an external flourish, to solace, a private experience even though it is also socially shared.

Rhetoricians call this procedure parataxis and distinguish it from a more exacting syntax. In syntax the unit is the clause, linked by particles to deliver an expression thought to be singular; in parataxis, the unit is a phrase, and one phrase is followed by another of similar provenance. There is no subordination of phrase to phrase, or any producible reason why the sequence ends when it does. The practice occurs in Hebrew poetry and in modern poets—Christopher Smart, Blake, Whitman, Ginsberg—given to the phrasal movement of the Psalms. Pater's version of parataxis is a technique of delay. Coordinate phrases hold the reader's mind in suspension, not in suspense. The matter in hand is resumed when Pater's sense of the tempo and duration of the sentence is ready to proceed.

The one thing Pater is determined not to do is to go directly from subject through verb to object. To defer the unhappiness of coming to a conclusion, he looks about for interpolations, however fanciful. Any occasion serves. In *Plato and Platonism* he describes how Berkeley's use of the dialogue as a discursive form differs from Plato's. His account of the matter mimes the difference between the two writers:

> Thus, with Berkeley, its purpose is but to give a popular turn to certain very dogmatic opinions, about which there is no diffidence, there are no half-lights, in the writer's own mind. With Plato, on the other hand, with Plato least of all is the dialogue —that peculiar modification of the essay—anything less than essential, necessary, organic: the very form belongs to, is of the organism of, the matter which it embodies. For Plato's dialogues, in fact, reflect, they refine upon while they fulfil, they idealise, the actual method, in which, by preference to anything like formal lecturing (the lecture being, so to speak, a treatise in embryo) Socrates conveyed his doctrine to others.[6]

The first sentence is as brisk as Pater is ever willing to be; his sympathy is not engaged by a writer "popular" and "dogmatic." The two clauses added to "opinions" tell us what Berkeley lacks; diffidence and half-lights anticipate Plato's better way. In the second sentence the kernel is simple: with Plato the dialogue belongs organically to the matter it embodies. But Pater qualifies virtually every word of this. Plato becomes "Plato least of all," the dialogue is compared with the essay, three adjectives ("essential," "necessary," "organic") call upon a romantic prejudice in favor of "organic form," and the word not yet given—"form"—is now produced along with two coordinate versions of its meaning. One of these is straightforward but is not allowed to go straight forward: "the very form belongs to" has to wait for a second thought of itself, "is of the organism of," before reaching its end, "the matter which it embodies." Pater is indifferent to an awkward phrase, the repeated "of," two partitive genitives calling more attention to themselves than they can sustain. He goes from qualification to qualification. In the last sentence he uses up four disparate verbs to join Plato's dialogues to their method. Taking the sentence as it comes, I can't know what the dialogues reflect, what they refine upon, what they fulfill, or what they idealize till I come to the object, "the actual method." Then I have to go back over the verbs and see what they have been doing. They have been moving from an objective to a subjective form of attention, by way of Pater's favorite process, refinement.

I idealize a method by taking personal possession of it, treating it as though it could be fulfilled in my mind and nowhere else. He wrote as if between the fate of the world and his mind there could be no conceivable relation and he might as well attend to his mind for the pleasure of it. What else could he do?

In the later essays especially, Pater is unwilling to let a noun go till he has revised it and, at least to his own satisfaction, refined it, sending it toward some higher form of itself. It was as if he had internalized the otherwise empty promise of redemption and set every noun, every adjective, moving toward an end never to be reached. In "Notre-Dame d'Amiens" we read of "an after-thought, an artificial after-thought," "by weather, by centuries of weather," "What, precisely what, is this to *me*?," "a curiosity, a very pleasurable curiosity," "this spirit, this 'free' spirit," and "a Greek—an unconscious Greek." In "Vézelay" virtually very word is in danger of attracting a scruple: "a reaction, a reaction against monasticism itself." "Beyond" cannot stand without the specious clarification of "far beyond."

These techniques of delay in Pater's sentences mark his quiet refusal to live by the rhythms of public life, commerce, and technology. Just as clearly as his indifference to the realistic novel, they express his distaste for bourgeois values. T. S. Eliot said that the invention of the internal combustion engine would alter literary forms and styles. Yeats circumvented the rhythm of efficiency and purpose by recourse to reverie, the mind bent upon itself as if there were nothing else. To the extent that public life in Victorian England was directed toward the rapid production of goods and services, Pater's style was antithetical to those purposes. Instead of moving swiftly from point to point, as in a newspaper or a guidebook, his sentences turn aside, replacing the repetitions of technology with activity entirely internal. They are busy with themselves, but not otherwise with the world. So their relation to the apparent theme is indirect. The sentences about the dialogue in Plato and Berkeley are informative on that matter, but their first loyalty is to the act of the mind in the process of negotiating the issue: they are responsive to a mind thinking rather than to the things being said. A phrase of Eliot's is useful here. In his first lecture on Milton he quoted a passage from *Paradise Lost* and one from *The Ivory Tower*, making an opportunistic comparison. The comment on Milton's style in *Paradise Lost* we may leave to Eliot. I want only the observation on *The Ivory Tower*. Both passages, as he said, depart from lucid simplicity:

The sound, of course, is never irrelevant, and the style of James certainly depends for its effect a good deal on the sound of a voice, James's own, painfully explaining. But the complication, with James, is due to a determination not to simplify, and in that simplification lose any of the real intricacies and by-paths of mental movement. . . .[7]

In James's sentences, as in Pater's on Plato and Berkeley, the apparent theme is respected, but only on the understanding that it serves a still higher value, the particular movement of a mind through these phrases and clauses. Mental movement is the real content of the passage.

The same prejudice affects Pater's diction, his favorite words which instead of specifying what they refer to indicate that the entire proceeding is problematic: "curious," "odd," "strange." As specifications, such words are nearly useless. They refuse to specify. They create a space in which a lesser mind would complacently denote objects and situations, but in which this mind, Pater's, will observe subjective scruple. As in a passage from the essay on Leonardo:

The year 1483—the year of the birth of Raphael and the thirty-first of Leonardo's life—is fixed as the date of his visit to Milan by the letter in which he recommends himself to Ludovico Sforza, and offers to tell him, for a price, strange secrets in the art of war. It was that Sforza who murdered his young nephew by slow poison, yet was so susceptible of religious impressions that he blended mere earthly passion with a sort of religious sentimentalism, and who took for his device the mulberry-tree —symbol, in its long delay and sudden yielding of flowers and fruit together, of a wisdom which economises all forces for an opportunity of sudden and sure effect. The fame of Leonardo had gone before him, and he was to model a colossal statue of Francesco, the first Duke of Milan. As for Leonardo himself, he came not as an artist at all, or careful of the fame of one; but as a player on the harp, a strange harp of silver of his own construction, shaped in some curious likeness to a horse's skull. The capricious spirit of Ludovico was susceptible also to the power of music, and Leonardo's nature had a kind of spell in it. Fascination is always the word descriptive of him. No portrait of his youth remains; but all tends to make us believe that up to this time some charm of voice and aspect, strong enough to balance the disadvantage of his birth, had played about him. His physical strength was great; it was said that he could bend a horseshoe like a coil of lead.[8]

This is extraordinary writing. It would be foolish to take it as merely mellifluous. In the first sentences it is hard to keep in mind that Sforza is a murderer: the murder is reported, along with the slow poison, so Pater can't be accused of concealing the fact. But he immediately surrounds it with the diction of sensitivity—"susceptible of religious impressions," "blended," "a sort of religious sentimentalism." Sforza's adoption of the mulberry tree as his symbol is mentioned as if it entailed moral as well as picturesque propriety. "Sudden and sure effect" means murder, but the euphemism is so well established that it is difficult to remember what the phrase means in Sforza's practice. Pater's diction discourages you from resolving the phrases into local reference, or from asking in what sense Leonardo's secrets in the art of war are strange, why the likeness of the harp to a horse's skull is curious, whether "capricious" quite meets the ethical case of Sforza, or how "a kind of spell" differs from a spell. Fascination is the word descriptive of Leonardo, he claims. It isn't; it has no force of description. What it describes is not Leonardo in any generally available sense but the impression in Pater's mind, thinking of Leonardo: the word doesn't otherwise describe anything. But Pater's rhetoric works by treating the impression in his mind as if it were visible and could be clarified by attaching to Leonardo's name further spectacular evidence. "Some charm of voice and aspect": as if it couldn't be specified. "Had played about him": like a spirit or a good angel. It is not surprising that the next paragraph refers to "brilliant sins and exquisite amusements." We are reading against the grain of this style if we ask what makes certain sins brilliant, certain amusements exquisite.

But a typical passage of Pater's would show more ardor than the one I've quoted from "A Study of Dionysus." Here is the finale to his essay on Raphael, where he is praising the artist's good taste as seen especially in a painting done at Florence of the Madonna and Child with St. Nicolas and John the Baptist in attendance:

Note this, for instance, in the familiar Apennine background, with its blue hills and brown towns, faultless, for once—for once only—and observe, in the Umbrian pictures around, how often such background is marred by grotesque, natural, or architectural detail, by incongruous or childish incident. In this cool, pearl-grey, quiet place, where colour tells for double—the jewelled cope, the painted book in the hand of Mary, the chaplet of red coral—one is reminded that among all classical writers Raphael's preference was for the faultless Virgil. How orderly, how divinely clean and sweet the flesh, the vesture, the floor, the earth and sky! Ah, say rather the hand, the method of the painter! There is an unmistakeable pledge of strength, of movement and animation in the cast of the Baptist's countenance, but reserved, repressed. Strange, Raphael has given him a staff of transparent crystal. Keep then to that picture as the embodied formula of Raphael's genius. Amid all he has here already achieved, full, we may think, of the quiet assurance of what is to come, his attitude is still that of the scholar; he seems still to be saying, before all things, from first to last, "I am utterly purposed that I will not offend."⁹

It is in a lecturer's manner: Pater delivered it in Oxford in August 1892. So the corrections and insistences are for the benefit of listeners. The repetitions, too, as the meaning of "faultless" on first hearing is negligible till it is pointed by being associated with Virgil. The nouns and verbs are expressive, but what they mainly express is the artist's subjective vision, exercised even at the risk of substituting himself for the persons and objects he is painting. Raphael's good taste is embodied in his knowing the risk his genius incurs, that of imposing his own mystery upon his subjects. Pater suggests this by giving impersonal words personal companions, as color "tells" and the cast of the Baptist's face is a "pledge."

This is the mark of Pater's style which Joyce emphasizes in the "Oxen of the Sun" chapter of *Ulysses*:

A scene disengages itself in the observer's memory, evoked, it would seem, by a word of so natural a homeliness as if those days were really present there (as some thought) with their immediate pleasures. A shaven space of lawn one soft May evening, the wellremembered grove of lilacs at Roundtown, purple and white, fragrant slender spectators of the game but with much real interest in the pellets as they run slowly forward over the sward or collide and stop, one by its fellow, with a brief alert shock. And yonder about that grey urn where the

water moves at times in thoughtful irrigation you saw another
as fragrant sisterhood, Floey, Atty, Tiny and their darker friend
with I know not what of arresting in her pose then, Our Lady
of the Cherries, a comely brace of them pendent from an ear,
bringing out the foreign warmth of the skin so daintily against
the cool ardent fruit.[10]

More nominatives, becoming vocatives because they are given nothing
to do but display their finery. No particular passage in Pater is tilted
at, unless Our Lady of the Cherries makes fun of "Our Lady's Church"
in *Gaston de Latour*. For the rest: Joyce's irony is gentle enough, the
pathetic fallacy not too heavily remarked. In truth, Pater doesn't indulge
himself in the fallacy more often than other Victorian writers. The
attribution of feelings to inanimate things—thoughtful irrigation, alert
shock, ardent fruit—is a standard device of the period. But Pater, unlike
Ruskin and Arnold, was unwilling to yield primacy to the object in
any experience, and purposed at every point to secure the artist's
privilege.

For the same reason, he tends to ascribe a chosen character to a
thing before saying what the thing is. By the time it arrives it has been
swaddled in its meaning and has no choice but to exemplify it. If as
Nietzsche said there are no facts, only interpretations, one could devise
a style in which the interpretation palpably comes first and the trace
of the fact brings up the dusty rear. In *Gaston de Latour* young Gaston's
guardians are not presented as looking at him but as interpreting him:
the narrator wonders what they would have divined if they had "read
below the white propriety of the youth." In the "Modernity" chapter
the narrator refers to "the amorous business of the birds," as if by
giving us the character of those intimacies in advance he might dis-
courage us from the indelicacy of visualizing them. In "The Bacchanals
of Euripides" we have "the dark-haired tresses of the wood," a phrase
that barely escapes redundancy since tresses are nothing but plaits or
braids of hair, and the compound adjective can only amount to dark:
we see the tresses before being told that they are figurative. In "A
Study of Dionysus" a rhetorical question—"And who that has rested
a hand on the glittering silex of a vineyard slope in August, where the
pale globes of sweetness are lying, does not feel this?"—is so leisurely
that we take our ease in deducing that he is talking about green grapes.
In "The Myth of Demeter and Persephone" Demeter at night hides
Metaneira's child "in the red strength of the fire," later "in the red heat

of the fire." Pater lets us have the thing, but on condition of receiving its purport a little in advance. Purport is what the mind gives the object; it must not be allowed simply to suffuse an object already given.

These techniques of delay issue from Pater's self-consciousness, but only in its mood of scruple. The air of labor is a sign of his determination to get the matter right, especially when the matter is the experience of a mind concentrated upon itself. It is well understood that modern languages are poor in registering experiences of the spirit. There are no words for spirit that aren't derived from words for matter; spirit itself merely means wind, and has to be treated euphemistically if a sublime meaning is intended. Pater's main device, where delay is proposed, is the second thought. The narrative voice keeps correcting itself, as if the mere words were at best approximate to the feelings they are called upon to serve. In *Gaston de Latour*, when Gaston and his friends are riding toward Ronsard's church, the narrative voice ascribes will to the road and then, speaking for Gaston, registers his second thought:

> He came riding with his companions towards evening along the road which had suddenly abandoned its day-long straightness for wanton curves and ascents; and there, as an owl on the wing cried softly, beyond the tops of the spreading poplars was the west front, silver-grey, and quiet, inexpressibly quiet, with its worn, late-gothic "flamings" from top to bottom, as full of reverie to Gaston's thinking as the enchanted castle in a story-book.[11]

A road that abandons straightness for wanton curves anticipates the next phase of Gaston's life. The visit to Ronsard marks Gaston's assent to new and dangerous feelings. Meanwhile the revision of "quiet" to "inexpressibly quiet" makes little semantic difference but enacts a residual scruple in every particular of Gaston's progress. On the same page, Ronsard's face is described as "all nerve, distressed nerve." In a later chapter about Gaston's mistress Colombe, we read that "for him, on the other hand, 'the pity of it,' the pity of the thing supplied all that had been wanting in its first consecration, and made the lost mistress really a wife."[12] The quoted words, Othello's to Iago, are held in the context of another sexual relation, and are revised, cooled by the unspecific "thing" until "consecration" establishes the feelings well enough to turn mistress into wife.

In some cases the second thought has mainly the effect of nagging a sentence into rectitude. In *Gaston de Latour* a paragraph deals with one of Giordano Bruno's lectures in Paris:

> The unity, the spiritual unity, of the world:—that must involve the alliance, the congruity, of all things with one another, of the teacher's personality with the doctrine he had to deliver, of the spirit of that doctrine with the fashion of his utterance, great reinforcements of sympathy. In his own case, certainly, when Bruno confronted his audience at Paris, himself, his theme, his language, were alike the fuel of one clear spiritual flame, which soon had hold of his audience also; alien, strangely alien, as that audience might seem from the speaker.[13]

The first sentence mimes an orator's emphasis, gives the theme—the unity of the world—and revises it at once: the spiritual unity. But it doesn't go straight to its main verb. The theme is detached by an unusual punctuation mark (:—) and picked up by a demonstrative construction, "that must involve. . . ." The revision of alliance to congruity has the acoustic value of following a word of three syllables with one of four; the semantic difference is otherwise slight. Three coordinate phrases document the congruity, and a final phrase—great reinforcements of sympathy—is a comment, narratively external to the whole. This triad is repeated in the second sentence, but with the sequence changed; an exact coordination would say his theme, himself, his language. The primacy of "himself" makes the "one clear spiritual flame," Pater's favorite metaphor of self, issue from the speaker and take hold of his audience. The tacked-on phrase, "alien, strangely alien," damages the sentence, because the adverb is weaker than the adjective it modifies. But the most insidious quality of Pater's style is its practice of invidious comparison: as in the essay on Leonardo, we hardly know that a judgment has been made till it has passed by. When we read a passage again we see that it has quietly enforced a system of values according to which ordinary minds are limited to the apprehension of ordinary things and are never given a chance to exceed themselves. Finer things, or ordinary things in some finer aspect, are reserved for the attention of superior minds. It's hard to quarrel with this practice, since it acts on the understanding that by definition only a few minds are remarkable. But one feels squeamish about making the distinction so boldly. Pater doesn't feel squeamish. "Finer" is his favorite word, when he separates swans from geese or one swan from a whiter one. As in the essay on Leonardo, where he describes Leonardo's type of womanly beauty:

> Daughters of Herodias, with their fantastic head-dresses knotted and folded so strangely to leave the dainty oval of the face disengaged, they are not of the Christian family, or of Raphael's. They are the clairvoyants, through whom, as through delicate instruments, one becomes aware of the subtler forces of nature, and the modes of their action, all that is magnetic in it, all those finer conditions wherein material things rise to that subtlety of operation which constitutes them spiritual, where only the finer nerve and the keener touch can follow. It is as if in certain significant examples we actually saw those forces at their work on human flesh. Nervous, electric, faint always with some inexplicable faintness, these people seem to be subject to exceptional conditions, to feel powers at work in the common air unfelt by others, to become, as it were, the receptacle of them, and pass them on to us in a chain of secret influences.[14]

"Subtler," "finer," "finer" again, and "keener." Pater's dealings with the comparative degree of the adjective call for comment, but not necessarily for Christopher Ricks's comment. Ricks has argued that Pater's comparative adjectives are deplorable; they issue from his dissatisfaction with states of being and his insistence on setting them in process of becoming other states to which, given a little time, he will feel the same aversion. Process alone is satisfying:

> Pater had a greed for fineness; but something other than greed is involved, as is clear from his not grinding on up to the word "finest." He uses "finest," as he uses every word cognate with "fine," but this one infrequently, perfunctorily. For, unlike the comparative, the superlative implies a climax, a completion, an outcome rather than an endless process and "a tension of nerve." . . . If what you desire is "ear and finger refining themselves infinitely, in the appetite for sweet sound," then you need, not "fine" or "finest" (each of which has its resting satisfaction), but "finer" and "refine."[15]

It is true that Pater is often found among dissatisfactions; the recognition that an object or a state is itself and nothing else does not gratify him.

It is also true that he shows no interest in the early state of a thing, before it developed to its present form. But it is possible to present this epistemological quirk more agreeably than Ricks does by noting Pater's favorite pattern of development. What he wanted for matter was that it should become form; for a form, that it should if possible be further developed or refined. He invariably had chemistry in view, as in his references to the "virtue" of a work of art, in the Preface to *Studies in the History of the Renaissance*. In the process of refinement, a chemist removes impurities from matter, bringing it to a higher form of itself; he is never interested in reversing the process. Pater thought of spirituality as the force with which the mind discovers higher possibilities in itself and embodies them. By definition, no degree of development was enough; a genius might discover something more. Pater was dismayed to think that an object or a state of being might have no need of a mind to sustain it, or that by reaching the superlative degree of its state it could have no further development. I share Ricks's irritation with "finer" and its insistence, but it would be harsh to rebuke Pater for tracing, by way of adjectives in the comparative degree, one of the fundamental patterns of desire—and not only of Pater's desire—to go from a state that is apparently the case to another that may yet be, or may become, a new and, yes, finer state. What is peculiar in Pater is that he apparently derived such satisfaction from the process that he wanted to prolong it indefinitely and to postpone forever his arrival at a destination. It is harsh to deny him the satisfaction of moving from one level of being toward a higher one, even though the claim for its being higher may be spiritually pretentious. In *The Poetics of Reverie*, Bachelard says that the imagination wants to have a future. Pater's imagination wanted the future of living among images, motifs, and desires finer than those at hand. He found satisfaction in the process of becoming: it was the other aspect of his restlessness. He regarded one level of being as higher than another to the extent that it answered to a "later" or more intense degree of sensibility: more freedom, less necessity; more spirit, less material imperative. So he often recognized three states: the common form of something, the better form of it which we deem to be beautiful, and a further refinement of this second form, available only to the artist. As in Leonardo's sketches:

> Some of these are full of a curious beauty, that remote beauty which may be apprehended only by those who have sought it carefully; who, starting with acknowledged types of beauty,

have refined as far upon these, as these refine upon the world of common forms.[16]

The ultimate refinement is to be seen in death, as in Leonardo's portrait of Beatrice d'Este—"full of the refinement of the dead." But there is a special thrill in approaching that end, short of reaching it.

The best defense of Pater's style is in Kenneth Burke's *Counter-Statement* (1931). Burke regards Pater as an adept of pure literature, a writer who devises his sentences from certain favored possibilities internal to the medium of prose rather than by considering the most cogent way of denoting an object or an event. He praises Pater's "superior adjustment of technique to aesthetic interests." Pater wanted to write in a certain style, so he looked about for themes that would make this possible. The themes didn't interest him for any other reason. His model in this practice was classical prose, the literature of Greece and Rome, which is rarely lifelike but has an interest in negotiating sentences with deftness meant to please:

> In *Marius the Epicurean* he has a scene of the somewhat godless court listening to an address by Fronto, an effulgent oratory in praise of the rigid Stoic doctrine; they sit about with their tablets ready to write down some especially happy phrasing, arranged comfortably among the images and flowers, and "ready to give themselves wholly to the intellectual treat prepared for them; applauding, blowing loud kisses through the air sometimes, at the speaker's triumphant exit from one of his long, skilfully modulated sentences." Pater's audience is expected to bring somewhat the same critical appreciation to bear, watching with keen pleasure as the artist extricates himself from the labyrinths of his material—a process which Pater loves so greatly that he often seems to make his labyrinths of his extrications.[17]

It follows that "ideology in Pater was used for its flavor of beauty, rather than of argument."

I agree with Burke, subject to one qualification. It is true that Pater was indifferent to ideas. He never thought of using ideas as Arnold used them, to win an argument and make people change their lives. Pater did not argue. He didn't believe that no truth can be known until it has been tried by the tooth of disputation. He was more inclined to believe that no truth can be known, except sufficiently for local purposes. The sadness in Pater's prose marks the occasions, numerous indeed, when he feels certain that he will never be seized by supreme belief, that he will merely move quietly from one uncertainty to another. Meanwhile he retained to himself the dignity of writing slow, intricate sentences, miming the process of passing from one unsatisfactory belief to another that might turn out to be just as doubtful. One pattern of experience held his attention, the plot by which a young man in a pilgrim's progress tries to discover how to live, what to do. One interest with such ramifying implication was enough. Besides, as Burke notes, Pater's "love of twilight, of emergence and evanescence, equipped him to symbolize transition."[18] Transition was his destined theme.

30

The Great Refusal

PATER RARELY SPEAKS for himself; normally he lets his feelings emerge from his attention to something else, a group of paintings, a story from Greece, Lamb's essays, Sir Thomas Browne's tone, Wordsworth's poems. Even then, we come upon his feelings only at the end; at the beginning, he seems merely to be looking at something, not very closely. The sequence is roughly this. First he chooses to pay attention to an object. The choice arises from his sense of kinship with it, a prejudice for the moment in its favor. He trusts the fortune that has brought the object and his mind into the same field of interest. Then he looks at it more carefully. But the care has a particular motive; he is looking at the object as a means to a certain end, the production of a new experience in himself. He values the experience for the intensity of the pleasure it provides. It is always a question of pleasure, and it is an achievement more than a gift. Pater asks these questions of any artist:

> What is the peculiar sensation, what is the peculiar quality of pleasure, which his work has the property of exciting in us, and which we cannot get elsewhere?[1]

When Pater looks at a painting, his aim is to enjoy the sensation the looking provides, the conviction of being alive in a further manifestation of his capacity. If he hadn't looked at that painting, he would have missed a particle of his genius for pleasure. Yeats said he did not know anyone of his generation who had a talent for conviction. Pater had a talent for the conviction of pleasure. Looking at a painting, he is not concerned with qualitative discrimination in the work or deciding that one pleasure is superior to another for reasons that may be produced. Pleasure is its own end, a new experience is its embodiment. But the production of a new experience does not depend on the self-evident existence of objects in the world. Pater is not a born novelist, but he can invent semblances of objects well enough and treat them as if they were already there. As in "The Child in the House": he imagines child and house and deals with them as if their semblances were palpable. The process differs from that of the realistic novel because Pater isn't exhilarated by the independent existence of a thing, even if that could be established. He is not interested in a thing apart from the mind that engages with it. He gives little or no credit to what is deemed to exist apart from him; credit is reserved for the production of new experiences, with or without the aid of prior existence. Finally, he is willing to see the object drift into his sense of it and be lost there. Even at the end, the object is required to serve the mind that looks at it.

Pater's way of looking at an object differs from the two forms of attention that Svetlana Alpers discusses in *The Art of Describing*, her study of Dutch art in the seventeenth century. Alpers maintains that the reason critics find it hard to say anything about Dutch paintings is that they bring to these works "the expectations of narrative action created by Italian art." Generally, paintings are expected to be Italian. Leon Battista Alberti's idea of a painting, according to Alpers, was of "a framed surface or pane situated at a certain distance from a viewer who looks through it at a second or substitute world."[2] Viewers try to understand such a painting by deducing a story from it: they assume that paint is applied to canvas because otherwise the story can't be told, a semblance of the second life or world can't be created in anyone's mind. The meaning of a painting is the second life that may be deduced from it. Dutch paintings proceed otherwise, they use what Alpers calls "the descriptive mode." Dutch artists in the seventeenth century were so entranced by the visible world newly made available to them through microscopes and maps that they were content to let the meaning of a thing consist in the look of it. A story was not required. No curiosity

incited the discovery of a second world behind domestic or rural appearances. Now, of these two forms of looking, Pater's wasn't quite
Dutch; his attention wasn't fulfilled, as Ruskin's was, or Hopkins's,
by the look of things or by sundry appearances. He was not given to
Dutch satisfactions. But his way of looking wasn't Italian either,
although most of the paintings he saw were Italian. He looked at them
not to deduce stories from them but to divine the artist's particular
genius behind surface and story. He didn't ask, What second life
does this picture imply? but rather, What is the particular character
of the artist such that he chose to create this semblance and tell this
story?

Pater construed genius as the quality of a particular form of energy
beyond local need that creates a new type of life for itself. He thinks
it wonderful to be alive to see such novelty, such profusion. A work
of art is an object added to the world, but not merely that; it is the
outward sign of a type of life that may be new, an original self-creation.
Leonardo, Botticelli, Michelangelo, and Giorgione are names of new
types of life. Many forces went into their making, but finally each
created himself through these semblances.

Sometimes the novelty is a matter of combining two attributes, as
in Pater's favorite conjunction, "strangeness and beauty." Sometimes
the genius is characterized by his dissent from both parts of an available
contrast: not quite this, not quite that. Of these types, the one that
Pater finds most congenial is Botticelli's. When he describes the type
named Botticelli, he describes—without the vanity of making a
comparison—himself. The difference is one of scale. According to this
motif, the world offers an artist two contrasting possibilities, ways of
working. An artist may choose one and work it without misgiving.
Another artist makes the second choice, and again without misgiving.
Pater recognizes these decisions, but he cherishes the misgiving more
than the choice. He would prefer to live without categories or definitions, or aside from them. When he refers to a category, a definite form
or bias, it is to say: no, that is not it at all; that is not what I meant at
all. In the essay on Botticelli, he distinguishes, as we have seen, between
the dramatic artist and the visionary artist. But the distinction is not
meant to be a sharp one, the blur surrounding it is much of its merit.
Pater takes Botticelli as an example of the visionary artist, one who
usurps the data before his eyes and makes them express chiefly his
mood and desire. A comparison with Dante is glanced at, but only to

qualify it and introduce an equivocation in Botticelli's behalf. Pater writes of him:

> But he is far enough from accepting the conventional orthodoxy of Dante which, referring all human action to the simple formula of purgatory, heaven and hell, leaves an insoluble element of prose in the depths of Dante's poetry. One picture of his, with the portrait of the donor, Matteo Palmieri, below, had the credit or discredit of attracting some shadow of ecclesiastical censure. This Matteo Palmieri, (two dim figures move under that name in contemporary history,) was the reputed author of a poem, still unedited, *La Città di Vita*, which represented the human race as an incarnation of those angels who, in the revolt of Lucifer, were neither for Jehovah nor for His enemies, a fantasy of that earlier Alexandrian philosophy about which the Florentine intellect in that century was so curious.[3]

Pater thinks prose a better medium than verse for representing mobility, ambiguity, modernity. But by prose in a poem he means some element in the imagined feeling that has not been sufficiently purified or charged to become poetry: it lies flat on the page, as on many of Wordsworth's pages. Or it remains opaque, resistant to the transfiguring act of the mind; it refuses to become aesthetic. By "an insoluble element of prose in the depths of Dante's poetry" Pater apparently means Dante's insistence on disposing every human action in one of his categories: hell, purgatory, heaven. Categories were never congenial to Pater, especially if they denoted an artist's ambition to take possession of the whole ground of reference; he valued more the shadowy spaces between them. So it is a tribute to Botticelli to say that he didn't accept Dante's categories. But the phrase we need for Botticelli's type is "those angels who, in the revolt of Jupiter, were neither for Jehovah nor for His enemies." In the original essay, published in August 1870, and in the first edition of the book in 1873, "Jehovah" appeared as "God." Pater made the change for the 1877 edition, taking this care not to offend Christian readers who profess belief in God and rarely invoke the Jewish or Masoretic name, Jehovah. He softened the blow of reminding them that the position of the neutral angels was one they should think about.

The reference to Matteo Palmieri's poem is apt. Pater never read

it. He got the title wrong, calling it *La Città Divina*, an error he transcribed from volume 39 of the *Nouvelle biographie générale* (Paris, 1863).
(The editor Donald L. Hill provided the correct title for the above
quotation.) In the poem, the angels who chose to remain neutral were
given through God's mercy a second chance, "*seconda prova*," as human
beings. They were made incarnate and allowed to return in human
form to their original place in the celestial hierarchy.[4] Pater associates
these angels with Botticelli and refers to "the peculiar sentiment with
which he infuses his profane and sacred persons, comely, and in a
certain sense like angels, but with a sense of displacement or loss about
them—the wistfulness of exiles, conscious of a passion and energy
greater than any known issue of them explains, which runs through
all his varied work with a sentiment of ineffable melancholy."[5] The
sentence is not as clear as it might be. The syntax refers to persons,
sacred or profane, but the adjectival phrases just as plausibly qualify
the angels. If the main reference is to persons, the sentence says that
they feel exiled from heaven, their first home: the sentiment is well
known through Vaughan's "The Retreat" and Wordsworth's "Ode:
Intimations of Immortality." These people are like the neutral angels
who were given human form and presumably would have preferred to
persist in their angelic state. They didn't want to have to make a choice
the first time, so the second chance is yet another exacerbation. These
beings are conscious of passion and energy in others greater than their
own; greater, too, "than any known issue of them explains," abundance
beyond need. They know passion they can't feel, and are melancholy
for that good reason. If the adjectival phrases refer to the neutral angels,
they mean that the angels exiled from heaven are conscious of a passion
and energy in their angelic colleagues that they can't feel. They see it
in those angels who made a choice for Jehovah or Lucifer. The neutral
angels feel exiled, too, from their former attributes. Scholastic theology
says that angels differ from men and women in having the power of
unmediated knowledge. If they once had that and lost it in taking human
form, they would feel dispossessed. William Empson's poem "This
Last Pain" makes grim play by ascribing these feelings to the fallen
angels:

> *This last pain for the damned the Fathers found,*
> *They knew the bliss with which they were not crowned.*[6]

The neutral ones who became human and were given a second chance could feel this, too. They would have preferred the bliss of not knowing.

Pater implies that most people agree with the neutral angels, even though they have moments in which they would love or kill from high passion and boundless energy if only they could:

> So just what Dante scorns as unworthy alike of heaven and hell, Botticelli accepts, that middle world in which men take no side in great conflicts, and decide no great causes, and make great refusals. He thus sets for himself the limits within which art, undisturbed by any moral ambition, does its most sincere and surest work. His interest is neither in the untempered goodness of Angelico's saints, nor the untempered evil of Orcagna's *Inferno*; but with men and women, in their mixed and uncertain condition, always attractive, clothed sometimes by passion with a character of loveliness and energy, but saddened perpetually by the shadow upon them of the great things from which they shrink.[7]

It was daring of Pater to claim that Botticelli's Madonna is like the neutral angels: "she too, though she holds in her hands the 'Desire of all nations,' is one of those who are neither for Jehovah nor for His enemies; and her choice is on her face."[8] It was ingenious of him, too, to identify the artistic capacity with the great refusal, since what is refused is the moral choice at every point: "art, undisturbed by any moral ambition." Presumably a moral ambition takes responsibility for moral judgments, acts upon a discrimination of right and wrong, good and evil. Pater is saying that an artist recognizes his responsibility, but that it is not a moral one. Botticelli established for himself the quiet privilege of the middle world, but Pater implies that this privilege may be resorted to by anyone at any time. Any artist may practice the rhetoric of "neither this nor that."

An artist's ambition is expressive, imaginative, creative; his aim is to take pleasure to himself and incidentally give occasions of pleasure to other people. But he is not quite the "subjective thinker," as Kierkegaard describes such a person, "essentially interested in his own thinking, existing as he does in his thought." It is true that in the essay on Winckelmann, Pater makes the subjective or visionary disposition "the basis of all artistic genius." But in the essay on Botticelli he doesn't show the artist reveling in his freedom from moral ambition. The "ineffable melancholy" of Botticelli's profane and sacred persons, "the shadow upon them of the great things from which they shrink," his Madonna's "trouble," her sense of "the intolerable honour": these sentiments correspond to a scruple in the artist which is hard to distinguish from moral ambition, until we think of it as the accepted cost of having put that aside. Artists are aware of the values they can't, as artists, practice. Botticelli is undisturbed by moral ambition, but he is disturbed by the verve with which he has relegated it. The trouble in his sacred and profane figures is his own, a scruple consistent with his being on principle an aesthete. So, too, Pater.

The passage in Dante to which Pater refers is in the third canto of *Inferno*. The scene is the vestibule of hell. Dante sees people in agony, wailing, crying, wringing their hands, and he asks Virgil who they are. Virgil tells him that they are the people who lived without infamy and without praise. They are mingled, too, with "that base band of angels who were neither rebellious nor faithful to God, but stood apart." Heaven drives them out, "so as not to be less beautiful." Hell rejects them "lest the wicked have some glory over them."

> Ed elli a me: "Questo misero modo
> tegnon l'anime triste di coloro
> che visser sanza 'nfamia e sanza lodo.
> Mischiate sono a quel cattivo coro
> de li angeli che non furon ribelli
> ne fur fedeli a Dio, ma per se fuoro.
> Caccianli i ciel per non esser men belli,
> ne lo profondo inferno li riceve,
> ch'alcuna gloria i rei avrebber d'elli.[10]

That is to say: the devils and wicked souls can't be allowed to take pride in their being greater evildoers than these lukewarm or Laodicean angels.

Within a few lines, we read of Dante recognizing "the shade of him who from cowardice made the great refusal":

> vidi e conobbi l'ombra di colui
> che fece per viltade il gran rifiuto

One of those who are displeasing to God and to His enemies. These wretches, Dante says, were never really alive: *"Questi sciaurati, che mai non fur vivi."*[11] The one who made the great refusal is usually taken to be Pope Celestine V, who was elected Pope at the age of nearly eighty, in July 1294, and gave up the post five months and nine days later.

Dante's phrasing implies that there are three possible moral positions, *ribelli*, *fedeli*, and *per se*:

> *Mischiate sono a quel cattivo coro*
> *de li angeli che non furon ribelli*
> *ne fur fedeli a Dio, ma per se fuoro.*

The *ribelli* and the *fedeli* are fully in Dante's moral universe, because they have chosen and acted. The *per se* have not, and therefore Dante drives them out of his consideration with contempt. John Freccero has commented on the state of those *per se*:

They simply did not act, but remained frozen in a state of aversion from God. It is pointless to ask whether they were better or worse than the lowest of sinners, for they do not fit into any category, after the initial division of heavenly light from infernal dark. With the aversion from God, the bond of charity was smashed; with the abstention from action, they deprived themselves of the one positive element that could win them a place in the cosmos. They are as close to nothing as creatures can be and still exist, for by their double negation, they have all but totally removed themselves from the picture. To be deprived of action is to be deprived of love, and love is the law of Dante's cosmos, determining all classifications. There remains nothing for them but the vaguely defined vestibule of hell, and they merit no more than a glance from the pilgrim before he passes on to the realm of love perverted.[12]

So they have, in effect, chosen Lucifer by virtue of their not having chosen God; they turned away from God's love. They have merely not declared their choice. But Dante did not give them the honor of having chosen Satan. Botticelli sympathized with them enough to retain and respect their difference. So did Pater.

The same passage from the *Inferno* was in Eliot's mind when he wrote his essay on Baudelaire. His motive was to present Baudelaire as a great sinner and for that reason as a man who knew that what really matters is not some political program but sin and redemption. For such a man, "the recognition of the reality of Sin is a New Life; and the possibility of damnation is so immense a relief in a world of electoral reform, plebiscites, sex reform and dress reform, that damnation itself is an immediate form of salvation—of salvation from the ennui of modern life, because it at last gives some significance to living."[13] So far as we are human, Eliot says in this Dantean tradition of moral doctrine, "what we do must be either evil or good; so far as we do evil or good, we are human; and it is better, in a paradoxical way, to do evil than to do nothing; at least, we exist."[14]

Eliot had the same passage of the *Inferno* in view again when he was writing the third section of "Little Gidding":

> *There are three conditions which often look alike*
> *Yet differ completely, flourish in the same hedgerow.* . . .[15]

He calls the three "attachment to self and to things and to persons," "detachment from self and from things and from persons," and indifference, "which resembles the others as death resembles life." It is according to Dante that Eliot presents indifference as removed from the structure of life: it falls outside the scheme of moral values. Attachment and detachment alike are subject to the liberating power of memory: under the sway of memory they are raised beyond desire; they cannot hurt or disfigure one's soul any longer. Indifference is the state of the neutral angels. Eliot, too, is thinking in categories and despising those people—Pater among them—who hold themselves apart or aloof from them. I have never been persuaded by Eliot's argument; his certitude is cruel.

Pater interpreted the passage in the *Inferno* differently and turned it to another purpose. He did not share Eliot's conviction that the work of politics must be displaced in favor of the work of religion. He had no interest in politics: "his blind side," as Saintsbury said of him. But he wanted to make space not for religion but for art and aesthetic criticism, both "undisturbed by any moral ambition." The forms of personal and civil life he speaks up for are those in which art and aesthetic criticism have a chance of thriving. They cannot thrive in competition with the zeal of moral or political ambition. Pater's aim is not, like Eliot's, the renewal of Christianity on a vocabulary of damnation, sin and redemption, but the justification of "that middle world in which men take no side in great conflicts, and decide no great causes, and make great refusals." These are difficult issues, as we know from arguments about countries that remain neutral during an apparently just war, or about the validity of conscientious objection. It is easy to present the inhabitants of "that middle world" as pusillanimous, like the neutral angels, and to drive them out of public recognition. In his quiet way, Pater set himself against that masculine rectitude. It is worth noting that in the passage I've just quoted, Pater insists on qualifying with the word "great" each of the otherwise disparate nouns, "conflicts," "causes," and "refusals." He is claiming for the refusals just as much respect as everyone gives to conflicts and causes.

Pater's reference to Matteo Palmieri does most of the work for him in this part of the essay. Freccero has noted that Palmieri, far from accepting Dante's contemptuous view of the neutral or lukewarm angels, "made these angels his heroes, and looked upon their neutrality as the essence of the human condition."[16] Pater made a good guess about Palmieri's poem, took the poet's position as endorsing the middle world, and covered that world with Botticelli's chief quality, sympathy. Botticelli then becomes, although Pater doesn't quite say this, a type of artistry that can be embodied at any time, as for instance in the later years of the nineteenth century, it was no disgrace to stand aside from the public realm. Or in the twentieth. As Yeats said in declining to write a war poem, "We have no gift to set a statesman right." Or to set an economist right, or a priest. "In our time the destiny of man presents its meaning in political terms," Thomas Mann said; whereupon Yeats transcribed Mann's sentence and subtended from it a poem, "Politics," in which he demonstrates that any vocabulary can aspire to be recognized as the crucial value in life and to claim privilege for that reason. When Mann shouts politics, Yeats shouts sex. In the middle world one may choose to live by nearly any values, so long as one doesn't overtly challenge the dominant forces in law and government. Or one can divide one's life into two parts, public and private, and live differently in each.

It is not necessarily a matter of shouting sex when an opponent shouts politics. Pater defined in his essay on Botticelli and exemplified in himself a type of life that became a paradigm for modern literature. As an Englishman and a loyal citizen, he was a member of the comfortable middle class, the *bourgeoisie*, except that the word "bourgeois" doesn't recognize that Pater was also a member of the intelligentsia, a cultural formation developed in England upon images carried from

France and Russia. As an artist, Pater was marginal to the *bourgeoisie* in which he was nonetheless content to take his social place. Walter Benjamin notes, in his book on Baudelaire, that "the theory of *l'art pour l'art* assumes decisive importance around 1852, at a time when the bourgeoisie sought to take its 'cause' from the hands of the writers and poets."[17] In France, and later in England, the *bourgeoisie* made separate peace with the state in terms that gave serious artists no particular recognition. Pater's affection for the late phase of a culture and his feeling for comely decadence marked his estrangement from a society with which in public he never quarreled. He lived by standing aside, making many little refusals on the authority of the great refusal he rescued from Dante's contempt. Within the limits of decorum he consorted with adepts of difference, bohemians, homosexuals, decadents, and while he rarely transgressed, he sympathized with those who did.

What did this form of life entail? Not necessarily bad faith. Baudelaire was the first artist to discover how to live among the socially enforced images of a city and preserve a mind of one's own. He did not despise those images, even though he didn't endorse them; he took an unofficial view of them. Benjamin has described the resourcefulness of the class to which Baudelaire belonged and their way with images:

> The very fact that their share could at best be enjoyment, but never power, made the period that history gave them a space for passing time. Anyone who sets out to while away time seeks enjoyment. It was self-evident, however, that the more this class wanted to have its enjoyment in this society, the more limited this enjoyment would be. . . . If it wanted to achieve virtuosity in this kind of enjoyment, it could not spurn empathizing with commodities. It had to enjoy this identification, with all the pleasure and uneasiness which derived from a presentiment of its destiny as a class. Finally, it had to approach this destiny with a sensitivity that perceives charm even in damaged and decaying goods. Baudelaire, who in a poem to a courtesan called her heart "bruised like a peach, ripe like her body, for the lore of love," possessed this sensitivity. To it he owed his enjoyment of this society as one who had already half withdrawn from it.[18]

Baudelaire managed to find charm in objects and images, however degraded. He invented the experience of being fascinated by appearances among which he did not feel obliged to choose. He was not impelled to give reasons. He practiced, instead, what Thomas Crow has called "the disjunction of sensation from judgment."[19] Among English writers, it was Pater who more than any of his peers made this disjunction available and thereby intuited one of the forms of modern literature, the one we find in the early work of Yeats, Joyce, and Eliot. It is axiomatic in that literature to regard a sensation as privileged, at least to begin with, and to postpone its moral anatomy. Readers hostile to this privilege are regularly heard denouncing Stephen Dedalus's vanity, J. Alfred Prufrock's ineffectuality, Yeats's yearning for Innisfreedom, Pound's medievalism.

To practice the disjunction of sensation from judgment, it was necessary to present the work of art as gratuitously produced, a gift, a flourish of energy beyond need. In the end it would become a commodity, but that evil day could be postponed. Meanwhile the production of a work of art could be valued as play, a satisfaction mostly intrinsic, its images blessedly useless to the state. The aesthetic life had to be conducted as if it were maintained in endless leisure, as it was in Pater's Long Vacations. Leisure was time spent in the perusal of images. Pater sought them mainly in England, France, and Italy, and valued them chiefly for their appearing not to minister to any public interest: medieval churches, old paintings, houses in comely decay.

Pater was rarely authoritative about these matters, he preferred to convey his sense of them by a phrase here, an adjective there. He did not develop a theory of the relation between art, leisure, play, and release from moral or ideological ambition. All he needed was to make a space for his interest within the larger space of his social and public life. He practiced by temperament what writers of his fellowship, a few years later, practiced on principle; usually they called the principle Symbolism. Symons's *The Symbolist Movement in Literature* explained an aesthetic mode that Pater chose to divulge only in occasional hints and guesses. Symbolism, according to Symons, blurs the distinction between reality and dream, and seeks to present the essences of things rather than things. Mallarmé's "Crise de vers" presented that aim, a theory of language as incantation, words as objects to be disposed on a page like jewels on velvet, not as vehicles for the elocutionist. In "The Symbolism of Poetry" Yeats made Pater explicit:

> If people were to accept the theory that poetry moves us because of its symbolism, what change should one look for in the man-

ner of our poetry? A return to the way of our fathers, a casting
out of descriptions of nature for the sake of nature, of the moral
law for the sake of the moral law, a casting out of all anecdotes
and of that brooding over scientific opinion that so often extinguished the eternal flame in Tennyson, and of that vehemence
that would make us do or not do certain things; or, in other
words, we should come to understand that the beryl stone was
enchanted by our fathers that it might unfold the pictures in its
heart, and not to mirror our own excited faces, or the boughs
waving outside the window. With this change of substance, this
return to imagination, this understanding that the laws of art,
which are the hidden laws of the world, can alone bind the imagination, would come a change of style, and we would cast out
of serious poetry those energetic rhythms, as of a man running,
which are the invention of the will with its eyes always on something to be done or undone; and we would seek out those wavering, meditative, organic rhythms, which are the embodiment
of the imagination, that neither desires nor hates, because it
has done with time, and only wishes to gaze upon some reality,
some beauty.[20]

Not that Yeats remained content with that rhetoric for long: when he
read Nietzsche, he consigned Pater and Mallarmé to his apprenticeship
and moved into a new vocabulary featuring conflict, theater, antinomies
of self and soul. But he was always ready to express a Paterian mood
or disposition; as in "In Memory of Major Robert Gregory":

> We dreamed that a great painter had been born
> To cold Clare rock and Galway rock and thorn,
> To that stern colour and that delicate line
> That are our secret discipline
> Wherein the gazing heart doubles her might.[21]

The gazing heart doubles her might when the mind looks at an object
without capitulating to it: it returns to itself, invigorated, having set
aside the temptation of losing itself in the object. As in Blake's concept
of vision, the mind sets the conditions upon which the act of seeing is
performed. The opposite state is naturalism, in which minds are help-
less before their contents at any moment, a state Yeats thought he saw

in Pound's *Cantos* and Joyce's "Anna Livia Plurabelle." In Yeats's poem color and line are formal properties issuing from an aesthetic sense of the object. The painter Robert Gregory looks at cold Clare rock and Galway rock and thorn as forms, not as geological or botanical specimens. They yield to his formal or aesthetic sense.

In the essay on Botticelli, Pater has his own version of the gazing heart, the mind that turns aside from the official syntax of things and chooses its own principle of order according to an aesthetic preference. The choice is like the work of dream according to Freud in *The Interpretation of Dreams*. Dream work "does not think, calculate or judge in any way at all; it restricts itself to giving things a new form."[22] In Botticelli and other visionary artists the "new form" answers to a demand in the subject, not in the object ostensibly depicted. The subject wants to express itself while appearing to depict something else. The imagination, as Bachelard said, wants to have a future. The Paterian imagination wishes to have such a future under the authority of its own motifs and rhythms.

But this authority is not absolute. Just as Botticelli's figures are saddened by the shadow upon them of the great privilege from which they shrink, so the Paterian imagination respects the world it turns aside from. Instead of duties, it seeks relations, especially with some mode of expression that is a superior form of itself. Donald Davie has suggested that there are three analogies for modern poetry: drama, as in Yeats; sculpture, as in Pound; and music, as in Eliot. These forms are paradigms to which the individual poet aspires. In *Studies in the History of the Renaissance* Pater says that each form of art wishes to transcend itself by attaining the typical virtue of another art, and that in the end all the arts constantly aspire toward the condition of music. The main difference between Pater and his contemporaries and successors in this respect was that their favorite paradigms were theater and dance. Wilde aspired not only to write plays but to be himself theater. The poets of Yeats's tragic generation found their ideal form in ballet and agreed to be entertained by its quotidian version, the music hall. Pater and Mallarmé sought their paradigm in the idea of music rather than in music itself, unity of form and matter achieved in the end, the emphasis falling now upon one of these, now upon the other. And in the meantime, to make the subjective emphasis clear, the aim of expression is to effect transition from one mobile state of feeling to the next, according to laws of genre and sequence not to be thought of as too firmly established. Pater, Mallarmé, Debussy: these names make the affiliation clear enough.

Of the writers who worked in this respect under Pater's auspices, Joyce is exemplary. It is true that in *Exiles* and parts of *Ulysses* he tried to write himself out of Pater's Aestheticism, but he remained susceptible to it. It is the subject of Stephen Dedalus's brooding in the third chapter of *Ulysses*, which begins with Aristotelian realism:

> Ineluctable modality of the visible: at least that if no more, thought through my eyes.[23]

But as the chapter proceeds, Stephen's mind usurps the data before it and determines the conditions of its seeing. He is idling on Sandymount Strand and at one point making an inventory of the scene:

> Broken hoops on the shore; at the land a maze of dark cunning nets; farther away chalkscrawled backdoors and on the higher beach a dryingline with two crucified shirts.[24]

The nets are cunning not only because they are designed to catch fish but because Stephen thinks of Ireland and its institutions, church and state, as nets set to catch him. In *A Portrait of the Artist as a Young Man*, Stephen says to Davin in the fifth chapter:

> When the soul of a man is born in this country there are nets flung at it to hold it back from flight. You talk to me of nationality, language, religion. I shall try to fly by those nets.[25]

His devices: silence, exile, and cunning. As for the crucified shirts, there are two of them, as if the apostate Stephen accompanied Christ to the end.

Even when the disclosure of Stephen's mind is not the main issue, Joyce's language is visionary according to Pater's sense of that capacity in the essay on Botticelli. The last sentence of the second chapter of *Ulysses* is a case in point. Stephen has been receiving his wages from Mr. Deasy, two pound notes, a sovereign, two crowns, and two shillings. Their conversation has alluded to money, domestic economy, borrowing, the nature of history, God, and a letter to *The Evening Telegraph* about foot-and-mouth disease. At the end, their business over, Mr. Deasy runs after Stephen to give him a parting sally about Ireland and the Jews. Then we read,

> On his wise shoulders through the checkerwork of leaves the sun flung spangles, dancing coins.[26]

These words are not spoken by anyone; there is no reason to think that the perception they express is Stephen's. That Mr. Deasy's shoulders are wise is nobody's notion in particular. Grammatically, the sentence speaks in the neuter. We are free to reduce it to its references: Mr. Deasy, the sun shining through the leaves. But what we have on the page is a putative situation as if it were seen by a language that has had other things on its communal mind and recalls them now. An event is reported, but the syntax that delivers it has other things, too, on its mind, embodied now in the internal rhyme of spangles and dancing, the assonance of flung and spangles, and an allusion to the coins transferred, ten pages back, from Mr. Deasy's savingsbox to Stephen's pocket.

Joyce's sentence draws to itself the object, the event, it apparently serves. Even if we assume, reading the sentence in the Italian manner, that there is an Ur-event that preceded these words in this order, we have only the words to divine it, and they have other commitments in mind. Joyce is writing sentences as Shakespeare wrote sonnets, working up the internal resources of a genre, a style, a form. The word "aesthetic" denotes an act by which a mind sees certain possibilities of form and rhythm in particular objects and events real or imaginary, and pursues these "to the end of the line." If we retain the vocabulary of subject and object, no other being available, it follows that there is a notional moment at which an object, attended to in this way, seems to lose its autonomy in favor of the mind that sees it. From that moment, aesthetic considerations are dominant. What do these entail? Crow has argued that a modern painting must fulfill two requirements: one, "it must be constructed only from an accumulation of single touches and cannot appear to subordinate immediate sensation to another system of cognition," and, two, "it must at the same time effectively close off the internal system of the picture and invest each touch with consistent descriptive sense in relation to every other touch."[27] So in Joyce's sentence: there is no appeal to "another system of cognition" beyond the one in place: "On his wise shoulders through the checkerwork of leaves the sun flung spangles, dancing coins." An adverbial phrase, followed by another one, each awaiting its subject and verb: subject, verb, and object in quick succession—the sun flung spangles—and the object is enhanced by verbal noun and noun doing the work of adjectives. There are no coins, only appearances of them, glinting through the leaves. No one is dancing, but spangles often adorn dancing girls and make them seem to shine. The sentence closes off any other considerations.

The disjunction of sensation from judgment has many consequences in the literature I'm referring to. According to the rhetoric of sensation and pleasure, we interpret desire not as sign or site of a lack but as a positive though equivocal and shadowed pleasure: it fulfills itself not in the achievement of a desired object but in the perpetual renewal of its own energy. Only the endlessness of desire satisfies it, while moment by moment desire incites it. And thwarts it. The most acute thwarting is effected by the human body, since the central nervous system pays no heed to desire's cry for intensities. Intensity is desire's business, but not the body's, except in the high moments it chooses for its own reasons. Proust says somewhere that it is a great weakness for a person to consist entirely of moments. No doubt; but Pater took the risk of it, and turned the weakness into a great refusal. Consciousness was the form of his desire, his chosen way of being alive. In that practice he wanted to live forever. So his desire is exactly opposite to the desire for oblivion which is expressed, intermittently anyway, by writers otherwise as different as Hardy and Beckett. In *Beckett's Dying Words*, Christopher Ricks has studied the provenance, in Beckett, Hardy, A. E. Housman, Larkin, and other writers, of Sophocles's conviction —if it is a conviction rather than a mood—that not to have been born is best. In *More Pricks than Kicks*, Beckett has Belacqua awaiting his operation and the doctors' award of "a new lease of apathy."[28] Pater stands apart from this quietus just as firmly, just as quietly, as from the positivist verities upon which the wheels of Empire ran.

The consciousness he practiced was not, then, a moral instrument. Still less was it the means by which a stable self lived life steadily by seeing it whole. Pater practiced what Michel Foucault came to the point of preaching in his last books, the three volumes of his *History of Sexuality*: an aesthetic sense of life, according to which—in Foucault's terms—we create ourselves as a work of art. Why, Foucault asks, should the lamp or the house be an art object, but not our life? The motto for this project is Nietzsche's: "we want to be the poets of our lives."[29] The method is improvisation. Neither in Pater nor in Foucault is it necessary to posit a stable self defending its coherence from every attack: it is enough that there is, sentence by sentence, a textual self in the act of becoming, of making itself, improvising itself from one intense moment to the next.

The syntax that corresponds to this process of self-making is Pater's "neither this . . . nor that." Or if we want to reason about it with a later reason we can quote one of Stevens's thirteen ways of looking at a blackbird:

> *I do not know which to prefer,*
> *The beauty of inflections*
> *Or the beauty of innuendoes,*
> *The blackbird whistling*
> *Or just after.*[30]

The preference is one on which little depends; it is best thought of as a further pleasure. I take it that inflections are distinctive ways of being present to an occasion, and the beauty is that of hearing the blackbird whistling just so, willfully, not as it might whistle otherwise. As in the distinctiveness of a certain voice, an accent, a tone or timbre—say, Brendel's phrasing in a particular performance of a Beethoven sonata. Innuendos come later, added on to the official meaning or subtracted from it, in any case an after-life, as in an image just going, going, gone. Thinking of Pater in this vocabulary: he lived by inflecting the official life offered him, and took pleasure in the sensuous occasions he chose; later he wrote innuendos. The life that counted for him was a count of impulses, impulsions. Like Stevens, he didn't know which to prefer, one beauty or the other, but he knew that the preference was not imperative.

It follows that Pater practiced consciousness not as a mode of knowledge but as an alternative to knowledge. Victorian culture was predicated upon an instrumental view of knowledge: officially, knowledge was pursued not as its own end and for its own sake—Newman was heretical in that emphasis—but as the great means of understanding and commanding the world. The rhetoric of Enlightenment remained in place, and it was officially optimistic, even though a few people knew that waste of human resources was inevitable. Arnold wanted young people to be trained to recognize the best that had been thought and said in the world; the best wasn't necessarily the same as the most useful. But he never doubted that the likeliest way out of chaos consisted in understanding things. One of the ways in which Pater was anti-nomian was in his being ready to think that understanding wasn't everything. He valued the experience of not understanding, and of feeling that it wasn't always necessary to comprehend.

An example of continuing to live while not understanding was revivalism in Victorian architecture. Richard Jenkyns has shown, in his *Dignity and Decadence: Victorian Art and the Classical Influence*, that the choice of a style was often capricious. Victorian architects adopted the classical style or the Gothic style for no grander reason than personal taste. Both styles were available, with various forms of ornament and allusion. In church architecture, Anglican and Roman Catholic churches were normally Gothic, while Congregationalists, Baptists, and Nonconformists went Greek. Schools and colleges were mostly Gothic, because their founders and benefactors were eager to maintain the religious basis of education against the secular drift. But an architect could practice whatever style he pleased or his patron wanted. William Wilkins is a case much in point. He designed University College, London, in Greek but changed to Gothic for his work at King's College, Cambridge. For Downing College he reverted to Greek for reasons entirely aesthetic, reasons of taste, not reasons of state.

The point of this excursus is to say that while there may be a deep relation between feeling and form—as Henry Adams thought, in his *Mont-Saint-Michel and Chartres*—it is often impossible to discern. When forms lack a vital relation to the forces from which they ostensibly arise, they become unmoored, unhinged, arbitrary; they seem to embody mainly caprice or whim. Revivalism in Victorian Britain was the practice of not having to understand, of doing something else rather than understanding. Allusion was a device, as it generally is, for filling spaces that could not be comprehended. It was a scandal to find such spaces, but they provided opportunities, too. In *The Great Tradition*, Leavis says of Conrad, with the windy insistence of "Heart of Darkness" in mind, that he is intent on making a virtue out of not knowing what he means. Leavis intended a rebuke. But there is more to be said about this. So far as modern literature is in question, the predicament of not knowing what one means while still saying something was first felt in Victorian Britain. The realistic novel is the crucial genre of that age because novelists tried to devise in it a language for understanding the forces new and old they had to deal with. Reference was its principle of faith. But many nuances of expression were achieved by writers who stood aside from that enterprise and took pleasure in the disjunction of sensation and knowledge. Pater was such a writer. Aestheticism was one form, one sad form, of the discovery that most of life could not be understood, it could only be lived. But there were pleasures to be invented in that predicament.

What then can we call his form of thinking? Adumbration is the best word for it. In the absence of a sustainable relation between consciousness and action in the world, Pater and other writers similar in temper settled to the work of adumbration, of working their sentences "towards a better life." They sought words for sensations, the first acts of sentient existence. Finding those words, they established a literature on the frail ground of a moment's sensation, intensely realized. Eliot never acknowledged his debt to Pater in this respect but chose instead to proclaim his indebtedness to F. H. Bradley. Joyce and Yeats were more generous in paying their debts to Pater. But Eliot's distinction between feeling—his word for sensation—and the later, congealed deformations of feeling he called ideas is entirely Paterian. And he noted, at least once, that a supreme moral achievement could be gained in a moment:

> Great simplicity is only won by an intense moment or by years of intelligent effort, or by both. It represents one of the most arduous conquests of the human spirit: the triumph of feeling and thought over the natural sin of language.[31]

Pater gave modern literature its first act. The major writers achieved their second and third acts by dissenting from him and from their first selves. Joyce shifted his interest from Stephen Dedalus, a Byronic version of Pater, to Leopold Bloom, whom Pater could not have imagined. Eliot inscribed in "The Love Song of J. Alfred Prufrock" Paterian tones and a determination to talk himself into contempt for them. In his later poetry, "the awful daring of a moment's surrender" is Eliot's repudiation of Pater, because the moment is retrieved from sensation and turned toward religious commitment. Yeats circumvented Pater by simultaneously discovering the vernacular and Nietzsche: the vernacular, as if it were a foreign tongue, which to Yeats for several years it was; Nietzsche, whom he read in Thomas Common's translation and assimilated to the vernacular before he achieved a new sense of both by mulling over Greek tragedy. Stevens annotated Pater's "Style" without liking it, but he was susceptible to Pater's Aestheticism and recognized it again when he read in an essay by Charles Mauron that art transforms us into epicures. And so on—there is no need to be further explicit; Pater's after-life is the first act of so many literary careers.

Should I feel misgiving about this, about the fact that the modern literature I most love has come from Baudelaire, Pater, and Mallarmé rather than from Newman, Arnold, and Ruskin? Yes, or at least I do. I think I appreciate the risks—triviality, exquisiteness, solipsism— entailed by Aestheticism. On the other hand, I regard as disastrous Arnold's proposal, a consequence of his high church atheism, as Eliot called it, that poets, novelists, and critics should take up the services that priests were allegedly no longer able to sustain, or rather the emotional residue of those services. Equally disastrous has been the subjection of literature and art to the censorship of blatantly reductive attention in behalf of political, social, and moral rectitude. Eliot was right: if you read literature, it is as literature you must read it and not as another thing. Another thing: politics, religion, democracy, any ideology one cares to name. If we read literature only to find in it evidence of bad faith, right-wing politics, the atrocities of Empire, racial and sexual prejudice, or any other attitude we disapprove of, we should give it up and confine our attention to TV and letters to the editor. If we no longer respect the difference between a work of art and an editorial, the game is up. Literature and art add objects to the world and, in so doing, call for aesthetic attention. If we had any reason to fear that such attention would bring the busy world to a standstill, or would seriously thwart its metaled ways, we might have to think again about art and literature and worry about their rhetoric of pleasure, delay, leisure, and antinomian care. But there is no danger of that. The world proceeds by force of its chiefly mundane interests, political, social, economic, ideological; it is an exercise of power and of responding to the power of others. Meanwhile we have literature, and the best way of reading it is by putting in parentheses, for the duration of the reading, the claims the world makes upon us. There will be time for those to assert themselves. We should read literature in the spirit in which we enter a concert hall. This is difficult, because literature is verbal and shares with other forms of discourse a semantic capacity. It is hard to say what a poetic sense of literature entails. But the best hope of practicing it is by showing aesthetic values—form, style, tone, pleasure, exercised in achieved conditions of freedom—as fundamental to the literature we care about, carry around with us, and hear whenever silence allows us to hear. In his subdued way, Pater is where these ladders start.

Notes

Unless otherwise indicated, references to Pater's published works are to the Library Edition of *Works of Walter Pater*, published by Macmillan in 1910 and reprinted by Basil Blackwell in 1967. The titles are:

The Renaissance: Studies in Art and Poetry
Marius the Epicurean: His Sensations and Ideas (two volumes)
Imaginary Portraits
Appreciations
Plato and Platonism
Greek Studies
Miscellaneous Studies
Gaston de Latour
Essays from the "Guardian"

Other references are abbreviated as follows:

Studies: Studies in the History of the Renaissance (London: Macmillan, 1873).
The Renaissance: The Renaissance: Studies in Art and Poetry: The 1893 Text, edited by Donald L. Hill (Berkeley: University of California Press, 1980).
Letters: Letters of Walter Pater, edited by Lawrence Evans (Oxford: Clarendon Press, 1970).
UC: Uncollected Essays (Portland, Maine: Thomas B. Mosher, 1903).
Benson: A. C. Benson, *Walter Pater* (London: Macmillan, 1906).

Seiler: *Walter Pater: A Life Remembered*, edited by R. M. Seiler (Calgary: University of Calgary Press, 1987).
CH: Walter Pater: The Critical Heritage, edited by R. M. Seiler (London: Routledge and Kegan Paul, 1980).
Sketches: Sketches and Reviews, edited by Albert Mordell (New York: Boni and Liveright, 1919).

CHAPTER 1

1. F. R. Leavis, *For Continuity* (Cambridge: The Minority Press, 1933), p. 144.
2. F. R. Leavis, *The Common Pursuit* (reprint, New York: New York University Press, 1964), p. 48.
3. Q. D. Leavis, "The Last Epicurean," *Scrutiny* 4, no. 3 (December 1935), p. 328.
4. W. B. Yeats, *Autobiographies* (London: Macmillan, 1955), p. 477.
5. Lucien Febvre, *La Terre et l'évolution humaine* (Paris, 1922), p. 438.

CHAPTER 2

1. Rayburn S. Moore, ed., *Selected Letters of Henry James to Edmund Gosse 1882–1915: A Literary Friendship* (Baton Rouge: Louisiana State University Press, 1988), pp. 114–15. A slightly different text of the letter appears in Henry James, *Letters*, vol. 3, 1883–1895, ed. Leon Edel (Cambridge: Belknap Press of Harvard University Press, 1980), p. 483.
2. Moore, *Selected Letters*, p. 114.
3. James, *Letters*, p. 484.
4. Moore, *Selected Letters*, p. 115.
5. Quoted in Seiler, p. 62.
6. Thomas Hardy, *The Life and Work of Thomas Hardy*, ed. Michael Millgate (Athens: University of Georgia Press, 1985), p. 187.
7. Edward Thomas, *Walter Pater: A Critical Study* (London: Martin Secker, 1913), pp. 121–22.
8. Moore, *Selected Letters*, 120. Gosse's essay appeared in *Contemporary Review* 67 (December 1894), pp. 795–810.
9. *Studies*, p. 210.
10. Moore, *Selected Letters*, p. 152.
11. Henry James, *Notes on Novelists* (1914; reprint, New York: Biblo and Tannen, 1969), pp. 246–47.
12. Ibid., p. 246.
13. Ibid., pp. 246–47.

14. Seiler, p. 261.

15. Henry James, *The Art of the Novel*, ed. R. P. Blackmur (Boston: Northeastern University Press, 1984), p. 96.

16. Edmund Gosse, *Portraits from Life*, ed. Ann Thwaite (Aldershot, U.K.: Scolar Press, 1991), p. 72.

17. Adeline R. Tintner, "Pater in *The Portrait of a Lady* and *The Golden Bowl*, including some unpublished Henry James letters," *The Henry James Review* 3 (1982), pp. 80–95.

18. Henry James, *The Princess Casamassima* (reprint, New York: Harper, 1959), p. 334.

CHAPTER 3

epigraph: George Saintsbury, *Prefaces and Essays* (London: Macmillan, 1933), p. 346.

1. *The Renaissance*, p. 89.

2. Ibid., p. 190.

3. *Appreciations*, p. 122.

4. *Miscellaneous Studies*, p. 200.

5. Seiler, pp. 2–3.

6. Quoted in William Gaunt, *The Aesthetic Adventure* (New York: Harcourt, Brace and Company, 1945), p. 58.

7. Ibid., p. 58.

8. Cf. Gerald Monsman, "Pater, Hopkins, and Fichte's Ideal Student," *South Atlantic Quarterly* 70 (1971), p. 366.

9. Ibid., p. 369.

10. Bernard Berenson, *Sunset and Twilight: From the Diaries of 1947–1958*, ed. Nicky Mariano (New York: Harcourt, Brace and World, 1963), p. 23. Entry for June 25, 1947.

11. Ibid., p. 526. Entry for April 13, 1958.

12. W. B. Yeats, *Autobiographies* (New York: Macmillan, 1927), p. 374.

CHAPTER 4

1. Gerard Manley Hopkins, *The Journals and Papers*, ed. Humphry House and Graham Storey (Oxford: Oxford University Press, 1970), p. 133.

2. Ibid., p. 138.

3. Gerard Manley Hopkins, *The Poems of Gerard Manley Hopkins*, ed. W. H. Gardner and N. H. MacKenzie (Oxford: Oxford University Press, 1970), p. 21.

4. Edward Dorn, *The Collected Poems 1956–1974* (Bolinas, Calif.: Four Seasons Foundation, 1975), pp. 209–10.

5. *Brasenose College Quatercentenary Monographs*, no. 14, pt. 2, pp. 74–75.

6. *Letters*, p. 16.

7. Bodleian MSS, Pattison 131, fol. 29. A somewhat inaccurate transcription is given in H. E. Wortham, *Oscar Browning* (1927), p. 59, and *Letters*, p. xxxiv.

8. *Greek Studies*, p. 42.

9. *Letters*, pp. 100–101.

10. John Addington Symonds: "Twenty-three Sonnets from Michael Angelo," *Contemporary Review* 20 (September 1872), p. 506.

11. John Addington Symonds, *Letters*, ed. Herbert M. Schueller and Robert L. Peters (Detroit: Wayne State University Press, 1967), vol. 2, p. 273.

12. *CH*, p. 60.

13. Ibid., p. 59.

14. John Addington Symonds, *Studies in Sexual Inversion* (privately printed, 1931), pp. 18, 19.

15. Ibid., p. 187.

16. *The Renaissance*, pp. 201–2.

17. Ibid.

18. *CH*, p. 124.

19. Ibid.

20. A. C. Benson, Diary, entry for May 18, 1905. Quoted in Laurel Brake, "Judas and the Widow," in *Walter Pater: An Imaginative Sense of Fact*, ed. Philip Dodd (London: Frank Cass, 1981), p. 45.

CHAPTER 5

1. *The Renaissance*, pp. 39–40.

2. Ibid., p. 152; cf. p. 252.

3. Quoted in William Walrond Jackson, *Ingram Bywater* (Oxford: Clarendon Press, 1917), p. 79.

4. *The Renaissance*, p. 160; cf. p. 250.

5. "Poems by William Morris," *Westminster Review*, October 1868, p. 309.

6. Ibid., p. 302.

7. Ibid., pp. 309–10.

8. Ibid., p. 310.

9. Ibid., pp. 310–11.

10. Ibid., p. 311.

11. Ibid.

12. Ibid.

13. Ibid.

14. Ibid., pp. 311–12.
15. Ibid., p. 312.

CHAPTER 6

1. *CH*, pp. 61–62.
2. Ibid., pp. 71–73.
3. Ibid., pp. 75–76.
4. Ibid., p. 91.
5. Ibid., p. 92.
6. Quoted in *The Oxford Undergraduates Journal*, November 27, 1873, pp. 98–99. Cf. Billie Andrew Inman, *Walter Pater's Reading: A Bibliography of his Library Borrowings and Literary References, 1858–1873* (New York: Garland, 1981), p. 329.
7. For the information on this episode I am indebted to Billie Andrew Inman, "Estrangement and Connection: Walter Pater, Benjamin Jowett, and William M. Hardinge," in Laurel Brake and Ian Small, eds., *Pater in the 1990s* (Greensboro, N.C.: ELT Press, 1991). Richard Ellmann's accounts of the episode, "Oscar at Oxford," *The New York Review of Books*, March 29, 1984, and *Oscar Wilde*, rev. ed. (New York: Knopf, 1988), pp. 60–61, are partially inaccurate, as Professor Inman has shown.
8. "Alexander Michaelson," "Giles and Miles and Isabeau," *Blackfriars* 9, no. 94 (January 1928), p. 25.
9. *CH*, p. 96.
10. Seiler, p. 190.
11. Ibid., p. 191.
12. W. H. Mallock, *The New Republic* (New York: Scribner, Welford and Armstrong, 1878), pp. 15, 27–28, 35, 196–97.

CHAPTER 7

1. *The Renaissance*, p. 232.
2. Ibid., p. 186.
3. Ibid., p. 318.
4. *Studies*, p. 194.
5. *Letters*, pp. 21–22.
6. Cf. *The Renaissance*, p. 373.
7. Ibid., pp. 90–91.
8. Letter of March 16, 1907, from Ed Dugdale to Thomas Wright: in Wright's scrapbook, Brasenose College Library. Cf. Thomas Wright, *Thomas Wright of*

Olney: An Autobiography (London: Herbert Jenkins, 1936), pp. 121–22. I owe this reference to R. M. Seiler.

9. "Alexander Michaelson," "Walter Pater: In Memoriam," *Blackfriars* 9, no. 101 (August 1928), p. 468n.

10. Arthur Symons, *Figures of Several Centuries* (reprint, Freeport, N.Y.: Books for Libraries Press, 1969), pp. 322–23.

11. Arthur Symons, *Selected Letters 1880–1935*, ed. Karl Beckson and John M. Munro (Iowa City: University of Iowa Press, 1989), p. 23.

12. *CH*, pp. 178–79.

13. *Letters*, p. 75. Letter of August 9, 1887.

14. *Essays from the "Guardian,"* p. 43.

15. *Letters*, p. 80. Letter of January 8, 1888.

16. Symons, *Selected Letters*, p. 39. Letter of August 8, 1888.

17. *UC*, p. 85.

18. Symons, *Figures*, p. 329.

19. Ibid., p. 329.

20. Ibid., pp. 330–31.

21. *Letters*, p. xl.

22. Arthur Symons, *Dramatis Personae* (Indianapolis: Bobbs-Merrill, 1923), p. 107.

23. Symons, *Selected Letters*, p. 236. Letter of August 10, 1915.

24. *Letters*, p. 81. Letter of March 4, 1888.

25. George Moore, *Avowals* (New York: Boni and Liveright, 1926), p. 229.

26. Ibid., p. 224.

27. *UC*, p. 142.

28. Cf. Moore, *Avowals*, p. 223.

29. Cf. *The Collected Poems of Lionel Johnson*, 2nd and rev. ed., ed. Ian Fletcher (New York: Garland, 1982), p. xxxiii.

30. Ibid., p. xxxiv.

31. Cf. *Letters*, p. 108.

32. Cf. Ibid, p. xxiii.

33. *CH*, p. 209.

34. Ibid., p. 321.

35. Seiler, p. 216.

36. Ibid., p. 322.

37. Oscar Wilde, *Selected Letters*, ed. Rupert Hart-Davis (Oxford: Oxford University Press, 1979), p. 199. Letter of January–March 1897.

38. *CH*, p. 163.

39. Ibid., p. 165.

40. Oscar Wilde, *The Artist as Critic: Critical Writings of Oscar Wilde*, ed. Richard Ellmann (London: W. H. Allen, 1970), pp. 366–67.

41. H. Montomery Hyde, ed., *The Trials of Oscar Wilde* (London: William Hodge, 1948), p. 124. Quoted in Donald Lawler, *An Inquiry into Oscar Wilde's*

Revisions of "The Picture of Dorian Gray" (New York: Garland, 1988), p. 55.

42. Lawler, *An Inquiry*, pp. 55–56.

43. Seiler, p. 157.

44. *UC*, p. 126.

45. Ibid., pp. 128–29.

46. Vincent O'Sullivan, *Aspects of Wilde* (London: Constable, 1936), p. 12.

47. Quoted in Richard Ellmann, *Oscar Wilde*, rev. ed. (New York: Knopf, 1988), p. 52.

48. Wilde, *Selected Letters*, p. 199.

49. Ibid., p. 357.

50. *The Renaissance*, p. 177.

51. Oscar Wilde, *Complete Works of Oscar Wilde*, with an introduction by Vyvyan Holland (New York: Harper and Row, 1989), p. 709.

CHAPTER 8

1. Benson, p. 26.

2. Seiler, p. 29.

3. Ibid., p. 30.

4. *CH*, p. 136.

5. *Letters*, pp. 64–65. Letter of December 23, 1885.

6. *Essays from the "Guardian,"* pp. 24–25.

7. Ibid., pp. 33–34.

8. Mrs. Humphry Ward, *Robert Elsmere*, ed. Clyde de L. Ryals (Lincoln: University of Nebraska Press, 1967), p. 558.

9. *Essays from the "Guardian,"* p. 66.

10. Ibid., pp. 66–67.

11. Ibid., p. 67.

12. Ibid., pp. 67–68.

13. Houghton Library (Harvard University) MSS, Eng. 1150 (12).

14. *Greek Studies*, pp. 54–55.

15. *Letters*, p. 69.

16. Ibid.

17. Ibid., p. 142.

18. Cf. Ernest Dowson's letter of August 22, 1890, to Arthur Moore, in *The Letters of Ernest Dowson*, ed. Desmond Flower and Henry Maas (Rutherford, N.J.: Fairleigh Dickinson University Press, 1967), p. 159.

19. *Letters*, p. 116 n. 3.

20. *Marius the Epicurean*, vol. 2, p. 127.

21. Oliver Elton, *Frederick York Powell: A Life* (Oxford: Clarendon Press, 1906), vol. 1, p. 158.

CHAPTER 9

1. *Letters*, p. 150.
2. *Greek Studies*, p. 108.
3. Simon Nowell-Smith, comp., *The Legend of the Master* (New York: Scribner's, 1948), p. 77.
4. Vera Brittain, *The Women at Oxford: A Fragment of History* (New York: Macmillan, 1960), p. 42.

CHAPTER 10

1. W. B. Yeats, "The Tragic Generation," *Autobiographies* (New York: Macmillan, 1927), pp. 385–87.
2. Henry James, "The Next Time," *The Complete Tales of Henry James*, vol. 9, 1892–1898, ed. Leon Edel (Philadelphia and New York: J. B. Lippincott, 1964), p. 229.
3. *Miscellaneous Studies*, p. 248.
4. Thomas Carlyle, *The French Revolution* (reprint, Oxford and New York: Oxford University Press, 1989), p. 294.
5. Johann Fichte, *Science of Knowledge (Wissenschaftslehre) with the First and Second Introductions*, ed. and trans. Peter Heath and John Lachs (New York: Appleton-Century-Crofts, 1970), pp. 69, 99.
6. *The Popular Works of Johann Gottlieb Fichte*, trans. William Smith (London, 1889), vol. 1, pp. 210–11, 284–85. Quoted in Gerald Monsman, "Pater, Hopkins, and Fichte's Ideal Student," *South Atlantic Quarterly* 70 (1971), p. 371.
7. *Miscellaneous Studies*, p. 251.
8. Ibid., p. 61.
9. *The Renaissance*, p. 152.
10. Ibid., pp. 175–76.
11. Ibid., pp. 174–75.
12. *Miscellaneous Studies*, p. 253.
13. Ibid., p. 254.
14. W. B. Yeats, *The Poems: A New Edition*, ed. Richard J. Finneran (London: Macmillan, 1984), pp. 134–35.
15. Edward Thomas, *Walter Pater: A Critical Study* (London: Martin Secker, 1913), p. 79.
16. *The Renaissance*, p. 185.

CHAPTER 11

epigraph: Ezra Pound, "A Shake Down," *The Little Review* 5, no. 4 (August 1918), p. 39.
epigraph: T. S. Eliot, "Eeldrop and Appleplex," *The Little Review* 4, no. 5 (September 1917), p. 17.
1. *The Renaissance*, p. xix.
2. *Miscellaneous Studies*, p. 18.
3. *The Levinas Reader*, ed. Sean Hand (Oxford: Basil Blackwell, 1989), pp. 77–78.
4. *The Renaissance*, p. 184.
5. Ibid., p. 108.
6. Ibid., p. 106.
7. Ibid., p. 109.
8. Ibid., p. 67.
9. Ibid., p. 119.
10. Ibid., p. 188.
11. Ibid., pp. 169–70.
12. Sharon Cameron, *Thinking in Henry James* (Chicago: University of Chicago Press, 1989), p. 3.
13. *The Renaissance*, p. 184.
14. Ibid., pp. 42–43, and cf. 218.
15. Ibid., pp. 18–19.
16. Ibid., pp. 98–99.
17. Quoted in *The Renaissance*, pp. 317–18.

CHAPTER 12

1. *The Renaissance*, p. 78.
2. Ibid., p. 83.
3. A. C. Swinburne, "Notes on Designs of the Old Masters at Florence," *Fortnightly Review*, July 1868, p. 17.
4. Ibid., p. 18.
5. Cf. *The Renaissance*, pp. 371–72.
6. *The Renaissance*, p. 86.
7. Ibid., p. 88.
8. Ibid., pp. 164–65.
9. *Plato and Platonism*, p. 8.
10. T. S. Eliot, *Knowledge and Experience in the Philosophy of F. H. Bradley* (London: Faber and Faber, 1964), pp. 22, 25.

11. *The Renaissance*, pp. 93–94.

12. James Joyce, *Ulysses*, ed. Hans Walter Gabler et al. (New York: Random House, 1986), 2, pp. 135–36.

CHAPTER 13

1. *Letters*, p. 41.

2. Ernst H. Gombrich, *Symbolic Images: Studies in the Art of the Renaissance* (London: Phaidon Press, 1972), pp. 31–81.

3. *The Renaissance*, pp. 46–47.

4. *Appreciations*, p. 18.

5. *The Renaissance*, p. 47.

6. Ibid., p. 45.

7. Herbert Horne, *Alessandro Filipepi, Commonly Called Sandro Botticelli: Painter of Florence* (1908), reprinted as *Botticelli: Painter of Florence* (Princeton: Princeton University Press, 1980), p. 152.

8. *Greek Studies*, p. 96.

9. *The Renaissance*, p. 42.

CHAPTER 14

1. *Studies*, pp. 191–92.

2. *Greek Studies*, p. 295.

3. Hegel, *Philosophy of Fine Art*, vol. 2, 143–44. Quoted in Wolfgang Iser, *Walter Pater: The Aesthetic Moment*, trans. David Henry Wilson (Cambridge: Cambridge University Press, 1987), p. 58.

4. *Studies*, p. 176.

5. Ibid., pp. 187–88.

6. Ibid., pp. 167–68.

CHAPTER 15

epigraph: D. H. Lawrence, *Phoenix: The Posthumous Papers of D. H. Lawrence*, ed. Edward D. McDonald (New York: Viking, 1936), p. 62.

1. Henry James, *The Portrait of a Lady*, in *Novels 1881–1886* (New York: Library of America, 1985), p. 500.

2. Henry James, *A Small Boy and Others* (New York: Scribner's, 1913), p. 415.

3. *Greek Studies*, p. 44.

4. Ibid., pp. 252–53.

5. Ibid., p. 29.

6. Ibid., p. 47.

7. Ibid., p. 59.

8. Edward B. Tylor, *Primitive Culture*, 3rd ed. (London: John Murray, 1891), vol. 1, pp. 424, 136, 137.

9. *Greek Studies*, pp. 99–100.

10. Ibid., p. 91.

11. Ibid., pp. 91–92.

12. Wallace Stevens, *Transport to Summer* (New York: Knopf, 1947), p. 117.

13. Philip Wheelwright, *The Burning Fountain*, rev. ed. (Bloomington: Indiana University Press, 1968), p. 50.

14. T. S. Eliot, "*Ulysses*, Order, and Myth," *Dial* 70, no. 5 (November 1923), p. 483.

15. Cf. Francis Haskell and Nicholas Penny, *Taste and the Antique* (New Haven and London: Yale University Press, 1981), pp. 199–202.

16. *Greek Studies*, p. 286.

17. *The Elder Pliny's Chapters on the History of Art*, trans. K. Jex-Blake, commentary by E. Sellers (1896; reprint, Chicago: Argonaut, 1968), p. 47.

18. *Greek Studies*, p. 286.

19. Ibid., p. 288.

20. Ibid., pp. 288–89.

21. Ibid., pp. 289–90.

22. Wallace Stevens, *The Necessary Angel* (New York: Knopf, 1951), p. 23.

23. *Studies*, p. 55.

24. *Greek Studies*, p. 287.

25. *Miscellaneous Studies*, p. 167.

26. Ibid., p. 164.

27. Ibid., pp. 164–65.

28. Ibid., p. 143.

29. *Imaginary Portraits*, p. 76.

30. *Miscellaneous Studies*, p. 150.

CHAPTER 16

1. Cf. *Letters*, p. xxix.

2. *Letters*, p. 30. Letter of April 17, 1878.

3. Rainer Maria Rilke, *The Notebooks of Malte Laurids Brigge*, trans. M. D. Herter Norton (New York: Capricorn Books, 1958), pp. 26–27.

4. Walter Pater, "Poems by William Morris," *Westminster Review*, n.s., 34 (October 1868), p. 307.

5. *Miscellaneous Studies*, p. 188.

6. *The Renaissance*, p. 44.

7. William Wordsworth, *Poetry & Prose*, selected by W. M. Merchant (London: Rupert Hart-Davis, 1955), p. 257.

8. Ibid., p. 173.

9. *Miscellaneous Studies*, p. 175.

10. Ibid., p. 70.

11. Wordsworth, *Poetry & Prose*, p. 316 (the 1805 text of *The Prelude*).

12. *Miscellaneous Studies*, p. 185.

13. Ibid., p. 186.

14. Ibid., p. 187.

15. Ibid., p. 189.

16. Ibid., p. 192.

17. Ibid., p. 195.

18. Ibid., p. 196.

CHAPTER 17

1. *Letters*, p. 52. Letter of July 22, 1883, to Violet Paget.

2. Ibid., p. 65. Letter of January 28, 1886, to Carl Wilhelm Ernst.

3. *Marius the Epicurean*, vol. 1, pp. 238–39.

4. Ibid., p. 14.

5. Ibid., p. 13.

6. Ibid., pp. 13–14.

7. Ibid., p. 15.

8. Ibid., pp. 151–52.

9. Ibid., pp. 53–54.

10. *The Communings with Himself of Marcus Aurelius Antoninus*, trans. C. R. Haines (Cambridge: Harvard University Press, 1979), p. 37.

11. *Marius the Epicurean*, vol. 1, p. 208.

12. Fredric Jameson, "Wallace Stevens," *New Orleans Review*, vol. 11 (1984), p. 16.

CHAPTER 18

epigraph: James Joyce, *The Critical Writings of James Joyce*, ed. Ellsworth Mason and Richard Ellmann (New York: Viking, 1959), p. 182.

1. *Imaginary Portraits*, p. 145.

2. Ibid., p. 144.

3. Henry James, "Nathaniel Hawthorne," *Literary Criticism* (New York: Library of America, 1984), p. 459.

4. *Imaginary Portraits*, p. 111.

5. Ibid., pp. 26–27.

6. Ibid., p. 24.
7. Ibid., p. 26.

CHAPTER 19

1. *Letters*, p. 126.
2. *Gaston de Latour*, p. vi.
3. *Studies*, p. 134.
4. *Gaston de Latour*, p. 54.
5. Ibid., p. 60.
6. Ibid., p. 71.
7. Ibid., p. 85.
8. Ibid., p. 106.
9. Jean Starobinski, *Montaigne in Motion*, trans. Arthur Goldhammer (Chicago: University of Chicago Press, 1985), p. 157.
10. *Gaston de Latour*, pp. 49–50.
11. Ibid., p. 10.
12. Ibid., p. 116.
13. Ibid., p. 129.
14. Ibid., p. 124.
15. Ibid., pp. 127–28.

CHAPTER 20

1. Walter Pater, "Poems by William Morris," *Westminster Review*, n.s. 34, (October 1868), p. 301.
2. Walter Pater, "Aesthetic Poetry," *Appreciations* (London: Macmillan, 1889), p. 215.
3. Pater, "Poems," p. 307.
4. William Morris, *Selected Poems*, ed. Peter Faulkner (Manchester: Carcanet Press, 1992), p. 88.
5. John Lucas, *England and Englishness: Ideas of Nationhood in English Poetry 1688–1900* (London: Hogarth Press, 1990), p. 202.
6. Pater, "Poems," p. 300.
7. Ibid.
8. Ibid., p. 305.
9. Ibid., p. 306.
10. Wallace Stevens, *Transport to Summer* (New York: Knopf, 1947), p. 138.
11. Pater, "Poems," p. 302.
12. Ibid.
13. Ibid., p. 306.

14. Ibid., p. 307.
15. T. S. Eliot, *Collected Poems 1909–1962* (London: Faber and Faber, 1963), p. 195.

CHAPTER 21

1. *Appreciations*, p. 3.
2. Ibid., p. 35.
3. Ibid., p. 21.
4. David de Laura, *Hebrew and Hellene in Victorian England* (Austin and London: University of Texas Press, 1969), p. 334. Cf. J. H. Newman, "Literature: A Lecture in the School of Philosophy and Letters," in *The Idea of a University*, ed. Charles Frederick Harrold (New York and London: Longmans, Green, 1947).
5. *Appreciations*, p. 8.
6. *Miscellaneous Studies*, pp. 52–53.
7. Ibid., pp. 24–25.
8. Ibid., p. 21.
9. Ibid., p. 18.
10. Ibid.
11. Ibid., p. 22.

CHAPTER 22

1. *Appreciations*, p. 227.
2. Ibid., pp. 172–73.
3. Ibid., p. 179.
4. Ibid., p. 181.
5. Ibid., p. 211.

CHAPTER 23

epigraph: W. B. Yeats, *A Vision* (London: Macmillan, 1962; New York: Macmillan, 1961), pp. 276–77. Reprint of the second edition of 1937.
1. *Appreciations*, p. 37.
2. Wordsworth, *Poetry & Prose*, p. 608.
3. *Appreciations*, p. 46.
4. Ibid., p. 47.
5. Ibid.
6. Ibid., p. 55.

7. Ibid., p. 57.

8. William Empson, *The Structure of Complex Words* (reprint, London: Hogarth Press, 1985), p. 290.

9. *Appreciations*, p. 54.

10. Ibid., p. 59.

11. Ibid.

12. Ibid., pp. 60–61.

13. Ibid., pp. 61–62.

14. Aristotle, *The Nicomachean Ethics*, trans H. Rackham (reprint, Cambridge: Loeb Classical Library. Harvard University Press and William Heinemann, 1975), p. 623.

15. John Ruskin, *Modern Painters: Complete Works*, ed. E. T. Cook and Alexander Wedderburn (London: George Allen, 1903–1912), vol. 4, p. 42. Cf. Frank M. Turner, *The Greek Heritage in Victorian Britain* (New Haven: Yale University Press, 1981), p. 354. Also *Oscar Wilde's Oxford Notebooks*, ed. Philip E. Smith II and Michael S. Helfand (New York: Oxford University Press, 1989), p. 15.

16. *Studies*, pp. x–xi.

17. Robert Crawford, "Pater's *Renaissance*, Andrew Lang, and Anthropological Romanticism," in *English Literary History* 53, no. 4 (Winter 1986), pp. 849–76.

CHAPTER 24

1. *Appreciations*, p. 246.

2. Ibid., pp. 257–58.

3. Ibid., p. 261.

CHAPTER 25

1. *Plato and Platonism*, p. 52.

2. Ibid., pp. 124–25.

3. Ibid., p. 72.

4. Ibid., pp. 175–76.

5. Ibid., p. 268.

6. Ibid., p. 271.

7. Ibid., p. 275.

8. Ibid., p. 115.

9. Ibid., p. 66.

10. Ibid., p. 120.

11. John Ashbery, *Selected Poems* (New York: Viking, 1985), pp. 231–32.

12. *Plato and Platonism*, p. 106.

13. Ibid., pp. 107–108.

14. Jacques Derrida, *Dissemination*, trans. Barbara Johnson (Chicago: University of Chicago Press, 1981), p. 77.

CHAPTER 26

1. *Letters*, p. 148. Letter of January 22, 1894.

2. John Ruskin, *The Bible of Amiens: Works*, eds. E. T. Cook and Alexander Wedderburn (London: George Allen, 1908), vol. 33, p. 246.

3. Marcel Proust, *On Reading Ruskin*, ed. and trans. Jean Autret, William Burford, and Phillip J. Wolfe with an introduction by Richard Macksey (New Haven and London: Yale University Press, 1987), p. 83.

4. *Miscellaneous Studies*, p. 110.

5. Ibid., p. 113.

6. Ibid., p. 139.

7. Ibid., p. 131.

8. Ibid., pp. 132–33.

9. *Miscellaneous Studies*, p. 131.

10. Quoted in Ruskin, *The Bible of Amiens*, p. xxxv.

11. Ibid., pp. 138–39.

12. Ibid., p. 127.

13. Henry Adams, *Mont-Saint-Michel and Chartres* (Boston and New York: Houghton Mifflin, 1913), pp. 92–93.

14. *Miscellaneous Studies*, pp. 128–29.

15. Henry Adams, *The Education of Henry Adams* (Boston: Houghton Mifflin, Sentry Edition, 1961), p. 435.

16. Ibid., p. 429.

17. Ibid., p. 384.

18. Adams, *Mont-Saint-Michel and Chartres*, p. 105.

CHAPTER 27

1. Matthew Arnold, *The Complete Poems*, ed. Kenneth Allott and Miriam Allott (London: Longman, 1979), p. 654.

2. Matthew Arnold, *The Complete Prose Works*, ed. R. H. Super (Ann Arbor: University of Michigan Press, 1960), vol. 1, pp. 18–37.

3. "Coleridge's Writings," *Westminster Review* no. 57, vol. 85 o.s., 29 n.s. (January 1866), p. 107.

4. *Plato and Platonism*, p. 174.

5. *Gaston de Latour*, p. 57.

6. *Studies*, pp. 205–206.

CHAPTER 28

1. A. C. Bradley, *Oxford Lectures on Poetry* (reprint, Bloomington: Indiana University Press, 1961), pp. 4–5.
2. T. S. Eliot, "Eeldrop and Appleplex," *Little Review* 4, no. 1 (May 1917), pp. 7–11.
3. T. S. Eliot, *Selected Essays* (reprint, London: Faber and Faber, 1976), p. 141.
4. T. S. Eliot, "Prose and Verse," *Chapbook* 22 (April 1921), pp. 7–8.
5. Crites, "A Commentary," *The Criterion* 3, no. 9 (October 1924), p. 1.
6. T. S. Eliot, *Selected Essays*, p. 434.
7. W. B. Yeats, *Autobiographies* (London: Macmillan, 1955), pp. 302–303.
8. T. S. Eliot, *Selected Essays*, p. 131.
9. Ibid., p. 439.
10. Ibid., pp. 442, 443.
11. Thomas Mann, *Last Essays*, trans. Richard and Clara Winston (London: Secker and Warburg, 1959), p. 175.
12. T. W. Adorno, *Aesthetic Theory*, trans. C. Lenhardt (London: Routledge and Kegan Paul, 1986), p. 76.
13. James Joyce, *A Portrait of the Artist as a Young Man* (reprint, London: Cape, 1964), p. 212.
14. Søren Kierkegaard, *Concluding Unscientific Postscript*, trans. David F. Swenson (Princeton: Princeton University Press, 1941), pp. 67–68.
15. J. L. Borges, *Labyrinths*, trans. James E. Irby (Harmondsworth, U.K.: Penguin Books, 1970), p. 223.
16. Walter Benjamin, *Illuminations*, trans. Harry Zohn (New York: Schocken Books, 1969), p. 242.
17. Adorno, *Aesthetic Theory*, p. 10.
18. Houghton Library (Harvard University) MSS, Eng. 1150 (7).
19. Ibid.; punctuation mine.
20. *Appreciations*, p. 38.

CHAPTER 29

1. Edward Thomas, *Walter Pater* (London: Martin Secker, 1913), p. 213.
2. Quoted in Linda Dowling, *Language and Decadence in the Victorian Fin de Siècle* (Princeton: Princeton University Press, 1986), p. 133.
3. *Greek Studies*, p. 15.
4. Ibid., p. 37.
5. Cf. Hugh Kenner, "Some Post-Symbolist Structures," in *Literary Theory*

and Structure, ed. Frank Brady, John Palmer, and Martin Price (New Haven: Yale University Press, 1973), pp. 379–93.

6. *Plato and Platonism*, p. 158.

7. T. S. Eliot, *On Poetry and Poets* (London: Faber and Faber, 1957), p. 142.

8. *The Renaissance*, p. 85.

9. *Miscellaneous Studies*, pp. 60–61.

10. James Joyce, *Ulysses*, ed. Hans Walter Gabler et al. (New York: Random House, 1986), p. 344.

11. *Gaston de Latour*, p. 61.

12. Ibid., p. 120.

13. Ibid., pp. 154–55.

14. *The Renaissance*, p. 91.

15. Christopher Ricks, *The Force of Poetry* (Oxford and New York: Oxford University Press, 1987), p. 393.

16. *The Renaissance*, p. 82.

17. Kenneth Burke, *Counter-Statement*, 2nd ed. (Los Altos, Calif.: Hermes Publications, 1953), p. 12.

18. Ibid., p. 10.

CHAPTER 30

1. *The Renaissance*, p. 39.

2. Svetlana Alpers, *The Art of Describing: Dutch Art in the Seventeenth Century* (Chicago: University of Chicago Press, 1983), pp. xix, xxi.

3. *The Renaissance*, p. 42.

4. Cf. Donald L. Hill's note in *The Renaissance*, p. 337.

5. Ibid., p. 43.

6. William Empson, *Collected Poems* (London: Chatto and Windus, 1977), p. 32.

7. *The Renaissance*, p. 43.

8. Ibid., p. 44.

9. Kierkegaard, *Concluding Unscientific Postscript*, pp. 67–68.

10. Dante Alighieri, *The Divine Comedy*, *Inferno*, trans. Charles S. Singleton (Princeton: Princeton University Press, 1971), p. 26.

11. Ibid., p. 28.

12. John Freccero, *Dante: The Poetics of Conversion* (Cambridge: Harvard University Press, 1986), p. 117.

13. *Selected Prose of T. S. Eliot*, ed. Frank Kermode (New York: Harcourt Brace Jovanovich, 1975), p. 235.

14. Ibid., p. 236.

15. T. S. Eliot, *Collected Poems 1909–1962* (London: Faber and Faber, 1963), p. 219.

16. John Freccero, *Dante*, p. 301.

17. Walter Benjamin, *Charles Baudelaire: A Lyric Poet in the Age of High Capitalism*, trans. Harry Zohn (London: NLB Press, 1973), p. 106. Quoted in Thomas Crow, "Modernism and Mass Culture in the Visual Arts," in *Modernism and Modernity*, ed. Benjamin H. D. Buchloh, Serge Guilbaut, and David Solkin (Halifax: Press of the Nova Scotia College of Art and Design, 1983), pp. 230–31.

18. Ibid.

19. Crow, "Modernism and Mass Culture in the Visual Arts," p. 242.

20. W. B. Yeats, *Essays and Introductions* (New York: Macmillan, 1961), p. 163.

21. W. B. Yeats, *The Poems*, ed. Richard J. Finneran (New York: Macmillan, 1983), p. 184.

22. Sigmund Freud, *The Interpretation of Dreams*, in *The Standard Edition of the Complete Psychological Works of Sigmund Freud*, ed. James Strachey et al. (London: Hogarth Press, 1953–1974), vol. 5, p. 507.

23. James Joyce, *Ulysses*, ed. Hans Walter Gabler et al. (New York: Random House, 1986), p. 31.

24. Ibid., p. 34.

25. James Joyce, *A Portrait of the Artist as a Young Man*, ed. Hans Walter Gabler with Walter Hettche (New York: Vintage International, 1993), p. 196.

26. Joyce, *Ulysses*, p. 30.

27. Crow, "Modernism and Mass Culture," p. 242.

28. Quoted in Christopher Ricks, *Beckett's Dying Words* (Oxford: Clarendon Press, 1993), p. 82.

29. Cf. Alexander Nehamas, "Subject and Abject," *The New Republic*, February 15, 1993, p. 34.

30. Wallace Stevens, *The Palm at the End of the Mind*, ed. Holly Stevens (New York: Vintage Books, 1972), p. 20.

31. T. S. Eliot, "The Post-Georgians," *Athenaeum*, April 11, 1919, pp. 171–72.

Index

Denis Donoghue was born in Tullow, Ireland, in 1928. He took his
B.A., M.A., and Ph.D. at University College, Dublin, and received
an M.A. at Cambridge University when he joined the teaching faculty
there. He was Professor of Modern English and American Literature
at University College, and is now University Professor at New York
University, where he also holds the Henry James Chair of English
and American Letters. Among Donoghue's many books there most
notably figure *The Third Voice*; *The Ordinary Universe*; *Thieves of Fire*;
The Sovereign Ghost; *Ferocious Alphabets*; *Connoisseurs of Chaos*; *The Arts
Without Mystery*; *We Irish*; *England, Their England*; *Reading America*;
Warrenpoint; *The Pure Good of Theory*; and *The Old Moderns*.

A NOTE ON THE TYPE

This book was set in Janson, a recutting made direct from type cast from matrices long thought to have been made by the Dutchman Anton Janson, who was a practicing type founder in Leipzig during the years 1668–1687. However, it has been conclusively demonstrated that these types are actually the work of Nicholas Kis (1650–1702), a Hungarian, who most probably learned his trade from the master Dutch type founder Dirk Voskens. The type is an excellent example of the influential and sturdy Dutch types that prevailed in England up to the time William Caslon developed his own incomparable designs from them.

Composed by PennSet, Bloomsburg, Pennsylvania
Printed and bound by Arcata Graphics/Martinsburg,
Martinsburg, West Virginia
Designed by Brooke Zimmer